MONTESQUIEU AND THE LOGIC OF LIBERTY

Montesquieu and the Logic of Liberty

War, Religion, Commerce, Climate, Terrain, Technology,
Uneasiness of Mind, the Spirit of Political Vigilance,
and the Foundations of the Modern Republic

Paul A. Rahe

Yale University Press
New Haven & London

Published with assistance from the Kingsley Trust Association Publication Fund
established by the Scroll and Key Society of Yale College.

Set in Electra and Trajan types by The Composing Room of Michigan, Inc.
Printed in the United States of America.

Library of Congress Cataloging-in-Publication Data

Rahe, Paul Anthony.
Montesquieu and the logic of liberty : war, religion, commerce, climate, terrain,
technology, uneasiness of mind, the spirit of political vigilance, and the foundations
of the modern republic / Paul A. Rahe.
p. cm.
Includes bibliographical references and index.
ISBN 978-0-300-14125-2 (hardcover : alk. paper) 1. Liberty. 2. Montesquieu,
Charles de Secondat, baron de, 1689–1755. I. Title.
JC585.R34 2009
320.01′1 — dc22
2008054927

A catalogue record for this book is available from the British Library.

This paper meets the requirements of ANSI/NISO Z39.48–1992 (Permanence of Paper).

10 9 8 7 6 5 4 3 2 1

Francesca Pia Rahe

Think of a genius not born in every country or every time: a man gifted by Nature with a penetrating, aquiline eye, — with a judgment prepared with the most extensive erudition, — with an Herculean robustness of mind, and nerves not to be broken with labor, — a man who could spend twenty years in one pursuit. Think of a man like the universal patriarch in Milton (who had drawn up before him in his prophetic vision the whole series of the generations which were to issue from his loins): a man capable of placing in review, after having brought together from the East, the West, the North, and the South, from the coarseness of the rudest barbarism to the most refined and subtle civilization, all the schemes of government which had ever prevailed amongst mankind, weighing, measuring, collating, and comparing them all, joining fact with theory, and calling into council, upon all this infinite assemblage of things, all the speculations which have fatigued the understandings of profound reasoners in all times. Let us then consider, that all these were but so many preparatory steps to qualify a man, and such a man, tinctured with no national prejudice, with no domestic affection, to admire, and to hold out to the admiration of mankind, the Constitution of England.

— *Edmund Burke*

CONTENTS

Book Three. The Modern Republic in Prospect

PREFACE

This volume is a sequel of sorts. Some seventeen years prior to its appearance, its author published a work entitled *Republics Ancient and Modern: Classical Republicanism and the American Revolution*. Although it was some twelve hundred pages in length, inevitably, it gave some figures short shrift, and others it neglected entirely. Niccolò Machiavelli was discussed and his importance underlined, but his thinking was not treated in depth. John Milton and Marchamont Nedham were not mentioned at all. Thomas Hobbes was accorded a chapter, but little was said about the evolution of his thought; and, while James Harrington's significance was emphasized, the foundations of his thinking were not discussed at length. These topics I addressed in a book entitled *Against Throne and Altar: Machiavelli and Political Theory under the English Republic*, which was published in April, 2008.

In that work, however, I did not make good other omissions, which may be of even greater significance. In an otherwise favorable review of *Republics Ancient and Modern*, James R. Stoner of Louisiana State University took me to task for neglecting Montesquieu, who was arguably the first to fully articulate the distinction between ancient and modern republicanism. In his review, Professor Stoner was kind. About my demerits, he could certainly have said considerably more. To be precise, he could have pointed to my similar neglect of Rousseau and Tocqueville, whom I quoted nearly as often as Montesquieu, but whose reflections on the subject I did not examine in detail and with the care that they deserved. He could have argued that my omissions left the story of modern republicanism — of its virtues, its vices, and, especially, its fragility — woefully incomplete. So I learned, to my dismay, some years after the publication of that heavy tome — when I took up the challenge he had issued and began to wrestle in all seriousness with the baron de Montesquieu.

This volume grew out of that wrestling match. With its companion volume, *Soft Despotism, Democracy's Drift*, to be published in the same year, it constitutes an attempt to round out the argument that I developed in my first book and restated in the sequel published in 2008, and the two new volumes are an attempt to extend and refine that argument as well. Above all else, they are an endeavor to flesh out, in light of the ruminations of Montesquieu and his most important heirs, a political science and an account of the political psychology of liberal democratic man sufficient to enable us to recognize the plight that we are now in so that we can come to grips with the peculiar maladies that give rise to the present discontents.

Hillsdale, Michigan
18 December 2008

ACKNOWLEDGMENTS

I am indebted, as always, to James W. Muller of the University of Alaska at Anchorage, who first steered me to Montesquieu, and to my former colleague Michael A. Mosher of the University of Tulsa, in whose company I first read *The Spirit of Laws* from beginning to end, and with whom I have had innumerable enlightening conversations concerning the French *philosophe*. I am indebted as well to David W. Carrithers of the University of Tennessee at Chattanooga, Catherine Larrère of the University of Paris (I), Stuart D. Warner of Roosevelt University, Henry C. Clark of Canisius College, Eldon Eisenach of the University of Tulsa, Diana J. Schaub of Loyola University, Baltimore, William B. Allen of Michigan State University, Rebecca Kingston of the University of Toronto, and Cecil Patrick Courtney of Christ's College, Cambridge, who were generous with their time and expertise on a multitude of occasions.

To Catherine Volpilhac-Auger, I am especially grateful. While I was laboring on this project, she patiently answered my queries concerning the working manuscript of *The Spirit of Laws*, which she was then preparing for publication in a critical edition, and when I began correcting my copy-edited manuscript, she kindly sent me the page proofs of that edition, which was published while the type in this volume was being set. In making Montesquieu's *manuscrit de travail* accessible and available to all for scrutiny, she has pointed the way forward for all future work on his *Spirit of Laws*.

In a fashion similarly generous, Graham Gargett responded to questions concerning Jacob Vernet; Daniel Gordon, Will Morrissey, Jon Fennell, and David Carrithers read and commented on the manuscript as a whole; and John Robertson, Peter Ghosh, Istvan Hont, Michael Sonenscher, Michael Mosher, Clifford Orwin, Ran Halevi, and Philippe Raynaud read (or listened to) and commented on one or more of its various parts. My devoted and long-suffering wife Laura more than once went over every word.

While on sabbatical from the University of Tulsa in the spring of 1999 at Clare Hall, Cambridge, I began this project in earnest. Later in 2005–6, while on sabbatical again, I received generous support from the Research Office at the University of Tulsa; from Thomas Benediktson, Dean of Henry Kendall College of Arts and Sciences at that institution; and from the Earhart Foundation, to which over the years I have come to owe a very large debt. I had the privilege of spending Michaelmas Term in 2005 and Hilary Term in 2006 in congenial company at All Souls College, Oxford — where, as a Visiting Fellow, I took ample advantage of library facilities unequalled anywhere else in the world, and there I had the opportunity to meet Ms. Ursula Haskins Gonthier, then of Worcester College, Oxford, and to read in various drafts the chapter in her dissertation dedicated to Montesquieu's *Considerations on the Causes of the Greatness of the Romans and their Decline.* In response to her argument, I made various small changes to the first book contained within this volume regarding the subtextual significance of Montesquieu's attack on Augustus, the incendiary character of the praise that Montesquieu bestowed on England's parliamentary regime, and the precise dates of the publication of Montesquieu *Considerations on the Romans* in English and in French. To her, to the Warden and Fellows of All Souls College, and to the librarians at the Codrington Library, the Taylorian Institution, and the Bodleian Library, I am especially grateful.

The spring and early summer of 2006, I spent in similarly congenial company at the American Academy in Berlin, where once again I was free to devote myself full-time to this project, and I did the same in the fall of 2006, when I was on leave from the University of Tulsa on a fellowship from the National Endowment for the Humanities. I owe a special debt to the Director and the members of his staff at the American Academy, who were helpful in a great many ways; to the National Endowment of the Humanities and the University of Tulsa for their generosity; and to Marc Carlson, Ann Blakely, Tamara Stansfield, and the staff at the interlibrary loan office at the McFarlin Library at the University of Tulsa, who performed miracles.

An earlier and considerably shorter version of Book One of this work appeared as Paul A. Rahe, "The Book That Never Was: Montesquieu's *Considerations on the Romans* in Historical Context," *History of Political Thought* 26:1 (Spring, 2005): 43–89. The bulk of it is reprinted here with the permission of the editors. Earlier and considerably shorter versions of Book Two appeared as Paul A. Rahe, "Soft Despotism: Democracy's Drift," in *Foundations of American Civilization,* ed. T. William Boxx and Gary M. Quinlivan (Latrobe, PA: Center for Economic and Policy Education, 1999), 15–54, and as Paul A. Rahe, "Forms of Government: Structure, Principle, Object, and Aim," in *Montesquieu's Science of Politics: Essays on the Spirit of Laws (1748)*, ed. David W. Carrithers, Michael A. Mosher, and Paul A. Rahe (Lanham, MD: Rowman & Littlefield, 2001), 69–108. A great deal of material from these is reprinted here with the permission of the Center for Economic Policy at Saint Vincent College and Rowman & Littlefield Publishers.

I would also like to register my gratitude to a scholarly organization. In the fall of 2003, when I finished the article that forms the basis of Book One of this work, I submitted it to the *Journal of Modern History*, and I was dismayed when it was returned within a week or two with a letter from the editor suggesting that "it would be better suited to a journal with a broader and more popular audience, such as *History Today*." Preferring my judgment to hers, I soon sent it off to *History of Political Thought*; and I was, needless to say, delighted in April 2006 when Professor Jeremy D. Popkin, Executive Director of the Society for French Historical Studies, wrote to me to tell me that his organization had awarded me the Koren Article Prize for the best article in French history published in 2005. I tell this story for two reasons. I am grateful to the Society for French Historical Studies for encouraging someone who was not trained in the field to continue with his studies in French history, and I offer my experience as encouragement to younger scholars — who should be urged to persevere when at first they do not succeed in finding a scholarly venue in which to publish work they think of genuine scholarly importance.

INTRODUCTION

Fortunately for all of us, the Cold War ended not with a bang but with a whimper. It is surprising, however, that its cessation inspired so little elation. Of course, there was a moment of euphoria and rejoicing twenty years ago when the Berlin Wall quite suddenly ceased to be a barrier. It seemed a miracle, and in a sense it was. But that moment quickly passed; and where one might have expected opinion leaders in the West to celebrate what was, after all, an astonishing and historically unprecedented victory, involving the utter defeat and ultimate dissolution of a powerful and threatening adversary in the absence of a major war, one encountered at best a cautious optimism and at worst a sense of resignation.[1] It was as if liberal democrats everywhere mourned the enemy they had known and were in fear of an enemy who had not yet appeared.

The French worried about the consequences of German reunification; the Germans fretted about its costs. In Czechoslovakia, the Velvet Revolution was followed by the Velvet Divorce. The revival of ancient religious and ethnic hatreds gave rise to armed struggle within and between some of the successor states to the Soviet Union and Yugoslavia; and, in time, Russia began to display an all-too-familiar species of belligerence. Throughout eastern Europe, people were less inclined to speak of revolution than of transition; and in many a country, the old communists with a name change and a face lift were soon returned to power by a newly liberated electorate nostalgic for a past offering in predictability what it had denied in the way of opportunity. Then, on the first occasion that presented itself, the French, the Germans, the Belgians, and many others within a Western Europe that had once been liberated from fascism by the United States and that had later been protected from communism by that same power turned on their former benefactor and set out to put as much distance as possible between themselves and that country, denouncing its policies, demonizing its leaders, and venting great rancor against its people and their way of life.

If, in and, for a brief time, after 1989, the prevailing mood was, nonetheless, one of relief, it was not unmixed with sadness, discontent, and a measure of world-weariness. When Francis Fukuyama announced "the end of history" and suggested that we may have entered the era of Nietzsche's "last man," he struck a nerve and caused a sensation — not just in the United States, but in France and in the rest of Europe as well.[2] A similar spirit pervaded Samuel P. Huntington's quite different — one might even say, contrarian — observations concerning the likelihood that there would be a great "clash of civilizations," wherein, as critics noted, there was more than a hint of the profound cultural pessimism that once suffused Oswald Spengler's *The Decline of the West.*[3]

When Ned Lebow and Janice Stein informed their fellow political scientists that "we all lost the Cold War,"[4] their claim was not immediately dismissed as preposterous. When Tony Judt denounced John Lewis Gaddis for focusing narrowly on grand strategy in a book charting the history of the Cold War, sneering that he had treated "the 'third world' as a sideshow, albeit one in which hundreds of thousands of performers got killed,"[5] no one from among his fellow historians stepped forward to point out that, from the perspective of grand strategy, the proxy wars that took place within the Third World really were a sideshow, and no one bothered to ask whether Professor Judt knew of a comparable epic struggle between rival coalitions lasting more than four decades in which the collateral damage had been less.[6] In keeping with the prevailing mood, triumphalism was also notably absent from the great outpouring of literature on liberal democracy and its prospects that appeared in the wake of the Soviet Union's collapse.[7]

There was also evidence of growing popular disaffection. In 2004, when a pollster named Scott Rasmussen asked Americans whether their country was "generally fair and decent," roughly a quarter of those planning to vote in the presidential election disagreed; and, when the Pew Trust asked whether American "wrongdoing" might have "motivated" the terrorist attacks in New York and Washington on 11 September 2001, a similar proportion of those who responded were persuaded that this might, indeed, have been the case. Even more to the point, polls taken that year revealed that something like a quarter of the American population doubted that the world would be better off if other nations were more like their own.[8] In February and March 2008, when the wife of a soon-to-be-successful American presidential aspirant repeatedly asserted in her stump speech that Americans are "cynical" and "mean" and have "broken souls" and that the lives "that most people" in the United States "are living" have "gotten progressively worse since I was a little girl," she deftly caught the sour mood of a substantial segment of the American electorate.[9]

In Europe, there have also been indications of the emergence of a deep sense of popular malaise. In February 2002, a Convention on the Future of Europe was convened to great acclaim under the chairmanship of former French President Valéry Giscard d'Estaing to draft a constitutional frame for the European Union. The following year a document, more than four hundred fifty pages in length, was placed before the public; and in June 2004, an amended version of the original draft was presented to the union's member nations for ratification. The following year, however, when the first referenda were held, despite the fact that the political class throughout the European continent was virtually unanimous in enthusiastic support for the constitutional project, the ordinary people of France and the United Provinces, founding members of the Common Market and leading members of the European Union, promptly and decisively rejected the proposal.

There is something altogether odd and not a little unsettling about these developments, for they leave us wondering where to turn. That the chattering classes should be inclined to sneer is hardly a matter needing extended comment: sneering is the coin in which the modern intellectual trades. But world-weariness and profound popular disaffection are something else again. Perhaps, however, the sobriety with which statesmen, peoples, and scholars have greeted liberal democracy's sudden and unexpected achievement of a seemingly unchallenged hegemony is entirely appropriate. After all, this sobriety jibes well with a conviction which informed the establishment of the modern world's first unequivocally liberal, undeniably republican regime: that an experiment of doubtful resolution had then been set in train. Perhaps, Americans and their European cousins can still echo the words that George Washington wrote to the governors of America's states in early June 1783 on the eve of his retirement as general of the armies — that "it is yet to be decided whether the [American] Revolution must ultimately be considered as a blessing or a curse: a blessing or a curse, not to the present age alone, for with our fate will the destiny of unborn Millions be involved."[10] If there is even a hint of justification for our strangely melancholy response to a set of events that seem, finally, to have made the world safe for democracy, it is worth pondering anew whether liberal republicanism, for all of its many obvious virtues, displays certain inherent defects as well.

For reflections of such a sort, there may be no occasion more appropriate than the interval between the 250th anniversary of the death of Charles-Louis de Secondat, baron de La Brède et de Montesquieu, and the 150th anniversary of the death of his disciple Alexis de Tocqueville — when this study was brought to completion. Tocqueville, whose contributions to democratic theory and to the analysis of bourgeois society are discussed in this book's companion volume, *Soft Despotism, Democracy's Drift*, needs no introduction. The pertinence of his work to the understanding of modern liberal democracy is well-known, and the same claim can arguably be made for Jean-Jacques Rousseau, whose oeuvre is discussed in the companion volume as well. The importance of their teacher Montesquieu — the subject of this tome — may, however, require a brief word of explanation.

That Montesquieu was a great man, graced with a comprehensive vision of the political universe, was once a fact universally known. In the eighteenth century, every major work that he ushered into print quickly found a wide audience. By 1800, his *Persian Letters*, which first appeared in 1721, had been published in ninety-three editions and had been translated into English, Dutch, German, Polish, and Russian — while his *Considerations on the Causes of the Greatness of the Romans and their Decline*, which was first published in 1734, had appeared in sixty-two editions and had been translated into English, Italian, Dutch, Swedish, Polish, Russian, and Greek. Neither of these bore comparison with Montesquieu's *Spirit of Laws*. This last work was in a self-evident way serious, and enormous it was as well. One purchased it expecting instruction and not diversion — diverting though it might be. And yet, from the moment of its release in the fall of 1748, it sold like hotcakes. By the end of the century, it had been published in one hundred twenty-eight editions, and it had been translated into English, Italian, German, Latin, Danish, Dutch, Polish, and Russian. To this one can add that, in the period stretching from 1748 to 1800, these three books were published together in editions of Montesquieu's complete works no fewer than thirty-six times.[11]

All in all, it would be fair to say that *De l'Esprit des lois* was a publishing phenomenon. It was that, and it was much, much more. For, as the eventful second half of the eighteenth century began, Montesquieu's great work became the political Bible of learned men and would-be statesmen everywhere in Europe, and beyond. In Britain, it shaped the thinking of Edmund Burke, Edward Gibbon, William Blackstone, Adam Smith, Adam Ferguson, William Robertson, John Millar, Lord Kames, and Dugald Stewart among others,[12] and in America, it inspired the Framers of the Constitution and their opponents, the Anti-Federalists, as well.[13] In Italy, it had a profound effect on Cesare Beccaria,[14] and in Germany, it was fundamental for Georg Wilhelm Friedrich Hegel.[15] In France, it was the starting point for all subsequent political thought.[16] Its impact can hardly be overestimated.[17]

This was especially true in the United States. In *The Federalist*, James Madison called the author of *The Spirit of Laws* an "oracle," and both Madison and Alexander Hamilton spoke of him as "the celebrated Montesquieu."[18] They sensed what subsequent scholarship has shown to be true: that no political writer was more often cited and none was thought to be of greater authority in the era of American constitution-making.[19] They knew, moreover, that in England and on the continent of Europe Montesquieu was thought to be of similar stature. Indeed, having carefully read his *Spirit of Laws* themselves, they knew why, throughout the Christian West, he was held in such regard.

If Montesquieu was so often consulted and cited by men of consequence in the eighteenth and early nineteenth centuries, it was largely because, in *The Spirit of Laws*, he had announced his discovery, on the very doorstep of his native France, of a new form of government more conducive to liberty and graced with greater staying power than any polity theretofore even imagined. As Madison put it, "The British constitution was to Montesquieu, what Homer has been to the didactic writers on epic poetry. As the latter have considered the work of the immortal Bard, as the perfect model from which the principles and rules of the epic art were to be drawn, and by which all similar works were to be judged; so this great political critic appears to have viewed the constitution of England, as the standard, or to use his own expression, as the mirrour of political liberty; and to have delivered in the form of elementary truths, the several characteristic principles of that particular system."[20] Students of the form of political liberty peculiar to modern republics may still have something to learn from considering what Montesquieu had to say a quarter of a millennium ago concerning the constitution of England—for, James Madison to the contrary notwithstanding, Montesquieu did not profess for "the particular government of England" an "admiration bordering on idolatry."[21] He was, in fact, a critic as well as an admirer, as sensitive to the imperfections inherent in the English form of government as he was to its many virtues; and, as we shall in due course see, the defects he and his heirs discerned in that polity and the propensities that arise therefrom are pertinent to understanding the political psychology of all modern republics and to tracing the sources of our present discontents.

If, then, we wish to understand whither we are tending, we would be well advised to reacquaint ourselves with a forgotten form of political science and to read with care Montesquieu and then those, such as Rousseau and Tocqueville, who closely followed his lead and expanded in crucial regards upon what he had to say. This is, however, easier said than done. For Montesquieu, in particular, wrote in a time now largely forgotten and unfamiliar, and he couched his arguments with an eye to an immediate public that has long since disappeared.

Moreover, he lived in an age of censorship, and he composed his works in conformity with unwritten rules of discretion, intimating that which could not with profit openly be said. It would be patronizing on our part for us to suppose him a "man of his time," condemned to think as his contemporaries thought; and it would be a grave error as well, for it would deprive us of the capacity to appreciate fully the force and the originality of what he had to say. But it is nonetheless true that to make himself understood Montesquieu had to make use of the vocabulary and the idioms spoken by his compatriots and redeploy them in a fashion suited to conveying what was novel in his reflections. In consequence, the challenge we face if we are to understand his thinking is not just intellectual; it is also literary, and it is unavoidably historical. One might even call our task archaeological. Before we can hope to be able to return to our own age; to rethink our situation in light of the penetrating analysis offered by Montesquieu, Rousseau, and Tocqueville; and to recognize it for what it is for the first time, we must undertake a journey into the past, to Montesquieu's day and, then, to that of his greatest successors, . . . in search of treasure that is buried there.

Journeys of this kind, whether through space or time, can be a liberation. Archaeologists of the ordinary sort may find it necessary to pack a great deal of luggage and equipment. Intellectual archaeologists generally do the opposite. As they proceed, they tend to lose the baggage that they have brought with them — and not to mind a bit. They find themselves jettisoning preconceptions, abandoning prejudices, and setting aside, at least for the length of the ride, their current pressing, confining concerns. Freed from the burden of present-mindedness and from the anxieties to which it gives rise, they enter imaginatively into ways of thinking that are decidedly foreign, and in the process, more often than not, they open themselves up to possibilities that they had never before even contemplated, and they secure for themselves a vantage point from which to view their own world. Such was the experience of Voltaire and of Montesquieu when they journeyed through space to England in the late 1720s; such was the experience of Rousseau when he sojourned in Paris in the late 1740s and the 1750s; and such was the experience of Tocqueville when he traveled with Gustave de Beaumont through Jacksonian America in the early 1830s. Moreover, when Montesquieu journeyed through time and gave himself over to Homer and Vergil; to Plato and Aristotle; to Herodotus and Thucydides; to Plutarch, Polybius, and Livy; and to Montaigne, Hobbes, Pascal, Locke, Mandeville, and a great many others, he had much the same experience — not just once, but repeatedly — as did Rousseau when he first read Plutarch and first studied Montesquieu's *Spirit of Laws*, and Tocqueville also, when on a daily basis he entered, as he tells us, into conversation with Pascal, Montesquieu, and Rousseau. Such, I hope, will be the experience of those who are led by this work and by *Soft Despotism, Democracy's Drift* to view the world, at least for a fleeting moment, through the eyes of Montesquieu, Rousseau, and Tocqueville.

Our intellectual odyssey we will begin, as is only proper, at the beginning — some three hundred years ago, at the moment when the world's first fully modern, first fully commercial republic first made its presence felt in the world and first demonstrated its viability in the sphere where aspiring polities meet their first, most decisive, and most grueling test — on the field of the sword. Then, after briefly considering the impact on the young Voltaire and on his slightly older contemporary Montesquieu of Great Britain's victories over France in the War of the Spanish Succession, we will set out on our way, as those two young men did on theirs. Our journey we will make in five stages, pausing at discrete intervals to dig deeply into the thinking of Montesquieu, Rousseau, or Tocqueville.

In the case of Montesquieu, to whom I have devoted the three books contained within this volume, we will start with his provocative analysis of the novel character of modern geopolitics and of the peculiar place occupied within that system by Great Britain. Then we will take up and explore in depth his regime typology — above all else, his description of the political psychology regnant within the various and strikingly different forms of government that existed in ancient and modern times and his account of the circumstances, practices, laws, and policies that sustain and subvert each polity — and, with an eye to the account of fallen man in Pascal's *Pensées* and to that of man in general in Montaigne's *Essays* and in Locke's *Essay concerning Human Understanding*, we will tease out the implications of Montesquieu's regime typology for the virtues, the vices, and the long-term prospects of Great Britain and of the colonies it established on the North American continent. Our ruminations on Montesquieu we will then conclude with a close examination of his penetrating and prescient assessment of the trajectory that European and world history were likely to take.

When we have finished these three stages of our journey and turn to this work's companion volume, we will briefly review what we have learned concerning Montesquieu and, then, pause to consider the impact that he had on his contemporaries. Thereafter, we will turn to his greatest admirer and most astute critic, Jean-Jacques Rousseau, and we will ponder the significance of the profound debt the latter owed his predecessor's analysis of the political psychology of the modern liberal republic. In this light, we will consider the substance of Rousseau's attack on the Enlightenment, his contention that progress in the sciences and the arts is likely to corrupt human beings and intensify their misery, and his suggestion that bourgeois society and popular enlightenment pose a threat to intellectual integrity and freedom. Then we will examine in detail the foundations of the savage critique he directed on other grounds at the commercial societies emerging in his time and weigh the eloquent argument that he made on behalf of intense civic engagement.

It is against this background that we will undertake the last stage of our journey—the one that will bring us home. Therein we will consider Tocqueville's application of the psychological insights of Pascal, the political science of Montesquieu and Rousseau, and that of Aristotle to the strange new world that emerged in the wake of the American and French revolutions. Here, once again, our focus will be first and foremost psychological, and we will examine the cast of mind promoted by the democratic social condition, the new species of despotism to which that condition gives rise, and the salutary remedies applied in the America that Tocqueville visited in the early 1830s. Then and only then will we return to our own time and, in light of what we have learned from Montesquieu, Rousseau, and Tocqueville, trace the trajectory of France, the European Union, and the United States; consider to what degree the world's modern republics are on the right course; and face up to what must be done if we are to recover from the profound sense of malaise to which we are now prone.

ABBREVIATIONS

In the notes, I have adopted the standard abbreviations for classical texts and inscriptions and for books of the Bible provided in *The Oxford Classical Dictionary*, 3rd edition revised, ed. Simon Hornblower and Antony Spawforth (Oxford, UK: Oxford University Press, 2003), and in *The Chicago Manual of Style*, 15th edition (Chicago: University of Chicago Press, 2003), 15.50–53. Where possible, the ancient texts and medieval and modern works of similar stature are cited by the divisions and subdivisions employed by the author or introduced by subsequent editors (that is, by book, part, chapter, section number, paragraph, act, scene, line, Stephanus page, or by page and line number). Cross-references to other parts of this volume refer to book and chapter and specify whether the material referenced can be found above or below.

In citing particular works by Machiavelli, to render my citations more precise I have added, in some instances, the paragraph numbers provided in Niccolò Machiavelli, *Discourses on Livy*, tr. Harvey C. Mansfield and Nathan Tarcov (Chicago: University of Chicago Press, 1996), and the sentence numbers provided in Niccolò Machiavelli, *Art of War*, ed. and tr. Christopher Lynch (Chicago: University of Chicago Press, 2003).

In citing Montesquieu, wherever possible, I have employed the splendid new critical edition being produced by the Société Montesquieu: Charles-Louis de Secondat, baron de La Brède et de Montesquieu, *Œuvres complètes de Montesquieu*, ed. Jean Ehrard, Catherine Volpilhac-Auger, et al. (Oxford, UK: Voltaire Foundation, 1998–), which I cite as VF. For works as yet unavailable in this edition, I cite Charles-Louis de Secondat, baron de La Brède et de Montesquieu, *Œuvres complètes de Montesquieu*, ed. Roger Caillois (Paris: Bibliothèque de la Pléiade, 1949–51), as Pléiade, and Charles-Louis de Secondat, baron de La Brède et de Montesquieu, *Œuvres complètes de Montesquieu*, ed. André Masson (Paris: Les Éditions Nagel, 1950–55), as Nagel.

For modern works frequently cited, the following abbreviations and short titles have been employed:

Montesquieu, *CEC*   Charles-Louis de Secondat, baron de La Brède et de Montesquieu, "Essai sur les causes qui peuvent affecter les esprits et les caractères" (ca. 1736), ed. Pierre Rétat, cited by line, in VF IX 219–70. For this work, there are two accessible English translations: see Montesquieu, "An Essay on the Causes That May Affect Men's Minds and Characters," tr. Melvin Richter, *Political Theory* 4:2 (May, 1976): 139–62, and Montesquieu, "An Essay on Causes Affecting Minds and Characters," tr. David W. Carrithers, in Charles-Louis de Secondat, baron de la Brède et de Montesquieu, *The Spirit of Laws: A Compendium of the First English Edition*, ed. David W. Carrithers (Berkeley: University of California Press, 1977), 417–54.

———, *CR*   Charles-Louis de Secondat, baron de La Brède et de Montesquieu, *Considérations sur les causes de la grandeur des Romains et de leur décadence* (1734), ed. Françoise Weil and Cecil Courtney, cited by chapter and, where appropriate, line from VF II 89–285.

———, *EL*   Charles-Louis de Secondat, baron de La Brède et de Montesquieu, *De l'Esprit des lois* (1757), cited by part, book, chapter, and, where appropriate, page from Pléiade II 225–995.

———, *LP*   Charles-Louis de Secondat, baron de La Brède et de Montesquieu, *Lettres persanes* (1721), ed. Edgar Mass, cited by number and, where appropriate, line from VF I 137–569—followed, where appropriate, by a backslash and the new number assigned the pertinent letter in the posthumous edition of this work published in 1758, which is reprinted in Pléiade I 129–373.

———, *MP*   Charles-Louis de Secondat, baron de La Brède et de Montesquieu, *Mes pensées*, cited by number and, where appropriate, page from Nagel II 1–677, who follows the enumeration provided by Montesquieu in the manuscript. This is the order that will be followed in VF XIV–

XV and in the English translation by Henry Clark scheduled for publication by Liberty Fund. This is also the order followed in Montesquieu, *Pensées, Le Spicilège*, ed. Louis Desgraves (Paris: Laffont, 1991), who provides a table of concordance, specifying the number assigned each corresponding entry in *Pensées et fragments inédits de Montesquieu, publiés par le baron Gaston de Montesquieu*, ed. Henri Barckhausen (Bordeaux: Publications de la Société des Bibliophiles de Guyenne, 1899–1901), and later reprinted in Pléiade I 971–1574, where the entries have been rearranged in topical order and renumbered.

———, *MS*   Charles-Louis de Secondat, baron de La Brède et de Montesquieu, *De l'Esprit des loix (Manuscrit de travail)* (ca. 1741/42–47), ed. Catherine Volpilhac-Auger, cited by page from VF III–IV.

———, *NA*   Charles-Louis de Secondat, baron de La Brède et de Montesquieu, *Notes sur l'Angleterre* (ca. 1729–31), cited by page from Pléiade I 875–84.

———, *RMU*   Charles-Louis de Secondat, baron de La Brède et de Montesquieu, *Réflexions sur la monarchie universelle en Europe* (1734), ed. Françoise Weil, cited by chapter and line from VF II 339–64.

———, *S*   Charles-Louis de Secondat, baron de La Brède et de Montesquieu, *Spicilège*, ed. Rolando Minuti, cited by number and, where appropriate, page from VF XIII 81–654.

Rahe, *ATA*   Paul A. Rahe, *Against Throne and Altar: Machiavelli and Political Theory under the English Republic* (New York: Cambridge University Press, 2008), cited by page.

———, *RAM*   Paul A. Rahe, *Republics Ancient and Modern: Classical Republicanism and the American Revolution* (Chapel Hill: University of North Carolina Press, 1992), cited by book, chapter, and section, which correspond with volume, chapter, and section in the three-volume paperback edition published in 1994.

Book One

THE MODERN
REPUBLIC DISCOVERED

Battles are the principal milestones in secular history. Modern opinion resents this uninspiring truth, and historians often treat the decisions in the field as incidents in the dramas of politics and diplomacy. But great battles, won or lost, change the entire course of events, create new standards of values, new moods, new atmospheres, in armies and in nations, to which all must conform.

—Winston S. Churchill

PREFACE

Roughly three hundred years ago, on 13 August 1704, an event took place that is today little remembered and even more rarely remarked on — though it signaled the beginning of a political and an ideological transformation that was arguably no less significant than the one marked in our own time by the fall of the Berlin Wall and the dismemberment of the Soviet Union. In the late spring and summer of that fateful year, two armies made their way from western to central Europe. The first, led by the comte de Tallard, marshal of France, aimed at upsetting the balance of power on the continent of Europe; at establishing Louis XIV's hegemony over the Holy Roman Empire by installing a French nominee on its throne; and at securing the acquiescence of the Austrians, the English, the Dutch, and every other European power in a Bourbon succession to the Spanish throne. The second army, led by John Churchill, then earl, later duke of Marlborough, with the assistance of Prince Eugene of Savoy, sought to preserve the existing balance of power, defend Hapsburg control of the imperial throne, and deprive Louis of his Spanish prize.

At stake, so Louis's opponents with some reason supposed, was the establishment of a universal monarchy in Europe and French dominion in the New World.[1] At stake for Englishmen, Scots, Irish Protestants, and Britain's colonists in the Americas were the supremacy of Parliament, the liberties secured by the Glorious Revolution in 1688 and 1689, the Protestant succession to the English crown, and Protestant hegemony in the British Isles and in much of the New World. James II, who had been ousted so unceremoniously from the English throne in 1688, had died in 1701. His Protestant daughter Anne was queen. But waiting in the wings, ready to claim his birthright when he came of age, was the French nominee — her fiercely Catholic younger brother James, known in France as the chevalier de Saint George.

3

There was every reason to suppose that Louis would attain for himself and his heirs the predominance within Europe that had been the object of his ambition during the entirety of his adult life. After all, on the field of the sword, France then enjoyed a pre-eminence that no one dared deny. The French had occasionally been checked, but on no occasion in the preceding one hundred fifty years had an army of France suffered a genuinely decisive defeat. It thus came as a shock when all of Europe learned that the army commanded by Marlborough and Prince Eugene had annihilated the French force and captured Marshal Tallard.[2]

Of course, had the battle of Blenheim been a fluke, had it been a genuine anomaly, as everyone at first assumed, Louis's defeat on this particular occasion would not have much mattered. At most, it would have marked a temporary, if severe setback for French arms. In the event, however, this great struggle was but the first of a series of French defeats meted out by armies captained by Marlborough, and it foreshadowed a series of setbacks that would bedevil monarchical France as the century wore on.[3] Sixty years later, an agent of the Minister of Foreign Affairs, when forced to acknowledge the "successes astonishing" and "incomprehensible" that William Pitt had just achieved in the Seven Years War, would console his principal by posing a series of highly revealing rhetorical questions. "In their foundations," he asked, "are these successes as considerable and of the same importance as were those of the Duke of Marlborough? Have the frontiers of France been blown open, have they been attacked? The Sovereign — has he been forced to consider whether he is to be buried under the ruins of the Monarchy?"[4] Such had been the achievement of Marlborough. This much everyone then knew.

If, today, we are astonishingly ill informed concerning the once famous battles that took place at Ramillies, Oudenarde, Lille, and Malplaquet in the brief span of years stretching from 1706 to 1709,[5] it is because we have become accustomed to resolutely averting our gaze from the fundamental realities of political life. In the United States, despite the leading role in the world our country long ago assumed, very few universities devote substantial resources to the study of armed conflict. Not one history department in twenty even offers a course focusing on the origins, the conduct, and consequences of war.[6] And yet Winston Churchill was surely right when he observed that "battles are the principal milestones in secular history," when he rejected "modern opinion," which "resents this uninspiring truth," and when he criticized "historians" who so "often treat the decisions in the field as incidents in the dramas of politics and diplomacy." "Great battles," he insisted, whether "won or lost, change the entire course of events, create new standards of values, new moods, new atmospheres, in armies and in nations, to which all must conform."[7]

It is in light of this bold claim that we must read Voltaire's *Philosophical Letters* and Montesquieu's *Considerations on the Causes of the Greatness of the Romans and their Decline*. For while it would be a gross exaggeration to say that, in comparison with the battle of Blenheim, the French Enlightenment and the French Revolution were little more than after-shocks, there can be no doubt that Marlborough's stirring victories over Louis XIV's France exposed the weakness of the *ancien régime* and occasioned the first efforts on the part of the philosophes to rethink in radical terms Europe's political trajectory.

One

AFTER THE FALL

That day at Blenheim, we lost the confidence that we had acquired by thirty years of victories. . . . Whole battalions gave themselves up as prisoners of war; we regretted their being alive, as we would have regretted their deaths.

It seemed as if God, who wished to set limits to empires, had given to the French this capacity to acquire, along with this capacity to lose, this fire that nothing resists, along with this despondency that makes one ready to submit to anything.

— *Charles-Louis de Secondat, baron de La Brède et de Montesquieu*

Events such as the fall of the Berlin Wall and the collapse of the Soviet Union have a way of altering the terms of public debate. Prior to 1989, Marxist analysis thrived in and outside the academy not only in the eastern bloc but even more so in the West. After 1991, it seemed—even to many of those who had once been its ardent practitioners—to be hopelessly anachronistic, at best a quaint relic of an earlier, benighted age, deserving of the species of contempt that Sir Francis Bacon, René Descartes, and the other proponents of the scientific revolution in the seventeenth century once reserved for the scholasticism of the high Middle Ages.[1]

So it was in France after 1713 when the treaty of Utrecht brought an end to the War of the Spanish Succession. By dint of diplomatic skill and a canny exploitation of the partisan strife that erupted between Whigs and Tories in Marlborough's England, Louis XIV had managed to preserve his kingdom intact and even to secure the Spanish throne for his grandson. But this achievement did not alter the fact that the Sun King's great project had proved unattainable. After all, French arms had been unequal to the task that they had been set, and the new Bourbon king of Spain had been required to renounce all claims to the French throne. Nor did the brilliance of Louis's diplomatic coup disguise the fact that overreaching on his part had bankrupted France and had very nearly brought down the polity.[2] A sense of foreboding gripped his countrymen as they slowly digested what there was to be learned from their repeated defeats on the field of the sword.

It is no accident that, as a thinker, Jacques-Bénigne Bossuet had in France almost no real heirs: comprehensive defeat is a solvent not only for Marxism but also for the species of Christian providentialism that the bishop of Meaux had deployed in defending the divine right of kings in his *Discourse on Universal History* (1681) and his *Politics Drawn from the Very Words of Holy Scripture* (1709).[3] Nor should it seem odd that the Regency—established with all due solemnity after Louis XIV's death on 1 September 1715 to govern France until his five-year-old great-grandson Louis XV should reach adulthood—quite quickly came to be synonymous with decay and disarray.[4] It was no longer possible to thrill to the vision that had informed Louis's great effort.

Whether Louis XIV ever actually aimed at universal monarchy is in dispute. He never publicly embraced such a goal. When his opponents lodged the accusation, he denied its truth, and historians today are inclined to the view that his aims were, in fact, considerably less grand.[5] It would, however, be an error to suppose that the charge leveled at him by his German, English, and Dutch antagonists was a mere slogan of their own invention. They first formulated the claim as a charge in response to its articulation as an aspiration by a figure at Louis's own court,[6] and later, when they restated this accusation, they could cite others within the royal entourage who had publicly embraced the same goal. As one particularly acute French critic of the Sun King subsequently observed, "Louis labored only to awaken against himself the jealousy of Europe. It seemed as if he had formed the project of arousing its fears [*l'inquiéter*] rather than of conquering it. The genius of a great statesman searches for a way to establish power before making it felt. Louis had a genius for making it felt before having established it."[7]

The blunders began in 1667, when Antoine Aubery, a member of the parlement of Paris, published—with formal approval from Louis XIV—a book articulating and defending the foreign policy which that monarch pursued. It bore the title *Of the Just Pretensions of the King to Empire*, and it included a passage that caught many an eye: praising the king's marriage to a Spanish infanta, intimating that this portended a union of the French and the Spanish thrones, and celebrating the birth of an heir "to whom all things seem infallibly to promise, in the ages to come, as great an Empire over the sea as over the land and universal Monarchy" to boot.[8]

Though the publication of this tract caused a furor throughout Europe, helped arouse opposition to the Sun King of France, and thereby landed its author for a time in the Bastille,[9] Aubery was by no means voicing sentiments solely his own.[10] The idea had been broached decades earlier by Tommaso Campanella, a long-time champion of Spanish ambitions in this regard.[11] Toward the end of his life, after the prospects of Spain had dimmed,[12] this visionary Calabrian friar had cast the horoscope of the "wonder child" born to Louis XIII, and he had predicted that Louis XIV would achieve the monarchy of the world.[13] Moreover, some three years before the publication of Aubery's tract, Jean de Lartigue presented to Louis and to his two principal ministers, Michel Le Tellier and Jean-Baptiste Colbert, a manuscript entitled "The Second Part of the Policy of the Conquerors," in which he articulated at considerable length a case for the king's adoption of universal monarchy as his goal.[14]

Nor was Aubery the last publicly to flatter the House of Bourbon in this fashion. For, in 1688, two decades after Aubery's involuntary sojourn in the Bastille, the grammarian Louis-Augustin Alemand would preface his book on the French language with a dedicatory letter addressed to the Grand Dauphin, the immediate heir to the French throne, in which he would heap extravagant praise on the French language, singling it out, first and foremost, as an instrument of imperial rule:

> It is, Monseigneur, with this beautiful & glorious language that Louis the Great gives laws not only to his own empire but also to Europe entire — so that other sovereigns appear to think it glorious & a matter for serious application to learn French solely in order better to understand the wishes of a prince whom they all recognize as their sovereign judge, and the peoples themselves, following the example of their princes, study it with a care, an attentiveness, & an expenditure so extraordinary that they abandon for this purpose country, well-being, parents, & all that they possess in the world that is most dear, expressing by this their recognition that one day they will be called upon to obey a French monarch. In effect, Monseigneur, whether due to destiny or reason, the French language has already established something like a universal monarchy not only over all the other languages but also over all the nations, where it has gone as if to mark out the places where our sovereigns shall one day make themselves heard & obeyed.[15]

It is no wonder, then, that François de Salignac de La Mothe-Fénelon, the Sun King's most articulate and thoughtful French critic, went to the trouble of composing for Louis, duc de Bourgogne, Louis's grandson and prospective heir, a brief treatise arguing that it was morally obligatory that one resist all attempts to establish universal monarchy. Although he refrained from commenting directly on current public policy, Fénelon knew perfectly well that the concerns he raised were more than merely academic, and he thought them a matter of sufficient moment to justify his taking what was, he knew, a very considerable risk.[16]

As all of this suggests, prior to the battle of Blenheim, thanks to the Sun King's eagerness to strike a pose, the view articulated by Campanella, Lartigue, Aubery, and Alemand constituted the common sense of the matter. By 1715, however, Louis's great dream had become a nightmare, and at that time hardly anyone in Paris would have dared to repeat claims so grandiose and vainglorious. Yet no one at that time had a viable alternative vision to proffer France.[17]

The regent, Philippe II, duc d'Orléans, was hard-working and canny, to be sure, but he was notoriously dissolute, and the reforms that he attempted either came to naught or wreaked havoc in France.[18] At the outset, to the delight of the Sun King's critics, he experimented with what he called *polysynodie*—the governance of France through aristocratic councils—but this expedient he soon abandoned for ministerial government along familiar lines, and the plan for managing the national debt that he subsequently concocted with the Scots adventurer and financier John Law proved to be a catastrophe, ruining many a Frenchman and ultimately tripling that debt.[19]

For inspiration in this time of dejection, the French could, of course, turn to *Telemachus, Son of Ulysses*, the wildly popular mirror of princes penned for the duke of Burgundy in the early to mid-1690s by Fénelon in his guise as tutor to that ill-fated prince.[20] But practical men, recognizing, as they did, that virtuous kingship is an object of prayer, not a program or policy, were for the most part left unmoved. By 1715, it was perfectly clear to anyone with a discerning eye that the French monarchy was bankrupt in more than one way. By the end of 1720, when John Law's "system" had collapsed and French banknotes were worth no more than the paper on which they had been printed, discernment was no longer required.

At this point, young Frenchmen of penetrating intelligence began to look elsewhere for workable models.[21] Prior to the first decade of the eighteenth century, the French had demonstrated very little serious interest in England. The execution of Charles I in 1649 had been noticed, of course, but it had evoked little but horror; and apart from the decade immediately thereafter—when, for a time, the Rump Parliament ruled Britain and, then, Oliver Cromwell came into the ascendancy—England played no very prominent role in the affairs of Europe or the New World. From the perspective of Louis XIV, the Restoration polity presided over by Charles II and his younger brother James in the period stretching from 1660 to 1688 was a mere pawn—a relatively inconsequential state virtually begging for manipulation from abroad. Nor was the Sun King aware of any other reason why the English should deserve attention or respect. He is said once to have asked an English ambassador whether, in his country, there had ever been any writers of note. Of Shakespeare and Milton he had apparently never even heard, and he was by no means peculiar in this regard. When Corneille was sent an English translation of *Le Cid*, he is said to have shelved it in his cabinet between the work's translations into such barbaric languages as Slavonic and Turkish.[22] In seventeenth-century France, England was nothing more than an object for idle curiosity, if even that. Hardly anyone thought England, the English, their language, their literature, their philosophy, their institutions, their mode of conduct, their accomplishments in science, and their way of seeing the world a proper object for rumination.[23] At the beginning of Louis XVI's reign, one well-informed observer jotted down the observation that forty years earlier, except in port cities such as Calais, there had been hardly anyone in France, even in the highest echelons of the government, who was capable of reading English.[24]

After Marlborough's great victories, however, attitudes changed; and, to an increasing degree, young Frenchmen of penetrating intelligence thought it necessary to read about and perhaps even visit the country that put together, funded, and led the coalition that had inflicted on the most magnificent of their kings so signal a defeat.[25] The first figure of real note to subject England and the English to close scrutiny and extended study, the first such political pilgrim, was an ambitious young poet of bourgeois origin named François-Marie Arouet, whom we know best by his pen-name Voltaire.[26]

FRANÇOIS-MARIE AROUET

Voltaire spent two and a half years in England, arriving in May 1726 and departing abruptly, under suspicious, perhaps legally awkward circumstances, in October or November 1728. His visit was occasioned by a scrape that he had gotten into in Paris, where he had insulted a member of the nobility, who had exacted revenge by luring the poet from a dinner party and having his minions administer to the bourgeois upstart a severe cudgeling. When word got around that Voltaire intended to challenge the noble master of his less-exalted assailants to a duel, a *lettre de cachet* was elicited from the authorities, and the poet was thrown into the Bastille. Ultimately, he was released on condition that he absent himself from Paris and its environs, which he did forthwith.

Voltaire had been thinking of visiting England in any case, for he knew that it would be impossible to publish openly in France his epic *La Henriade*, embodying, as it did, a diatribe against religious persecution, a defense of the Edict of Nantes, and an oblique but unmistakable attack on the religious policy of Henry IV's pious Catholic grandson Louis XIV. In England, while arranging for the publication of this work in a lavish edition, Voltaire dined out, circulating among poets — such as Alexander Pope, John Gay, and Jonathan Swift — who were on good terms with his controversial Tory friend Henry St. John, Viscount Bolingbroke. Voltaire did not, however, restrict himself to the circle of the erstwhile Jacobite. He hobnobbed as well with the Whigs. He arrived in London with an introduction in hand, written to the duke of Newcastle, England's foreign minister, by Horatio Walpole, the English ambassador in Paris and uncle to Bolingbroke's bête noire, Sir Robert Walpole. In time, Voltaire met Newcastle and was presented to King George I; he eventually became acquainted with the prime minister himself; he spent considerable time in the company of Walpole's great friend Lord Hervey; and, after the publication of his *Henriade*, he dined with George II, then quite recently crowned.

Nor did Voltaire limit himself to the world of the poets, politicians, and princes. When Sir Isaac Newton died, he attended the funeral and sought out thereafter the great man's niece, and in the course of his sojourn he made a point of calling on and becoming acquainted with the dowager duchess of Marlborough, widow to the warrior and statesman who, twenty years before, had very nearly brought Louis XIV's France to its knees. Much of the rest of his time Voltaire devoted to mastering the English language.[27] His accomplishment in this last regard was quite remarkable — for, by the time that he left Britain, he had published two essays in English, and he had begun writing a play in that language. Moreover, in French, he had composed in almost its entirety his celebrated *Lettres philosophiques*.[28]

This last work deserves attention. When he returned to France, Voltaire set aside the chapters that he had already penned and turned first to his play *Brutus*, which he had started in English and now recast in French, and then to his *Histoire de Charles XII*. It was not until 1732 that he took up again his letters on the English, which he dispatched to London in the spring of 1733 for translation by John Lockman. The collection was published there, in English, in August of that year to great acclaim, and the volume was reprinted again and again in the course of the eighteenth century. A year later, Voltaire's English publisher published Voltaire's French manuscript under the title *Lettres écrites de Londres sur les Anglois*. In the meantime, however, Voltaire in Paris — after adding a lengthy chapter in which he denounced the Jansenist Blaise Pascal as a "sublime misanthrope" and criticized in detail the deeply disturbing depiction of fallen man presented in his *Pensées*[29] — had rewritten the rest of the work with an eye to its potential audience in France. When it was clandestinely published in Rouen under an Amsterdam imprint with the title *Lettres philosophiques* in April of 1734, it caused so considerable a stir that, over the five years following, something like twenty thousand copies were put into circulation.[30] To his English audience, Voltaire had offered an elegant satire appreciative of their virtues but by no means devoid of humor and bite. To his compatriots, he presented, by way of invidious comparison, a savage critique of the polity under which they lived.[31] The early-twentieth-century scholar who dubbed it "the first bomb thrown at the *ancien régime*" was right on the mark.[32] As Jean-Antoine-Nicolas de Caritat, marquis de Condorcet, would observe in his biography of Voltaire, the *Lettres philosophiques* marked in France "the epoch of a revolution." It caused a "taste for English philosophy and literature to be born here." It induced "us to interest ourselves in the mores, the policy, the commercial outlook of this people." It even persuaded the notoriously self-absorbed French to familiarize themselves with the English language. Such was the book's effect.[33]

This was precisely what Voltaire had intended. Some years before, he had informed his English public that he had been "ordered to give an Account of my Journey into *England.*" It was, he continued, "the true aim" of such "a Relation to instruct Men, not to gratify their Malice. We should be busied chiefly in giving faithful Accounts of all the useful things and of the extraordinary Persons, whom to know, and to imitate, would be a Benefit to our Countrymen. A Traveller who writes in that Spirit, is a Merchant of a noble Kind, who imports into his native Country the Arts and Virtues of other Nations. I will leave to others the Care of describing with Accuracy, *Paul's* Church, the *Monument*, *Westminster*, *Stonehenge*, &c. I consider *England* in another view; it strikes my Eyes as it is the Land which hath produced a *Newton*, a *Locke*, a *Tillotson*, a *Milton*, a *Boyle.*"[34] This is evidently what Voltaire had in mind when, by entitling the Rouen edition of the completed work as he did, he suggested to his compatriots the unheard-of notion that England, the English, their language, their literature, their institutions, their accomplishments in philosophy and science, and their way of life constituted a subject genuinely worthy of philosophical reflection.

VOLTAIRE'S *LETTRES PHILOSOPHIQUES*

In the little book he eventually published, Voltaire did pretty much what he had promised: he introduced his compatriots to Newton, Locke, Tillotson, and Boyle, as well as to Bacon, Shakespeare, and Congreve, and he even took notice of Dryden, Pope, Swift, and Addison. But he did much more as well. He devoted the first seven of the book's twenty-five letters to religion: gently satirizing the practices of the Quakers, making that tolerant sect of religious enthusiasts seem quaint, morally attractive, and just a bit mad; mocking the religious and political pretensions of the Anglican establishment but hinting broadly that its clergymen were far less likely than their French counterparts to flaunt an amorous dalliance; savaging the Presbyterians for their fanaticism; and praising the Socinianism putatively embraced by Newton, Clarke, Locke, and Leclerc, "the greatest philosophers, & the ablest writers of their times."[35] All the while, he intimated that, in matters of religion, the great virtue of the English was that their devotion to Mammon rendered them as men of faith decidedly lukewarm. "Go into the *Royal-Exchange* in *London*," says Voltaire. It is a "place more venerable than many Courts of justice." There, he asserts,

> you will see the representatives of all the Nations assembled for the benefit of mankind. There the Jew, the Mahometan, & the Christian transact together as tho' they all profess'd the same Religion, & give the name of infidel to none but bankrupts. There the Presbyterian confides in the Anabaptist, & the Anglican depends on the Quaker's word. At the breaking up of this pacific & free assembly, some withdraw to the Synagogue, & others to take a glass. This man goes to be baptiz'd in a great tub, in the name of the Father, Son, & Holy Ghost. That man has his son's foreskin cut off, whilst a sett of *Hebrew* words (quite unintelligible to him) are mumbled over his child. Others retire to their Church to await the inspiration of God with their hats on, & all are satisfied.

Voltaire's compatriots can hardly have missed the significance for Catholic France of the lesson that in the end he drew: "If one Religion only were allowed in England, there would be reason to fear despotism; if there were but two, the people wou'd cut one another's throats; but there are thirty, & they all live happily in peace."[36]

In precisely the same spirit, Voltaire then examined England's government, tacitly juxtaposing it with the absolute monarchy ruling his native France. Though the English liked to compare themselves with the Romans, he expressed doubts as to whether the comparison was apt. "The Romans," he observes, "never knew the dreadful folly of religious Wars, an abomination reserv'd for Devout preachers of patience & humility. Marius & Sylla, Cæsar & Pompey, Anthony & Augustus did not go to war, merely to determine whether the *Flamen* should wear his shirt over his robe, or his robe over his shirt; & whether, for one to take the Augury, the sacred chickens should eat & drink, or eat only. In the past, the English reciprocally hang'd one another at their Assizes, & destroyed one another in pitched battles, for quarrels of as trifling a nature." By his day, however, this had all changed. "I don't perceive the least inclination in them now," he wrote, "to cut one another's throats over Syllogisms." In fact, he judged eighteenth-century Englishmen far superior to the pagans of ancient Rome, and, by appropriating for his own use a famous passage from Fénelon's *Telemachus* that the duc d'Orléans had paraphrased the day he established his prerogatives as regent, Voltaire implied that the English had achieved by way of institutions designed to check the power of their kings the species of ideal kingship that the duke of Burgundy's tutor had so heartily recommended to his young charge.

> The fruit of the civil wars at Rome was slavery, & that of the troubles of England, liberty. The English are the only Nation upon earth who have been able to prescribe limits to the power of Kings by resisting them; & who, by a series of struggles, have at last establish'd that wise Government, where the Prince, all powerful to do good, has his hands tied against doing wrong; where the Nobles are Great without insolence & Vassals; & where the people share in the government without confusion.
>
> The House of Lords & that of the Commons are the Arbiters of the Nation; the King is the Presiding Judge [*Sur-Arbitre*]. The Romans had no such balance. The Nobles & the People in Rome were perpetually at variance, with no intermediate power to reconcile them. The Roman Senate who were so unjustly & so criminally proud, as not to suffer the Plebeians to share with them in any thing, cou'd find no other artifice to keep the latter out of the administration than by employing them continually in foreign wars. They consider'd the People as a wild beast, whom it behov'd them to let loose upon their neighbours, for fear they should devour their Masters. Thus the greatest defect in the government of the Romans rais'd 'em to be Conquerors. By being unhappy at home, they became masters of the world, till at last their divisions sunk them to slavery.

England's government was not designed, Voltaire insisted, "for so great an *éclat* nor will its end be so fatal. Its aim is not the splendid folly of making conquests, but preventing its neighbours from doing so. This people is jealous not only of its own liberty, but of that enjoyed by others. The English were exasperated against Louis XIV, for no other reason but because they believed him ambitious."[37]

Voltaire was even willing to celebrate the bourgeois character of English society. In fact, he was more than eager to do so. "As Trade enrich'd the Citizens in England," he contended, "so it contributed to making them free, & this freedom extended their Commerce in turn, whence arose the grandeur of the State. Trade rais'd by insensible degrees the naval power, by which the English are masters over the seas." Moreover, commerce, which enabled a small island with little in the way of resources to marshal great fleets, also enabled it to finance great wars and to fight great battles, such as those, expressly mentioned by

Voltaire, in which England defeated France at Blenheim and Ramillies. The role, he adds, that the island's commercial classes played in funding the victories of Marlborough and Prince Eugene "raises a just Pride in an English Merchant, & makes him presume (not without some reason) to compare himself to a Roman Citizen." To those among his compatriots inclined to treasure aristocratic birth, Voltaire throws down an unanswerable challenge: "I cannot say which is most useful to a State; a Lord, well-powder'd, who knows exactly at what a clock the King rises, at what a clock he goes to bed; & who gives himself airs of Grandeur while acting the slave in the anti-chamber of a Minister; or a Merchant, who enriches his Country, dispatches Orders from his Compting-House to Surat & to Cairo, & contributes to the felicity of the world."[38]

Needless to say, not everyone in France was as pleased with sallies of this sort as was the author of the *Lettres philosophiques*. Upon first reading the book, the abbé Jean-Bernard Le Blanc, who was otherwise on excellent terms with Voltaire, protested in a letter to a common acquaintance that he was "shocked by a tone of contempt which holds sway throughout. This contempt pertains equally to our nation, to our government, to our ministers, to everything that is highly respectable — in a word to religion." In his little book, he adds, Voltaire displays "an indecency truly horrible."[39]

The authorities were similarly disposed. Under the Regency, there had been a relaxation of discipline and a flowering of frank political discourse. But the duc d'Orléans had died in December 1723, some ten months after Louis XV had attained his majority, and Louis-Henri, duc de Bourbon-Condé, who had succeeded him as prime minister, had not lasted long. From 1726 to 1743, André-Hércule Cardinal de Fleury was firmly in charge, and he was no more friendly to public political debate than had been Armand Jean du Plessis, cardinal-duc Richelieu; Jules Cardinal Mazarin; and Louis XIV.[40] Moreover, in the early 1730s, Paris had been in a great uproar, in large part as a consequence of the ongoing attempt by the crown and the Jesuits to restore unity to the French church by reining in and ultimately eliminating the Jansenists; and in April 1734 it was not yet certain that the crisis had passed.[41] Neither party to the dispute was amused by the antics of a libertine who evidenced a desire to dance in the ashes of both, and the civil magistrate was then, for understandable reasons, hyper-sensitive to any criticism that appeared to be subversive of the established order. Within a month of the book's appearance, a *lettre de cachet* had been issued ordering Voltaire's arrest; his house and that of his friend Jean Baptiste Nicholas Formont in Rouen had been searched; the printer had been arrested; and the remaining copies of the book had been confiscated. Soon thereafter, the parlement of Paris, already then a stronghold of Jansenist influence, denounced the

Lettres philosophiques as "scandalous, contrary to religion, good morals, and the respect due to authority," and it instructed the public hangman to lacerate and burn the book with all due ceremony in the courtyard of the Palais de justice, which he did on 10 June 1734.[42]

Voltaire, who was acutely sensitive to the change in political dynamics that had over time taken place, anticipated the storm.[43] By the time that it broke, he was far away from Paris in Champagne, near the border of Lorraine, safely and comfortably ensconced at Cirey, the chateau of his mistress, the marquise du Châtelet—where, in a kind of exile, he was to spend the better part of the next fifteen years.[44] As all of this transpired, however, another French visitor to England looked on with deep concern. He, too, upon his return from London, had written an ambitious book modest in its dimensions. He had arranged for its publication in Holland; and, now that Voltaire's *Lettres philosophiques* had been turned over to the public hangman, he wondered—and not for the first time—whether it was wise to usher into print some of the more controversial observations that he had very much wanted to convey.

CHARLES-LOUIS DE SECONDAT

Voltaire was a bomb-thrower. Charles-Louis de Secondat, baron de La Brède et de Montesquieu, was nothing of the kind.[45] He was trained in what can best be described as the common law of *ancien régime* France. He understood and sympathized with the legal profession's propensity for justifying decisions by means of an appeal to precedent, and he was inclined to be prudent and respectful of the dictates of long experience. When called upon for advice in crises, such as the one that threatened French finances at the death of Louis XIV, he tended to opt for modest reform.[46] Montesquieu was not attracted to extremes.

But, of course, Montesquieu was no more a traditionalist inclined to subject reason to the dead hand of the past than was Voltaire. During the Regency, some thirteen years before the appearance of the *Lettres philosophiques*, at a time when censorship was comparatively lax,[47] he had established his reputation as a wit and man of letters, and he had laid the groundwork for his eventual election to the Académie française by publishing his own philosophical letters—the *Lettres persanes*. In these, which later served as a model for Voltaire,[48] he too had none too gently satirized the foibles of his age, subverting inherited mores and obliquely criticizing both the Roman Catholic Church and the Jansenists, pointedly mocking the ambitions and despotic inclinations of Louis XIV, and intimating to all who cared to read between the lines that in France the *ancien régime* was on its last legs.[49]

In 1733, Voltaire paused briefly to consider what might ensue should he actually publish his *Lettres philosophiques*. "There are times," he mused, "when one can with impunity do the most daring things [*les choses les plus hardies*]; there are other times when something that is exceedingly simple and innocent becomes dangerous and criminal. Is there anything of greater force and strength [*de plus fort*] than the *lettres persanes*? Is there a book in which anyone has discussed [*ait traitté*] the government and religion with less tact and solicitude [*avec moins de ménagement*]? And yet this book has had no consequence, other than to cause its author to enter into the company called the Académie française."[50]

Montesquieu was born in 1689; Voltaire, in 1694. Both had witnessed the War of the Spanish Succession. Both had recognized the significance of Marlborough's victories. And both thought it essential to come to an understanding of the political regime that had so humiliated the nation into which they had been born. "Germany was made to travel in, Italy to sojourn in, . . . and France to live in," but "England"—she was made "to think in." Although the sentiment is attributed to Montesquieu,[51] the words could just as easily have been uttered by Voltaire.

Of the two, Montesquieu was the elder. At the time of his country's first great defeat, he was well past his fifteenth birthday—old enough to be thrilled at the prospect of martial glory, old enough to foresee a time when he might himself join the fray, old enough to take an interest in the welfare of his country and to mourn its loss. We do not know how he reacted to the news that Marlborough and Prince Eugene had annihilated his country's legions and captured their commander, but we can easily guess. Many years later, in the course of sketching out a history of France, Montesquieu recalled the events of that day and outlined their consequence. "Before the battle of Blenheim," he wrote,

> France had risen to a time of greatness [*grandeur*] that one regarded as immutable, although the country was then on the verge of decline [*touche au moment de la décadence*]. It is certain that the league [of those allied against Louis XIV] was in despair. That day at Blenheim, we lost the confidence that we had acquired by thirty years of victories. . . . Whole battalions gave themselves up as prisoners of war; we regretted their being alive, as we would have regretted their deaths.
>
> It seemed as if God, who wished to set limits to empires, had given to the French this capacity to acquire, along with this capacity to lose, this fire that

nothing resists, along with this despondency [*découragement*] that makes one ready to submit to anything. (*MP* 1306)[52]

Such were the sentiments that Frenchmen felt at the time; such appear to have been the sentiments that Montesquieu continued to feel throughout his life. And by the shocks that subsequently took place at Ramillies, Oudenarde, Lille, and Malplaquet, this despondency can only have been reinforced. Among other things, it helps explain why, during and immediately after his European tour, Montesquieu made repeated attempts to secure appointment as a French diplomat.[53] From the outset, he feared for the future of his native land. From early on, he hoped to make a contribution to rescuing it from its malaise.

Montesquieu was an aristocrat by birth. He traced his lineage to both the nobility of the sword and that of the robe.[54] He was anything but a *parvenu*. As a writer, he had no special need or desire for the passing applause of his contemporaries. His ambitions were, if anything, much grander than those of Voltaire, and today, at least in the United States, among those who read in order to understand, he enjoys a reputation far greater than that accorded his younger rival. Of course, Montesquieu could afford to be patient, and he generally preferred to be indirect—which is why, in the spring of 1734, as he contemplated the fate meted out to the *Lettres philosophiques* and visited upon its author, his hapless friend in Rouen, and the book's printer, he chose to censor a volume that he had the previous summer submitted to his publisher in Amsterdam,[55] a work for which the type had already been set.

MONTESQUIEU'S MYSTERIOUS BOOK

Montesquieu began his political pilgrimage to England in November 1729, roughly a year after Voltaire's departure, and he departed early in 1731. His sojourn there was much shorter than Voltaire's; he made no great effort fully to master the language and become an English author; and he made much less of an impression on those with whom he sojourned than had his more voluble compatriot—but he did circulate within aristocratic circles, and he paid close attention to everything that he was told.

Montesquieu was well connected. Like Voltaire, he had known Bolingbroke in France. When he set out on his European tour on 5 April 1728, he did so in the company of the first Earl Waldegrave, Great Britain's newly appointed ambassador to the Hapsburg court. On this tour, while in Vienna, he sought out Prince Eugene of Savoy and conversed at length on a number of occasions with Marlborough's old comrade-in-arms; and when he reached Venice, he made a point of interviewing John Law, erstwhile controller-general of the finances of France.

In Hanover, Montesquieu met King George II, and he arrived in England on the yacht of the earl of Chesterfield. While in the British Isles, he spent time with the king and with Queen Caroline, and he put together a collection of French ballads for their son Frederick, the prince of Wales. He almost certainly met the dowager duchess of Marlborough; he listened carefully when the future earl of Bath told stories concerning the deceased duke; and he befriended the husband of Marlborough's eldest daughter, the duke of Montagu. He also attended Parliament and paid close attention to the debates. He read with care Bolingbroke's *Craftsman*, and he perused the periodical press. He was elected to the Royal Society and inducted into the Free Masons. He used his time well.[56]

When he returned to France, Montesquieu retreated to his chateau near Bordeaux and devoted two years to writing. It was in this period of self-imposed solitary confinement that he composed his *Considérations sur les causes de la grandeur des Romains et de leur décadence*, the work that he was to publish in Holland in the late spring of 1734.[57] On the face of it, this work would appear to have next to nothing to do with his extended sojourn in England. In its pages, to be sure, if only for comparative purposes, there is occasional mention of the English and of the government under which they then lived, but neither the people nor the polity looms especially large. Montesquieu's chosen subject was Rome, after all, and for the most part he stuck to his last.[58] When viewed in this light alone, Montesquieu's *Considerations on the Causes of the Greatness of the Romans and their Decline* must be judged a minor masterpiece. There is no work on Roman history of comparable length, written before its author's time or since, that is as penetrating.

It remains unclear, however, just why Montesquieu thought it worth his time to write the book. It has neither a preface nor an introduction to inform us concerning his intentions;[59] and though it foreshadows in some respects the themes of his most famous work, *De l'Esprit des lois*, it evidences little to suggest a pertinence to public policy of the sort that was so central to the concerns that inspired the latter work. It would be tempting to conclude, as many scholars have,[60] that in the early 1730s Montesquieu was an antiquarian and a philosophical historian, intent on establishing his reputation within the republic of letters by writing a scholarly work on a noble theme.[61]

More can, however, be said, for in 1821 the existence of a second work, known from Montesquieu's catalogue but thought to be forever lost, was announced to the world; and seven decades thereafter it finally became available to the public.[62] Entitled *Réflexions sur la monarchie universelle en Europe*,[63] this brief essay survived only in printed form. As we learn from a note in Montesquieu's own hand placed at the top of the manuscript of yet another unpublished work, its author had originally had it "printed with" his *Considerations on the Causes of the Greatness of the Romans and their Decline*. His purpose had evidently been to publish the two together within the pages of a single volume. In fact, the paper on which his *Reflections on Universal Monarchy in Europe* is printed is of the same stock as that used by Montesquieu's publisher Desbordes in the first impression of the *Considerations on the Romans*. But, as Montesquieu goes on to indicate in his marginal note, certain "reasons caused" him "to suppress" the *Universal Monarchy*. These reasons he does not, in this particular marginal note, spell out. Elsewhere, however, in a note he penned on the first page of the printed copy of his *Universal Monarchy*, he is more forthcoming: he "suppressed" this work, he tells us, "for fear that certain passages would be interpreted ill [*de peur qu'on n'interpretat mal quelques endroits*]."

This was not, however, the end of the matter—for there survives yet another manuscript of significance for understanding Montesquieu's intentions in this regard, the so-called Bodmer manuscript, which is written partly in the hand of Montesquieu and partly in the hand of an amanuensis known to have worked for him in the period stretching from 1733 or 1734 to 1738 or shortly thereafter.[64] Within this manuscript, one finds a set of corrections laid out in preparation for the publication of a new and improved edition of the *Considerations on the Romans*. This revised version of the *Considerations on the Romans* was to contain two additional chapters not in the original version published in 1734, and these are drawn in their entirety from the sections of the *Universal Monarchy* most likely to offend. Moreover, in the manuscript of Montesquieu's *Pensées*, there are five entries graced with marginal notes indicating that they had been inserted in the *Considerations on the Romans*—entries which, in fact, appear nowhere except in the chapters of the *Universal Monarchy* that Montesquieu attempted to find place for in the projected revision of his little book on Rome.[65]

Nor is this the end of this story. On 10 March 1818, Joseph-Cyrille de Montesquieu, proprietor of La Brède, drew up a catalogue of the manuscripts, left unpublished at his grandfather's death, that he was sending to England to his cousin Charles-Louis de Montesquieu. Among the items listed was the printed version of Montesquieu's *Reflections on Universal Monarchy in Europe*. Also listed was a notebook, apparently no longer extant, with the following inscribed on the cover: "It will be necessary to finish this little treatise on *Universal Monarchy* and to cut out of it the articles concerning the mines of Spain that I placed in my book treating commerce in *The Spirit of Laws*. I will be able to add the treatise to [*joindre . . . à*] my *Romans* or my *Spirit of Laws*. Within this treatise it will be possible to enter those things which are the residue of my *Romans* or my *Spirit of Laws*."[66]

There can, then, be no doubt that Montesquieu originally intended to publish his *Reflections on Universal Monarchy in Europe* as a companion piece and sequel to his *Considerations on the Causes of the Greatness of the Romans and their Decline* and that he was dissuaded from doing so not by a change of opinion concerning their appropriateness for one another but solely by fear that a publication of the former work would cause him the sort of difficulties that Voltaire had brought on himself when he ushered his *Lettres philosophiques* into print. Moreover, there is evidence that, in the aftermath of 1734, Montesquieu persisted in wanting to complete the argument of the *Considerations on the Romans* with that of the *Universal Monarchy* and that he sought to incorporate much of the latter work within a revised edition of the former. Indeed, even after the publication of his *Spirit of Laws* in 1748, despite the fact that he had inserted within it a great deal of material drawn from the *Universal Monarchy*,[67] Montesquieu expressed yet again a desire to see his little book on the Romans and his short treatise on universal monarchy published in tandem.

In short, Montesquieu's *Considerations on the Romans* and his *Universal Monarchy* form a single work and must be addressed as such, for neither can adequately be understood apart from the other. In fact, when they are read together, as we shall soon see, Montesquieu's intentions become, in at least one crucial regard, exceedingly clear.[68]

MONTESQUIEU'S *REFLECTIONS* ON *UNIVERSAL MONARCHY IN EUROPE*

"It is a question worth raising [*une question qu'on peut faire*]," Montesquieu writes in the very first sentence of his *Reflections on Universal Monarchy in Europe*, "whether, given the state in which Europe actually subsists, it is possible for a People to maintain over the other peoples an unceasing superiority, as the [ancient] Romans did." For this question, Montesquieu has a ready answer—that "a thing like this has become morally impossible," and in support of this bold and unprecedented conclusion he gives two reasons: first, "innovations in the art of war," such as the introduction of artillery and firearms, "have equalized the strength [*forces*] of all men & consequently that of all Nations," and, second, "the *Ius Gentium* has changed, & under today's Laws war is conducted in such a manner that by bankruptcy it ruins above all others those who [initially] possess the greatest advantages" (*RMU* 1.1–9).

The second reason offered needs explication. In Machiavelli's *Art of War*, when the dialogue's protagonist, Fabrizio Colonna, laments the decline of martial virtue in Europe, he traces its disappearance to ancient Rome's elimination of the republics that had once flourished there. Europe's failure to recover after the fall of the Roman empire he explains partly with regard to the difficulty involved in restoring something that has been spoiled. Then he mentions a second, no less salient cause: "the fact that the mode of living today, as a consequence of the Christian religion, does not impose the necessity for self-defense that existed in ancient times." In antiquity, he explains,

> men conquered in war were either massacred or were consigned to perpetual enslavement where they led their lives in misery. Then, the towns conquered were either destroyed or the inhabitants were driven out, their goods seized, and, after being sent out, they were dispersed throughout the world. And so those overcome in war suffered every last misery. Frightened at this prospect, men kept military training alive and honored those who were excellent in it. But today this fear is for the most part lost. Of the conquered, few are massacred; none are held for long in prison since they are easily freed. Cities, even if they have rebelled a thousand times, are not eliminated; men are left with their goods so that most of the time what is feared is a ransom. In consequence, men do not want to subject themselves to military orders.

This alteration in the rules of war had an additional consequence, of particular interest to Montesquieu, which Colonna is no less inclined to regret: "That present wars impoverish the lords who are victorious as much as those who lose—for, if the one loses his state, the other loses his money and his possessions." In antiquity, he explains, war was for the victors a source of enrichment. In modern times, the costs all too often exceed the gains.[69]

To the changes in outlook effected by Christianity Montesquieu was no less sensitive than Machiavelli. He was, from the outset, fully aware of the fact that Christianity had "established the equality" of all mankind (*MP* 503), but, in his *Lettres persanes*, he questioned whether this had actually had any practical consequences (*LP* 73.22–32/75). In his *Universal Monarchy*, he would be considerably less tentative in this regard. There, the developments within the *ius gentium*—which Machiavelli's interlocutor traces to Christianity, laments, and evidently hopes to reverse—Montesquieu takes as an historic achievement,[70] and it is on this basis also that he judges universal monarchy a moral impossibility. "In earlier times," he explains, "one would destroy the towns that one had captured, one would sell the lands and, far more important, the inhabitants as well."

The sacking of a town would pay the wages of an Army, & a successful Campaign would enrich a Conqueror. At present, we regard such barbarities with a horror no more than just. We ruin ourselves [financially] in capturing places which capitulate, which we preserve intact, & which most of the time we return.

The Romans carried off to Rome in their Triumphs all the wealth of the Nations they conquered. Today victories confer none but sterile Laurels.

When a Monarch sends an Army into enemy country, he sends at the same time a part of his treasure so that the army can subsist; he enriches the country he has begun to conquer, & quite often he puts it in a condition to drive him out. (*RMU* 1.10–19)[71]

Herein lies what Montesquieu regarded as a delightful paradox, for in modern times imperial expansion tends to eliminate the conditions prerequisite for the imperial venture's success.

Having listed two reasons why universal monarchy cannot be achieved, Montesquieu then adds a third—emphasizing that there are "particular reasons responsible for the fact that in Europe prosperity cannot be permanent anywhere, & for the fact that there is a continual variation in [the distribution of] power, which, in the three other parts of the world, is, so to speak, fixed" (2.28–30).[72] These arguments deserve closer scrutiny as well.

In Montesquieu's view, Europe differs from the rest of the world in one crucial particular: "at present," it "is responsible for all the Commerce in the Universe & for the Carrying Trade [*Navigation*] in its entirety." He is persuaded as well that in his own day, at least in Europe, Machiavelli's famous dictum has been proven wrong and that money really has become the sinews of war: that, "to the extent to which a State takes a greater or lesser part in Commerce or in the Carrying Trade, its power necessarily grows or diminishes." In consequence, he contends, since war gets in the way of trade, "a State which appears to be victorious abroad ruins itself [financially] at home, while states which remain neutral augment their strength [*force*]." It can even happen that "those conquered regain their strength." In fact, "decline [*decadence*] generally sets in at the time of the greatest successes, for these can neither be achieved nor sustained except by violent means" (2.31–39).[73]

Poverty was once an advantage in war. In antiquity, when citizen armies were predominant, those from wealthy communities "were made up of men lost to flabbiness, idleness, & pleasure," and "for that reason" these cities "were often destroyed by the armies of neighbors accustomed to a life both painful & harsh, who were better suited to the war & military exercises of that time." In his own day, however, "the situation is not the same since no one group of Soldiers, the vilest part of every Nation, has a share in luxury greater than that of any other group, since in military exercises there is no longer need for the same strength & skill, and since it is now easier to form armies of regulars" (2.45–54).

In subsequent chapters, Montesquieu reinforces these claims, alluding to the shift in weaponry from arrows and spears to heavy artillery and firearms, touching on the motives that divide and paralyze modern monarchies, noting the relative stability that had taken hold in Europe, pointing to the depth of fortifications along France's border with Belgium, suggesting that the growth in communications attendant on trade denies anyone a lasting technological advantage, and contrasting the geography of Asia, which is favorable to empire, with that of Europe, which encourages the establishment of states of middling size. Along the way, he manages to remind his French readers of what had happened to their compatriots at Blenheim, Ramillies, Oudenarde, and Lille. It is at this point that he begins a brief survey of the abortive attempts, from Charlemagne's day forward, to found a universal monarchy in Europe on the lines of Rome's great empire—ending with the projects undertaken by the Hapsburgs and then, in his own day, by the Bourbons—and he shows why each and every one of these enterprises failed (3.65–17.382).

It is not difficult to discern why Montesquieu should have judged it imprudent to publish his *Universal Monarchy* in tandem with his *Considerations on the Romans.* In the seventeenth chapter of the former, with his tongue firmly in cheek, he piously denies the charge leveled by his opponents that Louis XIV had aimed at universal monarchy, and then he discusses events in a manner suggesting that this had been Louis's aim after all. "Had he succeeded," Montesquieu writes, in putative justification of his disclaimer, "nothing would have been more fatal to Europe, to his Subjects of old, to himself, to his family. Heaven, which knows what is really advantageous, served him better in his defeats than it would have in Victories, & instead of making him the sole King of Europe, it favored him more by making him the most powerful of them all." Had Louis won the battle of Blenheim, "the famous Battle in which he met his first defeat [*échec*]," Montesquieu tells us, "the undertaking would have been quite far from achievement, it would have hardly begun. It would have required a great increase in forces & a great expansion in frontiers." Moreover, he adds, the immediate prospect that the balance of power in Europe really would be overturned would have forced the lesser powers to enter the fray. "Germany, which had hardly entered the war except through the sale of Soldiers, would have taken the lead: the North would have risen; the neutral Powers would have taken sides, & his Allies would have changed sides [*changé d'interêts*]" (17.360–82).[74]

What the Sun King had failed to recognize was that "Europe is nothing more than one Nation composed of many" and that the rise of commerce had made his rivals for dominion his partners in trade. "France & England have need of the opulence of Poland & Muscovy," Montesquieu argues, "just as one of their Provinces has need of the others: & the State, which believes that it will increase its power as a consequence of [financial] ruin visited on another state on its border, ordinarily weakens itself along with its neighbor" (18.383–86).

The entire thrust of Montesquieu's argument throughout the *Universal Monarchy* is that offensive war does much more harm than good to the aggressive state. "If conquest on a grand scale is so difficult, so fruitless [*vain*], so dangerous," he asks, "what can one say of the malady of our own age which dictates that everywhere one maintain a number of troops disproportionate [*desordonné*]" to one's actual needs? We are not like "the Romans," he notes, "who managed to disarm others in the measure in which they armed themselves." In modern Europe, instead, where this endeavor produces an "Equilibrium" of sorts among "the great Powers,"

> this malady grows worse and worse [*a ses redoublemens*], & it is of necessity contagious, since as soon as one State augments what it calls its forces, the others of a sudden augment theirs, in such a fashion that one gains nothing thereby except the common ruin [attendant on insolvency]. Each Monarch keeps on foot all the Armies that he would be able to field if the Peoples he governed were in danger of being exterminated, & we confer the name Peace on this effort of all against all. Thus Europe is ruined [by bankruptcy] in such a fashion that, if three private Individuals were in the situation in which the three most opulent Powers in this Part of the World find themselves, they would not have anything on which to live. Thus we are poor with all the wealth & commerce of the entire Universe, & soon, on account of having soldiers, we shall have nothing but soldiers, & we will become like the Tartars.
>
> The great Princes, not content with buying troops from the lesser ones, seek on every side to purchase Alliances, which is to say: almost always to waste their money.
>
> The consequence of this situation is the perpetual augmentation of taxes, & that which prevents any remedy to come: they do not depend solely on their revenues but make war with their capital. It is not unprecedented for States to mortgage their incomes even in Peacetime, & to employ, in order to ruin themselves [by bankruptcy], means so extraordinary & so forceful that the scion of a good family, though he happens to be thoroughly out of control [*le plus derangé*], could hardly imagine resorting to such measures on his own behalf. (24.432–52)[75]

Montesquieu ends his *Universal Monarchy* by drawing a comparison in this regard between the modern monarchies of Europe and the despotisms of the Orient to the advantage of the latter. His final sentence, directed at Europe, is a Latin tag drawn from one of the epistles of Horace: "*Iliacos intra muros peccatur & extra*" (25.470). When one looks up the original, one finds that the tag is part of a larger whole: "By treachery, crime, and fraud," it reads, "crimes are committed both inside the walls of Troy and outside" (Hor. *Ep.* 1.2.16).

Although in retrospect Montesquieu denies that he "had in view any particular Government in Europe" and insists that he is expressing "reflections pertinent to them all" (*RMU* 25.468–69), had he actually published his *Reflections on Universal Monarchy in Europe,* everyone would have recognized in the work an angry diatribe against Louis XIV and everything for which the Sun King of France had once stood.[76]

Two

ROME ECLIPSED

To this first way of envisaging the subject, there succeeded in my mind another. It would no longer be a lengthy work but a book rather short, a single volume perhaps. I would no longer undertake a history of the Empire, so to speak, but an ensemble of reflections and judgments on that history. . . . The inimitable model of this genre is the book of Montesquieu on the greatness and the decline of the Romans. In it, one passes, so to speak, across Roman history without stopping; and nonetheless one perceives enough of this history to desire and comprehend the explanations offered by its author. . . . Occupying himself with an epoch quite vast and remote, he was, from time to time, able to choose only the greatest facts and to say apropos such facts none but very general things.

—Alexis de Tocqueville

When considered in light of its intended sequel, Montesquieu's *Considérations sur les causes de la grandeur des Romains et de leur décadence* reads like an extended introduction.[1] It was, after all, the image of Roman grandeur that had fired the ambition of Europe's greatest monarchs. Had it not been for Caesar's ruthless exploitation of the revolutionary potential inherent in his office as an *imperator* within the *imperium Romanum*, there never would have been a monarch who styled himself an emperor, a Kaiser, or Czar.[2] In the European imagination, the idea of universal monarchy was inseparable from a longing for imperial greatness on the Roman model.[3] If Montesquieu wished to find and apply an antidote for "the malady" besetting his own age, if he wished to defend against Machiavelli's assault the salutary changes in the *ius gentium* that had rendered universal monarchy a moral impossibility, he had to come to grips with the attraction exerted on his contemporaries by the glittering example of classical Rome.

Montesquieu fully understood Rome's allure. He felt this attraction quite powerfully himself. He had long felt its force. As an adolescent, he had studied its history at the collège de Juilly with the fathers of the Congregation of the Oratory.[4] On 18 June 1716, when, at the age of twenty-seven, he made his intellectual debut at the Academy of Bordeaux, he did so by reading a paper entitled "Dissertation on the Policy of the Romans in Religion."[5] A year or so later, he composed a "Discourse on Cicero," in which he displayed a profound admiration for the Roman as a statesman, orator, and philosopher and great regret at the demise of the Roman republic.[6] Four years thereafter, in his *Persian Letters*, Montesquieu had his Persian traveler Usbek report as the remarks of "a man of good sense" the observation that

> the Sanctuary of Honor, of Reputation, & of Virtue seems to be established in Republics & in the Countries where one is able to pronounce the word Fatherland. At Rome, at Athens, at Sparta, honor was the only compensation given for the most notable services. For a battle won or a City taken, a Crown of Oak or Laurel, a statue, a Eulogy was recompense on a scale immense [*une recompense immense*].
>
> There a man who had done something splendid [*belle*] thought himself to have received sufficient recompense from the act itself. He was not able to look on one of his compatriots without feeling the pleasure of being his benefactor: he reckoned the number of his services by that of his Fellow-Citizens. Every man is capable of doing another a good turn, but to contribute to the well-being of an entire Society is to resemble the Gods. (*LP* 87.15, 31–41/89)

A few years later, in his notebooks, Montesquieu paused to remark that, in the histories penned by the ancient Romans and Greeks, there is visible a "nobility," rooted in "love of the fatherland," and a "virtue dear to all those who possess a heart," which is utterly absent from the histories written in his own time. "When one reflects on the pettiness of our motives," he wrote, when one reflects "on the baseness of the means" to which we have resort, when one reflects "on the avarice with which we seek vile recompense," above all, when one assesses "this ambition, so different from the love of glory," it seems as if, with the disappearance of the ancients, mankind itself has been reduced in stature. So firmly was the French *philosophe* persuaded of the truth of these sentiments that, a decade later, he had the passage recopied in its entirety word for word and appended to a savage critique of Spanish imperialism in the New World.[7]

In 1748, when at long last he published his *Spirit of Laws*, Montesquieu was no less deeply in thrall. "One can never leave the Romans behind," he wrote therein. "So it is that still today, in their capital, one leaves the new palaces to go in search of the ruins; so it is that the eye which has taken its repose on the flower-strewn grasslands loves to look at the rocks & mountains" (*EL* 2.11.13). Some months after the publication of his magnum opus, when Montesquieu wrote to an old friend that "Rome *antica e moderna* has always enchanted me,"[8] in at least half of what he said, he was frankly speaking his mind. In politics, for Montesquieu, classical antiquity—above all else, Rome—represented the sublime.

Of course, nowhere in the various editions of the *Considerations on the Romans* that were published in French did Montesquieu even intimate that the ruminations contained therein had a present-day political point. Nowhere did he mention Dante's *De monarchia*.[9] Nowhere did he explicitly link Roman grandeur with the imperial project launched in Europe by the Holy Roman Emperor Charles V. Nowhere did he touch on the ambitions of that great monarch's son and heir. Only in the most oblique fashion did he allude to the aims generally attributed to the Sun King of France.[10] In fact, nowhere in that work did he even resort to the language customarily used in the sixteenth, seventeenth, and eighteenth centuries by admirers and detractors alike to describe the aspirations of Charles V, Philip II, and Louis XIV: nowhere did he identify the Roman empire as a *monarchie universelle.* Although he owned and had evidently read much of the literature on the subject, both pro and con,[11] assiduously he avoided that loaded term.

Montesquieu had not always been so circumspect. We know that he revised his *Considerations on the Romans* in the spring of 1734, after having had his Jesuit friend Louis-Bertrand Castel read the page proofs in search of passages that might offend the authorities,[12] and we know that he continued thereafter that year to make further adjustments by means of cancels and lists of errata.[13] There is reason to suppose that, prior to publication, he altered the text also in connection with his decision to suppress the *Reflections on Universal Monarchy in Europe,* changing the phrasing of the *Considerations on the Romans* where it too openly anticipated the outlook of the more controversial of his two essays. For, despite Montesquieu's efforts, traces of material that he deleted, in fact, survive—not in French, to be sure, but in the latter work's original English translation.

The anonymous English translator of Montesquieu's little book on Rome appears to have worked from the uncorrected or partially corrected page proofs, if not from a manuscript earlier yet;[14] and he worked with admirable alacrity. By early August 1734, just a few weeks after the book had been approved for distribution and publication in France,[15] Montesquieu had in hand copies of the translation suitable for presentation to the Royal Society and to its President and its Secretary,[16] and that month the translator's handiwork was available for purchase in bookstores in London.[17]

In the English translation, there are two passages that are highly revealing. Where the first impression of the version published in French read "*ce projet d'envahir tout*" and "*Les Romains parvinrent à commander à tous les Peuples*" (*CR* 15.86, 18.72), the English translation spoke of the "Schemes" responsible for the "Advances" that the Romans made "to universal Monarchy" and had Montesquieu remark, "The *Romans* arrived at universal Monarchy."[18] The translator's choice of language in these passages can hardly be fortuitous. It clearly reflects the version in French from which he had worked, and, in doing so, it confirms what can be inferred on the basis of other evidence: that, when Montesquieu's *Considerations on the Causes of the Greatness of the Romans and their Decline* was originally drafted, it was not intended to stand on its own. It was designed as part of a larger project—to which his *Reflections on Universal Monarchy in Europe* was also intended as a contribution.[19]

It should not, then, be surprising that, from the outset, Montesquieu had as his focus in the *Considerations on the Romans* Rome's imperial achievement. Nor should it seem odd that he at first thought it sufficient to write a brief account of the empire's origin. It would have been easy to suppose that his *Universal Monarchy* required nothing more in the way of an introduction. But, as Montesquieu discovered not long after he began, one cannot in so summary a manner do justice in the requisite fashion to Rome's allure; and so he invented the genre that so captivated Alexis de Tocqueville.[20]

In a preface that Montesquieu began drafting for his *Considerations on the Romans* and then eventually discarded, he remarked that, when he first undertook the project, he had intended nothing more than "to write a few pages on the establishment of sole rule by the Romans [*la monarchie chez les romains*]," but that he had strayed from that path. "The grandeur of the subject captured me," he explained. "Unawares [*insensiblement*], I climbed back to the first period of the republic, and I descended all the way to the empire's decline." En route, he investigated "the history of the Romans in their laws, in their customs, in their mode of maintaining order [*police*], in the letters of individuals, in the treaties they made with their neighbors, in the mores of the people with whom they had to deal, in the form of the ancient republics, in the situation in which the world subsisted before certain discoveries had been made"—all for the purpose of attempting "to explain what happened in the empire by what had happened in the republic." His book's aim was "to make sense of that famous usurpation of the world, which the Romans accomplished." Their "empire" was not, like that of

Alexander the Great, "the work of a day." Nor did it result from "the play of fortune." It was accomplished in the course of "a number of centuries" and was "a masterpiece of wisdom and conduct." It was achieved "through seven centuries of labor, with a vigor [*force*] and policy that remained constant, by means of following the same project in good fortune and bad, by a combination of causes that always lent themselves to this design." In the *Considerations on the Romans*, he sought "finally to make sense of a thing that has in history no counterpart at all and that, to all appearances, will have one never."[21]

AN ECONOMY OF WAR

The *Considerations on the Romans* begins abruptly with an admonition, contrasting the city of Rome in its early days with modern cities and suggesting that Rome came into being for the safeguarding of booty, first of all, then cattle and produce from the countryside. We are meant to envisage ancient Rome as alien—and as warlike in the extreme. Its statesmen were captains, and it was "a city without commerce, and nearly without arts." In consequence, Montesquieu tells us, "pillage was the sole means that individuals had for enriching themselves."

What distinguished Rome from other, similar communities existing at that time was its discipline and its systematic approach to the conduct of war. Booty was collected, then distributed to all who fought; a part of any land conquered was set aside for distribution to the Roman poor. The consuls, who led Rome's armies, could be honored with a triumph only if they were victorious on the field of the sword: no other accomplishments were thought worthy of the highest honor. Everyone had a compelling motive for the pursuit of war.

At Rome, as a consequence, distinctions were blurred: the practices that Montesquieu mentions were designed for the purpose of making it impossible for a citizen there to tell the difference between the virtues of "Constancy & Valor" and "the love he owed himself, his family, the fatherland, & all that is dearest to men." Not surprisingly, then, the Romans found themselves in "a war eternal & endlessly violent" (1).

In Montesquieu's judgment, there were two reasons for the Romans' success. To begin with, they looked on "war" as "the only Art" and devoted "mind entire & all their thoughts to its perfection." In the process, they imposed on themselves burdens and a type of discipline hardly imaginable in modern times. "Never," writes Montesquieu, "has a Nation made preparations for war with so much prudence & conducted it with so much audacity" (2).

In similar fashion, the Roman Senate remained resolute, displaying at all times "the same depth of understanding," and never allowing Rome's prosperity to occasion on its part a neglect of its responsibilities. While Rome's "Armies spread terror everywhere," its Senate "pinned those on the ground whom it found already crushed." To this end, the Senate "erected itself as a Tribunal to judge all the Peoples. At the end of every war, it decided on the punishments & rewards that each deserved. It took a part of its territory from a People vanquished in order to confer it on Rome's Allies and thereby accomplished two things: it attached to Rome Kings from whom it had little to fear & much to hope, & it weakened other kings from whom it had nothing to hope & everything to fear." The Romans employed their allies to defeat the foe, then laid them low as well. When faced with a coalition, they temporized, making a separate peace with its weakest member. In the midst of war, they put up with injuries of every sort, waiting silently for a time suited to retribution. When a people crossed them, they punished the nation, not just its leaders, and on their "Enemies" they inflicted "evils inconceivable." As a consequence, "war was rarely launched against" the Romans, "but always they waged war at the time, in the manner, & on those convenient" (6.1–29).

Since it was "the custom" of the Romans "to speak always as if they were the masters, the Ambassadors they dispatched to Peoples who had not yet had a taste of their power were sure to be mistreated, providing them with a pretext for making war anew." Peace they "never made in good faith," and "their Treaties were, strictly speaking, mere suspensions of war: they always put in them terms conducive to the ruin of the State which accepted them." When the Romans imposed a peace, it was designed to sow division—to set the members of a royal family against one another or the factions in a city at odds. When they learned of quarrels between states, they nearly always intervened, siding with the weaker party. "These customs" were not arrived at by accident. They were, Montesquieu insists, "invariable principles, as can easily be seen, for the maxims" the Romans "made use of against the greatest Monarchs were precisely those which they had employed in the beginning against the little Cities that surrounded them" (6.30–132).

The Romans were exceedingly patient. Theirs was, Montesquieu tells us, "a slow way of conquering: they defeated a People & contented themselves with weakening it; they imposed on it conditions that imperceptibly [*insensiblement*] undermined it; if it recovered, they beat it down once more; & it became a Subject without being able to date the Epoch of its subjection." On those they conquered, they imposed "no general Laws" lest the conquered develop "dangerous connections [*liaisons dangereuses*]" with one another. Their aim was that the conquered make up "a Body only by way of a common obedience." In this fashion, "without being Compatriots they would all be Romans." With their allies, the Romans dealt in much the same fashion, waiting until "all the Nations were accustomed to obey as free states & Allies before commanding them as Subjects," and then waiting again until these subjugated allies "little by little lost themselves in the Roman Republic" (6.211–19). In sum, Rome achieved greatness because the statecraft practiced by the Senate matched in cunning and ruthlessness the valor and skill of the soldiers and generals it sent into the field.

MONTESQUIEU AND MACHIAVEL

In his *Considerations on the Romans*, Montesquieu mentions neither Machiavelli nor Bossuet, but there can be no doubt that his Rome is modeled on the city described in the former's *Discourses on Livy* and not on its providentialist depiction in the latter's *Discourse on Universal History*.[22] Montesquieu does not situate Rome in the context of salvation history. His Rome owes its rise to grandeur not at all to a plan devised by God.[23] Montesquieu's Rome is a machine designed for conquest—and nothing more.[24]

As a consequence, in reading Montesquieu's *Considerations on the Romans*, we hear nothing of the civilizing mission of Rome. Cicero's analysis of the true greatness of the imperial city (*Off.* 2.8.26–27) is simply ignored, and Montesquieu nowhere quotes Vergil's celebrated juxtaposition of classical Greece with Rome:

> Others will cast with greater delicacy breathing bronze,
> So I firmly believe, and draw out from the marble faces that live,
> Speak in court with greater force,
> Trace the pathways of the heavens with an instrument
> And predict the rising of the stars.
> You! Roman! Remember to rule the world's peoples
> With imperious command—for these are the arts that will be yours:
> To impose the habit of peace,
> To spare the conquered, battle the haughty down. (*Aen.* 6.847–53)[25]

Montesquieu's Rome is not a benefactor conferring peace and prosperity: it is a predator. It achieved "the Empire of the World" and made of the Romans "Masters of the Universe." It "enchained the Universe" and "subjected" it "entire," and in the process it established a "universal Sovereignty" (*CR* 6.180, 9.31–43,12.85, 13.135). But no good came of it. Its subjects suffered more from its rule, Montesquieu tells us, than from the horrors of their original conquest (6.176–81). Like Machiavelli, Montesquieu intended to write "a thing useful for one who understands it," and he, therefore, thought it "more profitable" that he "go after the effectual truth of the matter [*andare drieto alla verità effettuale della cosa*] than" that he attend "to that matter as represented in the imagination [*che alla imaginazione di essa*]."[26] It is not an accident that at first he intended to call his work *Considerations on the Causes of the Aggrandizement of the Romans and their Decline.*[27]

There is, however, one great difference between Montesquieu and the Florentine,[28] and it is made explicit in a crucial passage within *The Spirit of Laws*, which echoes and elaborates on the significance of two earlier passages in the *Considerations on the Romans* that were evidently intended to foreshadow the argument of the *Universal Monarchy*. In his *Considerations on the Romans*, Montesquieu intimates what he openly says in the work's intended sequel: that the species of statecraft successfully applied by the Romans and both admired and recommended by Machiavelli has become in modern times utterly obsolete. In the book's first edition, he broached the issue toward the end of the first chapter: "The world of that time was not like our world today: the Voyages, the Conquests, Commerce, the establishment of great States, the Invention of the Postal System, of the Compass, & of Printing—these, along with a certain general orderliness and civilization fostered by Public Administration [*une certaine Police générale*], have facilitated communications & established among us an Art called Policy [*la Politique*]; everyone sees at a glance everything that is in motion throughout the Universe; & if a People displays a hint of ambition, it immediately arouses in all other peoples both caution and fear" (1.108–13).[29] In the book's antepenultimate chapter, he traces some of the consequences of this transformation. "Among us," he observes, "it seems to be more difficult than it was for the Ancients to carry out enterprises on a grand scale."

> It is difficult to hide them because communication among the Nations is such today that Princes have Envoys [*Ministres*] at all the Courts & can find traitors in all the Cabinets.
>
> The invention of the Postal System causes the News to take wing, so to speak, & to come in from every quarter.
>
> Given that great enterprises cannot be conducted without money & that Merchants [*Negocians*] became its masters as a consequence of the invention of Letters of exchange, the affairs of these merchants are always bound up with the secrets of State, & they neglect nothing [in their quest] to penetrate these.
>
> Variations in the rate of exchange without known cause induce many people to search out & in the end to find that cause.
>
> The invention of the Printing Press has placed Books in the hands of everyone; that of Engraving has rendered Geographical Charts commonplace; and,

finally, the establishment of the public Prints [*Papiers politiques*] gives to everyone a knowledge of the general interest sufficient that they can all more easily be enlightened concerning what has been done in secret.

Conspiracies within the State have become difficult because, subsequent to the invention of the Postal System, the Public has a capacity to learn all the secrets of Individuals [*tous les secrets des Particuliers sont dans le pouvoir du Public*].

Here, Montesquieu abruptly ends his discussion (21.89–105), in a manner appropriate to the Byzantine setting in which it arises (21.1–88), with the suggestion that the emergence of what is now sometimes called "publicity [*Öffentlichkeit*]" makes it more difficult for conspirators to form designs against a prince without being caught (21.106–9).[30] By drawing up short in this fashion, he whets the appetite of his more discerning readers and prepares them for his *Universal Monarchy* by causing them to wonder whether there are not other "enterprises on a grand scale" that have been rendered "more difficult" by the various revolutions that have taken place.[31]

In the parallel passage within his *Spirit of Laws*, Montesquieu asserts that there are, indeed, such enterprises, pointing to one particularly important consequence of the great transformation that has taken place, which he had left it to readers of the *Considerations on the Romans* to sort out for themselves. In making merchants the masters of money, he explains, the invention of the letter of exchange liberated commerce from political control, and thereby it rendered counter-productive a species of conspiracy once commonly engaged in by those already in power. "The richest trader," he remarks, can no longer be exploited as he had been in the past, for his expropriation has become difficult, if not impossible to achieve since he possesses "nothing but invisible goods," which can "be conveyed everywhere and leave not a trace in any place." Ever since the establishment of modern banking by merchants and the unrestricted flow of capital from one country to another, Montesquieu observes, "it has become necessary for princes" intent on securing the means to defend and even expand their domain to exercise self-restraint in the interests of promoting the commerce that enriches the subjects whose consumption and wealth they hope to tax. To be precise, it became necessary for them to establish the rule of law, to provide for the security of persons and property, and "to govern themselves" in all regards "with greater sagacity than they would themselves have thought possible—since, in the event, great acts of authority [*les grands coups d'autorité*]" of the sort advocated in France by Machiavelli's disciple Gabriel Naudé and engaged in by the latter's employer Cardinal Richelieu "proved to be so maladroit that experience gave rise to the recognition that only good government [*la bonté du gouverne-*

ment] brings prosperity." "We have," he concludes, "begun to cure ourselves of Machiavellianism, & we will continue the cure all the days of our lives. There is now greater need for moderation in councils. Those things which in other times one called *coups d'État* would today, apart from the horror, be blunders [*imprudences*]. Happy it is that men are in a situation in which, though their passions inspire them with the thought of being rogues, they have an interest in not being such" (*EL* 4.21.20, pp. 640–41).[32]

Moderation was Montesquieu's watchword, as even a cursory glance at his *Considerations on the Romans* will confirm.[33] The extreme measures that thrilled Machiavelli Montesquieu could not and would not countenance. His *Considerations on the Romans* is written in such a manner as to attract those inclined to admire Rome: it is designed at the outset to delight those who find Machiavelli's *Discourses on Livy* seductive.[34] In the end, however, Montesquieu's aim is to rob Rome of its allure. In the end, his aim is Machiavelli's defeat.

GREATNESS AND DECLINE

To this end, Montesquieu insists on the significance of a point that Machiavelli had readily conceded: that the Romans' loss of liberty was by no means an accident—that it was a natural consequence of the project of conquest which they undertook.[35] As Montesquieu puts it, "the greatness of the Empire destroyed the Republic." Rome's grandeur produced Roman decadence. In subjecting and enchaining "the Universe," in achieving "universal Sovereignty," the Romans subjected and enchained themselves (*CR* 9.29–43).

To begin with, this great expansion subverted the austerity traditional to Rome by exposing Roman soldiers to foreign temptations. In Syria, when battling Antiochus the Great, they first encountered "the luxury, the vanity, & softness" of the Asian courts, which had always been "contagious," and which were so "even for the Romans." This marked, we are told "the true Epoch of their corruption" (5.145–50); and as the wealth of the East poured into the conquering state, it subverted the spirit of equality and frugality that had always been the hallmark of Rome (4.19–34). By the time of the Gracchi half a century later, "the ancient mores no longer existed," and "individuals had immense wealth" (8.54–64).

For Rome, in Montesquieu's opinion, this development was an unmitigated catastrophe. "Bad examples," he writes, can be "worse than crimes." In fact, he argues, "more States have perished because of a violation of their mores [*moeurs*] than because of a violation of the Laws." In the past, before Rome's involvement in the Greek East, "the strength of the Republic" had always "consisted in discipline, austerity of morals [*moeurs*], & the constant observation of certain customs," and the Roman censors had always managed to "correct the abuses which the Law had not foreseen, or which the ordinary Magistrate was unable to punish." In those days, the censors stood in the way of "everything at Rome which was capable of introducing dangerous novelties, of changing the Citizen's heart or mind, & of preventing" the city's "perpetuation." Disorders, whether domestic or public, they could head off. From the Senate, they could expel anyone they wished; they could strip from a knight the horse that the city had hitherto maintained for him; they could reduce a citizen to the status of those who pay taxes to the city without having a share in its privileges. They could "cast their eyes over the actual situation of the Republic & distribute the People into the various Tribes in such a fashion as to" deprive "the Tribunes & the ambitious" of a mastery over the ballots, and thereby they could prevent the people from "abusing its power." These things the censors could do, and these things they did (8.64–79).

When the temptations and wealth that followed in the wake of Rome's expansion proved too much for the censors and deprived them of their capacity to stem the tide, Montesquieu tells us, "the Laws were no longer rigidly observed." Then, he adds, "the avarice of some Individuals & the prodigality of others caused property in land," which had once been more or less equally distributed, "to pass into the hands of a few; & immediately the Arts were introduced for the mutual needs of the rich & the poor." This meant that "there were hardly any Citizens or Soldiers left, for the property in land previously employed for the support of the latter served solely as a support for Slaves & Artisans, instruments of the luxury of the new proprietors." Such men, Montesquieu observes, do not make "good Soldiers." They are "cowardly" and corrupt, ruined by urban "luxury" and by the "Art" they practice. The very fact that they can make a livelihood anywhere means that, in war, artisans have "little to lose or to preserve." In practice, such men "have no fatherland at all" (3.16–31).

At the same time that it subverted mores and undermined the economic foundations of the martial order, Rome's great expansion occasioned a dilution of citizenship and a loosening of its bonds. It was with the help of the peoples of Italy that "Rome had subjected the entire Universe," and on these "at different times it had conferred various Privileges." Initially, Montesquieu reports, the Italians had not sought the right of Roman citizenship, preferring the institutions and practices that they had inherited from their ancestors in the distant past. But when Rome's expansion was more or less complete, when the "right" they once had spurned became tantamount to "universal Sovereignty, when one was nothing in the world if one was not a Roman Citizen & one was everything with that title," the Italians had occasion to reconsider. Having done so, they sought Roman citizenship; and, when it had been repeatedly and categorically refused, they "resolved to perish or to become Romans." Eventually, those who survived both the war that then erupted between the imperial city and its longtime allies and the civil war that followed thereafter did become full citizens of Rome. But for Rome itself this had grave consequences (9.31–43).

Prior to this time, Montesquieu remarks, Rome had been a city whose people had "but one and the same spirit [*qu'un même espirit*], one and the same love of Liberty, one and the same hatred for Tyranny," and if this people exhibited a "jealousy of the power of the Senate & of the prerogatives of the Great," it was nonetheless "mixed always with respect," for it "was nothing but a love of equality." Thereafter, the city lost the cohesion that had so long sustained it in the face of democratic envy. "When the Peoples of Italy became its Citizens, each Town brought with it its own genius, its particular interests, & its dependence on some great protector," and "the City, torn apart, formed no longer a united whole [*un tout ensemble*]." In effect, the Romans were now "Citizens solely by a kind of fiction"; and "since they no longer had the same Magistrates, the same walls, the same Gods, the same Temples, the same graves, they saw Rome with the same eyes no longer, they no longer had the same love for the fatherland, & Roman sentiments existed no more" (9.44–53).

The ultimate consequence of what was, in fact, a complete moral collapse was political anarchy. To vote in the assemblies at Rome—the *comitia centuriata*, the *comitia tributa*, and the *concilium plebis*—ambitious magnates brought entire cities and nations drawn from among their dependents. The assemblies themselves then became "veritable Conspiracies"; and on "a band of seditious men," one conferred the sacred title of *comitia*. "The authority of the People, its Laws—indeed, the People itself—become chimerical things," and the descent into "Anarchy" was so thorough that in late republican Rome one could never be quite sure whether "the People had passed an Ordinance or not" (9.54–59)

This was bad enough, but there was another development, far graver than those discussed thus far, to which it was nonetheless closely related—and it decisively affected the most crucial institution of all: the Roman army itself. "As long as Rome's dominion was restricted to Italy," Montesquieu explains, "the Republic could easily be sustained. Every Soldier was equally a Citizen; each Consul levied an Army, & the other Citizens went to war under the consul who succeeded him; the number of troops was not excessive; they were careful to accept into the Militia only those who had enough in the way of goods to have an interest in the City's preservation; the Senate exercised close oversight over the conduct of the Generals & prevented them from even thinking in a manner contrary to their duty." Once, however, Rome's legions crossed the Alps and passed over the sea, the republic was obliged to post its warriors abroad for extended periods, and Marius began what soon became a universal practice, enrolling as soldiers all without distinction—citizens and freedmen, those recorded in the Roman census as settled, propertied men, those listed as possessing children alone, and those who were counted solely by head. "Little by little" these soldiers "lost the spirit characteristic of Citizens, & the Generals, with Armies & Kingdoms at their disposal, sensed their strength & no longer found it possible to obey." The interplay between the army and its commander was such that soldiers "began to acknowledge" the authority of "no one but their General, to base their hopes entirely on him," and to think of Rome as something distant from their concerns. "They were no longer the Soldiers of the Republic," Montesquieu observes, "but those of Sulla, Marius, Pompey, Caesar. Rome could no longer tell whether the man who headed the Army of a Province was the city's General or its Enemy." When the Roman people, already by then corrupted by their tribunes, learned how "to confer on their favorites" so "formidable" an "authority abroad"—especially when the great magnates managed to persuade them to authorize "extraordinary Commissions, which annihilated the authority of the Magistrates, & placed all the great affairs in the hands of one alone or a few"—"all the sagacity of the Senate became useless, & the Republic was lost" (9.1–22, 11.33–36).

A DESCENT INTO DESPOTISM

What followed the republic's demise was not pretty, and it, too, followed logically and predictably from the fundamental character of Rome. To begin with, Montesquieu points out, there is the simple and undeniable fact that "there is no authority more absolute than that of the Prince who succeeds a Republic, for he finds himself in possession of all the power of a People incapable of putting limits on itself" (15.100–103). To this observation, Montesquieu added a stout denial that the "dreadful Tyranny of the Emperors" was an anomaly. It "stemmed," he argues, "from the general spirit of the Romans. Because they fell all of a sudden under an arbitrary Government, & because there was almost no interval between their being in command & their servitude, they were not at all prepared for the transition by a softening of mores. Their ferocious humor remained; the Citizens were treated as they themselves had treated the Enemies they vanquished, & they were governed on the same plan." It was, he suggests, "the continual sight of Gladiators in Combat" that had "made the Romans" so "ferocious." "Accustomed," as they were, "to making sport of human nature in the person of their Children & their Slaves, the Romans could hardly be cognizant of that virtue which we call Humanity" (15.16–32).

Montesquieu asks us to contemplate "the spectacle of things human," and he invites us to feast our imaginations on the grandeur that had so inspired Machiavelli. "How many wars do we see undertaken in the course of Roman History," he asks, "how much blood being shed, how many Peoples destroyed, how many great actions, how many triumphs, how much policy, how much sagacity, prudence, constancy, courage!" But, then, after giving classical Rome its due, Montesquieu asks us to pause and re-examine, with a more critical eye, the trajectory of the imperial republic: "But how did this project for invading all end—a project so well formed, so well sustained, so well completed—except by appeasing the appetite for contentment [*à assouvir le bonheur*] of five or six monsters? What! This Senate had caused the disappearance of so many Kings only to fall itself into the most abject Enslavement to some of its most unworthy Citizens, and to exterminate itself by its own Judgments? One builds up one's power only to see it the better overthrown? Men work to augment their power only to see it, fallen into more fortunate hands, deployed against themselves?" (15.83–92). Gradually, unobtrusively, Montesquieu weans us from the enticement of Rome—as our admiration gives way to horror and disgust.[36] And gradually and unobtrusively, at the same time, he lays the groundwork for the argument against continental empire that he intended to advance in his *Reflections on Universal Monarchy in Europe*.

Together, the *Considerations on the Causes of the Greatness of the Romans and their Decline* and the *Universal Monarchy* constitute Montesquieu's *Essay concerning Human Understanding*—which was, like them, a ground-clearing operation designed to prepare the way for the construction of a lasting edifice. Together, they were at one point expected to serve as an introduction to a third essay, which Montesquieu began drafting in, or not long before, 1733 with the intention of publishing it alongside them within the covers of a single volume.

THE CONSTITUTION OF ENGLAND

In the latter part of the eighteenth century, after the appearance of his *Spirit of Laws*, Montesquieu's name came to be synonymous with Anglophilia. For this propensity, there was considerable justification. Had the participation of Britain and France on opposite sides in the War of the Austrian Succession from 1740 to 1748 not rendered untimely his dedicating the work to Frederick, prince of Wales, as he had intended (MP 1860), his choice in the matter would certainly have seemed adroit. One friend, who had purportedly read *The Spirit of Laws* in manuscript three times through, is represented as having written to Montesquieu to praise him for his ingenuity and erudition—and to complain, "The example of the English government has seduced you."[37] Although the attribution of this letter to Claude Adrien Helvétius is almost certainly false, by 1789, when it appears to have been forged,[38] this was an opinion widely shared, especially in France. In fact, in 1788, James Madison was repeating what was by then the common sense of the matter when he wrote, "The British constitution was to Montesquieu, what Homer has been to the didactic writers on epic poetry. As the latter have considered the work of the immortal Bard, as the perfect model from which the principles and rules of the epic art were to be drawn, and by which all similar works were to be judged; so this great political critic appears to have viewed the constitution of England, as the standard, or to use his own expression, as the mirrour of political liberty; and to have delivered in the form of elementary truths, the several characteristic principles of that particular system."[39]

Prior to 1748, however, although penetrating readers of Montesquieu's *Persian Letters* and of his *Romans* might have thought their author quite friendly to England, they would have been hard-pressed to come up with evidence suggesting on his part a profound admiration.[40] Montesquieu's later reputation was, in fact, due to a single, comparatively long chapter that appeared in the eleventh book of *The Spirit of Laws*. What virtually no one knew was that Montesquieu had written this chapter shortly after his return from England to France, well before he started working on *The Spirit of Laws*, quite possibly before he had even conceived of the project. What virtually no one knew was that he had originally hoped to include it as the conclusion to the volume in which his *Considerations on the Causes of the Greatness of the Romans and their Decline* and his *Reflections on Universal Monarchy in Europe* were also slated to appear.

The evidence is compelling. To begin with, we have the testimony of a disinterested witness. Not long after Montesquieu's death, his son delivered a eulogy on his behalf in which, in passing, he revealed that his father's "book on the government of England, which had been inserted into *The Spirit of Laws*, was composed" in 1733, long before the publication of that great work, and that his father had entertained "the notion of having it printed with" his treatise on "*the Romans.*"[41]

In addition, there is material evidence. The manuscript of *The Spirit of Laws* that Montesquieu dispatched to his publisher does not survive, but in the Bibliothèque Nationale in Paris one can peruse an earlier version of the text replete with insertions and deletions, with rearrangements and revisions—some in the author's hand, others in the handwriting of his various amanuenses[42]—and this version is now available in a critical edition prepared by Catherine Volpilhac-Auger (*MS*). Robert Shackleton's pioneering work on Montesquieu's secretaries and that done since make it possible for us to date with some precision the handiwork of each.[43] Within this particular manuscript, as Shackleton points out, there are two chapters in a hand earlier than all of the others. One of these two (431–32) is an extract from a chapter originally composed for inclusion in Montesquieu's *Reflections on Universal Monarchy in Europe* (*RMU* 8.109–12, 122–34), which found its way into *The Spirit of Laws* (*EL* 3.17.6). The other (*MS* 228–39) is a draft of the longest and most famous chapter of *The Spirit of Laws*: Montesquieu's "Constitution of England" (*EL* 2.11.6). Both are largely, if not wholly in the hand of the amanuensis who served Montesquieu from 1733 or 1734 until 1738 or shortly thereafter.[44] It was this amanuensis who helped pen the Bodmer manuscript with its plan for inserting much of the *Universal Monarchy* within the *Considerations on the Romans*.[45] In short, there is every reason to suppose that, in the spring of 1734, when Montesquieu published his *Considerations on the Romans* and suppressed the *Universal Monarchy*, a draft of his little "book on the government of England" was ready to hand.

The two claims advanced by Montesquieu's son are not only, then, plausible; they constitute a possibility that we would be inclined to entertain even if he had never suggested it, and it is in this light that we need to reconsider the father's *Considerations on the Romans* and *Universal Monarchy*. We should not want to imitate the Romans, and in his *Considerations on the Romans* Montesquieu shows us why. And even if for some perverse reason we wanted to imitate the Romans, he then demonstrates in his *Universal Monarchy*, we could not succeed. We are left to wonder what alternative to the policy hitherto followed by states there might, in fact, be, and it is at this point that Montesquieu for a time intended to direct our attention to the polity that had recently emerged on the other side of the English channel.

Three

CARTHAGE ASCENDANT

In reading over the history of the last wars of England with France, one will conclude that the spirit of one nation could not be found to resemble that of another people more fully than the spirit of Carthage is found to resemble that of the British government today.

—*Abbé Séran de La Tour*

Montesquieu was inclined to anticipate. Well before he announced a theme and explored its implications, he was apt quietly and surreptitiously, without fanfare, to introduce the subject, touch on it briefly, and then pass on. As we have seen (I.1, above), he anticipated the discussion of universal monarchy in the second part of his triptych by characterizing classical Rome as a universal monarchy in his *Considerations on the Romans*. With regard to the English form of government, which formed the subject of the triptych's third part, he did the same.

Thus, for example, quite early in his *Considerations on the Romans*, while discussing the origins of the republic, Montesquieu had occasion to comment on the Servian reform and to allude to the prominent political role accorded the armed assembly by Servius Tullius, the penultimate Roman king. "Modern History," he wrote, "furnishes us with an example of what then happened at Rome." For "just as HENRY VII, King of England, augmented the power of the Commons in order to degrade the Great, SERVIUS TULLIUS, before him, extended the Privileges of the People in order to humble [*abaisser*] the Senate," and in each of the two cases the result was the same: "the People, at once becoming more audacious, overthrew the one Monarchy & the other" (CR 1.38–45). Read in isolation, the comparison seems an offhand remark; read in light of the subject to which the brief essay originally drafted to serve as the triptych's concluding part was devoted, it can be seen as a harbinger, inviting the reader to think of modern England as a worthy successor to classical Rome.

In similar fashion, when one returns once more to Montesquieu's *Considerations on the Romans* and re-reads its description of Rome's government in light of the analysis of the English constitution with its highly elaborated distribution of powers, which is articulated in what was once its intended sequel (*MS* 228–39; *EL* 2.11.6), there are moments when one realizes that, in the former, unobtrusively, England sometimes hovers in the background as a silent presence. Such is the case, for example, when Montesquieu singles out as one of the distinctive features of the Roman republic the fact that "the Laws of Rome wisely divided the public power [*la puissance publique*] among a great number of Magistracies, which stood by one another, arrested, & tempered one another" in such a fashion that "none possessed anything other than a power confined [*pouvoir borné*]" (*CR* 11.29–31).

There is, moreover, one passage, quite similar in spirit, in which the presence of England is anything but unobtrusive. In the first impression of the first edition of his *Considerations on the Romans,* before the authorities in France weighed in and he found himself forced to tone down the pertinent passage, Montesquieu allowed himself a highly revealing observation, which was evidently intended in an even more obvious way to foreshadow one of the principal themes of the third part of his literary triptych. After discussing the duties assigned the Roman censor, he remarked that, prior to Rome's acquisition of a transalpine and overseas empire, its "Government . . . was admirable in the fact that, from the time of its birth, its Constitution was such that, either by the spirit of the People, the strength of the Senate, or the authority of certain Magistrates, every abuse of power could always be corrected" (8.92–94).

Then Montesquieu asserted that Carthage, Athens, and the republics of medieval and modern Italy had failed this test, and he drew the attention of his readers to what was apparently the only modern analogue to classical Rome, observing,

> The Government of England is one of the wisest in Europe, because there is a Body [*Corps*] there that examines this government continually & that continually examines itself; & such are this body's errors that they never last long, & are useful in giving the Nation a spirit of attentiveness [*l'esprit d'attention*].
>
> In a word, a free Government, which is to say, a government always agitated, knows no way in which to sustain itself if it is not by its own Laws capable of self-correction. (8.101–6)[1]

This is a passage that should give one pause. As long as Montesquieu restricted his purview to classical antiquity and to the republics of medieval, Renaissance, and modern Italy, the authorities in Paris were loath to interfere. But with these words, the author of the *Considerations on the Romans* crossed a line.

A NERVE EXPOSED

It is quite possible that someone at the court of Louis XV who had perused the *Considerations on the Romans* took umbrage at Montesquieu's denunciation of Augustus therein as a "cunning Tyrant," who had "gently [*doucement*] conducted" the Romans not just "to servitude" but to "a durable servitude" (13.52–101). In 1734, the pertinent passages could all too easily have been read as a fierce, if oblique, assault on Cardinal Fleury's renewal of the policy of political pacification originally devised by Cardinal Richelieu and systematically implemented by Cardinal Mazarin and Louis XIV in the wake of the civil disorder that had gripped France under the Fronde.[2] After all, it had long been conventional for admirers of Louis XIV to celebrate his accomplishments by comparing him with the *princeps* who had brought peace, prosperity, and a flowering of the arts to a Rome hitherto bedeviled by civil war. In the circumstances, as Montesquieu was certainly aware, one could hardly attack the policy of Augustus without insinuating that there was something amiss with that of Louis as well.[3]

If this was not what Montesquieu had had in mind when he pointedly attacked the policy of Augustus, one could ask: why had he prefaced this attack with a brief allusion to the Wars of Religion and the Fronde (13.48–51), and why had he attributed to Augustus the rhetorical strategy so long pursued by the government of Bourbon France? "In a free State, where one is in the process of usurping Sovereignty," Montesquieu had observed, "one calls Orderliness [*Règle*] everything which is apt to establish authority without limits in an individual, & one gives the names trouble, dissension, bad Government to everything which is apt to maintain the liberty appropriate [*l'honnête liberté*] for Subjects" (13.53–56).

It is not at all unlikely that suspicions of such a sort were entertained. The author of the *Considerations on the Romans* was no stranger to the court. He was, in some measure, a known quantity. He had a history that justified suspicion. Voltaire had had good reason to doubt whether there had ever been "anything of greater force and strength than the *Persian Letters*" and to pose the rhetorical question whether there was any other "book in which anyone has discussed the government and religion with less tact and solicitude."[4] That Denis Diderot, co-editor of the *Encyclopédie, ou Dictionnaire raisonné des sciences, des arts, et des métiers*, should be of a similar opinion is precisely what one would expect.[5] Montesquieu was certainly aware of what he had gotten away with. In his later years, when he was inclined to speak of the letters as "juvenilia," he is said to have told "some friends that if he were actually going to put forth those letters now, he would omit certain ones in which the fire of youth had overwhelmed and transported him [*l'avait transporté*]."[6] Although, in preparing what was to be the posthumous edition of 1758, he chose, in the end, not to follow this course,[7] it is easy to see why he voiced such sentiments.[8] Moderation had not been his aim in the *Lettres persanes*.

After all, in this work, as Cardinal Fleury and everyone else at court no doubt remembered, Montesquieu had had Usbek's traveling companion Rica depict Louis XIV and his subjects in the most unflattering of terms. Upon arrival in Paris, after describing in comic fashion the multi-story buildings of the town and the continual rush of traffic, Rica turns to "the king of France," whom he quite rightly describes as "the most powerful prince in Europe." This king, he explains, has "more wealth" than the king of Spain. He "draws it from the vanity of his subjects," which is "more inexhaustible" than the gold mines in the New World on which the latter depends. The French king can undertake great wars, we are told, and he can sustain them by selling titles of honor. "By a prodigy of human pride, we find his troops paid, his strongholds fortified, & his fleets equipped."[9]

Had Montesquieu stopped at this point, he might not have incurred great annoyance, but he went on to display a species of irreverence more disturbing yet—by having Rica describe the Sun King as "a great Magician," who "exercises Dominion [*Empire*] even over the minds of his Subjects," making "them think as he wishes." He can persuade them to accept one ecu as payment for two ecus in goods, he reports. He can convince them to accept paper in place of silver. He can even "make them believe that, in touching them, he cures them of all sorts of maladies: so great is the force, & the power, that he has over their Minds." There is, moreover, "another Magician, stronger than" the French king, Rica adds, and he "is as much a master of the king's mind as the king is master of the others." This latter magician, who is called the Pope, makes Louis "believe that three is one, that the bread one eats is not bread, that the wine one drinks is not wine, & a thousand other things of this sort" (*LP* 22.24–42/24).[10] By way of ridicule, Montesquieu had set out to strike a powerful blow at the sacral character of the French monarchy, and to judge by the book's sales, at least within the class inclined to read, the blow appears to have struck home.[11]

Of this, Cardinal Fleury had an inkling, if not a full appreciation. To gain admission to the Académie française, Montesquieu was made to pay Louis XV's chief minister a brief visit in December 1727, ostensibly for the purpose of disavowing the very book that had occasioned his candidacy in the first place.[12] If, in the years immediately following his election to that august body, Montesquieu failed, despite repeated efforts, to secure for himself the diplomatic post that he craved, it may well have been due to the fact that, on his European tour, he allowed himself to be lionized as the author of the *Persian Letters* and that in conversation he was inclined to compare the government and court of France unfavorably with those of England, for his indiscretions in this particular regard were, in fact, reported to the authorities back home.[13]

It is also conceivable that, upon closer examination of the *Lettres persanes*, Cardinal Fleury had come to regret his indulgence. After all, in the book, Montesquieu had had Usbek debunk monarchy itself as "a violent State" with a perpetual tendency to "degenerate into a Despotism, or a Republic." It was not, he thought, possible for "power" to be "shared equally between the People & the Prince." He had regarded "the equilibrium" as "too difficult to maintain." He had expressed the view that "it is necessary that power diminish on one side while it grows on the other." In this struggle, he had added, the prince, as "head of the Armies," ordinarily had "the advantage." That monarchy could long subsist he had judged implausible (99.9–16/102).[14]

This Montesquieu had intimated in another fashion as well. In his depiction of the relations between Usbek and the harem that he had left behind in Ispahan, some among his contemporaries and friends recognized an elaborate burlesque of the French court—with obsequious prelates, priests, and ministers represented as eunuchs who have exchanged what, in a later edition, he would speak of as "a servitude in which one is obligated always to obey" for "a servitude in which one is obligated to command," and with fawning courtiers of both sexes parodied as concubines: all professing a love for and devotion to their master, all desperate for his favor, and all obsessed with outmaneuvering one another by way of manipulating the despot they served.[15] Some may even have discerned in Montesquieu's narrative of the chief eunuch's ultimately successful campaign for the acquisition of tyrannical power an account of the collapse of the system of government by councils, called *polysynodie*, which had been established by the regent after Louis XIV's demise, and a depiction of the rise to pre-eminence of his chief minister, Guillaume Cardinal Dubois, archbishop of Cambrai.[16] In a letter to the author, written not long after the appearance of Montesquieu's book, one such friend knowingly referred to this very minister on the occasion of his death as "the grand vizier" of France.[17]

Of course, the import of Montesquieu's elaborate conceit may well have escaped the notice of Fleury and his colleagues. They may not have had the time or inclination to read the work with the requisite attention, and they may have lacked the necessary acumen. In any case, the *Persian Letters* fell under their purview only tangentially: the book was published anonymously in Holland; wisely, no attempt was made to have it licensed for sale or publication in France, although someone did seek tacit permission for its circulation there and was denied.[18] The oblique, but extensive and unmistakable attack on Christian doctrine and practice that runs through the entire book may have given rise to considerable annoyance within the French church,[19] but it was not subjected to furious critical assault on the part of the clergy until after the publication of Montesquieu's *Spirit of Laws*.[20] Nor was it added to the *Index librorum prohibitorum* until 1762, four decades after its original appearance.[21] In large part because it was a novel and not a treatise, it was left alone.

Even, however, if the polemical thrust of the harem narrative escaped critical notice, there were, in Montesquieu's first published work, other letters no less provocative, and the political import of these the authorities can hardly have missed. In one, Montesquieu had had Rica quote a French savant who first denied that the barbarians who had overrun the Roman empire were "properly barbarians at all, since they were free," and then added that "they have become barbarians since—for, being submissive [*soumis*] for the most part to an absolute power, they have lost that sweet liberty, so conformable to Reason, to Humanity, & to Nature" (130.5–13/136). In another, Montesquieu had even had the audacity to have Usbek openly lampoon as a would-be despot on the Oriental model no less an eminence than the late, great Sun King of France (22/24, 35/37). When the author of the *Persian Letters* published his *Considerations on the Romans*, Cardinal Fleury and his minions had every reason to be on their guard.

It is, then, perfectly conceivable that someone among those in authority who read the latter work recognized something amiss in Montesquieu's fiery critique of "the project" that Justinian had "conceived of reducing all men to the same opinion in matters of religion" (CR 20.124–26). For this passage could easily have been read as an oblique attack on the policy of the French court—on Louis XIV's Revocation of the Edict of Nantes; on the campaign against the Jansenists that the Sun King, who regarded them as "a republican party in church and state,"[22] had launched in 1713 when he induced Pope Clement XI to issue the bull *Unigenitus* denouncing their doctrine;[23] and on Cardinal Fleury's revival of that campaign.[24] After all, in suggesting that Justinian's policy had divided and gravely weakened Rome's empire in the East (20, esp. 124–26), Montesquieu was merely echoing the criticism that he had had Rica and Usbek level at the religious policy of the Sun King thirteen years earlier in his *Lettres persanes* (LP 22.43–77/24, 57–59/59–61, 83/85, 98/101).[25]

One can also easily imagine that the courtiers who surrounded Louis XV were rendered nervous by Montesquieu's biting description of the peculiar "species of corruption" that in time came to grip the Roman court. For when he represented it as having been characterized by an all-pervasive "indolence," an "Asiatic splendor and pomp," and a poisonous atmosphere—in which "nothing was said, everything was insinuated," and men deservedly of great reputation, including officers and ministers of government, were at the mercy of "the sort of people who are able neither to serve the State nor to suffer others to serve it with glory" (*CR* 17, esp. 21–48)—Montesquieu was recasting as a fierce critique what he had had Usbek and Rica intimate in a jocular fashion concerning the royal court of France (cf. *LP* 35/37, 86.9–16/88, 104/107, with 87.42–49/89).[26]

But if the authorities were in any way discomfited by what Montesquieu had attempted to convey in these passages written concerning the history of Rome, they quite sensibly kept their misgivings to themselves—for the author of the *Considerations on the Romans* had constructed his analysis in such a fashion as to make efforts at censoring it seem like a public confession on their part that his account of imperial Rome really did read like an apt and devastating indictment of the political regime regnant in his native France. There was only one passage in the book they could not so easily choose to ignore. For, when Montesquieu lavishly praised the "Government of England," his focus was contemporary, and what he had to say touched a nerve quite recently exposed.

PARLIAMENT AND PARLEMENT

In 1733, when the British prime minister, Sir Robert Walpole, had proposed an excise tax on wine and tobacco, the commercial classes had risen up in high dudgeon, the newspapers in England had taken up their cudgels, and the Opposition in Parliament had seized on the opportunity to castigate the great man. The English had, in fact, displayed the "spirit of attentiveness" described by Montesquieu in the offending passage. England's government had then shown itself "capable of self-correction": the measure had been prudently withdrawn, and for a time it had even appeared that the Whig administration headed by Walpole would soon come to an end.[27] In the period stretching from 1730 to 1732, the government of France had faced comparable difficulties, and, in the judgment of Montesquieu and a great many others, it had fallen dismally short.

In early eighteenth-century France, there was no body quite like the English parliament. The Estates General had never exercised comparable leverage, and in Montesquieu's day it was for all intents and purposes defunct. It had last met in 1614, and in the first half of the eighteenth century hardly anyone, apart from Henri, comte de Boulainvilliers, and his disciples,[28] even dreamed that it would ever be summoned again. In its stead, as Montesquieu and many others saw it,[29] the French possessed a judicial body of great consequence, the Parlement de Paris, which, if adept, was in a position to play something like the same role. In its guise as a court—especially, in its capacity to discuss and determine whether royal edicts should be registered as laws consistent with justice, reason, virtue, and existing law—this body really was expected to subject the government and its measures to continual examination, to propose modifications, to negotiate with the ministers, and even to dig in its heels and refuse to register a decree—and this it regularly did.[30] Moreover, on occasion, the briefs (*mémoires judiciaires*) presented to it by barristers (*avocats*) arguing a case, and the remonstrances in which it defended its decisions, had something of the character of the *Papiers politiques* published on the other side of the English Channel. In contrast with books, journals, and the like, these legal documents were exempt from pre-publication censorship, and the more controversial among them circulated widely among the general public and formed a subject of conversation.[31]

Montesquieu, who had served for a time as a *président à mortier* on the Parlement de Bordeaux, possessed an intimate knowledge of the history and workings of the parlements and a profound appreciation for the constitutional role they could play.[32] In 1721, in his *Lettres persanes*, he had had the Persian visitor Rica observe, in response to the regent's decision to send the members of the parlement into exile at Pontoise, that these bodies are rendered "forever odious" by the fact that "they make their approach to the king only to tell him sad truths" and "to give the lie to the flattery" propagated by his courtiers (134/140). The Parlement de Paris he had had Rica's colleague Usbek praise as the very "image of public liberty" (89.20–23/92), and through the latter character, who is represented as having been forced into exile from Persia when his own propensity for carrying "truth to the foot of the throne" aroused the ire of the Sultan's ministers (8.4–25/8), Montesquieu had conveyed his own grave misgivings with regard to the parlements' seemingly irreversible decline and to the despotic implications of their all-too-predictable demise (89.13–19/92).[33] As he was already then acutely aware, this was the only body in France capable of arousing in the public "a spirit of attentiveness," and by means of the *mémoires judiciaires* of the *avocats* and the remonstrances it published in its own defense, it had done so in the not-so-far-distant past.[34] But all of this took place, as he well knew, before the early 1670s—when Louis XIV demonstrated for the benefit of his successors just how effective a resolute and skillful monarch could be in bringing the parlement to heel.[35]

In the early 1730s, in the midst of the long and involved controversy pitting the Jesuits and the crown against the Jansenists, the Parlement de Paris had performed its proper function. To begin with, it had deliberated as to whether Louis

XV's edict of 24 March 1730, accepting *Unigenitus* as a "law of church and state," was compatible with existing law. Then, having judged that the terms of the Papal bull contravened the Gallican Articles of 1682, which established the independence of the French church, the parlement had refused to register the edict and recognize it as binding, and it had explained its refusal in time-honored fashion by publishing a remonstrance against it. Moreover, in the aftermath, when Louis had held a *lit de justice* to register the edict himself, as was his right, the magistrates, spurred by the Jansenists in their number, had stubbornly resisted its enforcement by accepting appeals *comme d'abus* against episcopal directives denying the sacraments to recalcitrant Jansenists, and by remonstrating repeatedly against the evocation of such cases for adjudication by the king's council.

In the midst of all of this, there had occurred the *affaire des avocats*. It had begun with a group of barristers whose names had appeared on an incendiary *mémoire judiciaire*, written in defense of the Jansenists, which had seemed to assert as legal doctrine the republican claim that "all laws are contracts [*conventions*] between those who govern and those who are governed." When apprised of its contents, the ministry had demanded a disavowal and retraction from the signatories, and it had threatened them with a disqualification from legal practice. In response, the *avocats* had closed ranks, and the inability of intermediaries to come up with a formula capable of satisfying both sides had resulted in the barristers staging a dramatic, three-month-long strike, shutting down the courts in protest against what they took to be an infringement on the liberties properly accorded their order.

This series of closely related conflicts within the ruling order in France had aroused public opinion in a manner most remarkable. But in the end, after various half-hearted attempts at compromise, Louis and his ministers had dug in their heels. They had temporized in a great variety of ways, to be sure. They had even reached a compromise with the *avocats*, but they had not withdrawn the edict. At one point, the king had silenced his parlement. At another, all but those in the *grand'chambre* had resigned in protest en masse. In the end, the king had relegated one hundred thirty-nine of the *parlementaires* to exile in obscure and distant provincial towns; he had threatened to accept their resignations and even to treat them as rebels; and in due course, when the ministers had given them an opportunity to save face, the *parlementaires* had knuckled under.[36]

Montesquieu saw through the subterfuge. In the victory celebrated by the *parlementaires* upon their return from exile he recognized their defeat. In monarchical France, to his evident chagrin, there had been no genuine correction of course.[37] In praising the government of England so extravagantly for the particular qualities that he singled out, Montesquieu was alluding—obliquely, to be sure, but in a manner no one in France could have mistaken at the time—to events quite recent and much closer to home, and he was intimating that, under Louis XV and his minister Cardinal Fleury, the government of France lacked the capacity for self-correction that distinguished a polity as free.[38]

In doing so, Montesquieu overstepped, and, as a condition for securing royal permission for the distribution of his book in France and its publication in Paris,[39] he was made to drop his incendiary contention that "the Government of England is one of the wisest in Europe." In the volumes licensed for sale in France (and, tellingly, there only), he substituted the more muted and less threatening claim that in the crucial regard England's government is "wiser" than those that had once existed or still persisted in Carthage, Athens, and the various cities of the *regnum Italicum*.[40]

The brief passage in Montesquieu's *Considerations on the Romans* written in praise of "the Government of England" is, in fact, far more significant than this analysis suggests. It was not originally intended to stand alone, as we have seen. Its purpose was to foreshadow and pave the way for a much more extensive discussion of the English constitution. In fact, in the draft of what his son called his "book on the government of England," Montesquieu had set out to show what it was that occasioned the crucial process of self-correction. This he had done by discussing in detail the English constitution's institutionalization of a distribution of powers (MS 228–39; EL 2.11.6), and he had evidently intended to explore as well the consequences for England of the rivalries and tensions that this distribution introduces within its government, for he had set the stage for just such a discussion when, in his *Considerations on the Romans*, he had pointedly described this government as being "always agitated" (CR 8.105).

As should by now be abundantly clear, had he finished his "book on the government of England," and had he published it alongside his *Considerations on the Romans* and *Universal Monarchy* within a single volume, as he had at first intended, Montesquieu would almost certainly have found himself in dire straits. But he anticipated the danger—not just by dropping the *Universal Monarchy* in reaction to the uproar caused by Voltaire's publication of his *Lettres philosophiques*, but earlier as well when he ceased working on his "book on the government of England" and set it aside unfinished.

THE POLICY OF ENGLAND

When Montesquieu set out to write about England, it cannot have been the French philosophe's intention to stop where, apparently, he did. As we have seen, the common focus of his *Considerations on the Causes of the Greatness of the Romans and their Decline* and that of his *Reflections on Universal Monarchy in Europe* was empire. To round out and finish a work of which they were to form so signal a part, Montesquieu would have had to discuss at some point the imperial policy adopted by the English. He would have been required to demonstrate that, by the very nature of its polity, England was committed to a foreign policy that was, in modern circumstances, viable in a way that the Roman policy consistently followed by the continental powers clearly was not.

That Montesquieu recognized this need is evident in his *Universal Monarchy*, where, by way of anticipation, he took care to prepare the ground for just such a discussion. First, he briefly traced England's long history as a continental power intent on territorial aggrandizement in the age stretching from its conquest by William the Bastard, duke of Normandy, to Henry V (*RMU* 11.1–176). Then he remarked on the fact that, at long last, in and after the reign of Henry VI, the French learned how to take advantage of the "intestine divisions" of the English, to deploy their soldiers to advantage, and to profit from their opponents' distance from the territory in dispute (11.177–82). And, finally, he observed that when the English "were reduced to their Island & came to recognize the vanity of their ancient enterprises, they dreamt of nothing apart from enjoying a prosperity that they had always been able to possess & that they had not yet known" (11.182–84).[41] The precise character of the new foreign policy adopted by the English and the nature of the prosperity that they then hoped to enjoy Montesquieu deliberately left unspecified in a manner designed to tease his readers and whet their appetite for what was to come. And, as chance would have it, these are prominent among the issues that he did explore in the final and concluding chapter of what was, in the original edition of *The Spirit of Laws*, the first of its two volumes (*EL* 3.19.27).[42] It is to this chapter and to its treatment of the relationship between English commerce and England's empire over the sea that we now must turn.[43]

Even when fully fleshed out, the little essay on the English form of government, which Montesquieu is known to have drafted in, or shortly before, 1733 (*MS* 228–39), focused narrowly on institutions and said next to nothing about the actual operation of the polity (*EL* 2.11.6). This—perhaps also in the early 1730s, but certainly at some point prior to the production of a clean copy of the manuscript of *The Spirit of Laws* in 1741–42[44]—he set out to describe in a second essay aimed at showing the degree in which English mores, manners, and character derived from England's fundamental laws (*MS* 483–91). When one puts the final versions of these two essays (*EL* 2.11.6, 3.19.27) together—as an enterprising Edinburgh publisher, prompted by David Hume, did in English translation some two years after *The Spirit of Laws* first appeared in French[45]—one has an account of eighteenth-century England perfectly suited to what Montesquieu had in mind when he first designed his triptych. Although less historical and consequently much shorter than his extended essay on Rome, Montesquieu's two-part analysis of the English constitution and of the mores, manners, and character it inspired is no less ambitious in aim and equally comprehensive in scope.

Montesquieu's two essays on England have a character decidedly odd. They are not only the longest chapters in *The Spirit of Laws*; in them their author displays a measure of caution and a hesitation uncharacteristic of the tone he adopts in the work as a whole. In the first of the two, Montesquieu generally writes forthrightly in the indicative mood but frequently deploys the verb *devoir* in such a manner as to imply that the institutions which he is describing should operate in the way indicated but may not, in fact, do so (2.11.6). In the second of these chapters (3.19.27), in the brief chapter at the beginning of *The Spirit of Laws* in which he discusses the state of nature (1.1.2), and nowhere else in the book, Montesquieu persistently resorts to the conditional mood—as if to suggest that, in these chapters, he is exploring possibilities, even probabilities, which may not, strictly speaking, be real.[46] The title of the second of his two essays on England—"How the Laws Can Contribute to the Formation of the Mores, Manners, & Character of a Nation"—reinforces this impression (3.19.27, p. 574). It describes that which stands to reason, not that which always, of necessity, will in fact take place.

This seminal chapter falls neatly into four parts—a disquisition on the type of party conflict likely to arise under the English constitution, a study of the spirit that would guide such a polity's conduct abroad, a meditation on the role that religion would play in the lives of its citizens, and an account of the mores, manners, and character that its laws would produce. The first, third, and fourth of these parts have attracted notice,[47] but the second and arguably most important part has received little scholarly attention.[48] In it, Montesquieu demonstrates that England is—or, at least, ought to be—free from the "malady" that so threatens the powers on the continent with bankruptcy and ruin. In it, he allows us to comprehend how it is that, in modern times, a well-ordered Carthage, such as England, "whose principal strength consists in her credit and commerce," could "render fictive wealth real," equip "her Hannibal" with "as many men as she could buy," and "send them into combat," while Louis XIV's ill-ordered French Rome, "in a spirit of vertigo," patiently awaited "the blows" solely "in order to receive them" and fielded "great armies" only "to see" her "fortresses taken" and her "garrisons deprived of courage, and to languish in a defensive war for which" she had "no capacity at all" (MP 645).[49]

Montesquieu does not attribute any special rationality to the English. Given the character of their constitution, he imagines, they would be "always on fire" and "would be more easily conducted by their passions than by reason," and, for this reason, he adds, "it would be easy for those who govern the nation to make it undertake enterprises contrary to its real interests." The chief passion of the English, the only one which Montesquieu sees fit to mention in this particular context, would appear to be their fondness for liberty, which, he says, they "love prodigiously because this liberty is genuine [*vraie*]." In defending their freedom, Montesquieu intimates, this people would be no less resolute than were the citizens of classical Rome. This nation would "sacrifice its goods, its ease, its interests; it would burden itself with imposts quite harsh, such as the most absolute prince would not dare make his subjects endure." Moreover, possessing, as they would, "a firm understanding of the necessity of submitting" to these taxes, the English "would pay them in the well-founded expectation of not having to pay more; the burden would be heavier than the sense of burden" (*EL* 3.19.27, p. 577).

In this chapter, Montesquieu refrains from intimating, as he does repeatedly elsewhere, that the monarchies on the European continent find it well nigh impossible to inspire the confidence necessary to enable them to borrow the great sums of money needed for the conduct of war in modern times.[50] It suffices for him pointedly to remark that, given its laws, England should have little difficulty in sustaining the credit required. It could, after all,

> borrow from itself & pay itself as well. It would, then, undertake enterprises beyond its natural strength & deploy against its enemies immense fictional riches, which the confidence it would inspire & the nature of the government would render real.
>
> For the purpose of preserving its liberty, it would borrow from its subjects; & its subjects, seeing that its credit would be lost if it was conquered, would have yet another motive for exerting themselves in defense of its liberty. (3.19.27, p. 577)[51]

England could borrow from its subjects because, under the constitution that Montesquieu has in mind, its subjects would not, in fact, be subjects at all. They would be citizens, as Montesquieu quickly acknowledges (3.19.27, p. 577), in what he has already elsewhere described in *The Spirit of Laws*, in a fashion long familiar in Britain,[52] as "a republic concealed under the form of a monarchy" (1.5.19, p. 304).[53] And, as such, they could see to the payment of the debts that they owed themselves.

Though inclined, like Rome, to defend itself with a resoluteness and a vigor that beggar the imagination, this England would by no means be a nation intent on conquest. If it occupied an island, as it might, it would recognize that "conquests abroad" on the continent of Europe or elsewhere would serve only to "weaken it." If this island were blessed, as also it might be, with good soil, this nation "would have no need for war as a means for enriching itself." And since its laws would guarantee that "no citizen would be dependent on another, each would take his liberty more seriously than the glory reserved for a few citizens or one." In consequence, though the soldierly profession might be deemed useful and would no doubt often be dangerous, its members would be regarded as "persons whose services are burdensome [*laborieux*] for the nation itself, & civil status would be accorded greater regard."

The reason why Montesquieu's England would in this particular be so unlike Rome is simple. Situated, as it would be, on an island and blessed with the farmland and constitution with which it would be blessed, it would quite naturally be a seat of "peace & liberty"; and, when "liberated from destructive prejudices" —such as those rooted in otherworldliness, to which the Christian religion gives rise—it "would be inclined to become commercial" and to exploit to the limit the capacity of its "workers" to fashion from its natural resources objects of "great price." It would be inclined to carry on a great trade with those nations to the South that require its commodities and have much to offer that the English could not provide for themselves; and in flight from the excessive taxes it would impose, many of its citizens, on the pretext of travel or health, would seek their fortunes abroad "even in the lands of servitude itself" (3.19.27, pp. 577–78).[54]

Commerce these Englishmen would conduct as other nations conduct war. This people would have "a prodigious number of petty, particular interests." There would be "an infinity of ways" in which it could do and receive harm (*choquer et être choqué*). "It would become sovereignly jealous, & it would be more distressed by the prosperity of others than it would rejoice at its own." Its laws, "in other respects gentle & easy, would be so rigid with regard to commerce & the carrying trade . . . that it would seem to do business with none but enemies" (3.19.27, p. 578).[55]

Commerce would, in fact, be dominant in every sphere.[56] "Other nations," Montesquieu remarks elsewhere, "have made their commercial interests give way to their political interests: this one has always made its political interests give way to the interests of its commerce" (4.20.7). If England, he tells us, were to send out colonies far and wide, to places such as North America, "it would do so," precisely as had ancient Carthage and modern Venice, [57] "more to extend the reach of its commerce than its sphere of domination" (3.19.27, p. 578; 4.21.21). With these colonies, in keeping with its aim, it would be generous, as the

Carthaginians had been, conferring on them "its own form of government," which would bring "with it prosperity" so that "one would see great peoples take shape in the forests which they were sent to inhabit" (3.19.27, p. 578).[58] Nearer home, to be sure, England would be less forthcoming. If it subjugated the populace of a neighboring island, such as Ireland, it might "confer on" this nation "its laws" but then, out of jealousy regarding the island's location, the quality of its ports, & the nature of its resources, "retain" this nation "in great dependence in such a manner that the citizens there would be free while the state was itself a slave." The neighboring island's "civil government" might be "very good," but "its prosperity would be rendered quite precarious," for it would be little more than a "storeroom for its master" (3.19.27, p. 579).

As an island-nation, possessed of "a great commerce," Montesquieu's England "would have every sort of facility for fielding maritime forces." Safeguarding "its liberty would not require that it possess strongholds [*places*], fortresses, & armies on land," but "it would have need of an army at sea to guarantee it against invasion, & its navy would be superior to that of all the other powers, which, needing to employ their finances for war on land, would not have enough for war at sea."

England's supremacy at sea would not be without effect. "The empire of the sea has always given those peoples who possessed it a natural pride. Sensing themselves capable of insulting anyone anywhere," the English "would believe their power as unlimited as the ocean," and they would be inclined to exercise it when circumstances warranted. In consequence, "this nation would have a great influence on the affairs of its neighbors. Because it would not employ its power for conquest, they would be more inclined to seek its friendship, & they would fear its hatred more than the inconstancy of its government and its internal agitation would appear to justify." In consequence, although "it would be the fate of its executive power almost always to be uneasy [*inquietée*] at home," it would nearly always be "respected abroad" (3.19.27, pp. 579–80).[59] In short, thanks to the changes in the *ius gentium* that Christianity had inspired and to the liberation of commerce from political control effected by the invention of the letter of exchange, the tables had been turned, and Carthage now had the advantage over Rome.

NAPOLEON, HITLER, AND STALIN

As should by now be clear, Charles-Louis de Secondat, baron de la Brède et de Montesquieu, had a great deal in common with his countryman Voltaire. Both put a great deal of effort into pondering the revelation that took place 13 August 1704 on the battlefield of Blenheim when, contrary to all expectation, an army marshaled by Great Britain shattered Louis XIV's dream of universal monarchy by annihilating the legions deployed by France—and, after visiting England, the two reached quite similar conclusions. If, in 1734, circumstances conspired to prevent Montesquieu from spelling out in full detail the true focus of his critique of the imperial aspirations inspired by Roman grandeur, if they ruled out his making clear the depth of the admiration that he harbored for the peculiar species of commercial republicanism that had emerged in England in the course of the seventeenth century, they did not stop him from doing so in the slightly more relaxed political atmosphere of 1748, when Cardinal Fleury was dead, and the French philosophe included within his *Spirit of Laws* much of the material that he had suppressed on that earlier date and even contrived therein to juxtapose his beloved England with Rome.[60]

The understanding of the modern republic that Voltaire pointed to and that Montesquieu more fully articulated deserves careful consideration, for the two clearly were prescient, and over time they had a considerable impact on the thinking of their compatriots,[61] who came to think of England as a modern Carthage, just as they had long regarded France as a modern Rome. In the end, however, despite dramatic evidence, ultimately visible to all,[62] suggesting the existence of a profound gap between the scope of French ambitions and the magnitude of the resources that the monarchy could bring to bear in time of war;[63] despite the fact that, under Louis XV, France experienced repeated military defeats and was more than once brought to the brink of bankruptcy;[64] and despite the fact that the cost of France's support for the American War of Independence under Louis XVI had consequences for the monarchy's exchequer, for its capacity to project power in Europe, and for the stability of the regime even more dire,[65] these two authors failed fully to persuade Frenchmen of the superiority of English policy.[66] When the Physiocrats gave primacy to agriculture, denied that merchants could be citizens, praised France as a bellicose nation, and embraced enlightened despotism, it was the English model that they spurned;[67] and when—at the instigation of the French foreign ministry or on their own—writers, such as the abbé Séran de La Tour,[68] encouraged their compatriots to envisage England and France on the model of Carthage and Rome, as they persistently did during and after the Seven Years War, they invariably acted on the presumption that antiquity and modernity were for all practical purposes indistinguishable, that history could be trusted to repeat itself, and that in due course, therefore, the modern Rome would defeat and annihilate the modern Carthage.[69]

In no way did Voltaire and Montesquieu succeed in persuading the French to abandon their fatal longing for primacy and dominion on the continent of Europe; and, in the wake of the Revolution and the radical reorganization of the administrative state that accompanied it, a reinvigorated France forcefully renewed its quest for predominance.[70] Perhaps because Voltaire's *Philosophical Letters* was so quickly and firmly suppressed, perhaps because the critique Montesquieu directed at imperialism on the Roman model was buried and thereby rendered inconspicuous within his *Spirit of Laws,* perhaps because in the 1750s and the early 1760s Jean-Jacques Rousseau mounted a scathing and rhetorically compelling assault on commercial society,[71] classical antiquity retained its allure;[72] and, in subsequent generations, as religious and dynastic loyalties lost purchase and nationalism and universalist ideology were promoted as alternatives,[73] the most influential Frenchmen and those Germans and Russians who looked for inspiration to Paris, rather than to London, failed to take heed. Napoleon Bonaparte tried to establish a universal monarchy in Europe on the Roman model, and, when opportunity knocked, Adolf Hitler and Joseph Stalin followed suit. Even today, when Europe appears to have renounced war as an instrument of foreign policy, in some circles the dream of imperial grandeur persists: one need only peruse the book on Napoleon published in February 2001 by Dominique de Villepin—who was soon to become foreign minister, then prime minister of France—and ponder his assertion that, with Napoleon's defeat, Europe lost the most splendid opportunity ever to come its way.[74]

The simple fact that Great Britain withstood Napoleon proves the prescience of Voltaire and Montesquieu. Despite its diminutive size, its limited resources and population, Britain was able to put together, fund, and lead the various coalitions that ultimately inflicted on that would-be Caesar a defeat even more decisive than the one suffered by Louis XIV. Moreover, in 1940, Montesquieu's England stood up to Hitler, and for a time it did so alone. If, in the end, Great Britain did not put together, fund, and lead the coalition that eventually defeated the Nazi colossus, if it did not put together, fund, and lead the alliance that later contained, wore down, and ultimately dismembered the Soviet empire, it was because the British came to be overshadowed by another commercial people, which took "shape," just as Montesquieu had predicted, "in the forests" of the New World, a great people endowed by Britain with a "form of government, which brings with it prosperity."

As Winston Churchill foresaw quite early in the twentieth century,[75] this people was destined to be England's heir. For more than a century now, it has pursued a foreign policy modeled on the pattern of conduct pioneered by "the republic concealed under the form of a monarchy" that Voltaire and Montesquieu discovered when they crossed the English Channel. This people enjoys a supremacy not just on the sea but in the air, and, as a consequence, it exercises "a great influence on the affairs of its neighbors." Moreover, because it does "not employ its power for conquest" and never acquired a great empire, not even in a fit of absent-mindedness, other peoples are "inclined to seek its friendship," and they fear "its hatred more than the inconstancy of its government and its internal agitation would appear to justify." And while it is "the fate of its executive power almost always to be uneasy at home," its executive is nearly always respected abroad. Even now, when once again there is occasion to fear "the inconstancy of its government" and the "internal agitation" to which, like its predecessor, it is prone, this people finds itself compelled to follow the path opened up in the wake of the Glorious Revolution by the nation that contained Louis XIV, defeated Napoleon, and stood up to Hitler.[76]

In the Cold War with the Soviet Union, despite the propensity for "inconstancy" and "internal agitation" natural to a polity distinguished by a distribution of powers, and despite its inclination "to make its political interests give way to the interests of its commerce," the United States proved steadfast. Whether today it still possesses the spiritual resources, the prudence, and the resolve requisite if it is to play the role that circumstances have conspired to confer upon it remains an open question. In the last three hundred years, Carthage has repeatedly defeated Rome, but this need not always be the case. After all, at the outset, it was not a foregone conclusion that Louis XIV, Napoleon, Hitler, and Stalin would go down in defeat. On more than one occasion, what Montesquieu described as "morally impossible" very nearly took place.

Such thoughts are sobering. They serve as a timely reminder that we have no grounds for the complacency that we so often evidence. They suggest, moreover, that Montesquieu's assessment of the English polity is a matter of more than mere antiquarian interest. It is in light of what the French philosophe stopped short of saying in 1734 that we should read and ruminate on what he actually said fourteen years thereafter in the masterpiece for which he is generally remembered today.[77]

Book Two

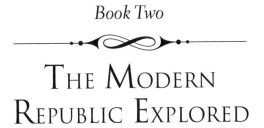

THE MODERN
REPUBLIC EXPLORED

The British constitution was to Montesquieu, what Homer has been to the didactic writers on epic poetry. As the latter have considered the work of the immortal Bard, as the perfect model from which the principles and rules of the epic art were to be drawn, and by which all similar works were to be judged; so this great political critic appears to have viewed the constitution of England, as the standard, or to use his own expression, as the mirrour of political liberty; and to have delivered in the form of elementary truths, the several characteristic principles of that particular system.

— *James Madison*

PREFACE

The tripartite book that Montesquieu set out to write in 1731, when he re-treated to his chateau in Bordeaux upon returning from his travels in Germany, Italy, and England, had the character of a polemic, as we have had occasion to observe. This is why, in the end, its author found it necessary to suppress its most salient, most controversial parts.

The book that Montesquieu then began writing, at some point in the mid-to-late 1730s after the publication of his *Considerations on the Causes of the Great-ness of the Romans and their Decline* in 1734,[1] was couched in an entirely differ-ent idiom. *The Spirit of Laws* had an air of impartiality. It was, its author intimated, a dispassionate analysis free from prejudice. Montesquieu's only goal was to "prove that the spirit of moderation should be that of the legislator" (*EL* 6.29.1). His aim was to "make it possible for human beings to cure themselves of their prejudices." He hoped to accomplish this largely by setting such an exam-ple himself (Préf.).[2]

On the face of it, then, one ought to regard Montesquieu's composition of *The Spirit of Laws* as a project distinct from and perhaps even opposed to the polem-ical effort initiated in 1731. But this is not at all the way in which the book's author conceived of his undertaking. When he published his *Spirit of Laws* in 1748, Montesquieu described its composition as "a labor [*travail*] of twenty years" and not as an effort of ten, twelve, or fourteen. "Many times I began this work," he wrote, "& many times I abandoned it; a thousand times I dispatched to the winds the pages I had penned; every day I felt the paternal hands drop; I followed my object without forming a design; I knew neither rules nor exceptions; I found the truth only to lose it. But when I discovered my principles [*mes principes*], every-thing that I had been seeking came to me; &, in the course of twenty years, I saw

my work begin, grow, advance, & come to completion" (Préf.). Early in the following year, in a letter addressed to a friend, Montesquieu repeated this claim. "I
can say," he explained, "that I have worked on this [project] my whole life; when
I left the *collège* they placed in my hands books dealing with right [*droit*]; I
sought its logic, sense, and aim [*son esprit*], I worked, I did nothing worthwhile."
Then, one day, everything became clear. "It was twenty years ago that I discovered my *principes*."[3] It was apparently during his travels, some two decades before the publication of his *Spirit of Laws*, that Montesquieu discovered the "principles," drawn from "the nature of things" and not from his "prejudices," which
enabled him to form his "design." (Préf.).

The precise timing of Montesquieu's discovery of his "principles" helps explain the point of his remark that, while "Germany was made to travel in, Italy to
sojourn in, . . . and France to live in," "England" was made "to think in." It justifies fully the claim, advanced in the *Encyclopédie, ou Dictionnaire raisonné des
sciences, des arts, et des métiers*, by that work's co-editor Jean Le Rond d'Alembert, that England was for Montesquieu the inspiration that "the isle of Crete
had been for Lycurgus."[4] And it suggests that it is in *The Spirit of Laws* that Montesquieu completes the project that he initiated in 1731 on his return to France
from his enlightening sojourn in the British isles. It was his purpose therein to articulate a new political science capable of making sense of the new world that he
had discovered when he crossed the English Channel, and he hoped to do so in
a manner that would stymie the censor and secure for its author the hearing that
he was denied in 1734.[5]

One

PRINCIPLES

We see next to nothing pertaining to justice & injustice that does not change in quality with a change in climate. Three degrees of Latitude overthrows all jurisprudence. A Meridian decides the truth; with a few years of possession the fundamental laws change. Right has its epochs. It is a ridiculous justice that has a river or a Mountain as its boundary. Truth on this side of the Pyrenees, error on that.

—Blaise Pascal

The first eight books of the work that Montesquieu entitled *De l'Esprit des lois* have one distinctive feature. It was there—after a brief introduction dealing with the problematic character of man's place in the universe and with the foundations of man-made law (*EL* 1.1.1–3)—that the French *philosophe* first introduced his novel typology of political forms. His stated purpose for doing so was to trace the *esprit*—the spirit, the mindset, the motive, the impetus, the purpose, the intention, the object, as well as the logic—behind the "infinite diversity of laws & mores" which are to be found in the larger world: his aim thereby was to refute skeptics and cynics inclined to agree with Pascal,[1] and to demonstrate to the satisfaction of all that there is a method to this apparent madness and that human beings "are not conducted solely [*uniquement*] by their fantasies" when they opt against "uniformity" and do not in every time and place adopt the same weights, the same measures, the same laws, and the same religion (Préf., 6.19.18).[2]

To this end, at the beginning of the second book of this great work, Montesquieu distinguishes, with regard to "nature," three species of government—republics, in which "the people as a body, or only a part of the people, hold the sovereign power"; monarchies, in which "one governs alone, but by laws fixed &

established"; and despotisms, in which "one alone, without law & without regulation [*règle*], draws everything in train by his will & by his caprices" (1.2.1). As Montesquieu's argument unfolds in the course of that book (1.2.2–3), he complicates this assertion, by further differentiating aristocratic republics, in which a part of the people hold the sovereignty, from democratic republics, in which the people hold the sovereignty themselves.

The typology deployed by Montesquieu is peculiar in two regards.[3] On the one hand, it abstracts from questions of moral character.[4] Where Xenophon, Plato, Aristotle, Polybius, and their medieval and Renaissance admirers had distinguished kingship from tyranny, aristocracy from oligarchy, and well-ordered popular government from the regime variously called democracy, anarchy, or mob rule and had done so chiefly with an eye to the character of the ruling individual or group,[5] Montesquieu insists that "the form of the constitution" is alone determinative; and when discussing one-man rule, he therefore treats as "accidental" matters such as "the virtues or vices of the prince" and as "external" questions such as "usurpation" and "the succession" (2.11.9).

At the same time, however, that Montesquieu jettisoned the contrast between aristocracy and oligarchy and that between well-ordered and ill-ordered popular government, he reasserted that between well-ordered one-man rule and tyranny.[6] He had long been sensitive to the fact that, with regard to their subjects, European monarchs exercised a species of self-restraint unknown in the Orient (*LP* 99–100/102–3), and he soon came to recognize that this was rooted in the fact that they did not themselves exercise the judicial power (*CR* 16.37–47). In consequence, where Thomas Hobbes had explicitly rejected regime distinctions of the sort espoused by the ancients as not just illusory but dangerous in the extreme,[7] Montesquieu insisted on restoring in the case of monarchy alone something like the classical understanding. But where the ancients and their medieval and Renaissance admirers had juxtaposed the lawful rule of an individual over willing subjects in the interest of those ruled with the lawless rule of an individual over unwilling subjects solely in the interest of the ruler himself, Montesquieu abandoned the focus on interest and consent while re-emphasizing the rule of law. If he ultimately eschewed political moralism, he was nonetheless a constitutionalist of sorts; and although he appears at one stage to have been inclined to criticize Machiavelli for confusing despotism and monarchy,[8] in the end, it was from the Florentine, who teaches that one should attend solely to "the effectual truth of the matter," that he took his cue.[9] As he saw it, monarchical government is distinguished from despotism solely by the presence of corporate bodies (*corps*) possessing the privilege of self-government, which is to say, by "the prerogatives of the lords, the clergy, the nobility, & the towns"[10]—above all, by the prerogatives accorded the "powers intermediary, subordinate, & dependent" which cause the monarch to "govern by the fundamental laws." There is, he contends, a sense in which "the nobility" with its *esprit de corps* "enters . . . into the essence of monarchy," for the "fundamental maxim" of this form of government is: "*no monarch, no nobility; no nobility, no monarch.*"[11] Where there is one-man rule in the absence of such a nobility, "one has a despot" on one's hands (*EL* 1.2.4).[12]

PRINCIPES

In the third book of his encyclopedic work, Montesquieu puts flesh on these constitutional bones by introducing a "distinction" which he thinks "very important" and which he describes as "the key to an infinity of laws." There is, he suggests, a "difference between the nature of the government & its principle [*principe*]: its nature is that which makes it such as it is, & its *principe*, that which makes it act. The one is its particular structure, & the other is the human passions that set it in motion" (1.3.1). The principle of democracy is virtue; that of aristocracy is moderation; that of monarchy is honor; and that of despotism is *la crainte* or fear (1.3.2–11). If Montesquieu rivals Aristotle as an analyst of political regimes, it is because he attends to the procedure followed by Plato in the eighth and ninth books of *The Republic* and supplements his strictly institutional analysis with an attention to political psychology which gives to his political science a suppleness, a flexibility, a subtlety, and range elsewhere unexcelled in modern times.[13] The bulk of the first eight books of *The Spirit of Laws* is devoted to a consideration of the manner in which the laws and customs reigning within a polity must be framed with an eye not only to the structure of that polity but to the passions setting it in motion (1.4–8). As Montesquieu explains when he first introduces the notion, the "principle" of a polity has "a supreme influence over the laws," and one can see them "flow from it as from a spring [*source*]" (1.1.3).[14]

THE SPIRIT OF LAWS, PART ONE

I. 1. Of Laws in General
    2. Of the Laws Which Derive Directly from the Nature of the Government
    3. Of the Principles of the Three Governments
    4. That the Laws of Education Ought to be Related to the Principles of the Government
    5. That the Laws Which the Legislator Provides Ought to be Related to the Principle of the Government

6. Consequences of the Principles of the Divers Governments, in Relation to the Simplicity of the Civil & Criminal Laws, the Form of Judgments, & the Establishment of Punishments
7. Consequences of the Different Principles of the Three Governments, in Relation to Sumptuary Laws, to Luxury, & to the Condition of Women
8. Of the Corruption of the Principles of the Three Governments

We would therefore expect that, when Montesquieu suddenly and without warning complicates his typology further by introducing yet another species of government,[15] he would not only discuss the structure of that government but take care to specify its principle and examine in detail the consequences that arise therefrom. After all, in mounting a defense of his *Spirit of Laws* against the charges laid against it by the faculty of theology at the Sorbonne, Montesquieu would later insist that his account therein of "the principles" distinguishing the various forms of government is "of a fruitfulness [*fécondité*] so great" that it can justly be said that these principles "give form to my book almost in its entirety."[16] But when the time comes and Montesquieu turns his attention to the question of "political liberty" in the eleventh book of *The Spirit of Laws*, he has nothing to say concerning the principle animating the new species of government that he describes therein.

His focus is what he terms elsewhere "a republic concealed under the form of a monarchy" (1.5.19, p. 304),[17] and he prefaces its discussion by introducing a category of distinction to which he has hitherto barely alluded (1.4.8): the "object" peculiar to each political community. That "all states have the same object in general, which is to maintain themselves," Montesquieu readily concedes. But he insists, as well, that "each state has an object that is particular to it."

Aggrandizement was the object of Rome; war, that of Lacedaemon; religion, that of the Jewish laws; commerce, that of Marseilles; public tranquillity, that of the laws of China; the carrying trade [*navigation*], that of the laws of the Rhodians; natural liberty was the object of public administration [*la police*] among the savages; in general, the delights of the prince was its object in despotic states; his glory & that of the state, its object in monarchies; the independence of each individual is the object of the laws of Poland, & what results from this is the oppression of all.

"There is also," he then adds, "one nation in the world which has for the direct object of its constitution political liberty," and he promises "to examine the principles [*les principes*] on which" this constitution "is founded" (2.11.5). This promise he keeps in the very next chapter by launching into an elaborate discussion of the "beautiful system" constituted by the pertinent nation's constitution and laws (2.11.6, esp. p. 407).[18] But neither here nor anywhere else does he tell us what is *the* "principle" and what are "the human passions that set in motion" what turns out to be the government of England.

It is difficult to know what to make of this. It is possible that, when he deals with England's constitutional monarchy in the eleventh book, Montesquieu abandons the mode of analysis that he had made extensive use of when he discussed democracy, aristocracy, monarchy, and despotism in Books Two through Eight. He may, in fact, be implying that it makes no sense to analyze the English polity in terms of "the human passions that set it in motion." But it is equally possible that Montesquieu has deliberately left it to his readers to discover on their own "the principle" exercising "a supreme influence over the laws" of England, which he had himself left unmentioned. At the end of the eleventh book of his magnum opus, Montesquieu remarks that "it is not necessary always to so exhaust a subject that one leaves nothing for the reader to do. The task is not to make him read but to make him think" (2.11.20).[19] To properly address these two questions, we will have to return to the first eight books of *The Spirit of Laws* and explore Montesquieu's political typology as a whole.

VIRTUE AS A PRINCIPLE

If, as Montesquieu more than once suggests, the English polity really is "a republic" of some sort (1.5.19, p. 304; 1.6.3; 2.12.19); and if, as he clearly implies, its government has a popular cast (1.2.4),[20] it should be set in motion by virtue—the principle that animates democratic republics.[21] This seems, however, not to be the case. To begin with, Montesquieu never attributes political virtue to the English: he touches on the subject only in referring to the brief republican experiment that took place after the execution of Charles I. The "impotent efforts" of the English "to establish among themselves democracy" on this occasion he regards as "a fine spectacle," noting that those "who took part in affairs had no virtue" and that the ambition that fueled their rivalries and gave rise to faction produced so "much of movement" and so "many shocks & jerks" that "the people," unable "to find anywhere" the democracy that "they were seeking," eventually "found repose in the very government that had been proscribed" (1.3.3).[22]

Moreover, Montesquieu nowhere suggests that political liberty is the object pursued by democracies and aristocracies. Indeed, he contends that these republics "are not in their nature free states" (2.11.4).[23] And he warns that it is a mistake to look for liberty "in democracies" where "the people seem pretty much to do what they wish" since to do so would be to "confound the power of the people with the liberty of the people" (2.11.2), for "political liberty does not at all consist in doing what one wants" (2.11.3). It is, in any case, "not to be found except" in what he calls "moderate governments"—and not always there. Political liberty, he observes, "is not present except where there is no abuse of power, & it is an eternal experience that every man who has power is drawn to abuse it; he proceeds until he finds the limits." It is in alluding to the human propensity for the abuse of power that he pointedly adds, "Who would say it! Even virtue has a need for limits" (2.11.4).

This claim should give us pause. If virtue has a need for limits, it is because the principle of democratic republicanism can itself become a motive for the abuse of power. It is "a misfortune attached to the human condition," Montesquieu later observes, but one cannot deny the fact:

> Great men who are moderate are rare; & as it is always easier to follow one's impulse [*force*] than to arrest it, within the class of superior people, one may perhaps with greater facility find people extremely virtuous than men extremely wise.
>
> The soul tastes so much delight in dominating other souls; even those who love the good love themselves so strongly that there is no one who is not so unfortunate as to still have reason to doubt his own good intentions: &, in truth, our actions depend on so many things that it is a thousand times easier to do good than to do it well. (6.28.41)

In this passage, Montesquieu describes one dimension of the problem: there is something inherently immoderate and perhaps even tyrannical at the heart of all forms of political idealism and public spiritedness. The other dimension of the problem stems from the nature of political virtue itself.

When Montesquieu speaks of democratic republics, he nearly always has foremost in his mind ancient Rome and the cities of classical Greece. His analysis of these communities and of their customs and laws in terms of constitutional structure and political psychology is, in one crucial regard, at odds with their self-understanding. As I have tried to demonstrate in fine detail elsewhere, the Greeks—and the Romans as well—took political rationality to be the fundamental principle of the classical republican regime. To be precise, their institutions and practices embodied the presumption that, with the proper civic education, human beings can rise to the task of sorting out through public deliberation the character of the advantageous, the just, and the good; and a quarter of a millennium before Aristotle fully articulated what this entailed, they evidenced that they were quite conscious of the fact.[24] Montesquieu stands opposed to the ancients and to those of their civic-minded, humanist admirers in the communes of Renaissance Italy who entertained similar presumptions concerning man's ca-

pacity for rational, public speech—for, like Machiavelli,[25] he has next to nothing to say concerning public deliberation. When he speaks of virtue, he is not interested in those qualities of character and intellect that enable the very best citizens (and perhaps even the ordinary citizens at their very best) to transcend
petty, private concerns and engage in public deliberation concerning the dictates of justice and the common good. Nor is he concerned with the liberation of
reason from passion. In stark contrast with the citizens of the ancient republics,
the classical philosophers, and their disciples the Christian theologians,[26] he
doubts whether "reason" ever "produces any great effects on the minds of men"
(3.19.27, p. 577). In this spirit, he has Usbek suggest in the *Persian Letters* that it
makes far more sense "to treat man as feeling [*sensible*] than to treat him as reasonable" (*LP* 31.22–34/33). As one would then expect, when Montesquieu mentions virtue, he has in mind the fostering of an irrational, unreasoning passion for
equality—for, in his judgment, it is this passion that sets the democratic republic
in motion (*EL* 1.5.2–7).

This passion in no way depends on, gives rise to, or is subordinate to anything
resembling moral, Christian, or even philosophical virtue as interpreted by Aristotle and his Christian successors,[27] and it is at odds with what Montesquieu
calls "moderate" government. It is perfectly possible for a republic to adopt some
of the institutional safeguards that the French philosophe considers essential to
"political liberty"; and as he demonstrates, something of the sort actually happened in classical Rome (2.11.12–19). But this cannot alter the fact that the democratic republic is not in its "nature" moderate. Popular government is rendered problematic by the fact that, in such a polity, the rulers are subjects at the
same time. In a monarchy, and surely also in "a republic concealed under the
form of a monarchy" such as the polity which Montesquieu found established in
England, "he who causes the laws to be executed" by appointing a public prose-
cutor "judges himself above the laws," and "one needs less of virtue than in a
popular government where he who causes the laws to be executed senses that he
must submit to them himself & that he will bear their weight" (1.3.3, 6.8, 2.11.6,
pp. 396–99). In a democracy, if civic virtue is lacking among the populace as a
whole, the laws will not be enforced—for, in the absence of self-discipline, there
will be no discipline at all.

The difficulty arises from the fact that self-discipline is, in Montesquieu's
judgment, unnatural. Virtue is not onerous at the outset and, then, somehow satisfying in the end. It is not what it was for Aristotle—a completion of nature's
work, a perfection of the soul.[28] Nor is virtue anything like what Homer (*Il.*
6.208, 9.443) and his successors took it to be: the product of self-assertion on the
part of a man who strives "always to be the best [*aristeúein*] and to be superior to

others." It, in fact, requires doing violence to oneself: "political virtue" is not an assertion, writes Montesquieu, it "is a renunciation of self"—and this is never pleasant, never satisfying. Virtue is "always a very painful thing" (*EL* 1.4.5).

According to Montesquieu, republican virtue is grounded in a "love of the laws & the fatherland"; it demands "a continual preference for the public interest over one's own"; in its emphasis on equality, which Montesquieu describes as "the soul" of the democratic state, it "restricts ambition to a single desire, to the sole happiness of rendering to the fatherland greater services than the other citizens." To produce this love, to so restrict the scope of ambition, and to inspire in the citizens of a republic the requisite spirit of self-renunciation, one must deploy "the complete power of education" (1.4.5, 5.3, 5).[29] In practice, this tends to require what Montesquieu calls "singular institutions"—of the sort established by the Greeks on Crete and in Thessaly, by the Spartans in Lacedaemon, by William Penn in Pennsylvania, by the Jesuits in Paraguay, by Plato in his *Republic* (1.4.7, 4.23.17), and by the Jews, the early Romans, and, we are told, the Chinese.[30]

The "singular institutions" that Montesquieu has in mind "shock all the received usages by confounding all the virtues," and they "confound" as well "things naturally separate" such as "laws, mores, & manners." By way of illustrating what this entails, Montesquieu invites us to admire "the extent of genius" found in the Spartan lawgiver Lycurgus who, by means of "harsh institutions," instilled a "warlike spirit" into the Lacedaemonians, rendered them "grave, serious, dry, taciturn," and produced a "people always correcting or being corrected, always giving instruction or being instructed, equally simple & rigid," more inclined "to exercise the virtues among themselves than to accord them [genuine] respect."

> By mixing larceny with the spirit of justice, the harshest slavery with extreme liberty, the most dreadful sentiments with the greatest moderation, he gave stability to the city. He seemed to deprive it of all resources—the arts, commerce, silver, walls: there, one had ambition without the hope of improvement; there, one possessed the natural sentiments without being a child, husband, or father; modesty itself was denied to chastity. By these roads Sparta was conducted to grandeur & glory—& with such an infallibility attending its institutions that one achieved nothing against it by winning battles if one did not succeed thereby in depriving it of its *police*. (1.4.6, 3.19.7, 16, 21)[31]

When instituted in democracies, Montesquieu observes, "singular institutions" of this sort are incompatible with "the confusion, the negligence, the extended affairs of a great people" situated on an extended territory; they find their "place" only "in a petty state" like the cities of ancient Greece where "all the citizens pay a singular attention to one another" and where "one can provide a general education & rear a people as a family" (1.4.7). In "small republics" such as these, especially in those graced with "singular institutions" dictating public supervision of affairs no less private than "the marriages" which take place "between the children of citizens," their "love of the public good can be such that it equals or surpasses every other love" (4.23.7). As Montesquieu had observed in his *Condierations on the Romans*, "there is nothing so powerful as a Republic in which the Laws are observed not out of fear, not because of reason, but by way of passion, as was the case at Rome & Lacedaemon — since there to the wisdom of good Government was joined all the force that faction can possess" (*CR* 4.60–64).[32]

In a large republic, Montesquieu adds in his *Spirit of Laws*, "interests become particular; a man senses then that he can be happy, great, glorious without his fatherland; & soon that he can be great solely on the ruins of his fatherland." One consequence of such a republic's size is that "the common good is sacrificed to a thousand considerations; it is subordinated to the exceptions; it depends on accidents." The situation "in a small" republic is more favorable: there, "the public good is more fully felt, better known, closer to each citizen; the abuses are less extensive there & as a consequence less well protected" (*EL* 1.8.16). Republics, if they are successfully to deploy shame as a reinforcement for the spirit of self-renunciation, must be comparatively simple and exceedingly small.

Here as in his *Considerations on the Romans*, Montesquieu evidences that he has much in common with Machiavelli. Like the Florentine, he wants his readers to stand in awe of the spiritedness and the ambition exhibited by the ancients.[33] This is why he writes, "One can never leave the Romans behind. So it is that still today, in their capital, one leaves the new palaces to go in search of the ruins; so it is that the eye which has taken its repose on the flower-strewn grasslands loves to look at the rocks & mountains" (2.11.13).[34] But, in contrast to the author of the *Discourses on Titus Livy*, Montesquieu is also intent that his readers recoil in horror and distaste at the price that the ancients paid for having what he regarded as great souls.[35] "It is necessary," he observes in one chapter, "to regard the Greeks as a society of athletes & warriors." The exercises that they engaged in were "suited to making men harsh & savage." They "excited" in the citizens "but one species of passion: severity, anger, cruelty" (1.4.8), and the code that they observed in conducting war, their *ius gentium*, was "abominable" (6.29.14). Later, he may begin by remarking that the "love of the fatherland" fostered by the ancient republics "is conducive to goodness in mores" and that "goodness in mores leads to a love of the fatherland," but he goes on to clarify what "goodness in mores" involves by invoking a disturbing analogy: "The less we are able to satisfy our private passions, the more we abandon ourselves to those of a more general nature. Why are monks so fond of their order? Precisely because of those things which make it insupportable. Their rule deprives them of all the things on which the ordinary passions rest: there remains, then, only that passion for the rule which torments them. The more austere the rule, that is, the more it curbs their inclinations, the more strength [*force*] it gives to the one inclination which it leaves them with" (1.5.2).[36] Classical virtue has something in common with Christian virtue: in both cases, Montesquieu contends, the self-renunciation required contains within itself the seeds of an ugly fanaticism.[37] Montesquieu may accept in its broad outlines Machiavelli's account of ancient citizenship and of the aggrandizement that he regarded as its raison d'être—but this does not make him an unabashed admirer of the severity, the cruelty, and the ferocity to which, both agree, it inevitably gives rise. In *The Spirit of Laws*, as in his *Considerations on the Causes of the Greatness of the Romans and their Decline* and his *Reflections on Universal Monarchy in Europe*, Montesquieu's aim is Machiavelli's defeat, and the critique that he directs at ancient republicanism is a crucial part of "the cure" that he has designed for the despotic temptations promoted by what he terms "Machiavellianism."[38]

In his moral and political outlook, Montesquieu has much less in common with the author of *The Prince* and the *Discourses on Livy* than with his fellow Frenchman Michel de Montaigne.[39] Both men enjoy contemplating "rocks & mountains," but both would prefer to reside in "flower-strewn grasslands."[40] The "beautiful system" admired by Montesquieu for taking political liberty as its "direct object" is not to be found among polities that are not in their nature free states. It must be sought among the forms of government that are intrinsically moderate.[41]

MODERATION IN GOVERNMENT

When he first introduces the notion of "moderate government," Montesquieu insists that it "is able, as much as it wishes & without peril, to relax its springs [*ressorts*]. It maintains itself by its laws & even by its strength [*force*]."[42] Such is not the case, he points out, with despotism, the quintessence of immoderate government—for if there were to appear in such a polity a "good citizen" and if, out of love of country, he were "tempted to relax the springs of the government" and then actually "succeeded" in doing so, "he would run the risk of losing himself, it, the prince, & the empire" as well. In fact, when "the spring [*ressort*]" of this species of government, "which is fear," is no longer present, "all is lost" and "the people no longer have a protector." For, in such a polity, "it is necessary that the people be judged by the laws & the great ones by the whimsy [*la fantaisie*] of the prince; that the head of the least subject be secure while that of the pasha is always exposed." If, when contemplating republics, Montesquieu at times betrays the same inclination "to shudder" that he ostentatiously displays when "speaking of these monstrous governments" (1.3.9, 4.3), it is because republics can only within limits approximate moderation: they cannot without danger relax their springs as much as they wish. Republics and despotic governments thus have this in common: they are fragile; they require apprehension; they must remain tense. "It is necessary," Montesquieu asserts, "that a republic dread something. The fear [*crainte*] of the Persians maintained the laws among the Greeks. Carthage & Rome threatened one another & rendered one another firm. It is a thing singular: the more these states have of security, the more, like waters excessively tranquil, they are subject to corruption" (1.8.5).

Moderate governments can profit from success and relax their springs because they encounter less friction than polities not in their nature moderate. Once set in motion, they possess a momentum all their own; like perpetual-motion machines, they do not run down.[43] "To form a moderate government," Montesquieu tells us, "it is necessary to combine powers, to regulate them, to temper them, to make them act, to give, so to speak, a ballast to one in order to put it in a condition to resist another; this is a masterpiece of legislation, which chance rarely produces & prudence is rarely allowed to produce." It may be more difficult to sustain and stabilize the government of any given despot, but it is much easier to institute despotic government in the first place. Though it constitutes an assault on human nature (1.2.4, 8.8, 21), despotism is, in a sense, natural. It "jumps up, so to speak, before our eyes; it is uniform throughout: as the passions alone are necessary for its establishment, the whole world is good enough for that" (1.5.14, p. 297).

In his initial discussion of moderate governments, Montesquieu is coy. For this, there is a reason. "I say it," he will later confess, "& it seems to me that I have composed this work solely to prove it: the spirit of moderation ought to be that of the legislator; the political good, like the moral good, is always to be found between two limits" (6.29.1). Political moderation is, in a sense, Montesquieu's cause.[44] Already, in 1721, when he published his *Persian Letters*, he was prepared to float the notion that the government "most in conformity with Reason" and "most perfect" is "a Government gentle [*doux*]," free from unnecessary "severity," which "moves towards its end with minimal expense" by conducting "men in the manner that accords best with their propensities & inclinations" (*LP* 78.4–10/80).

In *The Spirit of Laws*, Montesquieu's purpose is not simply to describe the political phenomena: description is, in fact, subordinate to prescription through-out. Because Montesquieu is persuaded that "extreme laws," even when de-ployed "for the good," nearly always "give birth to extreme evil" and that "it is moderation which governs men & not excess" (*EL* 4.22.21 and 22, p. 682), he is eager to teach legislators just how the spirit of moderation can be encouraged within each form of government. Thus, when treating despotism, he is quick to remark that religion, which may be otherwise politically malign, is useful as a check on arbitrary power: "as despotism subjects human nature to frightful evils, the very evil that limits it is a good" (1.2.4).[45] And when speaking of moderate governments, he implies that various polities may qualify. Sometimes he even treats republics as moderate states (1.5.15, 6.9, 15, 8.8), for to suggest that this is so is to justify and encourage their evolution in this direction.

ARISTOCRATIC MODERATION

Where Montesquieu is direct and clear from the outset is in his contention that monarchy, as exemplified by his native France, is moderate. In fact, monar-chy would appear to be moderate government par excellence.[46] This polity's moderation is not, however, a consequence of the moderation of the monarch and his nobility. As a "principle," moderation is peculiar to aristocratic republics: it is "the soul of these governments," and it is "founded on virtue"; it does not "come from a cowardice & a laziness of soul." Virtue is required in an aristocracy for the same reasons that it is required in a democracy: "those who are charged with the execution of the laws against their colleagues will sense that they then act against themselves. . . . The nature of this constitution is such that it seems to place the same people under the power of the laws that it exempts from them" (1.3.4).

Virtue is, however, exceedingly difficult to achieve in an aristocracy, for this species of government is "ill-constituted" (1.7.3).[47] In fact, as Montesquieu inti-mates, it is less a distinct form of government than a defective version of the de-mocratic republic—one that has a certain, unfortunate "connection [*rapport*] with the government of one alone" (3.18.1). When Montesquieu first speaks of this polity, he insists that "the more an aristocracy approaches democracy, the more perfect it is," and that "it becomes less perfect insofar as it approaches monarchy" (1.2.3, p. 247). Later he intimates that, to the degree that it ap-proaches the government of one alone, aristocratic government exhibits a spirit more despotic than monarchical. Thus, like despotism, it is extremely intolerant of "the satirical writings" that flourish under democracy. "In consequence of the fact that they are ordinarily composed against powerful individuals," these "satirical works" are welcome "in democracy" since there "they flatter the malignity of the people who govern." Within an aristocracy, however, the opposite is the case, for "the magistrates there are little sovereigns who are not sufficiently grand to despise insults." When a barb is aimed at a monarch, it rarely reaches so high, and he can easily laugh it off. "An aristocratic lord is pierced by it through & through" (1.6.15, 2.12.13).

The problematic character of aristocracy is due to the fact that its nature or structure runs counter to the principle required for sustaining it. Put simply, the inequality fundamental to an aristocracy militates against the inculcation of a love of equality. This explains why Montesquieu has absolutely nothing to say concerning the education in virtue given the citizen in an aristocracy.[48] As he will later have occasion to observe, "silence sometimes expresses more than any discourse" can (2.12.12).

Within an aristocracy, because one cannot hope to educate the citizens in virtue, one must rely, instead, on laws with teeth in them, and these must themselves instill "a spirit of moderation" in its rulers and work to insure that "everyone is as equal as the nature of the government permits." In an aristocratic republic, the nobles may have "riches," but they "are not supposed to spend them," and they become "so accustomed to miserliness that only courtesans can make them give money." As a consequence of the law, these nobles must display "modesty & simplicity of manners": they must "affect no distinction"; they must "confound themselves with the people"; they must "dress like them"; they must "partake of their pleasures"—and thereby make the people "forget their weakness."

Since all of this is contrary to the natural instincts of the well-born, there has to be within an aristocracy, "for a time or forever, a magistrate who makes the nobles tremble." Put bluntly, "this government has need of quite violent springs [*ressorts*]." One consequence, which would otherwise be counter-intuitive, is that there is "less liberty to be found in the republics of Italy" than in the "monarchies" of Montesquieu's Europe, for the former have to resort to "means as violent as the government of the Turks" if they are "to maintain themselves." If these aristocratic republics nonetheless fall short of corresponding "precisely with the despotism of Asia," it is only because "the multitude of the magistrates softens somewhat the magistracy." In Venice, Montesquieu tells us, it is a capital crime to bear arms, and it is necessary "that there be a hidden magistracy"—since the conspiracies "that it punishes, always profound, are formed in secrecy & in silence." For the letters of anonymous accusers, Montesquieu observes, there is "a mouth of stone open in Venice; you could say that it is the mouth of tyranny" (1.2.3, 5.8, 7.3; 2.11.6, pp. 397–98; 3.15.1; 5.26.24). In short, the state that inculcates and enforces the virtue of moderation is anything but moderate itself.[49]

HONOR AS A PRINCIPLE

Although monarchy and aristocracy both embrace inequality, they are, in at least one crucial regard, diametrically opposed: monarchy can be moderate —precisely because within it no one need be such himself.[50] "Monarchical government" can, in fact, "maintain & sustain itself" without "much in the way of probity," for "the force" possessed by its "laws" is sufficient. Severe self-discipline is not required where "he who causes the laws to be executed judges himself above the laws." If "bad counsel or negligence" prevents the monarch from "causing the laws to be executed, he can easily repair the evil: he need only change his counsel or correct the negligence itself" (1.3.3).

"In monarchies," Montesquieu explains, "policy makes great things happen with as little of virtue as it can, just as in the most beautiful machines, art also employs as little of movement, of forces, of wheels as is possible. The state subsists independently of love of the fatherland, of desire for true glory, of self-renunciation, of the sacrifice of one's dearest interests, & of all those heroic virtues which we find in the ancients & know only from hearing them spoken of." If virtue and moderation can be discarded, it is because in a monarchy "the laws take the place of all these virtues, for which there is no need; the state confers on you a dispensation from them." It is a good thing that monarchies have no need for the virtuous because therein "it is very difficult for the people to be so." Consider, Montesquieu urges, "the miserable character of courtiers. . . . Ambition in idleness, baseness in pride, a desire to enrich oneself without work, an aversion for truth, flattery, treason, perfidy, the abandonment of all one's engagements, contempt for the duties of the citizen, fear of the virtue of the prince, hope looking to his weaknesses, &, more than that, the perpetual ridicule cast on virtue form, I believe, the character of the greatest number of courtiers, as is remarked in all places & times" (1.3.5).[51]

If monarchy can nonetheless produce good government, it is because in it honor "takes the place of the political virtue" found in republics (1.3.6).[52] The honor that Montesquieu has in mind is an artifact: if it gives rise not to civic virtue but to the vices characteristic of courtiers, it is because it is a "false honor," more consonant with "vanity" than with "pride," which demands artificial "preferences & distinctions" and is grounded in "the prejudice of each person & condition" (1.3.6–7, 5.19, 2.19.9, 5.24.6).[53] The consequences of this all-pervasive "prejudice" are paradoxical but undeniable. "In well-regulated monarchies," Montesquieu contends, "everyone will be something like a good citizen while one will rarely find someone who is a good man" (1.3.6). Monarchy he compares to Newton's "system of the universe, where there is a force which ceaselessly repels all bodies from the center & a force of gravity which draws them to it. Honor makes all the parts of the body politic move; it binds them by its own actions; & it happens that each pursues the common good while believing that he is pursuing his own particular interests" (1.3.7).[54] Monarchies are ruled by something like what Adam Smith would later call the "invisible hand."[55]

It is essential, Montesquieu emphasizes, that social distinctions be maintained, for these artificial preferences and distinctions, and they alone, can work a transformation in the paltry vanity, which all men possess, and turn it into the socially useful and far more formidable passion for honor, glory, and renown which serves as monarchy's *principe*. Those who urge that, in France, the nobles be allowed to engage in commerce know not what they recommend. "This would be the means for destroying the nobility," he insists, and it confers "no utility on commerce." It is the prospect of advancing from trade to nobility that is the chief motive for engaging in trade. In similar fashion, he adds, there is much to be said for maintaining the distinction between "the estate of the robe" and "the great nobility." The former may lack "the brilliance" of the latter, but it has "all the" requisite "privileges." It may leave individuals in a state of "mediocrity," but the "body" drawn from among its members which serves as a "depository of the laws" basks in "glory." It is an estate "in which one has the means to distinguish oneself only by the achievement of a competency [*suffisance*] & by virtue." It provides one with an "honorable profession, but always lets one see another more distinguished: that of the warrior nobility, who think that, however rich one may be, one's fortune is yet to be made, but that it is shameful to increase one's goods if one has not begun by dissipating them." This latter body is a part of the nation, Montesquieu remarks, "which serves always with the capital of its goods; which, when it is ruined, gives place to another which will serve with its capital in turn; which goes to war in order that no one dare say that it was not there; which, when it has no hope for riches, hopes for honors, & when it does not obtain them, consoles itself because it has acquired honor nonetheless: all these things contribute to the greatness of the realm." If, during the previous two or three centuries, France has steadily increased its power, Montesquieu concludes, it is due to "the goodness of the laws" (4.20.22).[56]

On the face of it, monarchical government would appear to be absolute and entirely unchecked: such was certainly the English view of France.[57] But, according to Montesquieu, monarchical rule is far from arbitrary, and France is "the most beautiful monarchy in the world" (1.5.10).[58] "In states monarchical & moderate," he explains, the logic of absolute sovereignty is frustrated,[59] for "power is limited by that which is its spring or motive [*ressort*]; I mean to say honor, which reigns, like a monarch, over the prince & over the people." Honor reigns, "restrains [*arrête*] the monarch," and thereby limits the exercise of monarchical power—for "honor has its laws & regulations & knows not how to bend," and "it depends on its own caprice & not on that of another." Honor is an essential part of the "ballast" that puts the nobility "in a condition to resist" the court.

By this fact honor is linked with constitutional government: its rules and laws may be as irrational and capricious as honor is itself artificial and false, but, reinforced as they are by human vanity, they do persist; and honor, though it may be replete with "whimsicalities [*bizarreries*]," can therefore "be found only in states where the constitution is fixed & the laws are certain." This explains why a monarchy can relax its springs without danger as much as it wants: its nature or structure and its principle reinforce one another, for the love of honor is born of inequality. Relative to the "nobility," which is monarchy's distinguishing structural feature, "honor is, so to speak, both child & father." In consequence, as a form of government, monarchy is not fragile; it does not require apprehension; it need not remain tense; "it maintains itself by its laws"; and, like a well-made machine, it possesses a "strength [*force*]" all its own (1.2.3, 3.8–10, 5.9 and 14, p. 297), for the longing for honor that sets it in motion is in no way painful: it "is favored by the passions & favors them in its turn" (1.4.5).

This false honor is taught "not in the public establishments where one instructs children" but in "the world," and it teaches "three things: 'that it is necessary to introduce into the virtues a certain nobility, into mores a certain frankness, & into manners a certain politeness.'" The pertinent virtues arise from honor itself: they are "always less what one owes others than what one owes oneself: they are not so much what summons us towards our fellow citizens as what distinguishes us from them." With regard to monarchical government, it can be said that "honor, mixing itself through everything, enters into all the modes of thinking & all the manners of feeling & directs even the principles" governing conduct. Under its influence, these become a matter of fashion: "this whimsical [*bizarre*] honor causes the virtues to be only what it wishes & to exist in the manner in which it wishes; on its authority, it sets down rules for everything that is prescribed for us; it extends or limits our duties in accord with its fancy—even though they have their origin in religion, in policy, or in morals." Laws, religion, and honor emphatically prescribe "obedience to the will of the prince," but this same honor restricts royal power, for it "dictates to us that the prince should never prescribe to us an action which dishonors us—since that would render us incapable of serving him" (1.4.2).[60]

Monarchy is distinguished from despotism, Montesquieu insists, less by "the power" accorded the ruler than by "the manner" in which he is obeyed.[61] "In despotic states," he tells us, "the nature of the government demands an extreme obedience." All that matters is "the will of the prince. There is no tempering, and there are no modifications, accommodations, terms, equivalents, negotiations, remonstrances: nothing can be proposed on the grounds that it is as good or better. Man is a creature who obeys a creature who wills." Montesquieu is nowhere so indelicate as to suggest that, in a monarchy, the prince may be disobeyed. In fact, he asserts the opposite. When he contends that "honor . . . reigns, like a monarch, over the prince & over the people" alike, he merely infers that "from this fact there results certain necessary modifications in the obedience" accorded the prince. It is this alteration in "the manner of obeying" that apparently gives rise to the tempering, the modifications, the accommodations, the terms, the equivalents, the negotiations, the remonstrances, and the propensity to propose alternative policies that typify monarchy, distinguishing it not only from the singlemindedness of despotism but from that of republicanism as well. Throughout, however, Montesquieu insists that, "to whichever side the monarch turns, he prevails, tips the balance, & is obeyed." In short, "the entire difference" distinguishing the two forms of one-man rule is "that, in monarchy, the prince possesses enlightenment [*des lumières*] & the ministers are infinitely more skillful & expert in public affairs than in the despotic state" (1.3.10, 6.4).

Later, Montesquieu indicates by example what he means by the "modifications in the obedience" accorded the prince that are somehow made "necessary" by honor's reign: "Crillon refused to assassinate the duke of Guise, but he offered to Henry III to go into battle against him. After St. Bartholomew's day, when Charles IX wrote to all the governors to have the Huguenots massacred, the Viscount of Orte [Adrien d'Aspremont], who was commander in Bayonne, wrote back to his king, 'Sire, I have found among the inhabitants & the men of war only good citizens, brave soldiers, & not one hangman; for this reason, they & I beg Your Majesty to employ our arms & our lives in things that can be done.' This grand & generous courage regarded an act of cowardice as a thing impossible" (1.4.2). From Montesquieu's perspective, neither refusal counts as disobedience properly understood—for neither was aimed at overthrowing the monarchy or even the prince, and neither posed a challenge to the authority of the French king. In fact, in the very act of refusal, Crillon and the Viscount of Orte gave vital support to all three.[62]

One salutary consequence of the peculiar "manner of obeying" dictated by honor's reign is that in monarchies, as opposed to despotic states, "things are very rarely carried to excess." This arises from the fact that the leading men "fear for themselves; they fear being abandoned." In such a polity, "the intermediary, dependent powers" have almost as profound a stake in the existing constitution as the monarch himself and "consider it an honor to obey a king but regard it as sovereign infamy to share power with the people." Since the nobles "do not want the people to take too much," it is exceedingly "rare that the orders of the state are entirely corrupted. The prince depends on these orders: & the seditious, who have neither the will nor the expectation of overturning the state, neither can nor wish to overturn the prince." Instead, in times of disorder, when aristocratic resistance threatens to take a violent form, "the people who possess wisdom & authority intervene; temperings take place, arrangements are made, corrections are instituted; the laws regain their vigor & make themselves heard." Despotic states are characterized by "revolutions without civil wars," but the histories of the European monarchies are "filled with" the opposite. The histories of these "civil wars" and the conduct of those most responsible for fomenting them prove, as they did in the case of the Fronde, "just how little suspect ought to be the authority which the princes leave to certain orders in return for their service—for, even in their distractedness, the latter long for the laws & their duty, & they retard the ardor & impetuosity of the factious more than they can be of service to them" (1.5.11, 8.9).

A monarch who understands "the great art of ruling" will behave in such a manner as to take advantage of the proclivities of his subjects. Above all else, he will be accessible and easygoing, and he will never forget that, "in our monarchies, all felicity consists in the opinion that the people have of the gentleness [*la douceur*] of the government." "Towards his subjects," Montesquieu remarks, such a prince will "act with candor, frankness, & confidence," for "he who evidences a great deal of uneasiness [*inquiétudes*], suspicion, & fear [*craintes*] is an actor embarrassed & awkward in playing his role." In ordinary circumstances, he will refrain from employing domestic spies, and he will ignore anonymous accusations except where his own safety is at stake and in cases which "cannot suffer the tardiness of ordinary justice." Satirical writings he may prohibit, but he will not treat them as crimes, for "they can amuse the general malignity, console malcontents, diminish envy of those in public office, give to the people the patience to suffer, & make them laugh at their suffering." Such a prince will, however, be quite circumspect in resorting to raillery himself. In moderation, mockery may promote a pleasing familiarity. But when it is biting, it inflicts mortal wounds. A capable monarch will keep in mind the fact that he has it in his power "to make beasts of men & men of beasts" and that his "mode of conduct [*moeurs*] contributes as much to liberty as the laws" themselves. It is "an unskillful minister," Montesquieu remarks, who "always wants to inform you that you are slaves." The king who "loves free souls will have subjects" while he "who loves debased souls will have slaves." He should induce "honor & virtue" to draw near; he should "summon personal merit." At times, he may "even cast his eyes on tal-ent." His task is to "win the heart" but "not imprison the spirit. Let him render himself popular." A wise prince will be "charmed to have subjects for whom honor is dearer than life & no less a motive for fidelity than for courage" (2.12.13, 23–28).

Above all else, Montesquieu insists, the false honor that sets monarchies in motion is significant because it contributes to the rule of law. As we have seen, monarchy is distinguished from despotism by the presence of "powers interme-diary, subordinate, & dependent" constituted principally by the nobility. These sustain "the fundamental laws" of the kingdom "against the momentary & capri-cious will of one alone" by forming "intermediary channels through which power flows." The monarch creates the most important of these "intermediary channels" by delegating judicial responsibility: his "true function is to establish judges & not to judge himself." Were he or his ministers to act as judges them-selves, Montesquieu observes, "the constitution would be destroyed, the inter-mediary dependent powers would be annihilated: one would see all the formali-ties associated with judgments cease; fear would seize all minds [*esprits*]; one would see pallor on every visage; no longer would there be confidence, honor, love, security," or even "monarchy" (1.2.4, 6.5–6, 2.11.11). Were he, instead, to name commissioners to judge a particular case, the result would be no better, ar-guably worse, and "useless" to boot—for the subterfuge would be transparent, and he would thereby "attack" and "weaken liberty" more effectively than if he acted as a judge himself (2.12.22).

In Montesquieu's France, as we have seen (I.3, above), the most essential of the intermediary dependent powers are the parlements. These, he tells us, bor-rowing a religious metaphor customarily deployed by Jansenist barristers in de-scribing the courts,[63] are like certain, especially dependable interpreters of the Bible. They serve as a "depository for the laws," independent of the royal council and "the momentary will of the prince." These exercise the right of remon-strance: they "announce the laws when they are made"; they "recall them when they are forgotten"; and they "ceaselessly cause the laws to come forth from the dust where they are buried" (*EL* 1.2.4). These bodies, Montesquieu emphasizes, prevent the prince's salutary promptness in executing the laws from degenerat-ing into haste. They "never better obey than when they proceed tardily & carry into the affairs of the prince that reflection that one can hardly expect from the lack of enlightenment [*des lumières*] in the court concerning the laws of the state & from the precipitancy of its councils" (1.5.10). It is with the parlements in mind that Montesquieu writes, "Just as the sea, which seems to wish to cover the entire earth is brought to a halt by the seaweed & grasses [*herbes*] & the least bits of sand & gravel found on the shore, so monarchs whose power seems without limits are brought to a halt by the smallest obstacles & submit their natural haughtiness [*fierté*] to complaints & entreaty [*prière*]" (1.2.4).[64]

The existence of a depository for the laws independent of the prince does much more than encourage rational policy-making on his part. These bodies serve as "tribunals." They "render decisions," and these decisions, Montesquieu asserts, "ought to be preserved; they ought to be a subject for teaching & learning in order that one may judge here today as one judged here yesterday & the property & the lives of citizens here may be as secure & fixed as the constitution of the state itself." It is this that Montesquieu celebrates: the "fastidiousness [*délicatesse*]" of the judges, the manner in which jurisprudence becomes its own peculiar "art of reasoning," even the fact that confusion creeps in as different judges rule and suits are ably or poorly defended. Montesquieu admits that in the end there will be "an infinity of abuses," for these "creep into all that passes through the hands of men." But he dismisses this as "a necessary evil that the legislator will correct from time to time as contrary to the spirit of moderate government" (1.6.1). The crucial fact is that "the formalities of justice" give rise to "the liberty & security of the citizens," for "the pains, the expenses, the delays, even the dangers attendant on justice are the price that each citizen pays for his liberty." In "moderate states," Montesquieu insists, "the head of the least citizen is accorded consideration [*est considérable*]," and "one does not relieve him of his honor & goods except after an extended examination: one does not deprive him of his life except when the fatherland itself attacks it; & it does not launch such an attack without leaving him every possible means for defending" that life (1.6.2). Montesquieu makes much of the fact that monarchy is distinguished from despotism by "the security" that it confers on "the great" (1.6.21). Where Machiavelli was concerned chiefly with the integrity of the state and its success in conquest and war, Montesquieu gives priority to "the security of individuals."[65] It is "in moderate governments," where the obstacles to the abuse of power are many, that "gentleness [*la douceur*] reigns" (1.6.9).[66]

It would be tempting, then, to suppose that the government of England was conceived by Montesquieu as a variant form of monarchy.[67] In more than one passage, he seems to take this for granted (2.9.9, 11.7),[68] and the notion is by no means patently absurd.[69] After all, in England there reigned a king whose ministers saw to the execution of the laws; and though Great Britain was obviously too large to sustain itself as a republic, it possessed a territory of middling size, well suited, so Montesquieu says (1.8.17), to monarchy. Moreover, Montesquieu associates monarchy not only with political moderation but with liberty as well.[70]

To this hypothesis, however, there are insuperable objections. Quite early on, Montesquieu remarks in passing that "the English, in order to favor liberty, have eliminated all the intermediary powers that formed their monarchy" (1.2.4),[71] and, soon thereafter, he adds that "the English nobility were interred with Charles I under the debris of the throne" (1.8.9).[72] Nowhere does he even intimate that love of honor is the passion that sets the English polity in motion.[73] England may be, as he puts it, monarchical in disguise—but it is monarchical neither in its nature and structure nor in its principle.[74] It would appear, then, to be sui generis.[75]

Here, we must pause and contemplate another approach, for by a process of elimination we have demonstrated that the English polity cannot be understood in terms of the political typology introduced by Montesquieu with such fanfare at the beginning of his book. Before starting over, before attempting once again to determine whether England's government has a "principle" and just what this "principle" might be, before considering at length what is revealed by the fact that "political liberty" is this polity's particular "object," we must attend to Montesquieu's cryptic claim that, in *The Spirit of Laws*, "the author's design" cannot fully be discovered "except in the design of the work" (Préf.), and we must ruminate on the peculiar manner in which he structured his *Spirit of Laws*.

In this particular context, we must focus our attention on the meaning of Montesquieu's failure to include a full discussion of the English form of government within the eight books constituting what he designated as the first part of his work, where to the unsuspecting glance it would seem to belong; and we must sort out the significance of his decision to delay taking up this crucial matter until the central book of what he designated as Part Two, after what seems like an irrelevant digression on the capacity of the various polities to project power in time of war. It is in light of the architecture of the tripartite book that Montesquieu suppressed in 1734 that his design in 1748 can most easily be discerned, as we shall soon see.

Two

UNEASINESS

The patriotic spirit is an exclusive spirit, which makes us regard as a foreigner and almost as an enemy all other than our fellow citizens. Such was the spirit of Sparta and of Rome. The spirit of Christianity, on the contrary, makes us regard all men indifferently as our brothers, as children of God. Christian charity does not permit us to make an odious distinction between the compatriot and the foreigner; it is good not for making either Republicans or warriors, but solely for making Christians and men; with indifference, its ardent Zeal embraces the entire human race. It is, then, true that Christianity is, by its very holiness, contrary to the particularist social spirit.

— Jean-Jacques Rousseau

In the preface to his *Spirit of Laws*, Montesquieu makes a point of insisting that the work's architecture is deliberate, and he contends that, in attending to it, one is attending to his purpose overall. "If one wishes to search out the author's design," he tells prospective readers, "one cannot discover it fully [*bien*] except in the design of the work" (Préf.). Elsewhere in his preface, Montesquieu adopts another metaphor. It is, he writes, by reflecting "on the details" that one "will feel [*sentira*] the certitude of my principles," and he warns his readers that "many of the truths" he presents "will not make themselves felt [*se feront sentir*] until one has seen the chain that links them with others" (Préf.). The chain is not, however, evident to the unsuspecting glance.[1]

Winkling out the work's argument, as Jean Le Rond d'Alembert would later explain in the famous eulogy of Montesquieu that he penned for the *Encyclopédie, ou Dictionnaire raisonné des sciences, des arts, et des métiers,* is no easy task. "The author of *The Spirit of Laws* embraced within it a number of subjects so great & dealt with them with such brevity & depth," he observed, "that only an assiduous & meditative reading can give one a feeling for the merit of this book."[2] Some eighteen months after the publication of his *Spirit of Laws*, its author confessed as much. "That which renders certain articles of the book in question obscure & ambiguous," he told one correspondent, "is that they are often at a distance from the others which explain them & that the links in the chain which you have noted are very often at a distance the ones from the others."[3] To this one must add what Montesquieu tells us in the work's preface by way of an aside. As for the scattered "details" that make up the links in this chain, he wrote, "I have not provided them all: since who would be able to say everything without" incurring or inflicting (he does not say which) "a deadly *ennui?*" (Préf.).

Later yet, well after *The Spirit of Laws* had found its way into print, when critics, such as the abbé Joseph de La Porte, characterized the work as self-contradictory, disordered, and hopelessly obscure,[4] Montesquieu, after privately displaying his annoyance (MP 2057), took the trouble to sketch out for his own satisfaction a response specifying in detail the manner in which a work such as his should be studied. "When one reads a book," he insisted,

> it is necessary that one be disposed to believe that the author has seen the contradictions which, at first glance, one imagines that one encounters therein. In this fashion, it is necessary that one begin by distrusting rash judgments, that one take up again the passages which one asserts to be self-contradictory, that one compare them with one another, that one compare them again with those preceding and those following—all in order to see whether they derive from the same hypothesis, whether the contradiction is in the things or only in one's own particular manner of conceiving them. When one has done all of this properly [*bien*], one can pronounce as a master, "There is a contradiction."
>
> This is not always, however, everything that one must do. When a work is systematic, one must make sure that one has fully [*bien*] seized hold of the system in its entirety. Consider a great machine made to produce an effect. You see wheels turn in directions opposed; you believe at first glance that the machine is going to destroy itself, that the assemblage of wheels is going to get in its own way, that the machine is going to bring itself to a halt. It goes on forever: these separate parts [*pièces*], which appear at first to destroy themselves, unite together for the object proposed. (2092)

To this set of considerations, we must add what should now be obvious—the fact that Montesquieu had to write with the censor in mind, that indirection was sometimes required, that, in some measure, he had to conceal his design.[5]

Here, again, d'Alembert's observations are apt. In reading Montesquieu, he

insists, one must "distinguish genuine disorder from that which is only apparent." A work appears to be disordered but, in fact, is not "when the author, setting
in their true places the ideas he uses, leaves it to the readers to supply the intermediary ideas [*les idées intermédiaires*]: & it is this method that Monsieur de
Montesquieu believed he could & should use in a book destined for men who
think, whose genius could be expected [*doit*] to supply omissions deliberate
[*volontaires*] & reasoned. The order which makes itself apparent in the great
parts of *The Spirit of Laws* reigns no less in the details: we believe that the more
one penetrates the work's depths, the more one will be convinced of this." To
these observations, d'Alembert made one pertinent addition: "We will say concerning the obscurity that is permissible in such a work the same thing we said
about the lack of order; what would be obscure for vulgar readers is not so for
those whom the author had in view. In any case, deliberate obscurity is not a
species of obscurity: Monsieur de Montesquieu, having at times to present important truths whose absolute & direct declaration might have wounded without
bearing any fruit, had the prudence to shroud them, & by this innocent artifice,
veiled them from those to whom they would be harmful without causing them
be lost for the wise."[6] Unfortunately, d'Alembert's warning and Montesquieu's
advice to readers have not always been taken to heart, and this has proved to be
an obstacle to understanding not only the latter's cryptic account of the English
polity,[7] but also the dialectical structure of his overall argument and the stages in
which it unfolds.

MONTESQUIEU'S GREAT PARTS

Some aspects of the design of Montesquieu's *De l'Esprit des lois*, such as its division into thirty-one books and six hundred five chapters, are obvious. Some are
not. The most important and least discussed of the latter is the distribution of
these thirty-one books into what d'Alembert spoke of as its "great parts." Scholarly
neglect in this regard is not surprising. The parts, ultimately in number six, were
never given titles. They were not marked out as such in the first printed edition of
The Spirit of Laws, and this aspect of the work's architecture was similarly omitted
in the posthumous edition ushered into print by Montesquieu's son in 1757.[8]
That subsequent editors should often follow suit is only to be expected, and it is
only natural that it should become a scholarly convention to cite *The Spirit of
Laws* by book and chapter—and not at all by part. This is, nonetheless, a misfortune, for the work's six parts were distinguished as such when a final clean copy of
the manuscript was produced.[9] Moreover, Montesquieu was dismayed when he
learned that the printer and the editorial coordinator of the first edition had omit-

ted them;[10] and he saw to it that this aspect of the work's architecture was made explicit in the revised edition published in Paris under a false imprint in 1750,[11] the version that he described to a correspondent as being "the edition" of his *Spirit of Laws* that is "the most exact."[12] That Montesquieu regarded the work's articulation into parts as highly significant there can be no doubt.[13]

THE SPIRIT OF LAWS, PARTS FIVE AND SIX

V. 24. Of the Laws in the Relation Which They Have with the Religion Established in Each Country Considered with Regard to its Practices and in Itself
25. Of the Laws in the Relation Which They Have with the Establishment of the Religion of Each Country and its External Police
26. Of the Laws in the Relation Which They Ought to Have with the Order of Things on Which They Are to Pronounce Judgment

VI. 27. Of the Origin of & the Revolutions in the Roman Laws concerning Inheritance
28. Of the Origin of & the Revolutions in the Civil Laws of the French
29. On the Manner in Which Laws Are To Be Composed
30. The Theory of the Feudal Laws among the Franks in the Relation They Have with the Establishment of the Monarchy
31. The Theory of the Feudal Laws among the Franks in the Relation They Have with the Revolutions of Their Monarchy

In some respects, the structure of Montesquieu's magnum opus is relatively easy to discern. When, for example, one attends to the logic dictating the division between the two volumes published in 1748, it becomes clear that EL 3.19, with its focus on "the general spirit," was intended to serve as a summary and conclusion for the first volume and that, prior to Montesquieu's last-minute decision to add an appendix (6.28, 30–31) on the evolution of French law, EL 5.26, with its focus on the "relationship [*rapport*]" that laws "ought to have with the order of the things on which they are to pronounce judgment [*statuent*]," was designed to serve as a conclusion for the second volume—while 6.29, with its focus on "the manner in which laws are to be composed," was meant to serve as a conclusion for the entire work. By the same token, when one attends to the logic dictating the division between the three volumes published in Paris in 1750, one quickly recognizes that the thirteen books that make up Parts One and Two and formed its first volume have as their focus legislation; that the ten books that make up Parts Three and Four and formed its second volume have as their focus the natural environment and the dialectic between technology and commerce which enables human beings in some measure to reshape that environment and liberate themselves from it; and that Parts Five and Six re-examine the scope of legislation and consider how it, in fact, does and should take place. All of this suggests that Montesquieu's decision to delay making the English form of government thematic until Part Two was deliberate, but it does not clarify why he did so. To solve this problem one must attend to the less emphatic, but nonetheless crucial shift in perspective that distinguishes the first two parts from one another.

Montesquieu was a writer of consummate skill. Although he delighted in paradox and took pains to subject his readers to sudden and unexpected shifts in perspective, he was also inclined to prepare them surreptitiously for the great jolts to come. As we have seen (I.2–3, above), the triptych that, in 1734, he had wanted to publish illustrates both of Montesquieu's propensities. On the one hand, as originally designed, it would have required the reader to move without warning from a consideration of Roman aggrandizement to a reflection on the aspiration to universal monarchy in modern times and, then, to a meditation on the English polity. On the other hand, he consistently anticipated what was to come. In the first part of the trilogy, as it was originally designed, Montesquieu quietly laid the groundwork for his subsequent discussion by characterizing the Roman empire as a universal monarchy, by pausing briefly to reflect on the impact of modern communications on the formation of policy, and by suggesting that, as a consequence of its capacity for self-correction, the government of England was not only one of the wisest governments in Europe but deserved comparison with the government of republican Rome. And, in the trilogy's second part, he took care to indicate the manner in which England's emergence as a commercial, maritime power was prepared by the Anglo-Norman monarchy's loss of its vast domains in France.

In his *Spirit of Laws*, Montesquieu did much the same thing. He reserved his extended discussion of the English form of government for the work's second part. But he took care in its first part, especially toward the end, to whet the appetite of his readers for what was to come. Quite early on, as we have seen, he observed that "the English, in order to favor liberty, have eliminated all the intermediary powers that formed their monarchy" (EL 1.2.4). A bit later he even intimated that England is "a republic concealed under the form of a monarchy" (1.5.19, p. 304),[14] and he singled out as practices typical of those to be found in republics a set of procedures peculiar to the courts in England (1.6.3). But if, toward the end of the work's first part, he seemed to confirm the implications of these remarks by asserting that "the English nobility were interred with Charles I under the debris of the throne" (1.8.9), it does not make one forget his earlier comments concerning the "fine spectacle" constituted by the "impotent efforts" of the English "to establish among themselves democracy," his assertion that those "who took part in affairs had no virtue," and his contention that the ambition that fueled their rivalries and gave rise to faction produced so "much of movement" and so "many shocks & jerks" that "the people," unable "to find anywhere" the democracy that "they were seeking," eventually "found repose in the very government that had been proscribed" (1.3.3). It was evidently Montesquieu's intention in composing Part One to leave his readers for the time being perplexed.

To complicate matters further, Montesquieu also conspired to suggest on the part of the English a powerful propensity to political moderation. He mentioned England's jury system (1.6.3). He commented on the salutary consequences of the English king's use of his pardoning power and more generally on the relationship between letters of pardon and moderate government (1.6.16). He noted the absence of judicial torture in an England that was nonetheless "very well policed" (1.6.17), and he observed that the quality of its soil was conducive to luxury (1.7.6). Moreover, in the last reference to England as a country to be found in Part One, Montesquieu specifically referred to the "moderate" character of its government (1.7.17). If, in Part One, he tells his readers a great deal concerning England, it is for the purpose of making them want to learn a great deal more.

In similar fashion, in the last seven chapters of the final book of the first part of his *Spirit of Laws* (1.8.15–21), Montesquieu turned to the relationship between the form a government takes and the size of the territory it administers—a question, hitherto undiscussed in his work,[15] of so great an importance that its author insists that his overall argument will be incomprehensible to those who have not attended to it (1.8.15)—and this serves as a bridge to the ruminations on the projection of power that make up the first two books of the work's second part (2.9–10). If these two books seem to be a continuation of the last book of Part One, they nonetheless mark a shift in perspective.

THE SPIRIT OF LAWS, PART TWO

II.   9. Of the Laws in the Relation Which They Have with Defensive Force
    10. Of the Laws in the Relation Which They Have with Offensive Force
    11. Of the Laws Which Form Political Liberty in its Relation with the Constitution
    12. Of the Laws Which Form Political Liberty in its Relation with the Citizen
    13. Of the Relations Which the Levying of Taxes & the Greatness of Public Revenues Have with Liberty

It would no doubt be a blunder to say that the first part of Montesquieu's magnum opus is nothing more than a recapitulation of the argument advanced in his *Considerations on Rome*, and it would be equally misleading to suggest that the first two books of the second part are simply a restatement of the argument advanced in *Reflections on Universal Monarchy in Europe* concerning the transformation that has taken place in the *ius gentium* in modern times. But it is nonetheless true that in Part One of his great work Montesquieu does manage to exploit, then moderate, and ultimately subvert the allure associated with classical republicanism, and it is a fact that he accomplishes this feat just as he had done so in his *Considerations on the Romans*—by showing that antiquity, which seems to the unsuspecting glance so grand and glorious, is upon close examination distasteful, ugly, and grim. Moreover, it is no less true that early in Part Two, in Book Nine, Montesquieu explicitly debunks the aspiration to universal monarchy (2.9.7), using paragraphs lifted from the little treatise on that subject which he had suppressed in 1734 (*RMU* 17.360–65, 372–82); and it is also the case that, in Books Nine and Ten, he singles out for celebration the changes in the *ius gentium* (*EL* 2.9.1, 10.1–3) that he had treated in similar fashion in his *Universal Monarchy* (*RMU* 1.1–27).[16]

Put simply, Books Nine and Ten, the first two books of Part Two of Montesquieu's *Spirit of Laws*, are and are not a continuation of Book Eight, the last book of Part One. To the extent that they constitute a rumination on the relationship between the size of a polity and its capacity to project defensive and offensive force, they are a continuation. To the extent that they allude to the increasingly commercial, increasingly pacific character of modern republics and reflect on the changes in the *ius gentium* that have altered the conditions that determine the viability of different forms of government, they mark a real break with what has come before—and in this fashion they open the way for a consideration of a species of government that not only has no obvious ancient analogue and no self-evident principle but is also, as far as one can tell, subject to no territorial constraints.[17]

To grasp what Montesquieu is intimating, one must attend to the political significance of Christianity's sway. This was critical to understanding the argument of Montesquieu's triptych, as we have seen (I.1–2, above), and it is no less crucial for understanding the argument advanced in his *Spirit of Laws*. In Part One of the latter work, apparently in passing, Montesquieu pauses to lay stress on the alien character of ancient institutions, mores, and manners, implying that, in fact, they no longer even exist. When the virtue of the ancients was "in full force," he reports, "they did things that we no longer see & which astonish our little souls." If his contemporaries are unable to rise to the same level, it is, he suggests, because the "education" given the ancients "never suffered contradiction" while "we receive three educations different" from and even "contrary" to one another: "that of our fathers, that of our schoolmasters, that of the world. What we are told in the last overthrows the ideas imparted by the first two." In short, there is now "a contrast between the engagements" which arise "from religion" and "those" which arise "from the world" that "the ancients knew nothing of." This is why the moderns possess such "little souls" (1.4.4).[18] In short, there is nothing in the epigraph to this chapter to which Montesquieu did not subscribe.[19]

Here, of course, in keeping with the rhetorical posture that he adopts in much of Part One, Montesquieu seems to mourn the emergence of Christianity and the disappearance of classical republicanism in much the same manner as Machiavelli.[20] In Part Two, however, in the tenth book of *The Spirit of Laws*, where he briefly summarizes the central argument of his *Universal Monarchy*, Montesquieu abruptly reverses course. There he specifies the manner in which "the law of nations which we follow today" has set itself against "the arbitrary principles of glory, of decorum, of utility" sometimes recommended in "the councils of princes" (2.10.2). There he emphasizes that the *ius gentium* now rules out the legitimacy of offensive war except in self-defense and forbids conquest that eventuates, as ancient Greek and Roman conquest so often did, in the destruction of the conquered society and the enslavement, scattering, or extermination of its citizens. And there he adds, by way of conclusion, "Here is it necessary to render homage to our modern times, to the species of reasoning dominant at present [*la raison présente*], to today's religion, to our philosophy, & our mores" as well (2.10.3, 6.29.14).[21]

Moreover, later, in Part Five, where Montesquieu makes religion his theme, he will ask his readers to consider "the continual massacres" perpetrated by "the kings & chiefs" of the Greeks and the Romans; he will call upon them to contemplate "the destruction of peoples & cities" carried out "by Tamerlaine & Genghis Khan, the very chiefs who devastated Asia"; and he will then assert that, in the course of these ruminations, we will, of necessity, come to "see that to Christianity"—which, he will soon add, "softens the mores of men"—"we owe both in government a certain political right [*droit politique*] & in war a certain law of nations [*droit des gens*] for which human nature knows not how to be grateful enough" (5.24.3–4).[22] It is this shift—it is the achievement of hegemony by a religion which teaches that all men are brothers, which induces us to think of citizenship as a secondary matter, and which encourages peace on earth —that explains the discontinuity between the epochs called antiquity and modernity. And it is in light of this shift and of the transformation in the overall security environment that it effected that we can make sense of certain otherwise inexplicable claims put forward early in Book Nine—that confederations of cities "were more necessary in other times than they are today"; that in earlier times "a city without power ran greater risks"; and that "conquest" then caused such a city "to lose not only the executive & legislative power, as it does today, but also everything that there is that belongs to men," such as "civil liberty, goods, women, children, temples, & even tombs" (2.9.1). This profound shift in sensibility also explains why Montesquieu can now say what one could never say in antiquity: that "the spirit of the republic is peace & moderation" (cf. 2.9.2 with 1.4.8, 2.11.15, 6.29.14). And, as we have already seen (I.3, above), it accounts for the remarkable preeminence achieved by the new Carthage in the West.

LIBERTY AS AN OBJECT

In Part Two of *The Spirit of Laws*, after the interlude in which he obliquely addresses the manner in which Christianity and changes it inspired in the law of nations have profoundly altered the political prospects of man, Montesquieu takes the next logical step by making freedom, rather than virtue, his focus. There he informs us that monarchies, as represented in his regime typology, are peculiar to modern times (2.11.9), and there he suggests that they give rise to political liberty—but not in the course of its pursuit. Liberty is, as he demonstrates, an accidental byproduct of their pursuit of that polity's "direct object," which is "the glory of the citizens, of the state, & of the prince" (EL 2.11.7). In similar fashion, monarchies may achieve moderation by combining, regulating, and tempering powers so that one power possesses the ballast to resist another—but moderation is not that at which they aim. Thus, if the government of France is, in this regard, "a masterpiece of legislation" (1.5.14, p. 297), as it surely is, this fact is largely a matter of chance. After confessing, "I do not believe that there has ever been on this earth a government as well-tempered as that which existed in each part of Europe during the [feudal] period in which" the Gothic monarchy "subsisted," Montesquieu adds that he finds it "a matter for wonder [*admirable*] that the corruption of the government of a conquering people has formed the best species of government that men have been able to imagine" (2.11.8).[23]

One consequence of the fortuitous origin of Europe's monarchies is that they only "approach political liberty more or less." In this regard, England's government would appear to be quite different: if it actually provides for "political liberty"—as Montesquieu insists it does—it is because the form of government peculiar to England aims directly at it. English liberty is, at least in some measure, a product of "prudence" rather than "chance" (1.5.14, p. 297; 2.11.7). Montesquieu prefaces his initial discussion of the English polity with an account of the nature of "liberty," which he carefully distinguishes from "independence" of the sort possessed by those in the state of nature. His point is that the former is much more valuable than the latter. He begins, however, with a puzzling claim—that "liberty," properly understood, consists in "being able to do what one ought to want & in not being constrained to do what one ought not to want." Then, Montesquieu explains what this cryptic formula actually means—first, that "liberty is the right to do what the laws permit,"[24] and, then, that it is incompatible with genuine independence, for if a man is "able to do what the laws forbid, he no longer has liberty since the others would likewise possess this same power" and obstruct his freedom to do what the laws allow (2.11.3).[25]

To prevent those most likely to strive for this species of independence from being "able to abuse power," Montesquieu soon adds, "it is necessary that in the disposition of things power check power." It is his contention that "a constitution can be such that no one will be constrained to do things that the law does not require or prevented from doing those which the law permits him to do" (2.11.4). This would appear to be the object of the English polity, and it evidently constitutes what Montesquieu has in mind when he devotes the eleventh book of his tome to the laws which form "political liberty in its relation with the constitution" (2.11).[26] The government of England pursues this end chiefly through what eventually came to be called the separation of powers.[27] In its relation with the constitution, political liberty "is formed," we are told, "by a certain distribution of the three powers" (2.12.1).[28] But, as one learns while reading the second part of *The Spirit of Laws*, political liberty can be conceived in two different ways, and the second of these is no less important for understanding the modern predicament than is the first.

TWO CONCEPTS OF POLITICAL LIBERTY

Montesquieu distinguishes "political liberty in its relation with the constitution" from "political liberty in its relation with the citizen." The latter is the subject of the twelfth book of *The Spirit of Laws*. But because it is the central focus of Montesquieu's concern, it intrudes on that book's immediate predecessor as well. "In a citizen," Montesquieu explains therein, "political liberty is that tranquillity of mind [*esprit*] which comes from the opinion that each has of his security." If he is to possess "this liberty, it is necessary that the government be such that one citizen be unable to fear [*craindre*] another citizen" (2.11.6, p. 397). The

separation of powers is as essential to the elimination of this fear as it is to the
guarantee that "no one will be constrained to do things that the law does not require or prevented from doing those which the law permits him to do."[29]

In the working manuscript of *The Spirit of Laws*, there is an entry betraying
the fact that the two books ultimately numbered eleven and twelve were once
united as one (MS 291). On the face of it, this would seem to make perfect sense,
for the two forms of liberty that Montesquieu describes in these books would appear to be inseparable. Where the executive and the legislative power are united
in the hands of a single individual or corporate body, as they are in despotisms
and tend to be in republics, one has reason "to fear [*craindre*]" that the individual or body that "makes tyrannical laws" will "execute them in a tyrannical manner." In similar fashion, if "the power of judging" is not somehow "kept separate
from the legislative power & the executive power, there is no liberty." If it is
united with the legislative power, "the judge would be the legislator" and the citizen's life and property would be subject to "arbitrary power." If it is united with
the executive power, "the judge would have the strength [*force*] of an oppressor."
If the power "of making the laws" were united with "that of executing public res-
olutions & with that of judging crimes or the disputes of particular citizens,"
Montesquieu exclaims, "all would be lost" (2.11.6, p. 397).

After having set up this standard, Montesquieu applies it to the polities he has
earlier described. If "the kingdoms of Europe" tend to be "moderate," we are
told, it is because the prince, who exercises the legislative and the executive
power, leaves the power of judging to his subjects. The unity of the three powers
in the Turkish Sultan produces "a frightful despotism." That same unity causes
there to be "less liberty in the republics of Italy" than in Europe's monarchies:
these governments can sustain themselves only with "means as violent" as those
used by the government of the Turks. As a "witness" Montesquieu summons the
example of Venice with its "state inquisitors & the lion's mouth into which every
informer can at any time throw his accusation by letter," and he mentions the
"tyrannical magistracy of the ephors" at Sparta in the same regard. It was generally true of "the ancient republics," he later notes, that "there was this abuse: that
the people were at the same time judge & accuser." It was generally true that in
these republics "one citizen" could "fear another." Republics can be "despotic"
in more than one way (2.11.6, pp. 397–99, 404). Machiavelli to the contrary
notwithstanding,[30] they "are not in their nature free states" (2.11.4).[31]

Montesquieu's account of the English constitution has an odd tone. Instead of
describing, he resorts repeatedly to the language of prescription;[32] and he un-
derlines the point by issuing a disclaimer at the end: "It is not for me to examine
whether the English actually enjoy this liberty or not."[33] All that he will assert is

that "it is established by their laws" (2.11.6, p. 407). One is left with the impression that his England is less a reality than an ideal type suggestive of the potential inherent in England's laws: one is given the same impression later by his persistent resort to the conditional in describing the contribution of England's laws in forming "the mores, the manners, & the character" of the nation (3.19.27). He is far more concerned with what is likely to happen than with what, in fact, does. "I will be," he warns, "more attentive to the order of things than to the things themselves" (3.19.1).

Moreover, like Tocqueville in *Democracy in America*, Montesquieu seems to have his eye as much on the future as on the present or past, and though he betrays an enthusiasm for the political liberty embodied in England's laws, he qualifies this with a denial that it is his intention "to disparage the other governments or to say that this extreme political liberty should serve to mortify those who possess none but one that is moderate." "How could I say that," he exclaims, "I who believe that an excess even of reason is not always desirable & that men better accommodate themselves nearly always to middling things than to extremities?" (2.11.6, p. 407).

Montesquieu's refusal to issue a blanket endorsement of the English example should give us pause—for, however valuable political liberty may be, there may be something wrong with a polity that takes this liberty as its "direct object." In the chapter immediately following the one in which he celebrates the English constitution and then intimates that, for all its virtues, it somehow misses the mark, he adds to his readers' perplexity by singling out for praise "the monarchies which we know." Although, he explains, or perhaps because, we may add, these states "do not have liberty as their direct object," although or perhaps because they aim solely at "the glory of the citizens, the state, & the prince," they manage to instill in their citizens "a spirit of liberty"; and, in such states, this spirit is "able to accomplish things as great & to contribute perhaps as much to happiness as liberty itself" (2.11.7).

There is much in Montesquieu's description of the structure of the English polity which deserves discussion: his defense of the principle of representation, his endorsement of a bicameralism that leaves the initiative to the popularly elected branch and a veto to the hereditary nobility that stands in for the well-to-do, the case that he makes on behalf of a unitary executive armed with a veto and accountable to the legislature for his deeds solely through the principle of ministerial responsibility, the emphasis that he places on the linkage between taxation and representation, and the argument that he advances on behalf of an army of citizen soldiers commanded by the executive but ultimately dependent on the legislature (2.11.6).[34] If our primary focus were "the laws that form political liberty in its relation with the constitution," this would be our principal subject, and we would no doubt have to consider at length Montesquieu's ostentatious silence concerning the polity's territorial constraints.

More revealing, however, of the source of Montesquieu's reservations concerning the English polity is the fact that, when he discusses the English constitution, he singles out for particular attention the power of judging and the criminal law. He argues for fixed judgments determined by statute, and he praises the practice by which defendants help select their panel of jurors.[35] Security and fairness are obviously a concern. But repeatedly another theme thrusts itself into the limelight: Montesquieu's interests seem to be largely psychological.[36] Thus, in praising the jury system, he initially exclaims that "the power of judging" is "so terrible among men," and he then recommends that this power "be attached neither to a certain condition nor to a certain profession" and that it "become, so to speak, invisible & null." If this is the practice, "one does not continually have one's judges before one's eyes; & one fears [*craint*] the magistracy & not the magistrates." In much the same spirit, he adds that the jury should be made up of the peers of the accused so that "he cannot be of the mind that he has fallen into the hands of those inclined to do him violence" (2.11.6, pp. 398–99).

The emphasis placed on "fear" and on the defendant's state of mind is the feature of the argument that should catch and hold our attention. If Montesquieu can distinguish the liberty of the people from the power of the people, it is because he defines "political liberty in its relation with the citizen" in terms of "security, or, at least, the opinion that one has of one's security" (2.12.1–2). If anything, he seems more concerned with sustaining the citizen's "tranquillity of mind" than with sustaining his capacity "to do what the laws permit" him to do (2.11.3–4 and 6, p. 397). This explains why, in the end, he asks his readers to contemplate a paradoxical conclusion: that "it can happen that the constitution will be free & the citizen not" and that "the citizen will be free & the constitution not"; that while "only the disposition of the laws, & even the fundamental laws," can "form liberty in its relation with the constitution," liberty "in its relation with the citizen" can be made to arise "from the mores, from the manners, & from the received examples" prevalent within a political community and that it is less effectively promoted by political arrangements than by "certain civil laws" (2.12.1). It also clarifies why he can claim that "the knowledge which one has acquired in some countries and which one will acquire in others with regard to the surest regulations that one can hold to in criminal judgments interests human kind more than anything else that there is in the world" (2.12.2) and why he devotes so much attention to these regulations (2.12.3–30).[37] And it makes sense of his otherwise inexplicable concern with the psychological impact of taxation and his association of "duties," such as those "on commodities," that "the people least feel" with both "moderate government" and "the spirit of liberty" (2.13.7–8, 14).[38] If he claims that, "in our monarchies, all felicity consists in the opinion that the people have of the gentleness [*la douceur*] of the government" (2.12.25), it is because human happiness and, therefore, "political liberty in its relation with the citizen" is a state of mind.[39]

All of this helps explain why Montesquieu opted in the end to place the chapters focused on constitutional liberty in one book and those focused on the citizen's liberty in another, and it suggests something about human nature and something about the "principle" of the "republic concealed under the form of a monarchy" that he investigated during his extended sojourn in England. If, in contrast with its ancient counterpart, this modern republic can be situated on an extended territory, as Great Britain is, it is because it requires on the part of its citizens little or no virtue. Nowhere does Montesquieu suggest that "self-renunciation" is required to sustain it. Nor does he even intimate that it demands anything "very painful." And nowhere does he speak of the need to deploy therein "the complete power of education." His silence in this regard is explained by the fact that what Montesquieu says of monarchy can be said of England's government as well: it "is favored by the passions & favors them in its turn" (1.4.5). But though the passion that it favors and is favored by is as solid and reliable as the "principle" of monarchy, if not more so, this passion is not the longing for distinction. The "principle" of the modern republic is not honor; it is something very much like fear.[40] When, in 1753, the philosophe François Duverger Véron de Forbonnais insisted that "the principle" of Montesquieu's England "is terror,"[41] he was not far off the mark.

ENGLISH *INQUIÉTUDE*

The government of England is not a despotism comparable to the oriental states that Montesquieu so vehemently despised, but it has an undeniable kinship with despotism. It has as its object "political liberty," not "the delights of the prince." But it comprehends this political liberty in terms of the citizen's "opinion of his security." Where the "despotic state" in China takes as its object "public tranquillity" and other despotisms pursue "tranquillity" as their "aim [*but*]," if not their "object," England's government pursues the individual citizen's "tranquillity of mind."[42]

Despotisms sometimes attain their "object"; England's government generally fails to do so. If one were to examine the English constitution solely with regard to its "nature" or "structure," Montesquieu tells us, one would have to conclude that its three separated powers "form a condition of repose or inaction." But, of course, England's government is rarely, if ever, at rest (2.11.6, p. 405). In interpreting this fact, Montesquieu evidences something like an Epicurean understanding of the human condition,[43] comparable to that articulated by Machiavelli.[44] The foundation of the latter's teaching concerning politics is his claim that "all the things of men are in motion and cannot remain fixed." By this he meant to convey something closely akin to what Thomas Hobbes and David Hume had in mind when they subsequently asserted that reason is the slave of the passions. As Machiavelli put it by way of explanation, "the human appetites" are "insatiable"; "by nature" human beings "desire everything" while "by fortune they are allowed to secure little"; and since "nature has created men in such a fashion" that they are "able to desire everything" but not "to secure everything," their "desire is always greater than the power of acquisition [*la potenza dello acquistare*]."[45]

In writing of England, Montesquieu follows Machiavelli's lead—contending that "this nation" is "always inflamed" and that "it is more easily conducted by its passions than by reason, which never produces any great effects on the minds of men" (3.19.27, p. 577). And in speaking of "the three powers," he argues that when, "by the necessary motion of things, they are constrained to move [*aller*], they are forced to move in concert" (2.11.6, p. 405). One cannot say of the English constitution what Montesquieu says of despotism: that it "jumps up, so to speak, before our eyes"; that "it is uniform throughout"; that "the passions alone are necessary for its establishment." The modern republic is, after all, "a masterpiece of legislation," a product of chance and prudent artifice. One can say of it, instead, what he says of monarchy: that, in it, "policy makes great things happen with as little of virtue as it can" and that, "just as in the most beautiful machines, art also employs as little of movement, of forces, of wheels as is possible. The state subsists independently of love of the fatherland, of desire for true glory, of self-renunciation, of the sacrifice of one's dearest interests, & of all those heroic virtues which we find in the ancients & know only from hearing them spoken of." Moreover, one can say that, once a modern republic is instituted, "the human passions that set it in motion" are "alone" necessary to sustain it (1.3.5 and 5.14, p. 297)—and that the ruling passion that does so is closely akin to the very passion that is responsible for the "establishment" of despotism.

This helps explain, among other things, the tenor of Montesquieu's description of the contribution made by England's "laws" in forming "the mores, the manners, & the character" of the English "nation" (3.19.27).[46] One consequence of the laws' provision of liberty is that "all the passions there are free: hatred, envy, jealousy, the ardor to enrich & distinguish oneself appear to their full extent; & if things were otherwise, the state would be like a man struck down by a malady who has no passions because he has no strength [*forces*]." In a sense, the English citizen is unaccommodated man: like the individual trapped within the state of nature, he is "always independent."[47] He therefore follows "his caprices & his fantasies"; he and his countrymen are inclined "not to care to please anyone," and so "they abandon themselves to their own humors." Frequently, they even switch parties and drop one set of friends to take up another, having forgotten "the laws of love & those of hatred" (3.19.27, p. 575).

Precisely because the laws make no distinctions among men, each Englishman "regards himself as a monarch; & men, in that nation," are, in a sense, "confederates rather than fellow citizens." The fact that "no citizen ends up fearing [*craignant*] another" gives the Englishman a king-like "independence" that makes the English as a nation "proud." But, at the same time, "living," as they do "much among themselves" in a state of "retirement" or "retreat [*retraite*]," they "often find themselves in the midst of those whom they do not know." This renders them "timid," like those men in the state of nature truly graced with independence, but the recognition of "reciprocal fright [*une crainte réciproque*]" does not have on them the effect that it has on men in their natural state: it does not cause them to draw near, to take "pleasure" in the approach of "an animal" of their "own sort," and to become sociable. They are similarly immune to "the charm" of sexual "difference" and to "the natural appeal" which draws women and men to one another even in that aboriginal state. Instead of friendliness and longing, "one sees in" the "eyes" of these Englishmen, "the better part of the time, a strange [*bizarre*] mixture of ill-mannered shame & pride." Their "character" as a "nation" most clearly appears in the products of their minds—which reveal them as "people collected within themselves" who are inclined to "think each entirely on his own" (cf. 3.19.27, pp. 582–83, with 1.1.2, 2.11.3, 5.26.15).[48] In short, Montesquieu's Englishman is very much alone.

That so solitary a man should have an "uneasy spirit [*esprit inquiet*]" stands to reason (3.19.27, p. 582). Nor is it surprising that, unprompted by genuine peril or even by false alarm, he should nonetheless "fear [*craint*] the escape of a good" that he "feels," that he "hardly knows," and that "can be hidden from us," and that this "fear [*crainte*]" should "always magnify objects" and render him "uneasy [*inquiet*] in his situation" and inclined to "believe" that he is "in danger even in those moments when" he is "most secure" (3.19.27, pp. 575–76). The liberation of the passions does not give rise to joy. "Political liberty in its relation with the constitution" may well be "established" for the English "by their laws," but this does not mean that they "actually enjoy" what Montesquieu calls "political liberty in its relation with the citizen"—for the latter is constituted by "that

tranquillity of mind which comes from the opinion that each has of his security"
(2.11.1 and 6, pp. 397, 407), and the English are anything but tranquil of mind.

"Uneasiness [*inquiétude*]" without "a certain object" would appear to be the
Englishman's normal state of mind. He is rarely given reason to fear another citizen: fear is not deployed to secure his obedience as it is in a despotism. But he is
anxious and fearful nonetheless. Moreover, in such a country, "the majority of
those who possess intelligence & wit [*esprit*] would be tormented by that very *esprit*: in the disdain or disgust" that they would feel with regard "to all things, they
would be unhappy with so many reasons [*sujets*] not to be so" (3.19.27, pp. 576,
582).

PARTISANSHIP

Three

We never hold onto the present. We anticipate the future, as if it were too slow in coming, as if we could hasten its course, or we recall the past as if we could arrest its departure as too prompt. We are so imprudent that we wander in times which are not at all our own & think not at all of the only time which belongs to us, & we are so vain that we dream of times which do not exist & let escape without reflection the only time that really subsists. This is because ordinarily the present wounds us. We hide it from our view because it afflicts us, & if it is agreeable to us we regret seeing it escape. We attempt to shore it up with the future & think of arranging things which are not in our power for a time which we have no assurance of reaching.

— *Blaise Pascal*

In singling out *inquiétude* as the peculiar disposition of the English, Montesquieu is obliquely addressing an important contemporary debate, which was initiated in the previous century by certain Jansenists in France. The most important contributor to this debate was its instigator Blaise Pascal, a scientist and mathematician of the first rank and a loose adherent of Port Royal, who died in 1662. Pascal's thinking, like that of his Jansenist friends, had deep roots in Augustinian theology, and his influence on subsequent European political thought was not only profound: it was, as we shall eventually see in *Soft Despotism, Democracy's Drift*, long-lasting as well. Moreover, even at the outset, Pascal's influence was by no means restricted to France.

In the aftermath of Pascal's death, his sister Gilberte Périer and her son Étienne turned to Jansenist sympathizers, such as Antoine Arnauld, Pierre Nicole, and Artus Gouffier, duc de Roannez, who had been close to the deceased or had collaborated with him in the past; with their help, they saw to the editing of the loosely organized collection of *Pensées* that Pascal had left behind, and in 1670 they ushered these into print. The so-called Port Royal edition that this team produced was not, however, a faithful rendition of what they had found. For the most part, Pascal had jotted down his "thoughts" on large sheets of paper. Eventually, he cut up these sheets in order to isolate individual passages, which he then rearranged, stringing them together with thread run through a tiny hole made in the top left corner of each fragment. In this fashion, he produced sixty bundles, and to twenty-seven of these, by the time that he died, he had assigned titles. In the aftermath of his death, his relatives discovered this material laid out in no particular order that they could discern. They and the duc de Roannez were aware, however, that they were in the presence of genius and that their understanding might be inadequate and incomplete. Carefully, therefore, and cautiously, to the best of their ability, without rearranging the fragments, they had a clean copy made—from which other copies were made in turn. It was on the basis of these secondary copies, two of which survive,[1] that Arnauld, Nicole, and their colleagues did their work as editors. We cannot be sure what Pascal would have done with this material had he lived. But there is, in fact, a certain logic evident in the apparent confusion in which his *Pensées* were found, and this logic his editors, less cautious and respectful than had been those responsible for making the original copies of the work, deliberately ignored.[2]

Had Pascal's editors published the *Pensées* in the form in which they had originally been discovered, the French—and, before long, the European—public would have been presented with an apologetic work aimed squarely and bluntly at the irreligious and the lukewarm; at the followers of Michel de Montaigne, Pierre Charron, François La Mothe Le Vayer, and Pierre Gassendi; and at future heirs of the *libertins érudits*.[3] This work would have begun, in an empirical fashion, with ordinary human experience, and it would have subjected the vanity, the wretchedness, the boredom, and the desperate search for diversion characteristic of human life to an extended, penetrating, and moving psychological analysis. In the process, it would have restated in the most unsparing terms the Pyrrhonist critique of the human understanding, and it would have spelled out the psychological, moral, and political consequences of man's inability to find his way in an infinite universe beyond his ken. Only then would it have intimated that Pascal's chosen antagonist Montaigne had stopped well short of stating the full truth when, in passing, he had described "*inquiétude* and irresoluteness" as "our leading [*maistresses*] and predominant qualities." Only then would it have argued that the only plausible way to make sense of human restlessness—of the profound disproportion between human longing and aspiration, on the one hand, and human grandeur and achievement, on the other—is to explain it in terms of original sin, man's fallen nature, and his instinctive nostalgia for a repose in union with God that had evidently once been his. In short, it would have been a powerful restatement of the argument of Saint Augustine, as it was formulated in the very first paragraph of his *Confessions*, where, in addressing God, he wrote, "Thou hast made us for Thyself, and the heart of each of us will be uneasy [*inquietum*] until it rests in Thee."[4]

In practice, however, Arnauld and Nicole saw to it that Pascal's argument was redirected to the faithful. Under their influence, the editors cut much of what he had written illustrative of the human propensity for *inquiétude* and of man's intellectual failings. In the process, they eliminated the attacks on Descartes and the corrosive socio-political commentary contained therein,[5] and they gave precedence in the volume to the more narrowly religious argument that had originally served as its conclusion. In time, to be sure, the marquis de Condorcet would discover one of the manuscript copies, and in 1776 he would publish a collection of fragments arranged in such a manner as to suggest that Pascal was a religious skeptic or an atheist. Three years later, abbé Charles Bossut would publish a revised, slightly expanded edition of the *Pensées*, with twenty-eight hitherto unpublished fragments, in which he rearranged the material into two parts, the first devoted to philosophy, morality, and *belles lettres*, and the second dedicated to religion. It was not, however, until 1844 that there would be a more or less complete, more or less accurate edition of the *Pensées* available, and it was not until the second half of the twentieth century that readers would be able to peruse the *Pensées* in editions aimed at being faithful to the order established by Pascal himself.[6]

In abridging, censoring, and rewriting the text, and in restructuring the argument outlined in the twenty-seven bundles of Pascal's *Pensées* bearing titles, the editors obscured the work's focus and deprived it of much of its rhetorical force. In the end, however, this did not prove to be an insuperable obstacle to its assimilation. The book sold well, and from the outset it was widely read and discussed. If some figures, such as Jacques-Bénigne Bossuet, bishop of Meaux, failed to reply to Pascal, it can hardly be because they were unfamiliar with his *Pensées*. It can be shown that Nicolas Malebranche, who rarely mentioned Pascal by name, nonetheless paid exceedingly close attention not only to the great man's published works but also to fragments available at that time only in manuscript and that he responded in a pointed manner to what Pascal had said.[7] Moreover, the editors' mangling of the text, which was not materially corrected in the slightly augmented edition first published by Périer in 1678,[8] did not prevent a discerning reader, such as Voltaire, from gravitating to the material discussing the human condition that he found buried in the middle of the book, and, as we have seen, it did not deter him from denouncing its author as a "sublime misanthrope" who "writes against human nature," imputing to "the essence of our nature that which pertains only to certain men."[9] The way for readers of this sort was made considerably easier by the fact, well known at the time, that an argument almost indistinguishable from the one advanced by Pascal could be found fully developed in the *Essais de morale,* the first volume of which Pierre Nicole published a year subsequent to the appearance of the *Pensées.*[10]

Four years after Nicole began publishing his essays, John Locke arrived from England for an extended sojourn in France, which would last three-and-a-half years.[11] By this time, the Englishman was thoroughly versed in the history of philosophy. He had certainly read Thomas Hobbes's *Leviathan.* By then, he had also in all likelihood read Niccolò Machiavelli's *Prince* and *Discourses on Livy,* Sir Francis Bacon's *Advancement of Learning,* and *The Essays* of Michel de Montaigne; and he had embraced a conviction they all shared—that human desire is insatiable, and that reason is the slave of the passions.[12] By this time, he had also produced not one, but two preliminary drafts of what eventually came to be known as *An Essay concerning Human Understanding,*[13] and he had brought a copy of at least one of the two with him on his trip. In France, where he appears to have been operating as an emissary and intelligence agent on behalf of the Whig leader Anthony Ashley Cooper, first earl of Shaftesbury, Locke at first had time on his hands, and in Montpellier, early on, he devoted much of it to mastering French. It was in this period that he acquired and read the Port Royal edition of Pascal's *Pensées,* in which he displayed a keen interest; and it was in these years that he purchased the various volumes of Nicole's *Essais de morale* and translated for possible publication in English three of the essays contained therein.[14]

One may doubt whether Locke's encounter with the ruminations of these two Jansenists was decisive for the formation of his thinking, but there can be little doubt that they contributed mightily to the peculiar manner in which he formulated his argument. In 1690, when he finally published his *Essay concerning Human Understanding,* Locke introduced an observation not found in either of the drafts produced in 1671. That it owes a great deal to Hobbes's *Leviathan* is evident, but there is also language present suggesting on Locke's part an appropriation and transformation of the acute psychological analysis pioneered by Pascal, whom he tellingly praises in that work as a "prodigy of Parts."[15] It is this element, which was first fully developed by Nicole, that proved to be most pertinent to the concerns of Montesquieu.

Like Hobbes, Locke was persuaded "that the Philosophers of old did in vain enquire, whether *Summum bonum* consisted in Riches, or bodily Delights, or Virtue, or Contemplation," and in this context, he quipped that "they might have as reasonably disputed, whether the best Relish were to be found in Apples, Plumbs, or Nuts; and have divided themselves into Sects upon it." His point was that "Men may chuse different things, and yet all chuse right, supposing them only like a Company of poor Insects, whereof some are Bees, delighted with Flowers, and their sweetness; others, Beetles, delighted with other kind of Viands."[16]

To clarify just why this should be the case, Locke recast Hobbes's conclusion by resorting to formulations introduced by Pascal and taken up by Nicole, who had both argued that, as a consequence of the Fall, man lacks tranquillity of soul and a capacity for dwelling in the present and that he is condemned to a life of boredom (*ennui*) and uneasiness (*inquiétude*) relieved only by senseless diversion (*divertissement*). What men have in common, Locke explained, is not an orientation toward the good defined in any concrete way but "a constant succession of *uneasinesses*," such that "very little part of our life is so vacant from these *uneasinesses*, as to leave us free to the attraction of remoter absent good." Tellingly, Locke rips this characterization of the human condition from its theological context.[17] With regard to the Fall, he is strikingly silent. For him, as for Montaigne, "*uneasiness*" and the irresoluteness attendant upon it are the distinguishing characteristics of mankind as such: for him, in fact, *uneasiness* is the motive for all human action.[18]

In the French translation of *An Essay concerning Human Understanding* that Pierre Coste produced in close collaboration with Locke, *uneasiness* was appropriately rendered by the term originally deployed by Montaigne and Pascal. "By *inquiétude*," Coste remarked, "the author means *the state of a man who is not at ease, the lack of ease & tranquillity in the soul*, which is in this regard purely passive." When he deployed *inquiétude* to translate *uneasiness*, Coste added, he had consistently italicized the French word. Unless one kept in mind precisely what Locke meant by the term, he explained, "it would not be possible to comprehend with exactitude the matters treated in" his crucial chapter "Of Power" —matters which Coste considered "the most important and troubling [*délicates*] in the entire work."[19]

Locke's forceful restatement of Montaigne's broad claims in this regard stirred up considerable discussion, especially among those who spoke French,[20] and Montesquieu was well positioned to contribute to the debate. As one would expect, he owned the French translation of Locke's *Essay*.[21] With the translator, he was personally acquainted (MP 1108, 1231, 1441), and he even had occasion to hear him speak concerning the author of that renowned work (1105). Montesquieu's strategic redeployment of the pertinent term in *The Spirit of Laws* is intended to suggest three conclusions: that, while Locke was right to follow Montaigne in wresting the notion from its Augustinian theological context, he had erred in presuming that his countrymen were representative of all mankind; that, while *inquiétude* may, indeed, be natural to man, as a settled disposition it is specific to the citizens who live under a particular form of government;[22] and, most important of all, that the form of government "which has for the direct object of its constitution political liberty" characteristically fails to produce in its citizens the "tranquillity of mind" that constitutes "political liberty in its relation with the citizen."

AMOUR PROPRE

Montesquieu's point becomes even more obvious when one reads his extended description of the character of the English nation in the context of what he has just written a few pages before concerning his native France. "If there were in the world," he observes, "a nation which had a sociable humor, an openness of heart, a joy in living, a taste, a facility for communicating its thoughts, which was lively, agreeable, playful, sometimes imprudent, often indiscreet; & which had along with this courage, generosity, frankness, a certain sensitivity to honor, it would be necessary not to upset [*gêner*], by the laws, its manners lest one upset its virtues" as well (*EL* 3.19.5). One could certainly not say of the French what Montesquieu says concerning the English: that they evidence so great "a disgust for all things" that "they kill themselves without one being able to imagine any reason that would cause them to do so, that they kill themselves when in the bosom of happiness" (3.14.12–13).[23]

Just why the French should be exempt from *inquiétude* and from suicidal propensities required considerable rumination on Montesquieu's part. By the time in which he composed his *Spirit of Laws*, he had, in fact, devoted considerable time to the study of human psychology, as we have seen. He owned a copy of the 1678 Port Royal edition of the *Pensées* of Pascal;[24] and, like Locke, he had read the book.[25] He seems not to have owned a copy of Nicole's *Essais de morale*, but in his notebooks he demonstrates a close familiarity with this great, once celebrated, now neglected work (*MP* 1970). That he had closely examined and pondered the acute psychological analysis of human conduct hinted at by Pascal and developed in detail by Nicole there can hardly be doubt. In one passage in his notebooks (2064), he cites the latter's discussion of *amour propre*; in another (464), without mentioning his source, he restates the argument contained therein.

Above all else, Montesquieu was interested in the plasticity of human nature. In this connection, he seems to have paid especially close attention to Nicole's development of the implications of Pascal's description of the transformation worked by the Fall in man's "love for himself [*l'amour pour soi même*]." According to Pascal's account, after the Fall, this self-love, which had once been subordinated to the love of God, remained "alone" in what was a "great soul, capable of an infinite love"; and, in the absence of a proper object for human longing, by "extending itself & boiling over into the void that the love of God had left behind," this self-love metamorphosed into the species of vainglory that Pascal and the French moralists of the seventeenth century called "*l'amour propre*." This had, he contended, predictable consequences, for, in the process of becoming "infinite" in its scope, this self-love became both "criminal & immoderate" and gave rise to "the desire to dominate" others.[26] Then, after sketching what was a more or less conventional Christian account, Pascal went on—in a series of fragments omitted by Nicole and his colleagues from the Port Royal edition of the *Pensées*—to suggest a paradox: that men in their "grandeur" had somehow learned to "make use of the concupiscence" spawned by *amour propre*; and that, despite the fact that it dictates that "human beings hate one another," they had managed to deploy concupiscence in such a fashion as "to serve the public good." They had, in fact, "founded upon & drawn from concupiscence admirable rules of public administration [*police*], morality, & justice," and they had even succeeded in eliciting from "the villainous depths" of the human soul, which are "only covered over, not rooted up" by their efforts, a veritable "picture" and "false image of charity" itself.[27] To this paradox, Nicole devoted a seminal essay suggesting that Christian charity is politically and socially superfluous—that, in its absence, thanks to the particular Providence of God, *l'amour propre* is perfectly capable of providing a foundation for the proper ordering of civil society, of the political order, and of human life in this world more generally.[28]

Nicole's inspiration, and no doubt that of Pascal as well, was a passage in which Saint Augustine dilated on the propensity for human pride (*superbia*) to imitate the works inspired by Christian charity (*caritas*). It could, he claimed, cause men to nourish the poor, to fast, and even to suffer martyrdom.[29] At the beginning of his essay, Nicole specifies that, when he speaks of "*l'amour-propre*," he has in mind the fact "that man, once corrupted, not only loves himself, but that he loves himself without limit & without measure; that he loves himself alone; that he relates everything to himself"; in short, that "he makes himself the center of everything"; that "he wants to dominate over everything" and desires "that all creatures occupy themselves with satisfying, praising, & admiring him."

This "disposition," which Nicole attributes to all men, he calls "tyrannical." He acknowledges that it "renders human beings violent, unjust, cruel, ambitious, fawning, envious, insolent, & quarrelsome," and he readily concedes that, in the end, it gives rise to a war of all against all. He merely insists that, in the shocking manner so famously described by Thomas Hobbes, to whom he with approval alludes, instrumental reason, animated by *amour-propre* and by nothing else, can provide the polity with a firm foundation, and he contends that, by way of cupidity and vanity, *amour-propre*, with its "marvelous dexterity," can promote commerce, encourage civility, and even elicit from men a simulacrum of virtue, as those who desire security and prosperity are forced by the fear of death and the lust for gain to embrace justice and "traffic in works, services, favors, civilities," and as those who desperately crave admiration and love are driven to do admirable things. "In this way," he writes, "by means of this commerce" among men, "all the needs of life can in a certain fashion be met without charity being mixed up in it at all." Indeed, "in States into which charity has made no entry because the true Religion is banned, one can live with as much peace, security, & convenience as if one were in a Republic of Saints." Nicole is even willing to assert "that to reform the world in its entirety—which is to say, to banish from it all the vices & every coarse disorder, & to render man happy in this life here below—it would only be necessary, in the absence of charity, to confer on all an *amour-propre* that is enlightened [*éclairé*], so that they might know how to discern their real interests." If this were done, he concluded, "no matter how corrupt this society would be within, & in the eyes of God, there would be nothing in its outward demeanor that would be better regulated, more civil, more just, more pacific, more decent [*honnête*], & more generous. And what is even more admirable: although this society would be animated & agitated by *l'amour-propre* alone, *l'amour propre* would not make a public appearance [*paraître*] there; &, although this society would be entirely devoid of charity, one would not see anything anywhere apart from the form & marks of charity."[30]

When he read Pascal and Nicole, Montesquieu appears to have paid little, if any attention to what these two Jansenists had to say about Providence and the Fall. His concerns were, as Montaigne's and Locke's had been, political and psychological, not theological—and Nicole's discussion of the achievements of "*amour-propre éclairé*" had one crucial feature in common with Pascal's analysis of the role played within human life by *ennui*, *inquiétude*, and *divertissement*. As a descriptive account of the human condition, it was not in any way dependent upon the religious context within which it had originally been framed. Divorced from this context, recast as a metaphysically neutral depiction of human nature itself, it could easily serve as a starting point for secular political speculation, and serve in this fashion it did. It is by no means an accident that the leading Jansenists displayed a certain sympathy for Jean-Jacques Rousseau's *Social Contract*.[31] Nor is it at any way odd that, at the time of the French Revolution, many within their number welcomed the confiscation of church property and the Civil Constitution of the Clergy and that the regions in France most sympathetic to Jansenism in the seventeenth and eighteenth centuries tended to do so as well.[32] From early on, Montesquieu had foreseen that something of the sort might come to pass (273). When Louis XIV decried the Jansenists as "a republican party in church and state" (I.3, above), he was, for reasons that David Hume would in due course specify,[33] more prescient than he knew.[34]

To get an inkling of the moral significance of the vision of human nature that the Jansenists and their irreligious admirers propagated, one need only consult the seemingly secular *Réflexions, ou Sentences et maximes morales*, of François, duc de La Rochefoucauld,[35] a work that Montesquieu greatly admired (*MP* 667). To get a sense of the political implications of this way of thinking, one need only work one's way through *Various Thoughts on the Occasion of a Comet* by Nicole's great admirer Pierre Bayle and ponder his notorious contention that *amour propre*, if properly deployed, would be sufficient to provide a foundation for a well-governed society of atheists,[36] as Montesquieu did (104, 989, 1946, 1993; S 488; *EL* 5.24.2–6).[37] To explore these implications more fully, one need only read *The Fable of the Bees* by Bayle's student Bernard Mandeville and contemplate the argument underpinning his scandalous and highly influential assertion that private vices, properly managed, can make for public virtues,[38] as Montesquieu did as well (*MP* 1553; *EL* 1.7.1, 3.19.8). And, to begin to measure its long-term impact, one need only turn to *The Wealth of Nations* by Montesquieu's admirer Adam Smith.[39] For our purposes here, however, it would be sufficient that one simply peruse Part One of Montesquieu's *Spirit of Laws*, for Nicole's penetrating discussion of the "marvelous dexterity" of *amour propre* and the variations on this theme articulated by La Rochefoucauld in 1665, by Bayle in 1682, and by Mandeville in and more fully after 1705 appear to have inspired the ruminations that eventuated in Montesquieu's remarkable analysis of the salutary role played in monarchies by the ethos of what he insists on calling "false honor."[40]

Nicole's analysis may also have prepared the way for Montesquieu's assimilation and appropriation of another exceedingly important passage in Pascal dealing with the effects on human conduct of *amour propre*, which can be seen to cast light on the psychological foundations of the "sociable humor" so evident among the French. "We are not content with the life that we have in ourselves & in our own being," Pascal observed. "We wish to live an imaginary life in the thinking of others. And to this end we endeavor to show ourselves to advantage [*de paraître*]. We labor incessantly to embellish & preserve this imaginary being & neglect the true one. And if we possess either tranquillity or generosity or loyalty, we hasten to make it known in order to attach these virtues to this being of the imagination; we detach them from ourselves in order to join them to it; & we would willingly be cowards [*poltrons*] in order to acquire the reputation for being valorous." It is, Pascal contended, "a great mark of the nothingness of our own being that we are not satisfied with the one without the other & often renounce the one for the other! For he who would not die to preserve his honor would be infamous."[41]

This discussion of the manner in which *amour propre*, with what Nicole had called its "marvelous dexterity," can produce a species of false consciousness and induce a thoroughgoing forgetfulness of self appears to have fascinated Montesquieu. In its light, at one point in his *Considerations on the Romans*, he paused to ponder the Roman propensity for suicide, which, tellingly, he did not trace to a disgust with life. Instead, he focused on the manner in which "the soul" of a human being can be so "totally preoccupied with the action that it is about to engage in, with the motive determining it, with the danger that it is going to evade that it does not properly see death—since passion makes us feel: it never makes us see." In this context, he remarks on the "many ways" in which "*l'amour propre*, the love of our own conservation, transforms itself," and he observes that it "acts by principles so much opposed to one another [*si contraires*] that it induces us to sacrifice our Being for the love of our Being." We take ourselves so seriously, he explains, "that we consent to cease living by an instinct natural & obscure that causes us to love ourselves more than we love even our lives" (*CR* 12.90–110).[42]

This was not the first such discussion in Montesquieu. Earlier, in his *Persian Letters*, he had applied to his own countrymen this very analysis of the manner in which a capacity for self-forgetting is inherent in *l'amour propre*. There he had had Usbek remark that it is impossible to distinguish "the desire for glory" from "the instinct that all Creatures have for their own conservation."

> It seems that we expand our Being when we find it possible to convey [*porter*] it into the memory of others: it is a new life that we acquire, & for us it becomes as precious as the life that we have received from Heaven.
>
> But just as all men are not equally attached to life, so they are not equally sensitive to glory. This noble passion is always firmly engraved on the Heart: but imagination & education modify it in a thousand ways.
>
> This difference, which is found to distinguish one man from another [*se*

trouve d'homme à homme] makes itself felt even more between Peoples [*de Peuple à Peuple*].

One might even posit as a maxim that in each State the desire for glory grows in tandem with the liberty of the Subjects & diminishes with that: glory is never a companion of servitude.

Having made this observation, Usbek then quotes the opinion of "a man of good sense," who had traced the exaggerated French love of glory to the fact that "in France in many respects one is more free than in Persia." It is, he adds, "this fortunate fantasy" that "causes a Frenchman to do with pleasure & gusto [*goût*] what your Sultan is not able to obtain from his Subjects except by placing always before their eyes torments & rewards." This is especially evident in the conduct of French, as opposed to Persian, troops. The armies of the Sultan are "composed of slaves who, being cowardly by nature, do not surmount fear [*la crainte*] of death except in the face of Punishment [*Châtiment*], which produces in the soul a new species of terror & thereby renders it stupefied." French soldiers, in stark contrast, "present themselves for combat [*coups*] with delight & banish fear [*la crainte*] by means of their satisfaction in being superior" (LP 87.1–30/89).

In short, one could say of the French two things that Montesquieu never quite says himself in *The Spirit of Laws*: first, that, in pursuing "glory" rather than "political liberty" as their "direct object," they become inattentive to their natural insecurity as men; and, second, that the forgetfulness rooted in the "fortunate fantasy" to which they fall prey enables them to cultivate in themselves "a spirit of liberty" (EL 2.11.7) and "a tranquillity of mind" which contribute far more to their happiness than the political liberty "established" by England's laws but not "enjoyed" by her citizens (2.11.6, pp. 397, 407). One could say this of the French because it is consistent with Montesquieu's overall argument in the book. One could say it as well because early on, in his notebooks, where he jotted down observations for future consideration, Montesquieu himself said the like.

"The sole advantage that a free people has over another," Montesquieu began, "is the security wherein each is in a position in which the caprice of one alone will not deprive him of his goods or his life." He then added that "a subject people, which has this security, well or badly founded, would be as happy as a free people, the mores otherwise being equal: for mores contribute still more to the happiness of a people than the laws." And in this context he concluded, "This security of one's condition [*état*] is not greater in England than in France" (MP 32). All of this helps explain why Montesquieu once remarked that France was made "to live in" and England "to think in."[43] It was his conviction that, as a settled disposition, *inquiétude* is the distinguishing feature of modern republican man.

THE TWO VISIBLE POWERS

Inquiétude is not, however, the principle of Montesquieu's modern republic, for in and of itself uneasiness can do little more than keep a polity on edge. It cannot animate it and give it a definite direction and orientation. Like vanity, the disposition that the French moralists called *amour propre, inquiétude* is too shapeless: it is too plastic, too protean, too apt to succumb to whimsy and fashion, too much a creature of circumstance. If it is to assume the status of a political principle, *inquiétude* must undergo a metamorphosis—comparable to the one by which the presence of a nobility with all of its artificial ranks and distinctions transforms vanity into the love of honor, giving it a focus and a more precise and stable form.[44] In Montesquieu's England, as we have seen, the laws are primary: they are themselves almost sufficient to give form to the nation's mores, manners, and character (*EL* 3.19.26 and 27, p. 574). In practice, then, it must be the separation of powers itself, the fundamental law of the English constitution, that transforms the characteristic uneasiness of the English into a passion capable of setting their polity in motion.

England's constitution works this transformation by providing a focus for the *inquiétude* that makes modern republican man so inclined to "fear the escape of a good" that he "feels," that he "hardly knows," and that "can be hidden from us," and so prone to "believe" that he is "in danger even in those moments when" he is "most secure" (3.19.27, pp. 575–76). In the political realm, Montesquieu observes, the characteristic uneasiness of the English gives rise to occasional panic, and the separation of powers gives direction to these popular fears. It does so by way of the partisanship that it fosters.[45]

Partisanship is, in Montesquieu's judgment, the fundamental fact of English life. In consequence, it is with this fact that he begins his analysis of the influence of the laws on English mores, manners, and character: partisanship is the premise from which his argument unfolds. "Given that in this state, there would be two visible powers, the legislative & the executive power," he observes at the outset, "& given that every citizen would have a will of his own & would value his independence according to his own pleasure, the majority of people would have more affection for one of these powers than for the other, since the great number is not ordinarily equitable or sensible enough to hold the two in equal affection." This propensity would only be exacerbated by the fact that the executive had offices in his gift, for his dispensing of patronage would alienate those denied favor as it turned those employed into adherents (3.19.27, p. 575).

"The hatred" existing between the two parties "would endure," Montesquieu tells us, "because it would always be powerless," and it would forever be powerless because "the parties" would be "composed of free men" who would be inclined to switch sides if one party or the other appeared to have "secured too much." The monarch would himself be caught in the toils of partisan strife: "contrary to the ordinary maxims of prudence, he would often be obliged to give his confidence to those who have most offended him & to disgrace those who have best served him, doing out of necessity what other princes do by choice." Not even the historians would escape with their judgment intact: "in states extremely free, they betray the truth on account of their liberty itself, which always produces divisions" such that "each becomes as much the slave of the prejudices of his faction as he would be of a despot" in an absolute monarchy (3.19.27, pp. 575, 583).

Like David Hume, who had in 1741 articulated a strikingly similar analysis of the manner in which, in England, the separation of powers gives rise to a species of partisanship that explains many of the features of public life,[46] Montesquieu finds this spectacle droll but in no way distressing. In a polity so caught up in partisanship, he notes, "every man would, in his way, take part in the administration of the state," and "the constitution would give everyone . . . political interests." One consequence of this widespread political participation would be that "this nation would love its liberty prodigiously since this liberty would be true." To "defend" its freedom, "it would sacrifice its well-being, its ease, its interests," subjecting itself to taxes that no prince, however absolute, would dare impose, and deploying against its enemies in the form of a national debt owed its own citizens "an immense fictional wealth that the confidence & nature of its government would render real." Another side-effect of the party struggle would be that everyone "would speak much of politics," and some would "pass their lives calculating events which, given the nature of things & the caprice of fortune, . . . would hardly submit to calculation." It matters little, Montesquieu intimates, whether "particular individuals reason well or ill" concerning public affairs: in a nation that is free, "it suffices that they reason," for from their reasoning arises "the liberty" that provides them with protection against the unfortunate "effects of this same reasoning" (3.19.27, pp. 577, 582).[47]

In a country governed in this manner, Montesquieu hastens to add, the charges lodged by the party inclined to oppose the executive "would augment even more" than usual "the terrors of the people, who would never know really whether they were in danger or not." The modern republic is, however, superior to its ancient predecessor in that "the legislative power," which is distinct from the people, "has the confidence of the people" and can, in times of crisis, render them calm.[48] "In this fashion," Montesquieu observes, when "the terrors impressed" on the populace lack "a certain object, they would produce nothing but vain clamors & name-calling [*injures*]; & they would have this good effect: that they would stretch all the springs [*ressorts*] of government & render the citizens attentive" (3.19.27, p. 576).

In circumstances more dire, however, the English would comport themselves in a manner reminiscent of the various peoples of ancient Crete—who showed how "healthy principles" can cause even "bad laws" to have "the effect of good." In their zeal "to keep their magistrates in a state of dependence on the laws," the Cretans are said to have "employed a means quite singular: that of *insurrection*." In a procedure "supposed to be in conformity with the law," Montesquieu reports, "one part of the citizenry would rise up, put the magistrates to flight, & oblige them to re-enter private life." One would naturally presume that "such an institution, which established sedition for the purpose of preventing the abuse of power, would . . . overturn [*renverser*] any republic whatsoever," but Montesquieu insists that this was not the case in Crete because "the people possessed the greatest love for the fatherland" (1.8.11).

In England, where the citizens exhibit a love of liberty as prodigious as the patriotism of the citizens of Crete, something quite similar transpires. In his *Persian Letters*, Montesquieu had Rica observe that in England's historians "one sees liberty constantly spring forth from the fires of discord & of sedition" and that one finds "the Prince always tottering on a throne" which is itself "unshakeable." If the "Nation" is "impatient," this character remarks, it is nonetheless "wise in its very fury" (*LP* 130.30–33/136).[49] In his *Spirit of Laws*, he returns to this theme. If the terrors fanned by the party opposed to the English executive were ever "to appear on the occasion of an overturning [*renversement*] of the fundamental laws," he observes, "they would be muted, lethal, excruciating & produce catastrophes: before long, one would see a frightful calm, during which the whole would unite itself against the power violating the laws." Moreover, if such "disputes took shape on the occasion of a violation of the fundamental laws, & if a foreign power appeared," as happened in 1688, "there would be a revolution, which would change neither the form of the government nor its constitution: for the revolutions to which liberty gives shape are nothing but a confirmation of liberty" (*EL* 3.19.27, p. 576). As Montesquieu remarks elsewhere, the "impatience" characteristic of a people such as the English, "when it is joined with courage," gives rise to an "obstinacy [*l'opiniâtreté*]" that makes a "free nation" well suited "to disconcert the projects of tyranny." If their characteristic restlessness renders the English incapable of taking repose, it renders them vigilant at the same time (3.14.13).

Paradoxically, then, the fact that Englishmen do not "actually enjoy" the sense of "security" and "tranquillity of mind" which Montesquieu describes as

"political liberty in its relation with the citizen" helps account for the ethos of political distrust and the spirit of watchfulness and wariness which guarantee that
"political liberty in its relation with the constitution" remains "established by
their laws" (2.11.6, pp. 397, 407). The partisan conflict inspired by the separation
of powers transforms the *inquiétude* characteristic of the English into a vigilance
directed against all who might be tempted to encroach on their liberty. This vigilance is the passion that sets the English polity in motion, and it serves as a substitute for the republican virtue that the English need not and generally do not
possess.

Here once again we must pause—for our analysis thus far leaves one crucial
question unanswered and, in fact, as yet unposed: whether, to what extent, and
under what circumstances the spirit of vigilance essential to the modern republic can be sustained. It is to Montesquieu's reflections on the question of political corruption that we must now turn.

Four

CORRUPTION

Misfortune comes upon a republic when there are no longer intrigues; & this takes place when the people have been corrupted with a bribe of silver: they become cold-blooded; for silver they display an affection, but they no longer have any affection for public affairs: without care for the government & concern regarding the proposals it entertains, in tranquillity they await their pay.

—*Charles-Louis de Secondat, baron de La Brède et de Montesquieu*

Near the end of the long and elaborate chapter embodying Montesquieu's famous celebration of the virtues of England's constitution, in the paragraph immediately preceding the one in which he suddenly and unexpectedly intimates that the English may not actually "enjoy" the "liberty" that is "established by their laws," the author of *De l'Esprit des lois* advances yet another arresting claim, which attentive early readers found far more disturbing than the reservations suggested by the puzzling distinction that he had drawn between the establishment and the enjoyment of liberty. "Just as all human things come to an end," Montesquieu there observes, "the state of which we speak will lose its liberty; it will perish. Rome, Lacedaemon, & Carthage have in fact perished. This state will perish when the legislative will be more corrupt than the executive power" (*EL* 2.11.6, p. 407).

The meaning of these cryptic remarks is by no means self-evident. Just as Montesquieu nowhere explicitly discussed "the human passions that set in motion" the English government, so nowhere in his great tome, apart from this one passage, did he explicitly address the question of this particular polity's "corruption." If we are to elicit what he had in mind from the few things that he did, in fact, deign to say concerning the vulnerabilities of the modern republic and if we

118

are then to assess the significance of his thinking in this regard, we will first have to examine in some detail the account that he gave at the end of the first part of his magnum opus concerning the multifarious species of corruption that beset the various forms of government, and we will eventually have to explore the sometimes unspoken implications of his scattered remarks concerning the natural and the historical preconditions for the existence of these divers polities.

In pursuing these questions, we must never for a moment lose sight of one crucial fact. Throughout his discussion of the various species of corruption, Montesquieu insists that what counts as corruption in political affairs is relative to the form of government.[1] "The corruption of each government," he explains, "begins nearly always with that of its principles," and "once the principles of the government are corrupted, the best of its laws become the worst & turn against the state . . . for the strength of the principle drives everything" (1.8.1, 11–12). The source of the pertinent species of corruption need not be internal to each form of government as such, but, as we shall see, quite frequently it is.[2]

CORRUPTION IN A DEMOCRACY

The effects of political corruption in a democratic republic are exceedingly unfortunate and quite dramatic. When republican virtue is utterly and completely lost, Montesquieu tells us, "ambition enters the hearts able to receive it, and avarice enters every heart."

> The desires change their objects: that which one loved, one loves no longer; one was free under the laws & wishes to be free against them. Each citizen is like a slave who has escaped from the house of his master: what was a *maxim*, one calls *rigor*; what was a *rule*, one calls an *awkwardness*; what was *watchfulness*, one calls *fear*. There it is frugality that passes as avarice, & not the desire to possess. Beforehand the wealth of particular citizens made up the public treasury, but now the public treasury becomes the patrimony of particular citizens. The republic is a layer of skin sloughed off [*dépouille*], & its force is no more than the power of a few citizens & the license of all. (1.3.3)

The situation would be less dire if republican virtue were stable and reliable. But, as we have already had occasion to notice, the self-discipline demanded in a democracy is unnatural, and virtue is "always a very painful thing" (1.4.5). This means that republics are fragile and easily subject to corruption. "It is not only crimes which destroy virtue," Montesquieu observes, "but also negligence, blunders, a certain lukewarmness in love of country, dangerous examples, the seeds of corruption; that which does not shock the laws but eludes them; that which does not destroy them but weakens them" (1.5.19). In consequence of virtue's vulnerability, Montesquieu finds it necessary to describe nearly every feature of republican government with an eye to the prevention of corruption.

Thus, for example, he supplements his discussion of education and of the "singular institutions" devised by the Greek republics for the purpose of "inspiring virtue" by emphasizing the need to "proscribe silver, whose effect is to fatten the fortunes of men beyond the limits that nature has set for them, to teach men to conserve uselessly that which they have amassed in the same fashion, to multiply infinitely their desires, & to supplant [*suppléer*] nature, which has given us very limited means for irritating our passions & for corrupting one another." With regard to Epidamnus, he then quotes Plutarch's report that its citizens, "sensing that their mores [*moeurs*] were being corrupted by their communication with the barbarians," opted to elect a magistrate to conduct all trade in the city's name and on its behalf. Where trade is administered in this fashion, he explains, "commerce does not corrupt the constitution, & the constitution does not deprive the society of the advantages of commerce" (1.4.6). That Montesquieu should later add that republics possessed of "singular institutions" need to institute "a general prohibition" against travel abroad should not surprise us, for there is every likelihood that citizens who have lived elsewhere will "bring back home foreign customs & ways [*les moeurs étrangères*]" and thereby corrupt their fellow citizens while undermining the ethos of the community as a whole (2.12.30, p. 458, n. a). Republican virtue cannot endure that which Montesquieu was the first to specify as "communication." It is a hothouse flower best cultivated in an isolated and controlled environment.

One feature of the requisite environment is the institution of equality and frugality. Both are acquired tastes: they can excite love if and only if first "established by the laws" (1.5.3–4). It is best, we are told, that lands be divided into equal allotments at the time of a republic's foundation. Thereafter, care should be taken to prevent subsequent concentrations of wealth. Otherwise, "the constitution" will be "transitory; inequality will enter on the flank where the laws provide no defense, & the republic will be lost." To prevent this from happening, Montesquieu remarks, "it is necessary that one regulate the dowries of women, gifts, inheritances, testaments—in short, every species of contract" (1.5.5). Equality, however, is insufficient on its own, for "the portions of land" awarded the citizens must also be "small." Equality and frugality are essential to one another: "each of them is cause & effect; if one of them is removed from the democracy, the other always follows" (1.5.6).

Sumptuary laws are, thus, necessary as well—especially where an absolute equality of fortune is not in the offing and poverty fails to guarantee an extreme frugality. Given that an "equality of distribution makes for the excellence of a republic," Montesquieu argues, "it follows that the less there is of luxury in a republic, the more perfect it is." The reasons are straightforward. "In so far as luxury establishes itself in a republic, the mind turns itself towards particular interests. For people who feel no need for anything but the necessary, there remains only the desire for the glory of the fatherland and for the glory that is properly one's own. But a soul corrupted by luxury has many other desires. Soon it becomes an enemy of the laws that stand in its way" (1.7.2). In fact, when luxury prevails, it "marks the end for a republic" (1.7.4). For this reason, "the spirit of sumptuary laws in republics" is such that they have as their "object an absolute frugality" (1.7.5).

To sustain frugality and republican mores in the absence of a precisely "equal division of lands," Montesquieu also suggests the establishment of a senate or council of elders elected for life—for the old, when distinguished in this fashion as such, feel compelled to demonstrate that they are "attached to the old institutions" of the city, and they therefore dedicate themselves to seeing "that the people & the magistrates never depart from them." In this connection, Montesquieu argues that "nothing contributes more to maintaining the mores than an extreme subordination of the young to the old. Both are restrained: the former by the respect that they have for the old, & the latter by the respect that they have for themselves." The task of the old is like that assigned the censors at Rome: "to re-establish in the republic all that has been corrupted, to take note of lukewarmness, to judge negligence, & correct blunders in the manner in which laws punish crimes" (1.5.7, 19). This "censorship" loses its "force," however, when "corruption becomes general" (4.23.21, p. 697).

In Montesquieu's judgment, it is particularly important that the women be supervised. "In a popular state," he explains, one ought to look "on public incontinence as the final evil indicating the certainty of a change in the constitution." In consequence, "good legislators there have demanded of women a certain gravity in mores. They have proscribed from their republics not only vice but even the appearance of vice. They have banished even that commerce of gallantry which produces laziness—which causes the women to corrupt even before they have themselves been corrupted, which gives a price to every nothing & lowers the value of what is important, & which causes one to base one's conduct solely on the maxims of ridicule that women understand so well how to establish." In this particular, republics are opposed to monarchies where women take up "the spirit of liberty" associated with the court, become the arbiters of taste, and cause "vanity" and "luxury" to come into their own. In republics, though "free by law, women are held captive by mores; luxury is banished & with it corruption & vice" (1.7.8–9, 14, 6.28.22).[3]

THE SPIRIT OF EXTREME EQUALITY

In the book in which he makes corruption thematic (1.8), Montesquieu re-examines the fragility of the democratic republic from a different and unexpected perspective. "The principle of democracy is corrupted," he warns his readers, "not only when the spirit of equality is lost"—as it nearly always is in a republic situated on an extended territory in which "interests become particular" and "a man senses . . . that he can be happy, great, & glorious without his fatherland & soon that he can be great solely on the ruins of his fatherland." Democracy's principle is corrupted also "when the spirit of extreme equality is seized on & each wishes to be equal to those chosen for command." If, in this book, Montesquieu devotes more attention to the latter of the two possibilities than to the first, it is because he is persuaded of two things: that, "even in popular government, power [*la puissance*] should not fall into the hands of the lower orders [*les bas peuple*]," and that "the spirit of extreme equality" reflects powerful proclivities inherent within democratic republicanism itself. It is only natural, he concedes, that a democratic people should find "insufferable even the power that they confide" and that they should "wish to do everything on their own hook: to deliberate for the senate, to execute for the magistrates, & to strip all the judges" of their functions (1.8.2, 16, 3.15.18).

When a democratic people give way to "the spirit of extreme equality," the magistrates, the senators, the old, and fathers all lose respect; husbands are denied deference and masters, submission. Instead of being satisfied to have "for masters only one's equals," one seeks to have no master at all. All will then be equal not only in their capacity as citizens but regardless of the fact that a particular citizen may be "a magistrate, senator, judge, father, husband, or master." "Everyone will come to love this libertine life [*libertinage*]," Montesquieu laments. "The difficulty of command will be as fatiguing as that of obedience. The women, the children, the slaves will submit to no one. No longer will there be mores [*moeurs*] & love of order, & in the end there will be virtue no more" (1.8.2–3).

The process of dissolution begins when "those to whom the people have entrusted themselves, wishing to conceal their own corruption, seek to corrupt the people." That their own ambition and avarice be not seen, these demagogues "speak to the people of their grandeur alone," and "they flatter their avarice unceasingly." Thereafter, "corruption will grow among the corruptors, & it will grow among those who are already corrupted. The people will distribute all the public moneys to themselves. And just as they will have joined to their idleness the administration of affairs, they will join to their poverty the amusements of luxury." Given the taste that they have developed for idleness and luxury, the people will then make the public treasury their "object" and sell their votes to the highest bidder. This marks the crucial turning point: for, when "people have been corrupted with a bribe of silver [*à prix d'argent*]," the political "intrigues" essential to the vigor of democratic government disappear: the people "become cold-blooded [*de sang-froid*]. For silver, they display an affection, but they no longer have any affection for public affairs: without care for the government & concern regarding the proposals it entertains, in tranquillity [*tranquillement*] they await their pay." But "the more they seem to draw advantage from their liberty," Montesquieu warns, "the more they approach the moment when they will lose it." At first, within the republic, there will appear "petty tyrants possessing all of the vices of a single tyrant." In time, even "the remains of liberty become insupportable, a single tyrant arises, & the people lose everything—even the advantages of their corruption" (1.2.2, 8.2).[4]

CORRUPTION IN AN ARISTOCRACY

Montesquieu's account of aristocratic corruption is, in most respects, quite similar to his account of corruption in democracies. In its republicanism, after all, his aristocracy is just like his democracy: it knows no restraint but self-restraint (1.3.3–4), and it can be sustained only if its territory is small (1.8.16). Even then, however, it becomes "corrupted when the power of the nobles becomes arbitrary" and "the ruling families" no longer "observe" the laws. What had been a monarchy with many monarchs then becomes a despotism with many despots. The republic may continue to exist with regard to and among the nobles but it will be "despotic" with regard to "the governed."

When such a nobility becomes hereditary, "extreme corruption" is the natural result, for then the nobles "can hardly possess moderation," and "the aristocracy is transformed into" something very much like what Aristotle had in mind when he spoke of the lawless rule of "an oligarchy" over unwilling subjects solely in the interest of the ruling clique.[5] If the members of this hereditary aristocracy are few in number, their power may be great but they will be insecure. If, however, they are numerous, as they are in Venice—the city "which has by its laws best corrected the inconveniences" that arise from "hereditary aristocracy"—their power will be diminished and their security increased. The fact that a large membership in the ruling order renders their "government less violent" does not, however, alter the fact that this government will evidence "little in the way of virtue," for hereditary aristocracies are prone to fall prey to "a spirit of nonchalance, idleness, & abandon," and a state under the control of the dissolute will "possess neither strength [*force*] nor incentive to act [*ressort*]." For an aristocracy to "sustain the strength [*force*] of its principle," Montesquieu insists, the laws must be such as to "make the nobles sense the dangers & tiresomeness of command more than its delights" and the state must be "in such a situation that it has something to dread." Security must "come from within & uncertainty from without" (1.8.5).

In this last regard, democracies and aristocracies are again alike. "Confidence" subverts them, for it is necessary that "a republic dread something." The more successful a democracy is, the more the people have contributed to its success, the more prone they are to an "arrogance" that renders it impossible "to guide them." It is in this context that Montesquieu remarks that the more democracies and aristocracies "have of security, the more, like waters excessively tranquil, they are subject to corruption" (1.8.4–5).

CORRUPTION IN MONARCHIES

In Montesquieu's estimation, monarchies are less vulnerable to corruption than are democracies and aristocracies: the principle of honor that governs them is far less fragile than the virtue required of democratic citizens and the moderation demanded from their aristocratic counterparts. In consequence, as we have had occasion to observe (II.1–2, above), monarchies are suited to territories of a considerable, if not unlimited size. Of course, if they conquer a territory as vast as that encompassed by the empires of Alexander the Great and of Charlemagne, it becomes impossible for the intermediary powers to assert themselves with any effect against the will and caprices of the one who is alone. One cannot deny that "promptness in decision-making is required to compensate for the distance of the places to which orders are sent"; that "fear [*crainte*] is required to prevent negligence on the part of the governor or magistrate operating at a great distance"; that, in such circumstances, "law must be lodged in a single head" and that "it must change unceasingly," for "accidents" really do "multiply in a state in proportion to its magnitude." When monarchies grown to this extent do not break apart, they soon succumb to despotic rule (*EL* 1.8.17, 19).

Of dread, however, monarchies have no need. In fact, the "confidence" that tends to be fatal to republics "constitutes the glory & security of a monarchy" (1.8.5). The ruin of monarchies derives from another source. If democracies succumb to corruption "when the people strip the senate, the magistrates, & the judges of their functions," monarchies suffer the same fate when they lose their *esprit de corps*—to be precise, "when, little by little, they deprive the corporations [*des corps*] of their prerogatives or the towns of their privileges" and thereby eliminate the intermediary powers (1.8.6).

It is obvious that Montesquieu has in mind here the policy devised by Cardinal Richelieu—of whom he writes, "When this man did not have despotism in his heart, he had it in his head" (1.5.10). If he does not pause to specify that Richelieu's policy was systematically implemented at the first opportunity by Louis XIV and that this policy was revived by Cardinal Dubois and taken up again by Cardinal Fleury, it is only because this is a truth that everyone in France, if not also in Europe as a whole, already comprehends.[6] It is Montesquieu's contention that

> a monarchy is lost when the prince believes that he demonstrates his power more in changing the order of things than in following it; when he deprives one group of its natural functions in order to give them arbitrarily to others, & when he loves his fantasies more than what he wills.
>
> A monarchy is lost when the prince, ascribing everything solely to himself, summons the state to his capital, the capital to his court, & the court to his person alone.
>
> Finally, it is lost when a prince misapprehends his authority, his situation, the love of his peoples; & when he does not sense that a monarch ought to judge himself secure just as a despot ought to believe himself in peril. (1.8.6)

With an eye to Tacitus' celebrated depiction of the decadence prevailing in imperial Rome, Montesquieu subsequently adds that monarchy's "principle" has itself been corrupted when "pre-eminent [*les premières*] dignities are marks of a pre-eminent servitude, when one deprives the great of popular respect, & when one renders them the vile instruments of arbitrary power. It has been corrupted even more when honor has been set in contradiction with honors, & when one is able to be covered at the same time with infamy & with dignities." In such circumstances, honor as a political principle ceases to be a force (1.8.7).

Later, Montesquieu adds, by way of illustration, that "nothing is more contrary to the spirit" of monarchy than making "the lucrative profession of tax-farmers" into "an honored profession." Where this is done, "disgust seizes all the other estates; honor loses every consideration; the slow & natural means by which to distinguish oneself lose their hold; & the government is struck down along with its principle." In a healthy monarchy, "the lot of those who levy the taxes" will be "wealth" and wealth alone. "Glory & honor" will be reserved for the "nobility who know, who see, who sense as a real good only honor & glory," and "respect & consideration" will be accorded only "the ministers & magistrates who, finding nothing but labor after labor, are watchful night & day over the well-being [*bonheur*] of the empire" (2.13.20).[7]

There is an irony in this, which seems to have been lost on the courtiers and monarchs of the time. "If it is true (as one can see in every age) that to the degree that the power of the monarch becomes immense, his security diminishes," Montesquieu asks, "is it not a crime of *lèse-majesté* to corrupt this power to the extent of causing its nature to change?" (1.8.7). Montesquieu openly worries that "a long abuse of power" or "a great conquest" will undermine "the mores" that sustain liberty and that there will be established on the continent of Europe a "despotism" such that "human nature" there will "suffer at least for a time the insults to which it is subject" elsewhere (1.8.8). There are, he insists, "natural limits" to the conquests which can be accomplished by a monarchy, and "prudence" dictates that "it come to a halt as soon as it passes these limits" (2.10.9). Nothing, Montesquieu asserts, repeating what he had written long before in the second part of the trilogy suppressed in 1734 (*RMU* 17.360–82, cited in I.1, above), "nothing would have been more fatal to Europe, to his original subjects, to himself, to his family" than the success of Louis XIV's putative "project" for the establishment of a "universal monarchy" in the West. This king of France was better served by his "defeats" on the field of battle than he would have been "by victories" (*EL* 2.9.7).

DESPOTIC CORRUPTION

Montesquieu contends that "there are two species [*genres*] of corruption: the one, when the people do not observe the laws; the other, when they are corrupted by the laws." The latter he regards as "an incurable evil, because it is in the remedy itself" (1.6.12). For this reason, he finds it difficult to speak of corruption within a despotism without resort to paradox. The "principle" of this form of government, he explains, "is ceaselessly corrupted because it is in its nature corrupt. The other governments perish because particular accidents violate their principle; this one perishes by its own interior vice when accidental causes fail to impede its principle of self-corruption." Despotism can sustain itself without a frequent collapse into anarchy "only when circumstances drawn from its climate, religion, situation, or from the genius of its people force it to follow some order & to submit to some regularity [*souffrir quelque règle*]. These things force its nature without altering it; its ferocity remains; for a certain time, it is tamed" (1.8.10).[8] Circumstances of just this sort, he soon adds, provide an explanation for the remarkable stability of the despotic polity that governs the Chinese (1.8.21).

China is, in fact, the exception that proves Montesquieu's rule.[9] In certain passages, he treats this tempered despotism as an example of monarchy (1.8.6, 2.12.25). Once he speaks of it as a republic and monarchy (1.6.9, n. a).[10] He is even prepared to list it as an example of "moderate government" (3.18.6). But he suffers no illusions in China's regard. It is a despotism, he repeatedly insists (1.5.19, p. 306; 1.6.20, 7.7; 2.9.4, 10.15–16, 11.5, 12.7, 29, 13.19; 3.15.19, 16.9, 18.6, 18, 19.4, 10, 13, 16–20; 5.25.15).[11] Those Christian missionaries to China who described that "vast empire" as "an admirable government which mixed together in its principle fear, honor, & virtue" were clearly on to something highly significant, but they failed to penetrate to the true reason for the quality of Chinese governance (1.8.21).

The ordinary pattern in despotism is self-indulgence, carelessness, and neglect: "a man whose five senses say unceasingly that he is everything & that others are nothing is naturally indolent, ignorant, voluptuous." He is, in consequence, quite apt to "abandon public affairs [les affaires]" and appoint a vizier. "The more extended is his empire," Montesquieu writes, "the larger his harem grows, the more, in consequence, the prince is inebriated with pleasure. In these states, therefore, the more peoples the prince governs, the less he thinks of government; the grander his affairs, the less he deliberates concerning affairs" (1.2.5).

The vizier has no more interest in the long-term welfare of the empire than the despot. He is "a slave chosen by his master to tyrannize over the other slaves." Because he is "uncertain of enjoying today's good fortune tomorrow, he has no felicity other than quenching the pride, the desires, & the sensual longings [les voluptés] of each day" (1.7.4). The same can be said for his subordinates. In the absence of the system of checks that one finds in monarchies and republics, "all power passes entirely into the hands of the one to whom it is confided." There are, in fact, "an infinity of people who will for the prince & in the same manner as the prince," and since "the law is the momentary will of the prince, it is necessary that those who will on his behalf will in a peremptory manner [subitement] as he does" (1.5.16).

The enlightened despotism envisaged by Hobbes and Voltaire Montesquieu considers a contradiction in terms. Within the despotic polity, there is nothing to encourage reflection on anyone's part. As we have seen (II.1, above), "there is no tempering, & there are no modifications, accommodations, terms, equivalents, negotiations, remonstrances: nothing can be proposed on the grounds that it is as good as or better" than the latest object of the prince's passing whim. Under despotism, "man is a creature who obeys a creature who wants." He "can no more publish his fears regarding a future event than excuse his lack of success on the grounds of fortune's caprice." It matters not a whit whether he "reasons well or ill." From the perspective of despotism, both are "equally pernicious." That he "reasons" at all is, in fact, "sufficient to shock the principle of the government."

Within this polity, then, man's "portion" resembles that of "the beasts": all that he can count on is "instinct, obedience, chastisement." One might even say that despotism aims at degrading him further, at reducing him to something inanimate, incapable of conduct, confined to a species of behavior fully explicable in terms of the principles of the new physics articulated by Galileo, Descartes, and Newton,[12] for "the will of the prince, once known, is supposed to have its effect as infallibly as one ball [*boule*] hurled against another." It is supposed to produce the sort of "extreme obedience" that "presupposes ignorance on the part of the one who is to obey." More telling yet, "it presupposes ignorance even on the part of the one who commands: he has no need to deliberate, to doubt, to reason; he has only to want." In a despotic state, there is no occasion for discussion, much less deliberation, and no possibility of enlightenment: the public will is informed by private appetite alone (*EL* 1.3.10, 4.3, 3.19.27, p. 582).

From the perspective of despotism, "the conservation of the state is merely the conservation of the prince or, rather, that of the palace in which he is enclosed." Distant provinces are, for this reason, frequently placed in the hands of "a vassal prince" or, if they lie on the frontier, they may be "ravaged" and left "deserted" so that "the body of the empire becomes inaccessible." In general, however, inattention is the norm. "On minds ignorant, proud, & biased, everything which does not directly threaten the palace or the capital city makes no impression; & as for the chain of events, they are unable to follow it, foresee it, even think about it." Despotism's "aim [*but*]" may be a species of "tranquillity," but this tranquillity, grounded as it is on an "extreme subordination," is by no means reflective of a genuine "peace." It is nothing more than "the silence of the towns which the enemy is ready to occupy" (1.5.14, pp. 293–94; 2.9.4; 3.16.9). "When the savages of Louisiana want fruit," Montesquieu explains, "they cut the tree down to the ground & gather the fruit: there you see despotic government" (1.5.13).

One consequence is demographic implosion. In the *Persian Letters*, Montesquieu has Usbek single out population growth as a sign of good government. "The propagation of the species" is, he tells us, promoted by "gentleness [*douceur*] in Government" of the sort found in "all Republics." There, "the Equality of the Citizens itself, which ordinarily produces an equality in fortunes, brings abundance & life to all parts of the Body Politic & spreads them everywhere." By the same token, procreation is hindered in "Countries subject to arbitrary power," where wealth is concentrated in the hands of "the Prince, the

Courtiers, & certain individuals," and "all others groan in an extreme poverty."
Human beings, Usbek observes, "are like plants, which never grow well if they
are not well cultivated: among peoples in misery, the Species loses ground &
sometimes even degenerates" (*LP* 118/122). In "countries left desolate by despotism," Montesquieu intimates in his *Spirit of Laws*, the propensity toward "depopulation" is an "evil almost beyond cure" (*EL* 4.23.28).[13]

If the Chinese government is able to achieve a measure of moderation in government, it is solely because China itself is more immediately and obviously vulnerable to anarchy when faced with the despotic ethos of luxury and indiscipline
than are the other despotic governments. In Montesquieu's estimation, the Middle Kingdom is distinguished from other imperial polities by two accidents
which turn out to be decisive: its climate so favors reproduction that, despite the
despotic character of its government, its population rarely, if ever, falls short of
the carrying capacity of the land; and, "like all countries in which rice is grown,
China is subject to frequent famines" (1.7.6, 8.21, 4.23.16).

> When the people are dying of hunger, they disperse to seek something to eat;
> they form themselves in every district into bands of three, four, or five thieves.
> The majority are then exterminated; other bands grow larger & are also exter-
> minated. But, in so great a number of provinces, so distant from one another, it
> can happen that some troop has good fortune. It maintains itself, fortifies itself,
> forms itself into the body of an army, goes straight to the capital, & its chief
> mounts the throne.
>
> The nature of the thing is such that bad government there is punished forth-
> with. Disorder there comes into being suddenly because the population is
> prodigious & lacks subsistence. That which, in other countries, makes it so dif-
> ficult to stage a comeback after a time of abusive governance is that abuses
> there have no sensible effects; the prince is not alerted in as prompt & striking
> a manner as in China.
>
> He does not sense as do our princes that, if he governs badly, he will be less
> happy in the next life, less powerful & rich in this one. He knows that if his gov-
> ernment is not good he will lose his empire & his life. (1.8.21)

In China, Montesquieu contends, "virtue, attention, & vigilance are necessary"
(1.7.7). Fortunately for the Chinese, their lawgivers learned this lesson quite early
in the country's history before their empire had become large—soon after the
emperors had built dikes and recovered from the sea two provinces which turned
out to be fertile in the extreme. To keep these dikes in repair and thereby retain
this prize demanded "continual care"; and, as these early lawgivers were quick to
discern, this in turn required "the mores of a people wise rather than those of a

people voluptuous, the legitimate power [*pouvoir*] of a monarch rather than the tyrannical power [*puissance*] of a despot." In short, "it was necessary that power there be moderated." Despite the climate, despite the country's great extent, "the first legislators of China were obliged to make very good laws, & the government was often obliged to follow them" (3.18.6).[14]

That the government did not always follow these laws goes without saying. According to Montesquieu, the "virtue, attention, & vigilance" requisite for sustaining the Chinese polity tend to be present "at the beginning of a dynasty, & they are lacking at its end." It is only "natural," he remarks, that rulers "nourished on the fatigues of war, who succeeded in causing a family drowned in delights to descend from the throne, should conserve the virtue that had proven to be so useful & fear the sensual pleasures [*les voluptés*] that they had seen to be so lethal." After, however, the first three or four princes of the new dynasty have passed from the scene, China's despotism reverts to the norm: "Corruption, luxury, laziness, delights lay hold of their successors; they shut themselves up in the palace, their spirits weaken, their lives grow short, the family declines, great magnates [*les grands*] raise themselves up, the eunuchs secure credit, none but children are placed on the throne, the palace becomes the enemy of the empire, the lazy people who live within it ruin the people who work without, the emperor is murdered or destroyed by a usurper who founds a family, & his third or fourth successor goes into the same palace & shuts himself up once more" (1.7.7).[15]

Because the Chinese are so numerous, Montesquieu observes, it is necessary that they work untiringly in order to produce on the land that with which to nourish themselves (1.8.21). To get them to do so, however, is no mean feat—for the weather in China is exceedingly hot and enervates the soul. The need to overcome the untoward effects of China's climate helps explain the intensely practical bent of Chinese religion, philosophy, and law as well as their antipathy to the contemplative life. "The more the physical causes encourage in men repose," Montesquieu observes, "the more the moral causes should distance them from it" (1.7.6, 2.14.5). This concern provides a rationale also for the elaborate ceremony performed by the emperor each spring to open up the fields for cultivation, and it makes sense of the practice by which he heaps honors annually on "the laborer who has most distinguished himself in his profession" (2.14.8).

As these two examples suggest, in China the formation of a people who are both "submissive & tranquil" and "diligent & industrious" not only "demands great attention on the part of the government." It secures it. Above all else, Montesquieu observes, it is understood to be in the interest of the ruling order "that everyone at every moment be able to work without fear of being deprived of the fruits of his labor [*frustré des peines*]." To this imperative, he traces "the regulations" so much discussed in the literature on China available in Europe (1.8.21, 3.19.20).

> The legislators in China had for their chief object—making the people live in tranquillity. They wished that they would show great respect for one another, that each would sense at every instant that he owed much to the others, that there would be no citizen who did not depend in some regard on another citizen. They gave, then, to the rules of civility the greatest sway.
>
> In this fashion, one sees, among the Chinese people, village folk observe among themselves ceremonies as if they were people of an elevated condition: this is a means very appropriate for inspiring in them gentleness [*la douceur*], for maintaining among the people peace & good order, & for removing the vices which arise from a spirit that is harsh. In fact, freeing oneself from the rules of civility—is this not how one seeks the means for becoming comfortable with one's own defects?

Civility is, in Montesquieu's estimation, worth more than politeness: instead of being a means by which one flatters the vices of others, it prevents men from making a display of their own. "It is a barrier that men place between themselves to prevent their corruption" (3.19.16).[16]

To inculcate the rules and regulations that give rise to the requisite civility, the lawgivers of China—Confucius, first of all (CEC 632–36)—did something quite similar to what Lycurgus had done at Sparta. They established "singular institutions" which confound "the principles that govern men," treating laws, mores, manners, and even religion as if they were all one, reducing them all to "practices," and "engraving" them as "rites in the hearts & minds of the Chinese" (EL 3.14.5, 19.16–17, 21). "A number of things [*plusieurs choses*] govern men," Montesquieu remarks: "the climate, religion, the laws, the maxims of government, the example of things past, mores, & manners—from which, as a result, a general spirit [*esprit général*] is formed" (3.19.4). It is a measure of the success of China's lawgivers in teaching the Chinese "rites" as "precepts" or "rules of common practice" that, in China, "these rites" were themselves sufficient to "form the general spirit of the nation." In consequence, even when conquered, the Chinese retain "their laws," and the "manners" which "govern the Chinese" are "indestructible" as well (3.19.4, 13, 17–19).

The extraordinary achievement of China's lawgivers Montesquieu attributes to their establishment of "an infinity of rites & ceremonies for honoring fathers during their lives & after their deaths." The government of China is, in consequence, less a "civil government" than a "domestic" one: "this empire is formed on the model [*sur l'idée*] of a family government," and "the prince is regarded as the father of the people." In China, "respect for fathers is necessarily linked with everything which represents fatherhood: the old, the teachers, the magistrates, the emperor. This respect for fathers presupposes a reciprocal love for one's children &, in consequence, the same reciprocal love on the part of the old for the young, on the part of magistrates for those who submit to their rule, on the part of the emperor for his subjects." A diminution in paternal authority would weaken respect for the magistrates; and bereft of that respect, they would have less care for the people whom they are supposed to think of as their children. In turn, "the relationship of love between the prince & his subjects would disappear little by little." "Remove one of these practices," Montesquieu warns, "& you overturn the state" (1.8.21, 2.12.29, 3.19.19). Attempt to accomplish in China by "dint of torments [*supplices*]" what can be accomplished only by "governing through rites," and you are bound to fail. Chinese authors repeatedly remark that "the more, in their empire, one sees of an augmentation in the resort to torture [*supplices*], the nearer" one approaches "revolution." Of China, one can say something like what can be said of ancient Sparta and Rome—that, when "mores" fail, nothing can suffice to guarantee the requisite orderliness, civility, and industriousness (1.6.9, 3.19.17).

ROME AND THE DISTRIBUTION OF POWERS

To do full justice to republican Rome, Montesquieu intimates that one must pay careful attention to institutions as well as to mores. This stems from the fact that, in one crucial particular, Rome resembled England. It, too, possessed an elaborate and ingenious distribution of powers and a set of checks and balances to support it. In one passage in his *Considerations on the Causes of the Greatness of the Romans and their Decline*, as we have seen (I.3, above), Montesquieu observes, "the Government of Rome was admirable in the fact that, from the time of its birth, its Constitution was such that, either by the spirit of the People, the strength of the Senate, or the authority of certain Magistrates, every abuse of power could always be corrected" (CR 8.92–94). In another, as we have also seen (I.3, above), he adds, "The Laws of Rome wisely divided the public power among a great number of Magistracies, which stood by one another, arrested, & tempered one another" in such a fashion that "none possessed anything other than a power confined" (CR 11.29–31).

Rome was, to be sure, a republic of virtue, and it was subject to corruption in the same manner as other republics of the same sort. Its conquest of the Mediterranean world and its expansion well beyond the limits requisite for sustaining republican virtue subverted its mores in any number of ways—by exposing its citizens to irresistible temptation, by undermining the economic foundations of the city's military power, by forcing it to dilute its citizen body and loosen civic ties, and by requiring that it deploy its legions for extended periods far from home in such a manner as to render it virtually inevitable that its soldiers would become clients of their generals and forget the city that had sent them abroad. All of this Montesquieu explores in his *Considerations on Rome*, and to it he traces the Roman republic's demise, as we have seen (I.2, above).

In Part One of *De l'Esprit des lois*, Montesquieu makes the same argument in passing,[17] but, in Part Two, he retells the story from another perspective—that of the distribution of powers. In his *Considerations on the Romans*, he had already observed that, "while Rome conquered the Universe, there was within its walls a hidden war: its fires were like those of Volcanoes which shoot forth as soon as some matter comes along to augment their fermentation," and there he had explored the reasons why Rome's plebeians contracted so "immoderate a desire for Liberty," the reasons why it was inevitable that the patricians' retention of privileges better suited to a monarchy than to a republic should give rise to "odious comparisons," and the manner in which by a slow process, skillfully obstructed by the Senate at every turn, the plebeians used the leverage that they had to strip the patricians of their privileges one by one (*CR* 8.1–53). There also Montesquieu insisted, as Machiavelli had in his *Discourses on Livy*,[18] that this struggle did Rome a great deal more good than harm. "One hears Authors discuss only the divisions that ruined Rome," he wrote,

> but one sees that these divisions were necessary to it, that they had always been there, & that they needed to be there at all times. It was solely the greatness of the Republic that produced the evil & turned the popular tumults into Civil wars. It was necessary that there be divisions at Rome, for Warriors so haughty, so daring, so terrible abroad could not have been very moderate at home. To ask that there be in a free State men bold in war & timid in peace—this is to wish for things impossible; & as a general rule, every time that one sees everything tranquil in a State which calls itself a Republic, one can be certain that there Liberty does not exist.
>
> That which one calls union in a Political Body is a thing very equivocal; the true sort is a union of harmony, which causes all the parties, however opposed they may seem to us, to come together for the general good of the Society, as dissonances in Music come together for an overall accord. It is possible for there to be union in a State where one believes that one sees only trouble —which is to say, a harmony from which there results the happiness which is alone true peace; it is as with the parts of this Universe, eternally joined together by the action of some & the reaction of others. (9.60–76)

What Montesquieu did not explain in his *Considerations on the Romans* was how all of this was managed. That is the task that he undertook in the second part of *The Spirit of Laws*.

There, Montesquieu began by emphasizing that what distinguished the Roman republic from other ancient republics was twofold: it originated as a limited monarchy, and it inherited that monarchy's practice of dividing and distributing the three powers (*EL* 2.11.12). He might have compared its trajectory in this regard with that of England, as he had in his *Considerations on the Romans* (*CR* 1.38–45), but, given the fact that his chapters on Rome follow almost immediately upon his discussion of "the constitution of England" (*EL* 2.11.6) and take as their subject the principal theme announced in that chapter, he saw no need. It was sufficient that he allow his readers to see that Rome derived much of its energy from the political struggle mounted by the plebeians jealous of the prerogatives that the patricians, out of place as an hereditary order within a more or less democratic republic, had nonetheless managed to retain. First, he observed, "the situation of things then demanded that Rome become a democracy, & yet it was not one." Then, after alluding to the fact that "it was necessary to temper the power of the leading men [*principaux*]" and to make sure that "the laws inclined towards democracy," he added, "States often flourish more fully during the passage unfelt [*insensible*] from one constitution to another than they do under one constitution or the other. It is then that all the springs [*ressorts*] of the government are taut [*tendus*], that all the citizens lodge claims [*prétentions*]; that one is attacked or one is doted on [*qu'on se caresse*]; & that there is a noble emulation among those who defend the constitution in decline & those who advance the one that prevails" (2.11.13).

Initially, Montesquieu devotes a chapter to the enormous number of changes that took place in the distribution of the three powers during the centuries subsequent to the expulsion of the kings (2.11.14). Then, after glancing briefly at the short-lived tyranny of the Decemvirs (2.11.15), he considers each of the three powers in turn (2.16–18). In the first of these chapters, he remarks on the manner in which the *concilium plebis*, an assembly of plebeians organized by tribes under the presidency of the tribunes, came to have legislative power. In this context, he describes the exclusion of the patricians from such a body as "a delirium of liberty," remarking that "to establish the democracy, the people shocked the very principles of democracy," and arguing that had it not been for the censorship and the dictatorship the Senate would have quickly had its authority reduced to nothing (2.11.16).

In the second of these chapters, Montesquieu suggests that the people left the executive power to the Senate and the consuls because Rome's aggressive policy required that it conduct itself not only "with an heroic courage" but also "with a consummate wisdom" that only a body like the Senate could provide. As Montesquieu puts it, "the people disputed with the Senate over all the branches of the legislative power, because it was jealous of its liberty; it did not dispute with it over the branches of the executive power because it was jealous of its glory." It was not until they were caught up "in the drunkenness of their prosperity" that the people insisted on electing the military tribunes and on reserving for themselves "the sole right to declare war" (2.11.17).

In the last and most important of these chapters, Montesquieu attempts to locate "the power of judging in the government of Rome," and in the process he identifies a cause for the decline and collapse of the Roman republic that he had not touched on in his *Considerations on Rome*. The story is complex, and Montesquieu tells it in some detail (2.11.18, pp. 421–25). But, after doing so, he devotes the bulk of his attention to one crucial fact. "It is necessary to remark," he writes, "that the three powers can be well distributed in relation to the liberty of the constitution although they are not so well distributed in relation to the liberty of the citizen." With this possibility in mind, he then goes on to explain that "at Rome, because the people had the better part of the legislative power, a part of the executive power, & a part of the power to judge, theirs was a great power which needed balancing by another" and that "the Senate evidently had a part of the executive power" and "a certain branch of the legislative power" but that "this did not suffice to counter-balance" the power held by the people. In consequence, he added, "it was necessary that it have part of the power of judging," and that, in fact, it possessed just such "a part when the jurors were chosen from among the Senators" as was the case for many years (2.11.18, pp. 425–26).

Things went awry, however, "when the Gracchi deprived the Senators of the power of judging." Thereafter, Montesquieu explains, "the Senate was no longer able to resist the people," and there resulted from this "ills infinite" in number. The Romans "changed the constitution in a time in which, in the fire of civil discords, there was hardly a constitution." At the very moment when the Roman republic most needed the wisdom and resolve that the Senate had evidenced in earlier times—just before Marius first enrolled men lacking property in the Roman army and the Italians began demanding citizenship—the people gravely weakened that body. "At that time," according to Montesquieu, "they shocked the liberty of the constitution in order to favor the liberty of the citizen." What they did not expect is what then transpired: "the latter" species of liberty "was lost with the former" (2.11.18, p. 426).

This is not Montesquieu's last word. He ends by pointing to the dangers associated with the fact that Rome's governors in the provinces combined all three

powers and were, in effect, despots each in his bailiwick (2.11.19). But it is the previous discussion that should arrest our attention—for the phrase that Montesquieu uses in describing the propensity of the plebeians for excess—"a delirium of liberty"—will reappear in the chapter that he devotes to the impact of
England's fundamental laws in forming the nation's mores, manners, and character (3.19.27, p. 581), and in that chapter one learns, as we have seen (II.2–3,
above), that the English constitution is in one crucial respect like the Roman
constitution prior to the Gracchi: it does a much better job of providing for political liberty in relation to the constitution than it does in inspiring the sense of security and the tranquillity of spirit that constitute political liberty in relation to
the citizen.[19]

Nowhere does Montesquieu expressly make the comparison. Nowhere does
he explicitly suggest that in England the populist impulse might eventuate in an
overturning of the delicate balance provided by the distribution and separation
of the three powers under the English constitution. He leaves this as a matter for
his readers to consider. Tellingly, it is in the chapter immediately following his
extended discussion of the distribution of powers in republican Rome that he
writes, "it is not necessary always to so exhaust a subject that one leaves nothing
for the reader to do. The task is not to make him read but to make him think" (*EL*
2.11.20).

ENGLISH CORRUPTION AND THE SEPARATION OF POWERS

Initially, at least, few appear to have taken notice of Montesquieu's acknowledgment of the fragility of England's government and of his puzzling suggestion
that it would "perish" when "the legislative" power became "more corrupt than
the executive power" (2.11.6, p. 407).[20] But, within a year of the book's publication, an Anglo-Irish acquaintance named William Domville—who was then
busy on Montesquieu's behalf securing the publication of a corrected edition of
De l'Esprit des lois in London and arranging for Thomas Nugent to translate the
book into English[21]—did write to its author to express dismay at the licentiousness of his own compatriots and to ask whether Montesquieu thought that England was in any immediate danger of succumbing to corruption and thereby
losing its liberty.[22]

Montesquieu was not immune to the fears voiced by Domville.[23] As early as
1721, he had evidenced an interest in "the impatient humor" of the English, in
the manner in which it underpinned their refusal to give allegiance to a despotic
king (*LP* 101/104), and in the peculiar fashion in which "the Historians of England" depicted "liberty arising ceaselessly from the fires of discord & of sedi-

tion" in "a Nation" not only "impatient," but "wise in its very fury, which, Mistress of the Sea (a thing hitherto unheard of), mixes Commerce with Empire" (130.30–33/136). Moreover, in what survives from the journal that he kept during his sojourn in England from November 1729 to early 1731, Montesquieu exhibited a keen appreciation for the peculiar advantages of English liberty (NA 876, 884), an awareness of its dependence on the delicate balance achieved in the division and distribution of powers between Parliament and the King (884),[24] and genuine shock and dismay at the pervasiveness in England of political corruption. "Here," he wrote in one passage, "money is sovereignly esteemed and honor and virtue are little esteemed." "The English," he sputtered elsewhere, "are no longer worthy of their liberty. They sell it to the King; and if the King were to give it back to them, they would sell it to him again. A minister dreams only of triumphing over his adversary in the lower chamber; and to accomplish this, he would sell England and all the power in the world" (878, 880).

At some point during the same visit, however, Montesquieu appears to have shifted his ground, for there is a passage in his notebooks in which he puzzles over the mysterious process by which "the most corrupt of parliaments" was, nonetheless, the very one "that most assured the public liberty" by passing a bill severely punishing corruption, a bill that hardly anyone then holding public office actually wanted to see become the law of the land (881). Montesquieu appears to have been much impressed by what took place in Parliament on this particular occasion, and, as we have seen (I.3, above), there is reason to think that he was no less surprised and delighted by the manner in which a vigilant public forced Sir Robert Walpole in 1733 to withdraw his proposal for an excise tax on wine and tobacco and threatened to drive the great man from office—for it was in that very year, shortly after his return to Paris, that he first drafted the highly laudatory discussion of the English constitution that would appear fifteen years later, in revised form, in his *Spirit of Laws*. Moreover, as we have also seen (I.3, above), in 1734, when he first published his *Considerations on the Causes of the Greatness of the Romans and their Decline*, he buried within the book what was then an exceedingly controversial claim—that "the Government of England is one of the wisest in Europe," and that its wisdom arises from two closely related circumstances: that "it has a Body which subjects it to continual examination, & which examines itself continually," and that the "errors" of this body "are such that they never last long & are often useful in giving to the Nation a spirit of attentiveness" (CR 8.101–6).

It was to the underpinnings of this argument that Montesquieu returned in the course of preparing a reply to Domville's query. First and foremost, he wanted to reassure his correspondent that "in Europe the last sigh of liberty will be heaved by an Englishman." He also wanted to suggest to him that England's peculiar position within the concert of Europe and the character of its foreign policy conferred on it a capacity and an inclination to conduct its affairs in such a fashion as to "slow down the velocity [*promptitude*]" with which "other nations" made their way to "total collapse [*chute entière*]." And, finally, he wished to draw Domville's attention to the intimate connection between English liberty and English commerce.[25] In pursuing the first and the last of these aims, Montesquieu sketched out in his notebooks in preliminary fashion a series of reflections elaborating what he had come to understand in pondering the political dynamic that had once guided "the most corrupt of parliaments" onto an unintended path (*MP* 1960).[26]

In assessing the materials jotted down in what served Montesquieu as a kind of a commonplace book, we must exercise considerable caution. At the head of the collection entitled *Mes pensées* in imitation of Pascal, he affixed a "warning [*avertissement*]" intended to alert future readers with access to his private papers to the fact the numbered items contained therein were nothing more than "some detached reflections or thoughts that I did not place in my [published] works." "These are," he explained, "ideas which I have not plumbed to the depths [*approfondies*], and I keep them to think them through if and when the occasion presents itself. I carefully refrain from taking responsibility for all the thoughts that are here. I placed them here for the most part because I have not had the time to reflect on them, and I will think about them when I make use of them" (1–3).[27]

This is a warning that we ignore at our own peril. To rely on the material in Montesquieu's notebooks to any great degree, to treat it as more than a supplement sometimes useful for fleshing out themes prominent already in his published works, is to court error—for, except in those rare cases in which Montesquieu spells out in his notebooks an idea too controversial to be explicitly addressed and fully explored in his published works, such a procedure could easily result in our giving his passing impressions preference over his considered conclusions, and it invites on the part of his modern students indulgence in a vice to which scholars in all times are quite prone. Left to their own devices, freed from the discipline that Montesquieu as a writer imposes on readers of his published works, and inclined (as is only natural) to concentrate their attention on those of Montesquieu's passing comments which seem most attractive and penetrating, they are led by imperceptible steps to recast the great man's thinking along the lines of their own predilections.[28]

On the face of it, the notes that Montesquieu penned in preparation for writing back to Domville would appear to be undigested or half-digested reflections of just the sort that he warns us against holding him responsible for. If they deserve respectful consideration, nonetheless, it is because we know in their regard what we almost never know with regard to any of the other entries in his *Pensées:* their precise provenance. To be specific, we know when they were written and why; we know that they were composed in the immediate aftermath of the publication of *The Spirit of Laws* and that they constitute an attempt on Montesquieu's part to flesh out and clarify for the purposes of his own understanding the thinking that lies behind an especially cryptic and important passage in his masterwork. As such, even in their half-digested form, they come as close as we are ever likely to get to Montesquieu's final judgment on a matter of considerable and continuing importance, and they can, therefore, serve as an appropriate occasion for rumination on our part.

Montesquieu begins this draft of his letter to Domville by remarking that it is "good" that England's monarch believes in the stability of the polity and "that the people believe that the foundations on which it is established are subject to disturbance [*peuvent être ébranlés*]": that it is "good" that "the prince renounces the idea of augmenting his authority" while "the people dream of preserving the laws." "I believe, sir," he then explains, "that what will conserve your government is the fact that the people basically have more of virtue than those who represent them." In England, he explains, "the soldier is worth more than his officers, and the people are worth more than their magistrates and those who govern them." The pay given officers is so great that it seems as if the English wanted to corrupt them, and there are so many ways in which a man can make his fortune in and through government that it seems as if the English really wanted to corrupt their magistrates and representatives. "It is not the same with the whole body of the people," Montesquieu then adds, "and I believe that I have noticed a certain spirit of liberty that always flares up and is not readily extinguished."

Montesquieu acknowledges that corruption plays a role in parliamentary elections but he denies that it affects the whole—for this species of corruption is limited to certain localities. Even more to the point: what Parliament lacks in probity, it possesses in what Montesquieu terms "enlightenment [*lumières*]." The attempts of the executive to corrupt individual members of Parliament cannot successfully be covered up; and however much a given member may wish to be a rogue, he wishes as well to pass himself off as a good man. Indeed, even "those who betray their duty hope that the evil that they do will not extend as far as the members of the contrary party want to make men fear it will." In consequence, the evil that flows from the corruption that does exist is severely constrained.

From Montesquieu's perspective, the crucial fact is that within the populace there is a large and vigorous "middle class [*l'état moyen*]" which "still loves its laws and its liberty." As long as these "middling men [*gens médiocres*] preserve their principles," he avers, "it will be difficult" for England's "constitution to be overthrown." The steadfastness of these middling men is made possible by the fact that England is a mercantile society in which the chief "sources" of "wealth" lie in the private sphere: the ordinary Englishman, intent on making his fortune, looks not to high office, but to "commerce and industry," which are "of such a nature that he who draws on them is unable to enrich himself without enriching many others." Rome was more vulnerable to this species of corruption because it was a martial society and the principal "sources" of its wealth were public and political — "the profits from the levying of tribute and the profits from the pillaging of the subject nations." That which enriched an individual Roman impoverished an infinite number of others. In consequence, Rome was distinguished by extreme wealth and extreme poverty, and whether one possessed the former or was subject to the latter was largely a consequence of the distribution of political power. Rome lacked not only "middling men" but "the spirit" of independence and "of liberty" that, characteristically, they and they alone display. In England, Montesquieu concludes, liberty will be secure as long as "great fortunes . . . are not drawn from military employment and as long as those drawn from civil employment [*l'état civil*] remain moderate" (1960).[29]

To begin to grasp the import of the observations that Montesquieu sketched out in preparation for writing back to his English correspondent, one must remind oneself that he is elaborating on his cryptic claim that England will continue to exemplify "political liberty in its relation with the constitution" as long as its legislature is less corrupt than its executive — and that he is doing so in a manner intended to be easily understood by someone conversant, as both he and his correspondent were, with the principles espoused and the vocabulary customarily deployed by England's radical Whigs and their Country Tory imitators. In this context, therefore, Montesquieu does what he pointedly refrains from doing in his book: he attributes "virtue" to the English middle classes. Nowhere, however, does he specify what constitutes this virtue: nowhere does he attribute to these Englishmen a passion for equality or a spirit of self-renunciation; nowhere does he describe the "singular institutions" by which the English provide for their education. Nor could he do so: for, as we have already noted, the "singular institutions" ordinarily necessary for the production of virtue of this sort are incompatible with the spirit of commerce and inconsistent with "the confusion, the negligence, the extended affairs of a great people" possessed of an extended territory. They can be found only in "petty" states, such as the cities of ancient Greece, where "one can provide a general education & rear a people as a family" (*EL* 1.4.6–7). The virtue that Montesquieu celebrates in his discussion of the English middle class amounts, then, to little more than the watchfulness typical of spirited men who are wary lest they be robbed of a prize possession.[30] Diminished though it may seem, this virtue deserves respect, for, as a political principle, vigilance is compatible with political moderation in a manner that republican virtue is not,[31] and this spirit is sufficient as a safeguard for sustaining in full vigor the distribution and separation of powers that guarantee the liberty established by England's laws.[32]

As Montesquieu and his English correspondent are both aware, the source of the pertinent corruption can be found in the military and civil offices and honors that are in the gift of England's executive.[33] These are, as the former readily confesses, exceedingly lucrative, and they can be and frequently are used to influence voting in Parliament. But this public largesse is nothing, he insists, in comparison with the money to be made by private initiative in industry and commerce; and given the fact that this corruption extends to only a few members of Parliament, that the press and the Opposition are poised to expose and denounce it,[34] and that the multitude of those within the electorate who are of middling wealth are beyond corruption's reach, naturally fearful of executive encroachment, and inclined to be vigilant in the Constitution's defense,[35] there is no immediate danger that the legislature will fully succumb to executive influence and that there will for all practical purposes cease to be a separation of powers. Free enterprise provides the foundation for the peculiar species of virtue that sustains English liberty.[36]

In reaching this conclusion, Montesquieu was guided by experience. While in England, as we have seen, he had watched with amazement from the sidelines as "the most corrupt of parliaments" passed a bill severely punishing corruption, and he had taken time to reflect on the political dynamics that had produced a result that virtually no one in Parliament at the time had genuinely desired. Then, from a greater distance, after his return to France, he had observed the excise crisis unfold in 1733, and he had recognized the decisive role played in Walpole's humiliating defeat by great merchants, tradesmen, and retailers aroused to great fury by what they took to be a tyrannical attack on their well-being.[37] The answer to Domville that Montesquieu sketched out in his notebooks was an extended rumination on these two events.

A BRIBE OF SILVER

In Montesquieu's judgment, the legislature within a modern republic would be in serious danger of succumbing fully to executive influence only in the un-

likely event that the management of commerce and industry within that republic were somehow, to a very considerable extent, entrusted to the executive. In
such a polity, should the populace in general and the middle class in particular
ever be beholden to government for their economic well-being, the situation of
the citizens would indeed be grim—rather, we must suspect, like the circumstances confronted by their counterparts in a democratic republic in which "the
people have been corrupted with a bribe of silver." Where this has taken place,
we have already learned, partisan "intrigues come to an end," the people cease to
be passionately involved in the rough and tumble of political life, and they "become cold-blooded" and completely indifferent with regard to public policy.
"For silver, they display an affection, but they no longer have any affection for
public affairs: without care for the government & concern regarding the proposals it entertains, in tranquillity [*tranquillement*] they await their pay" (1.2.2).

    All of this helps explain why, on the very first occasion in which Montesquieu
mentions England, he makes two surprising observations: that if you "abolish in
a monarchy the prerogatives of the lords, the clergy, the nobility, & the towns," as
England's Parliament did, "you will soon have a state popular—or, indeed, a
state despotic"; and that the English who, "in order to favor liberty, have eliminated all the intermediary powers which formed their monarchy, . . . have good
reason to conserve this liberty"—for, "if they should come to lose it, they would
be one of the most fully enslaved peoples on the earth" (1.2.4).[38] In issuing this
pointed warning, which elicited warm approbation from David Hume and,
decades later, public affirmation on his part,[39] Montesquieu is doing more than
merely reiterating the point that he had advanced earlier in his *Considerations
on the Causes of the Greatness of the Romans and their Decline*. He is, indeed, re-
asserting, as he asserted then, that "there is no authority more absolute than that
of the Prince who succeeds a Republic," and part of his point is that such a
prince "finds himself in possession of all of the power of a People incapable of
putting limits on itself" (CR 15.100–103). But in the case of England there is
much more that needs to be said.

    The principle of the English polity, the passion that sets it in motion, is by no
means unnatural, and it is generally reliable. On more than one occasion in the
centuries that followed the appearance of *The Spirit of Laws*, at the time of
Napoleon Bonaparte and in the epoch of Adolf Hitler, Montesquieu's prediction
that "in Europe the last sigh of liberty will be heaved by an Englishman" was
proven apt.[40] But the principle of the English polity is not utterly impervious to
corruption. The uneasiness, the fear, the anxiety, the impatience, and the restlessness that contribute to the spirit of obstinacy and vigilance which enables the
English to defend their liberty might take another, less salutary, and quite omi-

nous form should they fail, by chance, to succeed in that defense and should their failure in this particular deprive them thereafter of the sense of sturdy independence that has hitherto sustained their courage. Because the modern republic and despotism are in the passions that set them in motion akin, the former can easily degenerate into the latter.

These observations should give us pause—for subsequent history suggests that Montesquieu was overly sanguine in supposing it highly unlikely that modern republics would be inclined to take over or regulate the management of commerce and industry. To understand fully the import of his analysis of the prospects for corruption in the modern republic, we will have to consider what he has to say concerning the evolution of commercial society.

Book Three

The Modern Republic in Prospect

Reason has a natural empire; she even has a tyrannical empire: one resists her, but this resistance is her triumph; just a little time, & one is forced to return to her side.

— *Charles-Louis de Secondat, baron de La Brède et de Montesquieu*

PREFACE

If, in exploring the question of political corruption, one were to confine one's attention to the scattered chapters and the one book within *The Spirit of Laws* in which Montesquieu makes this subject thematic, one would be missing a great deal. Although Montesquieu does not speak of historical contingency when he touches on the question of fundamental transformation over time, it is clear that he is sensitive to the manner in which changes that lie beyond any statesman's control can destroy a polity and make possible the emergence of forms of government not just unprecedented but hitherto unimagined as well.

In the first eight books of *The Spirit of Laws*, Montesquieu mentions many events and examines many institutions and practices, and he describes in some detail the alterations that take place as one form of government becomes corrupt, collapses, and is replaced by another. Rarely, however, does he advert to the great subterranean currents which scholars in the centuries following would treat as a source of fundamental and irreversible historical change. To the unsuspecting glance, Montesquieu's initial discussion of the various forms of government would appear to be static in the extreme. One is left with the impression that he regards the political typology that he identified at the outset as a permanent feature of the human condition; and one finds oneself drawn almost irresistibly to the conclusion insisted on by the progressive American jurist Oliver Wendell Holmes: that Montesquieu "was not able to see history as an evolution" and that "he looked at all events as if they were contemporaneous."[1]

This impression may persist even as one peruses the next five books of Montesquieu's great tome. Here, to be sure, after exploring the import of war for the various forms of government and drawing attention to the changes that have taken place in the *ius gentium*, he does introduce, in his discussion of the constitution of England, an example which would appear to explode the rigid scheme previously laid out. Nowhere, however, does Montesquieu explicitly indicate that his initial typology needs to be abandoned or even amended, and he still has little to say concerning the manner in which development over time can render a species of government an anachronism.

It would, nonetheless, be a blunder to interpret Montesquieu's reticence in this regard as a sign of ignorance on his part or even as an indication that, for reasons bad or good, he rejects the very notion that fundamental historical change can so alter the circumstances in which men conduct their affairs as to transform their political options beyond recognition. After all, as we have seen (I, above), the triptych that Montesquieu suppressed in 1734 was designed to argue the very opposite, and, as one would expect, in *The Spirit of Laws* he follows suit. His initial reticence is temporary, tactical, and rhetorical—aimed at drawing in eighteenth-century readers steeped in the Aristotelian tradition, who will be presented at the outset with an approach to political affairs that seems to be a variation on familiar themes. These same readers will then be confronted with phenomena that force them to rethink their inherited presumptions over and over again as Montesquieu's argument unfolds and he gradually makes them aware that the ground on which they stand is moving, with increasing rapidity, beneath their feet. Montesquieu did not look "at all events as if they were contemporaneous"; and though he may not have been a philosopher of history in the strict sense—on the model of Anne-Robert-Jacques Turgot, baron d'Aulne; the latter's disciple Jean-Antoine-Nicolas de Caritat, marquis de Condorcet; Georg Wilhelm Friedrich Hegel; Karl Marx; or even Immanuel Kant[2]—he was, like Giambattista Vico, of whose work he was aware,[3] among the very first to think of history in strictly secular terms as "an evolution," and he was arguably the first to attempt to identify the motor driving it, as we shall soon see.

To understand Montesquieu's argument, we must follow it step by step, recognizing that each stage is provisional. In doing so, we will once again have to recall to mind the advice he offers readers of *The Spirit of Laws*: "If one wishes to search out the author's design, one cannot discover it fully [*bien*] except in the design of the work" (Préf.). In order to make his overall scheme easier to discern, Montesquieu divided its thirty-one books into six discrete parts, as we have seen (II.2, above). Within the first part, he grouped the first eight books of his great tome—those devoted to his political typology. Within the second, he included the next five books—those in which he initially explored what is entailed for each of the polities in different epochs by the presence or possibility of war and then examined the relationship between political liberty and constitutional government, the institutions established in the one nation which took liberty as its direct object, and the contribution of both criminal law and taxation to the formation of liberty as it pertains to individual citizens. Although these two parts are in considerable tension with one another, as we have had occasion to note, they have this in common: both emphasize human agency; both focus on that which lies within a legislator's control.

It is, therefore, easy to see why, in 1747, Montesquieu pondered whether he should publish the first two parts of his *Spirit of Laws* together in a discrete volume;[4] it is easy to see why he did just that when he brought out a revised edition of his magnum opus in 1750.[5] After all, what followed Parts One and Two represented a dramatic shift in Montesquieu's argument—for it was in the third part of *The Spirit of Laws* that he laid the essential groundwork for his argument concerning history by isolating a set of influences, not obviously subject to alteration by man, that he took to be the supreme obstacles to human agency and to the capacity of the lawgiver to shape a polity as he thought fit. It is here that he asks us to assess the importance of what we would now call the environment and to ponder the impact of climate and terrain on the human condition and the prospects of the modern republic.

NATURE'S DOMINION

We ought to be extremely careful with regard to the fibers of our brain. As moderate movements promise us an infinity of other movements, so violent movements circumscribe those which one would expect to follow. The Orientals make themselves giddy with a concoction from hemp, which procures for them ideas so agreeable and pleasures so lively that, for some hours, they are transported outside themselves. The consequence of this is total dejection and a condition that approaches lethargy. The effect of this liquid is to tug at the fibers, which become incapable of being moved by a lesser action. One dose stupefies only for a time; long usage stupefies forever.

— *Charles-Louis de Secondat, baron de La Brède et de Montesquieu*

Montesquieu was by no means the first to have noticed liberty's absence from much of the world and to have wondered whether this sad fact had anything to do with nature's provision. Aeschylus and Herodotus had drawn the attention of their listeners and readers to the prevalence of despotism outside Europe; and in Aristotle's day, the great minds of the age were disputing whether the peoples of Asia subject to the Great King of Persia were obsequious by nature, by education, or because of the climate.[1] In France, before Montesquieu's day, Jean Bodin and the Jesuit traveler Father Chardin put great emphasis on the influence of climate. Even among his countrymen, then, Montesquieu stands out less for his originality than for the thoroughness and seriousness with which he examined the question and for the systematic character of his attempt to ground his argument in human physiology.[2]

Montesquieu's thoroughness in this regard was an indication of the depths of his concern. He had long been interested in the question of human agency.[3]

From very early on, he had been a devotee, if not a virtuoso, of the new science.[4] He had a penchant, as we have had occasion to note, for describing despotism, monarchy, and moderate government more generally in the new mechanical and hydraulic language of Galilean, Cartesian, and Newtonian physics,[5] and, from the outset, he was exceedingly sensitive to the difficulties that anyone would inevitably face who attempted to make sense of human agency in a world that seemed to be governed by what he eventually termed "the necessary relations [*rapports*] which derive from the nature of things" (*EL* 1.1.1). Moreover, as a young man, Montesquieu had read and admired Lucretius' *De rerum natura.*[6] He had then pondered the implications of Epicurean physics (*MP* 206, 211); he had marveled at the degree to which the Roman poet's contention that religion is a source of monstrous crimes (Lucr. 1.80–101) was proven by Spanish colonialism to be applicable to the Christian faith (*MP* 207);[7] and to this work, in due course, he would with renewed interest return (*S* 561).

In his early years, Montesquieu had also read Thomas Hobbes and wrestled with the *Ethics* of Baruch Spinoza,[8] and in the early 1720s, when he made an abortive attempt to compose a work entitled *A Treatise of Duties,* modeled on Cicero's *De officiis,*[9] he had briefly explored the consequences for human conduct of a denial of Providence; he had drafted a critique of Hobbes's harsh depiction of man's natural condition; and, in responding to Spinoza's attempt to situate man within a nature governed by necessity, he had displayed a mix of fascination and horror. "A great genius," he then wrote,

> has promised me that I will die like an insect. He seeks to flatter me with the idea that I am merely a modification of matter. He employs a geometrical order and lines of reasoning [*des raisonnements*]—which are said to be very strong, but which I have found very obscure—to elevate my soul to the dignity of my body; and, in place of this immense space that my mind [*esprit*] embraces, he hands me over to the matter that is properly mine and confines me to a space in the universe of four or five feet.
>
> According to him, I am not a being distinguished from another being; he relieves me of everything that I believe most personal. I no longer know where to find this "me" in whom I interest myself so much; I am more lost in the sphere of extension [*dans l'étendue*] than a particle of water is lost in the sea. Why glory? Why shame? Why this modification which is not one at all? . . . [I]n the universality of substance, the lion and the insect, Charlemagne and Chilperic have been, have passed without distinction.

What most bothered Montesquieu at the time, or so he said, was that "this same philosopher strongly wishes, on my behalf, to destroy in me liberty. . . . He deprives me of the motive for all my actions and relieves me of morality altogether [*de toute la morale*]" (MP 1266, esp. pp. 342–43).[10]

GENERAL CAUSES

Natural necessities and man's place in the cosmos were not for Montesquieu a passing concern. At the outset, in his *Persian Letters,* he had had Usbek insist on man's utter insignificance in the greater scheme of things and mock the very propensity that Montesquieu would subsequently display in the material he sketched for inclusion in his *Treatise of Duties.* "We do not sense our pettiness," Usbek observed. "We want to count in the Universe, figure in it, & be in it an object of importance. We imagine that the annihilation of a Being as perfect as we are would degrade all of nature: & we do not conceive that one man more or one man less in the world—what do I say? All human beings together, one hundred million Earths such as ours—are only an atom insubstantial [*subtil*] and slender, which God perceives only because of the immensity of his knowledge" (*LP* 74.36–43/76).

In the *Persian Letters,* after having drawn a distinction between moral and physical causes (99.45–48/113), Montesquieu also had Usbek touch on the power of climate to effect human beings (117.1–36/121), and there he had both Rica and Usbek refer to the human body as a machine (22.10–13/24, 31.22–34/ 33). In *Mes pensées,* he repeatedly did so himself, sometimes even speaking of man more generally as a machine (*MP* 30 [esp. p. 10], 58, 220, 2035), and there, as well, he restated the distinction between moral and physical causes (811, 1296). In his *Considerations on the Causes of the Greatness of the Romans and their Decline,* he paid almost no attention to individual agency. Events and political developments he persistently explained in quite general terms.[11] "It is not," he insisted, "Fortune that holds dominion over [*domine*] the World." When the Romans followed one plan, they were consistently prosperous; when they conducted themselves on another, they suffered reverse after reverse. "There are," he explained, "general causes, either moral or physical, which operate in every Monarchy, raise it up, maintain it, or throw it down; all accidents are subject to these causes, & if the hazard of a battle, which is to say, a particular cause, has ruined the State, there was a general cause responsible for the fact that this State could be expected [*devoit*] to perish in a single battle." "In a word," he concluded "the principal tendency [*allure*] draws with it all the particular accidents" (*CR* 18.52–60).

Soon thereafter, when, in preparation for writing the first three parts of his *Spirit of Laws,* Montesquieu drafted his *Essay concerning the Causes Which Can*

Affect Minds and Characters, he explored therein the impact on "the general character [*caractère général*] of a people" of the environment, of sexual difference, of the diversity in "the physical constitution" of the human "machine," of the practice of celibacy, and of a prolonged and persistent indulgence in hashish and alcohol (CEC passim, esp. 365–427, 559–78).[12] In the same work, he once again distinguished "physical causes, which depend" for the most part "on the climate," from what he termed "*causes morales,*" which he described as "a combination of the laws, the religion, the mores and manners, and that peculiar emanation [*cette espèce d' émanation*] of the mode of thinking, the atmosphere [*air*], and folly of the Court and Capital, which spills over into the laws" (623–30). On this occasion, he insisted on the capacity of the *causes morales* to overwhelm the *causes physiques* (677–736); and to clarify the predicament of man and indicate the limited scope of his capacity for agency, he borrowed from the world of insects an arresting image. In its relationship with the body, he argued, "the soul" of man resembles "a spider in its web."

> The spider is not able to move without shaking one of the threads extended outward, and, by the same token, one cannot move one of these threads without upending the spider. One cannot touch one of these threads without moving another, which responds to it. The tauter the threads, the better informed and more fully warned the spider. If some of these are loose, communication will be less from the thread to the spider or from one thread to another, and the spider's fate [*providence*] will depend almost entirely on the web itself [*suspendue dans sa toile même*]. (359–65)[13]

In reaction against the rigid metaphysical monism of Spinoza, in rejecting—as incompatible with the appearance within the universe of "intelligent beings" —Lucretius' contention (Lucr. 1.265–92, 329–98, 418–634, 951–1051, 1102–13, 2.62–164, 4.26–28, 5.186–94, 351–877) and Spinoza's presumption that "*a blind fatality has produced all of the effects that we see in the world*" (EL 1.1.1),[14] Montesquieu turned back to the distinction between *res extensa* and *res cogitans* drawn by René Descartes,[15] whose work he regarded not only as an antidote to "destructive prejudices" inspired by superstition,[16] but also as a corrective to an unmitigated Epicureanism (MP 1508). And on this foundation he articulated an account of the relationship between the soul and the body closely analogous to the one outlined by Descartes in the first part of his book *The Passions of the Soul.*[17] It is easy to see why David Hume should detect in Montesquieu's attempt to found "right" on "certain *rapports* or relations" an echo of the Cartesian "system" devised by Père Nicolas Malebranche, and it is no less difficult to understand why the skeptic who penned *A Treatise of Human Nature* should regard this and every other brand of Cartesian metaphysics as irreconcilable "with true philosophy."[18] In the end, as we shall soon see, this may have been Montesquieu's considered opinion as well.

In *The Spirit of Laws*, Montesquieu returned once again to what was for him the central question. In Parts One and Two, he focused primarily on the *causes morales*; in Part Three, he turned to the *causes physiques*. His aim was to do justice to both.[19] Throughout, he displays a studied ambiguity. In the first chapter of this great work (*EL* 1.1.1), he brazenly lifts lines from Descartes' *Discourse on Method*,[20] and he hints at the species of Cartesianism developed by Malebranche and taken up by his English disciple Samuel Clarke,[21] but this may be a smokescreen designed to pacify the ecclesiastical authorities, for he does more to draw attention to the dilemma posed by the reductionist, mathematical physics of modernity than to resolve it.[22] In the original Invocation to the Muses, penned for inclusion in *The Spirit of Laws*, which his editorial coordinator persuaded him to suppress,[23] Montesquieu seems not to have spoken of "reason" in materialist terms as "the most perfect, the most noble, and the most exquisite of our senses,"[24] but he certainly did so in the version copied in 1754 by an amanuensis and inserted at some point thereafter by Montesquieu or someone else into what had once been the working copy of his *Spirit of Laws*.[25] Moreover, in Part Two, when he touches briefly on the question of "philosophical liberty," Montesquieu leaves it open whether it "consists in the exercise of one's will" or merely "in the opinion" that one is so engaged (*EL* 2.12.2). And when he discusses the English form of government, he justifies the lodging of "the legislative power" in "the people as a body" with the remark that, in "a free state, every man who is thought to have a free soul ought to be governed by himself" (2.11.6, p. 399). Carefully, and tellingly, he refrains from making self-government dependent on a freedom that the soul may not, in fact, possess. As is so often the case in Montesquieu's thought, what matters politically is less the fact than the presumption. The metaphysical question he acknowledges as a matter most serious, and then, in a manner reminiscent of Hume,[26] he quietly and firmly sets it aside. If, in articulating his argument, Montesquieu remains within a horizon that accommodates the presumption of human freedom, he nonetheless remains open to the possibility that, philosophically speaking, this freedom is as illusory as the "false honor" that animates monarchies.

Like the Scottish philosopher whom he evidently admired and would eventually befriend,[27] Montesquieu was persuaded of two things: that Thomas Hobbes was more right than wrong in contending that human reason is the slave of the passions,[28] and that the English philosopher erred in supposing that there are no grounds for human sociability other than the fear of violent death.[29] Because,

again like Hume, he had reflected deeply on the consequences of man's possession of social as well as anti-social passions and on the character of their interac-
tion, Montesquieu was convinced that man is more "flexible," more pliable, and
malleable than Plato, Aristotle, and even Hobbes had supposed, and he therefore focused his attention not only on the import of man's inclination to "accommodate himself in society to the thoughts and impressions of others" but
also on the degree to which his passions render him subject to nature's vagaries
as well. "If," he writes in his *Spirit of Laws*, "the character impressed on the mind
& spirit [*esprit*] & if the passions of the heart are extremely different in the divers
climates, the laws ought to be relative to the variation in these passions & to the
variation in this character" (Préf., 3.14.1).

THE SPIRIT OF LAWS, PART THREE

III.   14. Of the Laws in the Relation Which They Have with the Nature of the Climate
15. How the Laws of Civil Slavery Have a Relation with the Nature of the Climate
16. How the Laws of Domestic Slavery Have a Relation with the Nature of the
Climate
17. How the Laws of Political Servitude Have a Relation with the Nature of the
Climate
18. Of the Laws in the Relation Which They Have with the Nature of the Terrain
19. Of the Laws in the Relation Which They Have with the Principles Which
Form the General Spirit, the Mores, & the Manners of a Nation

In studying the *causes physiques*, Montesquieu proceeds methodically—examining, from the perspective of the scientific knowledge and the travel literature of his day, the impact of climate on human physiology; speculating as to its
importance for the shaping of the laws more generally; and then exploring the
manner in which the climate can encourage and perhaps even dictate the establishment of slavery, the subjection of women, and the institution of despotism
(3.14–17). As this list of topics should suggest, his interest is more than merely
academic: here in the third, as in the second part of his work, the subject that pre-
occupies him is political liberty, and his purpose is to elucidate the degree to
which nature stands in liberty's way.[30]

THE CONDITIONS OF FREEDOM

There were, of course, some who doubted whether the climate exercised great sway. David Hume was one among these. He believed sympathy, the "contagion of manners" natural within a polity or insular sect, and other *"moral* causes" of a like sort more than sufficient to explain the peculiarities of national character, and in an essay published late in 1748, within weeks of the appearance of Montesquieu's *Spirit of Laws*, he flatly denied that *"physical causes,"* such as the climate, have any "discernible operation on the human mind"—except, perhaps, he puckishly added, in encouraging in men a marked taste for strong liquor where the temperature is cold and a weakness for the amorous passions where it is persistently hot.[31]

Montesquieu was of the opposite opinion. In his judgment, men in cooler climates have a great deal "more vigor" than those who live in warmer climes. In consequence, they display "greater self-confidence, which is to say, more courage"; they possess "a fuller understanding of their superiority, which is to say, less desire for vengeance"; and they evidence "a greater opinion of their security, which is to say, more frankness, less suspicion, policy, & cunning [*ruse*]." Heat has the opposite effect. Just as an indulgence in hashish tends to eventuate in dejection, lethargy, and stupefaction (*CEC* 403–12), so heat produces in human beings "a very great faintness of heart," a paralyzing diffidence, "an imagination so vivid that everything strikes them to excess," and an extreme sensitivity to erotic pleasure. In the tropics, he explains, "the heat of the climate can be so excessive that the body there is entirely without strength. Exhaustion will, then, pass to the spirit itself: no curiosity, no noble enterprise, no generous sentiment. There the inclinations will all be passive; idleness will constitute happiness; most chastisements will be less difficult to bear than the action of the soul, & servitude will be less insupportable than the strength of spirit needed for conducting one's own affairs [*se conduire soi-même*]." Nations of men living in such a climate have a particular need for "a wise legislator" of the sort found in early China, who will set himself against "the vices of the climate," for not only are these vices considerable; in hot climates, "impressions once received" are not readily changed. "The more easily & forcefully," Montesquieu writes, that one is "stamped [*frappé*]" by the education that one is initially given by the laws, "the more important it is to be stamped in a suitable manner: to receive no prejudices & to be conducted by reason" (*EL* 3.14.2–5, 8, 18.6, 19.16–20).

Wise legislation may in some measure be able to ameliorate the ill effects of the climate, but it cannot overcome these entirely. "There are climates," Montesquieu remarks, "in which the physical has such a force that morality [*la morale*] can accomplish almost nothing there. Leave a man alone with a woman: temptation will be a fall, attack sure, resistance nil. In such a country, in place of precepts, it is necessary to have bolts" on one's doors. In one Chinese classic, he tells us, it is regarded "as a prodigy of virtue for a man to find himself in a remote apartment alone with a woman without doing her violence" (3.16.8). In places such as Guinea, and in Indonesia where "the lechery [*la lubricité*] of the women" is so overpowering that men have to devise means to protect themselves from "their designs, one sees to what point the vices of the climate, when allowed great liberty, are able to carry disorder. Nature has a force there & our sense of decency [*la pudeur*] a weakness that one cannot comprehend" (3.16.10).

The manner in which Montesquieu assesses the significance of this atmosphere of sexual licentiousness conveys much regarding his deeper concerns. "All nations are equally agreed," he contends, "in attaching contempt to the incontinence of women: this is because nature has spoken to all nations. She has established defense, she has established attack; & having placed desires on both sides, she has placed in the one temerity & in the other shame. . . . It is not, then, true that incontinence follows the laws of nature: on the contrary, it violates them. It is modesty [*la modestie*] & restraint which follow these laws." Feminine reserve and the sometimes grudging masculine appreciation that it procures Montesquieu traces not only to natural instinct but also to the crucial quality which distinguishes man from the other animals. "It is in the nature of intelligent beings," he explains, "to be aware of their imperfections: nature has placed in us a sense of decency [*la pudeur*] —which is to say, a sense of shame with regard to our imperfections." This leads the French philosophe to speak of "the physical power [*puissance*] of certain climates" as a phenomenon which "violates" not only "the natural law of the two sexes" but "that of intelligent beings" as well. It is this fact that explains why, in hot climates, "the legislator" finds himself called on to devise "civil laws" that will "bring force to bear against the nature of the climate & re-establish the primitive laws" grounded in human nature (3.16.12). Although he is no admirer of polygamy and the enclosure of women, Montesquieu admits their inevitability (3.16.2–10). If Islam has established itself in Asia and Christianity has not, it is because only the former sanctions practices required by the climate there. As Montesquieu puts it, "human reasoning [*les raisons humaines*] is always subordinate to this supreme cause, which does all that it wishes & makes use of everything that it wishes" to use (3.16.2).

One additional indication of the power that Montesquieu accords to climate is his willingness to contemplate the possibility that slavery may also be a necessity in the tropics. Montesquieu was no friend to the peculiar institution. Among intellects of the very first rank, he has the great distinction of having been the earliest to have denounced the practice;[32] and in *The Spirit of Laws,* he did every-thing that he could to convey his distaste and to persuade readers that slavery is not only unjust but contrary to the interests of masters and slaves alike and quite likely to corrupt both (3.15.1–5, 8–9, 11–13). His starting point is the fundamen-tal premise of John Locke's *Two Treatises of Government,*[33] and from it he draws an obvious conclusion that Locke seems deliberately to have sidestepped.[34] "Given that all men are born equal," he insists, "it is necessary to say that slavery is contrary to nature" (3.15.7). It is only after an extended discussion of the ills to which slavery gives rise that Montesquieu acknowledges the possibility that, "in some countries," slavery "may be founded on a natural reason," pointing to places where "heat enervates the body & so forcefully weakens courage that men are brought to perform a painful duty only by the fear of chastisement" (3.15.7). To his reluctant admission that in this sphere as well the climate appears to vio-late natural law, we should apply the warning that Montesquieu issues when dis-cussing the subjection of women. "In all of this, I do not justify usages, but I do give their rationale [*en . . . les raisons*]" (3.16.4).

Long before the time when he turns from a consideration of slavery and do-mestic servitude (3.15–16) to "the connection [*rapport*]" between "the climate" and what he calls "the laws of political servitude" (3.17), even before he makes these three subjects thematic, Montesquieu has made it abundantly clear that he believes despotism unavoidable in hot climates (1.5.15). In the third part of his great work, he prepares us for what is to come—first by asserting that it is only in despotisms, where one's "liberty is worth nothing," that it can be rational for a man to think that enslavement might improve his prospects (3.15.6), and then by explicitly asserting that "the servitude of women conforms very well with the genius of despotic government" and that "when the climate" requires such an "empire over women," then "the government of one alone is most convenient" (3.16.9).

When he treats political servitude, Montesquieu never loses sight of Africa and the districts in the Americas near the equator (3.17.2, 6), but his real focus is Asia—which is suited, he says, to despotism because of both the climate and the terrain. Asia is distinguished by broad plains, and it knows very few natural divi-sions: "if servitude there were not extreme," the polity "would soon undergo a partition that the nature of the country cannot tolerate" (3.17.6).[35] Asia's climate is also peculiar since it has no temperate zone. "The places situated there in a cli-mate quite cold touch immediately on those which are in a climate quite hot, which is to say Turkey, Persia, the Mogul empire, China, Korea, & Japan." The crucial consequence is that "in Asia the strong & the weak nations sit opposite one another; the peoples warlike, brave, & active touch immediately on the peoples effeminate, idle, & timid: it is necessary then that the one be the conqueror & the other, the conquered," and conquest along the lines described has taken place over and over again no less than eleven times (3.17.2–4).

Such a pattern would matter much less if the peoples of the north were themselves free, but the Tartar people, "the natural conquerors" of Asia, are "themselves enslaved." Their plight is due to the terrain. Situated, as they are, in the wastelands of northern Asia, the Tartars "have no towns, they have no forests; they have little in the way of marshes; their rivers are almost always frozen; they inhabit an immense plain; they have pastures & herds &, in consequence, goods: but they have no space for retreat or defense." Defeat for them means political subjection because there is no refuge, no exit, and no escape, and they have, therefore, no leverage on the basis of which to negotiate terms favorable to their autonomy.[36] The peoples subject to the great empires of Asia are "governed by the cudgel"; their Tartar conquerors, "by the lash" (3.17.5, 18.19). "In Asia," because of nature's tyranny, "there reigns a spirit of servitude which has never abandoned it; & in the entire history of the country, it is not possible to find a single trait that marks a free soul: there one never sees anything but the heroism of servitude" (3.17.6).

Montesquieu's purpose is neither to denigrate Asia, Africa, and the equatorial regions of the Americas nor to elevate Europe: his aim is to achieve an understanding of the special conditions that made possible and perhaps even encouraged the emergence of republics and monarchies in the one place in the world where they happen to have appeared. He explores the regions afflicted with slavery and domestic and political servitude in order to be able to isolate and then illustrate the circumstances conducive to their absence.

To begin with, in Europe, the terrain is favorable to freedom. There are no broad plains: there are towns, forests, marshes, rivers, and mountains. "Nature's partition [of the continent] formed a number of states of moderate extent, in which a government of laws is not incompatible with the maintenance of the state: on the contrary such a government is favorable to such a state since without the laws this state falls into decay [*décadence*] & becomes inferior to all others. It is this which has formed a genius of liberty which renders it very difficult for each part to be subjugated & subjected to a foreign force—other than in accord with the laws & with that which is useful to its commerce" (3.17.6).[37]

The climate is also conducive to liberty. Europe is neither too cold nor too hot. There are climactic differences, to be sure. Spain and Italy are considerably warmer than Norway and Sweden, but "the temperate zone is of considerable extent," and though the weather grows colder as one moves north, it changes so gradually that one can hardly sense the difference. "Each country is more or less similar to the one that is its neighbor," and "notable differences there are none." As a consequence, "in Europe, strong nations sit opposite one another," and "those which touch have more or less the same endowment of courage." This is, Montesquieu insists, "the great reason for the weakness of Asia & the strength of Europe, for the liberty of Europe & the servitude of Asia." And if it never happens that liberty increases in Asia, "in Europe it increases or diminishes according to circumstances." Thus, if Muscovy and Denmark are despotic, it is not a matter of natural necessity (3.17.3).

On similar grounds, Montesquieu argues that nature gives no sanction to slavery in Europe. "However painful the work that society demands, one can do everything with free men." Once it was thought that only slaves or criminals could be induced to become miners, but experience has shown that by doling out "small privileges" one can provide sufficient encouragement, compensating free men for "an increase in work with an increase in gain" and leaving them satisfied and tolerably happy with their lot. In any case, as has been shown in the mines of Hungary, "by the convenience of machines which art invents or applies, one can provide a substitute for the forced labor that otherwise one would have had done by slaves." Montesquieu is even willing to contemplate the possibility that there is no "climate on earth where one cannot engage free men to work" and that it is only because "ill-fashioned laws" produced "lazy men" that human beings have been "placed in slavery" (3.15.8).

In Europe, women are also very much better off. In hot climates, Montesquieu observes, girls mature at a very young age, and childhood and marriage go hand in hand. By the time they reach twenty, they are already old: "in such places, therefore, reason is never found in beauty's company." This puts women at a decided disadvantage. "When beauty demands empire, reason causes it to be refused; when reason could obtain it, beauty no longer exists." The resulting lack of leverage contributes mightily to the subjection of women—since "reason cannot procure for them in their old age an empire that beauty did not give them even in their youth." The result is polygamy. In temperate climates, however, "where women's charms are better preserved, where they reach physical maturity later, & where they have children at an age more advanced, the aging of their spouses follows in a certain fashion on their own; & since they have more of reason & knowledge when they marry, if only because of having lived longer, it is natural that there be introduced a species of equality between the two sexes, &, in consequence, the law specifying that there be only one wife" (3.16.2).

Montesquieu considers himself fortunate to live in a climate which violates neither the natural instincts of the two sexes nor the consequences of human intelligence, "where the mores of women are naturally good; where all their passions are calm, just a little bit active, just a little bit refined; where love has an empire over the heart so regulated that the least bit of policing [*la moindre police*] suffices to guarantee their conduct." Such climates are, he suggests, conducive to happiness because they "allow one to communicate" and because the taste for communication makes of refined women the arbiters of male conduct. There, "the sex which has the most charm seems to adorn society," and "women, reserving themselves for the pleasures of one alone, serve nonetheless for the amusement of all" (3.16.11–12, 6.28.22).

Of course, whether Montesquieu really thought that, in such a society, adultery would be rare is open to question. He had often lived in Paris, and there is evidence suggesting that, as a young man, he had been by no means averse to illicit *amours*.[38] In his *Persian Letters*, he had Rica report in one letter that "the French hardly ever speak of their wives . . . because they fear speaking of them in front of people who may know them better than they do" (*LP* 53.8–9/55), and in another he had him quote Frenchmen as saying that "while we may be unfortunate in our capacity as husbands, we always find the means for consoling ourselves in our capacity as Lovers" (36.17–18/38). Elsewhere in the book he has his Persian visitors indicate an awareness that certain exceedingly elegant young men and clerical confessors have a well-known capacity for providing comfort of an unspecified but easily identified sort to the disconsolate wives and daughters of French men (36/38, 46.46–58, 110–45/48, 108/110).[39]

To this, one can add that, in his subsequent ruminations on French history, Montesquieu returned to this theme, devoting particular attention to tracing the process by which, as royal power "fortified itself" in France, "the nobility left its lands" for the capital and the court, mores underwent a revolution, and to an ever increasing degree marriage came under assault. "Girls," he wrote, "no longer paid attention to the traditions followed by their mothers."

> Women, who hitherto had come only by degrees to a certain liberty, obtained it in its entirety in the first days of their marriage. The women and the idle young men stayed up all night, and often the husband began his day as his wife finished hers. Vices were no longer recognized as such; only ridicule was felt, and numbered among the objects of ridicule were modesty thought to be in the way and virtue traced to timidity.
>
> Each stage in the evening meal concealed some new arrangement; but the secret lasted only long enough for matters to be brought to a conclusion. In dealing with women of rank, one no longer steered clear of dangers. Amidst this continual change, taste became tiresome, and, in the end, one jettisoned it for the purpose of pleasure's pursuit.
>
> The education of children was no longer ranked among the cares of moth-

ers. The wife conducted her life in an attitude of total indifference regarding the affairs of her husband. All the ties of kinship were neglected; all consideration was abandoned; no more visiting for decorum's sake. All conversations became audacious; all that one dared to do was openly avowed, and the only thing regarded as impolite was a deficiency in daring, will, or capacity.

The virtue of a woman was for her a total loss; it was even at times something like a species of persecuted religion.

Nor was all this the final extent of the disorder. The women were as unfaithful in games as in their love affairs, and they joined to that which dishonors their sex everything capable of debasing ours. (*MP* 1272) [40]

It is, of course, conceivable that with regard to this subject Montesquieu changed his mind regarding the facts or their larger import before publishing his *Spirit of Laws*. But this is hardly likely. When it suited his rhetorical needs, the author of the *Persian Letters* continued to display a knack for disingenuousness. He never forgot how to elicit laughter from his countrymen by the audacity with which he advanced on their behalf a preposterous claim, and he never championed sexual license. If Montesquieu firmly opposed the subjection of women and even sanctioned no-fault divorce, it was above all because he favored love in marriage. To a recourse to *filles de joie* on the part of men, to a "violation of modesty [*pudeur*]" on the part of women, and to "illicit unions" on the part of either or both, he was markedly unfriendly. In his judgment, "infidelity" on the part of a married woman presupposed "a renunciation of all the virtues" and a rejection of her "state of natural dependency" as a mother and wife. "Public continence" was everywhere to be preferred because it "is naturally linked with the propagation of the species," a project that Montesquieu thought central to the well-being of both women and men (*LP* 112/116, *EL* 3.16.12, 15–16, 4.23.2, 5.26.3, 8).[41] For the denial to women of full freedom in choosing a mate, for the laws prohibiting divorce and remarriage, and for the libertinism to which such a state of affairs naturally gives rise, Montesquieu's compatriots paid, in his opinion, a considerable price.

There was, of course, the other extreme. When Montesquieu remarked that "Germany was made to travel in, Italy to sojourn in, England to think in, and France to live in,"[42] one of the things that he no doubt had in mind was the fact, already well-known in his day, that in England "the women . . . hardly live among the men" (*EL* 3.19.27, p. 582). But if Montesquieu's Englishmen are less sociable and less inclined to take pleasure in the intercourse between women and men, they are no less free than the inhabitants of his native France. Here, too, the climate and terrain seem to play a prominent role. To begin with, the English are an island people, and such "peoples are more disposed to liberty than the peoples of the continent." The sea protects them against the "great empires" which otherwise might be inclined to become their "conquerors"; internal divisions are fewer and pose less of a threat; and their relative isolation contributes also to the preservation of their laws (3.18.5). The climate is no less important. It makes "the English" exceedingly sensitive to "the weight of life" and causes them to feel "a certain difficulty in existence." In consequence, they "kill themselves" for no apparent reason—even when "in the very bosom of happiness" (3.14.12). Undesirable though it may be in and of itself, this propensity is quite favorable to liberty—for "the government best suited to people who find everything intolerable would be the one . . . in which laws rather than men govern" and the citizens "would be unable to pin the blame for their woes on any one individual." Such a government would similarly suit quite well a nation endowed by the climate with "impatience"—for, as we have already had occasion to remark (II.3, above), when backed by "courage," this impatience gives rise to the sort of "obstinacy" that can help "a free nation . . . disconcert the projects of tyranny." It is "with slumber," Montesquieu tells us, that "servitude always begins," and "a people who take their repose in no situation, who never stop pinching themselves, who find every place uncomfortable [*douloureux*] can hardly be induced to sleep" (*EL* 3.14.13).

We should not, then, be surprised that, when, at the beginning of the exceptionally long chapter that concludes the third part of his work, Montesquieu intimates that the general spirit of the English nation derives from its fundamental laws, he qualifies this claim in one particular, by pointedly refraining from denying that "the climate has . . . in large part produced the laws, mores, & manners of this nation" (3.19.27, pp. 574–75). By this, he does not mean to repudiate or even call into question his claim that the peculiar distribution of powers under the constitution of England, described in his eleventh book (2.11.6), contributes decisively to shaping the mores and manners of the English. His point is, rather, that England's climate is permissive—that "the principles" embodied within England's "constitution" would be ineffective were the English not predisposed by the climate to accept them (3.19.27, pp. 574–75). As he points out at the very beginning of his discussion of the connection between a nation's laws and its climate, "in temperate countries, you see peoples inconstant in their manners & even their vices & virtues: the climate there has not a quality sufficiently determinate to stabilize these" (3.14.2).

A favorable climate opens up options. It does not change the fact that the formation of a "moderate government" is "a masterpiece of legislation, which chance rarely produces & prudence is rarely allowed to produce." Nor does it in any way alter the fact that despotic government "jumps up, so to speak, before our eyes" and that "the passions alone are necessary for its establishment" so that "the whole world is good enough for that" (1.5.14, p. 297). In fact, for many centuries, following the collapse of the Roman republic, civilized Europe knew nothing but despotism. The question that Montesquieu poses is whether modern Europe, especially England and France, can succeed where ancient Europe failed. "The majority of the peoples of Europe are still governed by mores [*moeurs*]," he notes. "But if by a long abuse of power, if by a great conquest, despotism at a certain point were to establish itself, neither mores nor the climate would hold things in check; & in this beautiful part of the world, human nature would suffer, at least for a time, the insults that she endures in the world's three other parts" (1.8.8).

In an earlier chapter in which he celebrates the barbarian conquest of imperial Rome, Montesquieu pointedly ignores ancient Greece and republican Rome and singles out, as "the spring [*source*]" from which flows "Europe's liberty," Scandinavia instead. In this context, he then quotes, without obvious disapproval, the judgment of the Goth Jordanes—who dubbed northern Europe "the manufactory of human kind." This opinion he corrects only in suggesting that this part of the continent is even more aptly described as "the manufactory of the instruments which break the chains forged in the south." Northern Europe "forms the valiant nations, which venture forth from their countries to destroy tyrants & slaves & to teach men that, as nature has made them equal, so reason cannot render them dependent, except insofar as is requisite for their happiness." The claims advanced by Jordanes and by Montesquieu are by no means incompatible—for it is in the favorable environment of Europe that man managed to free himself from the tyranny of climate and terrain, develop his natural capacities as an intelligent being subject to shame and capable of deliberation and choice, and thereby discover himself as man (3.17.5).[43]

L'ESPRIT GÉNÉRAL

Montesquieu brings the third part of his *Spirit of Laws* to its conclusion with a book (3.19) intended to draw together the various strands of the argument he has presented in the work's first three parts. Here he turns from "the things themselves" to what he calls "the order of things." "It is necessary," he explains, "that I open up space to the right & to the left [*que j'écarte à droite et à gauche*], that I break through, that I reveal myself [*que je me fasse jour*]" (3.19.1). It is in this context that he provides his readers with a summary discussion of what he calls "the general spirit"—the *esprit général* formed for each nation by "the climate, the religion, the laws, the maxims of government, the example of things past, the mores, & the manners" (3.19.4).[44]

Montesquieu had long been persuaded that "human societies" are constituted as such by "a union of outlook and spirit [*une union d'esprit*]," and he believed that in them "a common character is formed." In the early 1720s, when he set out to write his *Treatise of Duties*, he spoke of this "common character" as a "universal soul," and he suggested that it "takes on a way of thinking that is the effect of an infinite chain of causes, which multiply themselves and combine together from age to age." As soon as "the tone is given and received," he argued, "it is this tone which governs, and all that the sovereigns, the magistrates, the peoples are able to do or imagine, whether they seem to shock the tone or to follow it, is related to it always," and its dominion ceases only with "a total destruction."[45]

Initially, Montesquieu's outlook had been resolutely political. In his *Persian Letters*, he had had Rhedi observe that, in France, "the Monarch impresses the character of his Mind [*Esprit*] on the Court, the Court follows suit with respect to the Town, the Town with respect to the Provinces. The soul of the Sovereign is a mold, which gives form to all the others" (LP 96.25–29). At about this time, in his notebooks, he remarked, "I call *the genius of a nation* the mores and the character of mind [*esprit*] of different peoples directed by the influence of one and the same court and one and the same capital" (MP 348).

A few years later, he was prepared to qualify this claim, observing that "states are governed by five different things: by religion, by the general maxims of the government, by particular laws, by mores, and by manners," and concluding that "these things all have a mutual relation [*rapport*] with one another. If you change one of them, the others do not follow except slowly; this produces everywhere a species of dissonance" (542). It was not long thereafter that he produced another list of five variables, in which he tellingly substituted "the climate" for "the general maxims of government," suggested that in a given nation one of the variables could predominate, and observed that for savages, the Chinese, the Japanese, the Romans and Spartans, and those living in central Europe the dominant variables were, respectively, climate, manners, laws, mores, and religion (854).

Initially, Montesquieu uses the phrase *esprit général* in various ways—to describe the patriotic, as opposed to the particular, spirit required within a republic (968), and to allude to the "common character" and "universal soul" shared by a people (957). In 1734, in his *Considerations on the Causes of the Greatness of the Romans and their Decline*, he settled on the latter usage, tracing the formation of an *esprit général* within a nation to "the multitude of examples received" therein. These, he observed, give rise to "mores which rule as imperiously as the Laws" (*CR* 21.87–88). Then, by way of explanation, he brought up the notion again, denying that there is, has been, or can ever be anywhere "in the world a human authority that is in all regards despotic." Even "the power that is most immense is always," he contended, "in some fashion limited." The Grand Seigneur of Turkey cannot impose a new tax in Constantinople without provoking an out-cry, and the king of Persia cannot make his subjects drink wine. "In each Na-tion," Montesquieu explained, "there is a general spirit on which power [*la puis-sance*] itself has its foundation. When power shocks this spirit, it shocks itself & brings itself of necessity to a halt" (22.207–15).[46] In *The Spirit of Laws*, Mon-tesquieu returned to this theme, contending that it is "a maxim of capital impor-tance that one must never change the mores & the manners in a despotic state," for "nothing would be more promptly followed by a revolution." Indeed, he added, "if you turn these upside down, you will turn everything upside down" (*EL* 3.19.12).

In the latter work, however, despotism is only on occasion Montesquieu's fo-cus; and, when he once again takes up the *esprit général*, he is interested in its significance for other forms of government as well. There, he argues that, even in republics and in monarchies, an attempt on the part of "those who govern" to "establish" institutions or practices "that shock a nation's way of thinking" is likely to backfire, for it will instill in the governed the "opinion" that they live un-der a "tyranny." It is, he insists, incumbent on "the legislator to follow the spirit of the nation when it is not contrary to the principles of the government, for we do nothing so well as that which we do freely while following our natural genius" (3.19.3, 5). And he prefaces this discussion with a series of anecdotes illustrating his central concern—the degree in which "liberty itself has seemed intolerable [*insupportable*] to peoples unaccustomed to its enjoyment." Even for "the best laws," he contends, "it is necessary that minds and spirits [*esprits*] be prepared" (3.19.2).

Montesquieu was extremely sensitive to the difficulties involved. Early in this discussion, he observed that, in so far as any one of the elements that contribute to the formation of the general spirit "acts with greater force, the others give way." Over savage peoples, he explained, "nature & the climate exercise an almost complete dominion," and moral causes can do the same in civilized societies as well: "manners govern the Chinese; the laws tyrannize in Japan; in bygone days, mores set the tone in Lacedaemon; the maxims of government & ancient mores set it in Rome" (3.19.4). Montesquieu was persuaded that, within civilized soci-eties, this imbalance is an aberration.[47] "Laws, mores, & manners" he regarded as "things naturally separate." Each has a different focus. "Laws have more to do with regulating the actions of the citizen; mores have more to do with regulating the actions of the man." Mores and manners differ in that for which they have "greater regard": the former pay more attention to "interior conduct," and the latter to "external conduct." Of course, Montesquieu did acknowledge that they are never radically separate. "Between them," he wrote, there are always "close relations [*grands rapports*]." But he insisted that they could not be "confounded" except by means of what he called "singular institutions" (3.19.16, 21).[48] In Sparta, as Montesquieu had already pointed out in his discussion of republican government,[49] Lycurgus instituted "singular institutions" by fashioning "a single code" to establish "the laws, the mores, & the manners" (3.19.16). In China, following Confucius' lead (*CEC* 632–36), "the lawgivers did the same" and "more: they confounded religion, the laws, mores, & manners" by means of what "one calls rites." Moreover, in ancient Israel, Moses fashioned "a single code for the laws & religion"; and on the river Tiber, "the first Romans confounded the ancient customs with the laws" (*EL* 3.19.16–17, 20–21).[50] After reading Montesquieu's extended rumination on Chinese "rites" (3.19.16–21), one is left with the impression that, concerning religion in Israel and mores in Sparta and very early Rome, one could say something analogous to what he says concerning "manners in China"—that they are "indestructible" (3.19.13).

"When one wishes to change the mores & the manners" of a nation, Montesquieu insists, "one must not do so by laws," for "that would seem excessively tyrannical: it is better to change them by other mores & other manners" (3.19.14). This may be impossible in a polity endowed with singular institutions, but it can be done in a moderate government of the sort depicted so vividly by Montesquieu in *The Spirit of Laws*, for such a government "is able, as much as it wishes & without peril, to relax its springs" (1.3.9), and there laws, mores, and manners are left separate. Moreover, "the vanity" that is predominant in a monarchy such as France inspires "luxury, industry, the arts, fashion, politeness, taste" (3.19.9), and on the part of such a nation it favors a certain "facility in communicating their thoughts" (3.19.5). This capacity Montesquieu regards as politically crucial.[51] "The more peoples communicate," he observes, "the more easily they change manners, because each is more a spectacle for another; one sees better the singularities of individuals" (3.19.8).[52]

Despotism represents the other extreme. "In a country where each, both as superior & as inferior, exercises & endures [*souffre*] an arbitrary power," Montesquieu observes, "one communicates less than in countries where liberty reigns in every station [*dans toutes les conditions*]," and "there one is less apt to change manners & mores" (3.19.12). But even in such a polity, especially if the climate is favorable, alterations of this sort can be induced. Peter the Great ran into trouble in Muscovy and behaved in a tyrannical fashion when he ordered his compatriots to shorten their beards and clothing, but he found it quite easy to give to the Russians "the mores & the manners of Europe" when "he summoned to his court" the well-born women of the land, who had been "kept confined & were in a certain fashion slaves," and when he "made them dress in the German mode" and "sent them fabrics." As Montesquieu put it, "this sex immediately developed a taste for a style of life which flattered so powerfully their taste, their vanity, & their passions, & they caused the men to develop the same taste" (3.19.14).[53] Here, as often, Montesquieu is sly. It is not until the next chapter that he adds that "this change in the mores of the women will without a doubt have a great influence over the government of Muscovy." It is only then that he interprets this alteration as a harbinger of Russia's transformation into a monarchy (3.19.15). If, in a despotic state, he had warned, you turn the mores and the manners "upside down, you will turn everything" else "upside down" as well (3.19.12).

It is no doubt the case that, on occasion, "liberty itself has seemed intolerable [*insupportable*] to peoples unaccustomed to its enjoyment." It is also without a doubt true that, even for "the best laws, it is necessary that minds and spirits [*esprits*] be prepared" (3.19.2). It is, however, less clear how such preparations are to be made. But, in analyzing the success of one of Peter the Great's reforms, as we have just seen, Montesquieu does hint at the manner in which this can be done, and elsewhere he touches on the question as well. Sometimes, he tells us, "a wise legislator" eager "to restore by a just tempering of punishments & rewards the spirits" of a people "opinionated, capricious, resolute [*determiné*], whimsical [*bizarre*]," and inured to laws of very great cruelty, will find it insufficient or even impossible to proceed "by maxims of philosophy, morals, & religion suited to their character; by a just application of the rules of honor; by deploying shame as a punishment;" or even by encouraging their "enjoyment of a constant happiness & a sweet tranquillity." Then, he will have to conduct himself "in a manner *sourde et insensible*—muted, muffled, well-concealed, & unfelt" (1.6.13, p. 323). Moreover, in the course of tracing the evolution of French law, Montesquieu tellingly observes that "the supreme skill [*habileté*] is to invite when it is requisite that one not constrain, to provide guidance [*conduire*] when it is requisite that one not command." The key presumption that he insists on throughout is that "reason has a natural empire; she even has a tyrannical empire: one resists her, but this resistance is her triumph; just a little time, & one is forced to return to her side" (6.28.38). In the fourth part of his great work, Montesquieu will provide further indications why a lawgiver—interested in fostering liberty, prepared to rely on reason's possession of a natural empire, and satisfied with an issuing of invitations and a provision of guidance—should exhibit patience and not lose heart.

The original edition of *The Spirit of Laws* appeared in two volumes, as we have had occasion to note. The first of these, which included the first three of the work's six parts, concluded with the book containing Montesquieu's summary account of the general spirit (3.19), and this book concluded with the long chapter in which he attempted to situate England in this regard (3.19.27). The second volume of this initial edition marked a new beginning. Montesquieu signaled this to his readers by giving it its own epigraph, adapted from Vergil's *Aeneid*, and by providing a map of the world to serve as its frontispiece. In later editions, the map is omitted and the epigraph appears at the beginning of Montesquieu's twentieth book, the first of the four books dealing with commerce and demography that he had grouped together and designated as the fourth part of *De l'Esprit des lois*.[54]

Apart from signaling a new beginning, the epigraph suggests that there is more to *The Spirit of Laws* and to its last three parts than may meet the eye and that the scope of Montesquieu's inquiry somehow includes, at least in principle, all that Atlas, the Titan who supports the heavens on his shoulders, taught Iopas—the bard who sings to Dido's Carthaginians and to Aeneas' Trojans of "the wandering moon and the labors of the sun," clarifying "whence came the race of men and the beasts, whence rain and fire, Arcturus, the stormy Hyades, and the twin Oxen," and explaining "why the wintry sun hastens to touch Ocean" and "what delay then obstructs the course of the lingering nights" (Verg. *Aen.* 1.740–46). Montesquieu will once again draw attention to the epic quality of his *Spirit of Laws* when he ends the work with another quotation from *The Aeneid*—the words "Italy, Italy" (EL 6.31.34), which, first, Aeneas' close companion Achates and, then, his other men call out when these refugees from Troy first heave into sight of that mountainous peninsula on which, it has been foretold, they are destined to found Rome (Verg. *Aen.* 3.523).[55]

It is here, in the fourth part of his great work, that Montesquieu first indicates with full clarity his awareness that the world of man is in motion and that there is a logic to history's unfolding. There is a key to understanding this phenomenon and, with it, the new Rome, which will be founded by the author of *De l'Esprit des lois* with the assistance of those among his readers who foresee that, like it or not, they, too, will soon be refugees from an *ancien régime* that has admitted within its walls a Trojan Horse—and this key is what Montesquieu calls *commerce*. To begin to comprehend what he means by the term, however, one must return to his discussion of the *rapport* that exists between a nation's laws and the terrain that it occupies (EL 3.18).

Two

COMMERCIAL CIVILIZATION

In former times, each nation remained more closed in on itself. There was less communication. There were fewer voyages; fewer interests, common or opposed; fewer political and civil connections between peoples. There were not so many of those petty royal annoyances called negotiations and no ordinary Ambassadors continually in residence. Great sea voyages were rare. There was little in the way of far-flung commerce and the little that there was at that time was conducted by the Prince himself, who employed foreigners for it, or by people held in contempt, who set the tone for no one and did nothing at all to bring the nations together. There are a hundred times as many connections today between Europe and Asia as there were formerly between Gaul and Spain: Europe alone was more diverse than is the entire world today.

—*Jean-Jacques Rousseau*

When Montesquieu speaks of the climate (*EL* 3.14–17), his emphasis falls almost exclusively on its capacity to dictate to man. When he turns to the terrain (3.18), he pays at least as much attention to the manner in which men make use of and even transform their environment.[1] "Nature & the climate" may "exercise an almost complete dominion over the savages," as he suggests (3.19.4),[2] but everyone else appears to one degree or another to have escaped their tyranny. To the technology by which this is achieved, Montesquieu is no stranger. Earlier in the third part of his work, he has already alluded to the invention of labor-saving devices (3.15.8), and he will soon do so again (4.23.15). Although he does not dwell on the matter, he is exceedingly sensitive to the manner in which the application of reason and science (*lógos*) to the mechanical arts (*technaí*) is producing a technological revolution in his own day. We live "in a time," he ob-

170

serves, "when the arts communicate with one another, in a time when one corrects by art both the defects of nature & the defects of art itself" (4.21.6, pp. 609–10).[3]

For some time, Montesquieu had been interested in man's capacity consciously to alter the environment.[4] On 1 January 1719, some two decades prior to the appearance of his *Spirit of Laws*, he had publicly announced his interest in composing "a physical history of the earth" from antiquity to modernity; and in appealing to the world's savants for help in completing this project, he had indicated that he was interested in charting not only the changes effected by earthquakes, maritime inundations, and the like, but also those resulting from "Works produced by the hand of man which have given a new face to the Earth."[5] In a related passage, which appears in his notebooks, he explains that, while "certain places on the earth are uninhabitable" and "others are habitable without any inconvenience," there are others yet, which are subject to "certain inconveniences, that would not be habitable had remedies not been found for these inconveniences." These remedies, he adds, are not the work of "particular providence." In these cases, man had to provide for himself (S 298).

It is in light of these long-standing concerns that we should read, in Montesquieu's *Spirit of Laws*, the book on terrain—wherein he pays particularly close attention to the manner in which the Egyptians, the Dutch, and the Chinese have carved out for their use entire provinces once buried beneath the sea (*EL* 3.18.6), and then alludes to the elaborate systems of irrigation by which the ancient Persians brought water from the mountains to make the desert bloom. "By their care & by good laws," he remarks, "men have rendered the earth better suited for their residence. We see rivers flow where there were lakes & marshes; it is a good that nature has not made but which it sustains. . . . Industrious nations there are which have conferred benefits that do not come to an end when they themselves disappear" (3.18.7).

In economic matters, as we should by now expect, Montesquieu's outlook is thoroughly modern. Twenty years prior to the publication of *The Spirit of Laws*, in his *Considerations on the Wealth of Spain*, he had puzzled over the fact that her acquisition of gold mines and silver mines in the New World and their systematic exploitation had left Spain impoverished rather than enriched. In the brief treatise that he had then penned, in paragraphs that he subsequently adapted for insertion in the twenty-second book of his masterpiece (4.22.21), he charged the Spanish with having succumbed to the confusion that had bedeviled King Midas. Under the supposition that gold and silver constitute genuine wealth, they had neglected "merchandise" and "produce [*denrées*]," which are "the sources of natural wealth," in order to pursue a species of "fictional wealth [*richesses de fiction*]" arising from the invention of coinage and the use of precious metals in commercial exchange as wealth's "sign." Because these precious metals are durable, he argued, a great increase in the amount in circulation serves to reduce dramatically the value of all gold and silver—including that subsequently mined. Because the value of this gold and silver depends on demand, the Dutch and the English were able to reduce their value further by resorting to "new fictions" and monetizing "public credit" as an alternative medium of exchange. Moreover, because the Spanish mines were located abroad, the employment of labor in them did little, if anything, to promote commerce and industry in metropolitan Spain; and, in their confusion, the Spanish failed to capitalize on the highly profitable trade between Europe and their holdings in the Americas.[6] In a later work (pertinent to the plight of the oil-producing countries today), in which Montesquieu summarizes the argument of his *Considerations on the Wealth of Spain*, he casts aspersions on every "form of wealth" that is "a reward conferred by chance [*un tribut d'accident*]" and "depends neither on the industry of the Nation nor on the number of its inhabitants nor on the cultivation of its Land" (*RMU* 16.348–51). By his day, he added in another work that he then wrote, the consequences were utterly clear: by its own policy, Spain had been reduced to a state of such "weakness" that it would have been unable "to maintain itself" had it not been for "the treasures of the Indies" (*CR* 23.36–37).[7]

In his master work, Montesquieu argues in much the same spirit: that labor, not lucre, is the foundation of wealth; that one is better off inheriting a "trade [*métier*]" than a modest parcel of land; and that "the worker who has given his children a skill [*art*] for their inheritance has left them a good which is multiplied in proportion to their number" (*EL* 4.23.29). He regards as nonsense the notion that nothing but burdensome taxes and "poverty" can make men "industrious." These, he asserts, have the opposite result: those "discouraged by exhaustion [*accablement*] from work" are inclined to make "their entire happiness consist in idleness [*paresse*]." In general, "the effect of wealth in a country is to inspire ambition in every heart. That of poverty is to give birth to despair. Ambition is aroused by work; poverty finds its consolation in idleness" (2.13.2). From the start, then, as one would expect, Montesquieu's discussion of the terrain is an analysis of the modes by which human beings manage to subsist.

MODES OF SUBSISTENCE

There are, Montesquieu suggests, four such modes—not just hunting, herding, and agriculture, as he initially implies (1.1.3), but, as he ultimately reveals, commerce as well (3.18.8).[8] At the very outset, even before he has presented us with the other three alternatives, Montesquieu links the cultivation of the soil with the spirit of subservience and with "the government of one alone." As he puts it,

> the goodness of a country's land naturally establishes dependence there. The people of the countryside, who make up the principal part of the people, are not especially jealous of their liberty; they are too much preoccupied, filled with their own particular affairs. A country gorged with goods fears pillage, it fears an army. "Who is it that forms the party of the good?" said Cicero [*Att.* 7.7] to Atticus. "Are they the men of commerce & of the countryside? Not unless we imagine that they are opposed to monarchy—they for whom all governments are equal as long as they provide for tranquillity." (3.18.1)

Fertile countries are distinguished by their broad plains. In such a terrain, "one can dispute nothing with the strong man: one submits to him; & when one has done so, the spirit of liberty knows not how to return; the riches of the countryside are a pledge of one's fidelity." One tends to find "a more moderate government" among the impoverished peoples of the mountains who have little to lose but their "liberty," who are better situated for defense, and who have less need for "all the laws," restrictive of freedom, that are made "for the safety of the people" in countries more vulnerable to invasion (3.18.2). In any case, Montesquieu adds, fertile lands are rarely well tended. Their very fertility promotes, "alongside ease, softness & a certain love for the preservation of life." Where the inhabitants are free, they work much more diligently. Moreover, where the land is sterile, as it generally is in mountainous terrain, one can expect men to be "industrious, sober, inured to work, courageous, & fit for war: for they have to procure for themselves what the terrain refuses them" (3.18.3–4).

The "savage peoples," who subsist by hunting and fishing, and the "barbarian peoples," who live off their herds, make less efficient use of the land than those who cultivate the plains. They have more frequent occasions for war, and they tend to be governed by mores as opposed to laws (3.18.10–13). But they do boast of one considerable advantage over those who practice agriculture: despite their subjection to nature and the climate, in their relations with men "these people enjoy a great liberty." There are two reasons for this. To begin with, because these savages and barbarians are "wanderers" and "vagabonds," they ordinarily have options unavailable to those burdened with real estate. Except when overawed by superstition, they are generally able to walk away from "a chief" who "wishes to deprive them of their liberty" and seek an alternative leader; and unless they live in a vast wasteland, as the Tartars do, they can always "retire into the woods." Among savages and barbarians, Montesquieu tells us, "the liberty of the man is so great that it of necessity brings with it the liberty of the citizen" (3.18.14, 18–19).

The second reason that these primitive hunters and herdsmen find it easy to retain their freedom is that they have no real need for or interest in money. In Montesquieu's view, agriculture presupposes "much in the way of arts & knowledge, & one always sees the arts, knowledge, & needs progress at an equal pace. All of this is conducive to the establishment of a sign for value." The creation of money opens the way for trickery [*la ruse*], and this, in turn, makes civil laws necessary. Where men live from hunting, fishing, or herding, no one can assemble goods in sufficient quantity with sufficient security "to be in a condition to corrupt all the others, but where one has signs for wealth, one can amass these signs & distribute them to whomever one wishes. Among peoples who have no money, each has little in the way of needs, & these they satisfy with ease & in an equal manner. Equality is then inevitable [*forcée*], & so their chiefs are emphatically not [*point*] despotic" (3.18.15–17).

Montesquieu's account of the first three modes of subsistence embodies a tacit critique of the agrarian republics of classical antiquity and prepares the way for an assertion of modernity's superiority. Free and equal in the fashion of the herders, hunters, and fishermen described above were the German barbarians who put an end to the despotism that had long flourished among the agricultural nations governed by imperial Rome—venturing "forth from their countries," as we have seen (III.1, above), "to destroy tyrants & slaves, & to teach men that, as nature has made them equal, so reason cannot render them dependent, except insofar as is requisite for their happiness" (*EL* 3.17.5,18.23–30).[9]

COMMERCIAL SOCIETY

Had Montesquieu ended *The Spirit of Laws* with its third part or published the first volume some years before the second, some among his readers would almost certainly have been left with the impression that he believed that we must choose between civilization and subservience, on the one hand, and barbarism and liberty, on the other. Others would have taken him for a precursor of Jean-Jacques Rousseau.[10] This misconception Montesquieu rules out when he turns his attention, in the fourth part of his opus, to the fourth and last mode of subsistence.[11] Here, for the first time, he directly addresses the question of commerce and its connection with the capacity of the human race for moral and political progress.[12]

THE SPIRIT OF LAWS, PART FOUR

IV.　20. Of the Laws in the Relation Which They Have with Commerce, Considered with Regard to its Nature & its Distinctions

　　21. Of the Laws in the Relation Which They Have with Commerce, Considered with Regard to the Revolutions That It Has Had in the World

　　22. Of the Laws in the Relation Which They Have with the Use of Money

　　23. Of the Laws in the Relation Which They Have with the Number of Inhabitants

In preparing the ground for what he will later say, Montesquieu makes it clear that social interchange has the capacity to transform the general spirit, as we have seen. In one passage, he remarks, "The more the peoples communicate, the more easily do they change their manners. Since each human being is more a spectacle for another, one sees better the singularities of individuals. The climate that causes a nation to love communication makes it also love change" (3.19.8). In another passage, he suggests that there is a definite direction to the changes likely to take place. "Certain laws are required in a nation in which men communicate a great deal," he contends, "and others, among a people where no one communicates at all" (3.14.10).

Crucial to understanding the logic of social interchange is one fact: that "the history of commerce" is the history of "communication between peoples" (4.21.5). Precisely because commerce promotes communication across national boundaries, it is quasi-medicinal. It "cures destructive prejudices." In fact, Montesquieu contends, "it comes close to being a general rule that everywhere there are gentle mores [*moeurs douces*], there is commerce, & everywhere there is commerce, there are gentle mores." Commercial intercourse causes "the mores of all the nations" to "penetrate everywhere." It enables men to "compare them with one another." And from informed comparison "great goods" result (4.20.1).[13]

These goods are acquired, however, at a price. To begin with, there is something about commerce that is undignified and utterly grim. As Montesquieu puts it, "This commerce is a species of lottery, & each is seduced by the hope of a black ticket. Everyone loves to play, & the wisest people play willingly, when its character as gambling, its obsessiveness [*ses égarements*], its violence, its dissipation, the loss of time, & even of one's whole life, is not apparent" (4.20.6). Moreover, although commerce may resemble and even reinforce Christianity in its propensity to soften mores and to promote a species of cosmopolitanism (cf. 5.24.3–4), it is not conducive to moral and social solidarity in any form. It "does not unite the individuals" who live within particular states. Instead, it disaggregates human communities by setting their members apart and by reminding them of their particularity. "In the countries," such as Holland, "where one is affected by nothing but the spirit of commerce," Montesquieu observes, "we see that one traffics in all human activities & in all the moral virtues: the smallest things, which humanity demands, are done there or given for money." By way of explanation, he adds that "the spirit of commerce produces in human beings a certain sentiment of exact justice, opposed on one the side to brigandage & on the other to the moral virtues which cause one to not always restrict one's discussion rigidly to one's own interests, & which enable one to neglect one's interests for those of others" (4.20.2).[14] To the extent that it penetrates and permeates a traditional polity, the spirit of commerce will subvert it by encouraging the reconfiguration of what had been a community based on a sense of moral mission and purpose into a society grounded in contract and held together by self-interest alone.[15]

This helps explain why commerce is no less incompatible with the "singular institutions" deployed by many classical republics than is the Christian faith. Precisely because these polities presuppose on the part of their citizens an intense public-spiritedness and a willingness to neglect and even sacrifice private interest for communal good, they require, as we have seen (II.4, above), a proscription of "silver, whose effect is to fatten the fortunes of men beyond the limits that nature has set for them, to teach men to conserve uselessly that which they have amassed in the same fashion, to multiply infinitely their desires, & to supplant [*suppléer*] nature, which has given us very limited means for irritating our passions & for corrupting one another." For similar reasons, these republics regard as a threat to "their mores" the "communication" with "barbarians" that commerce and travel ordinarily promote (*EL* 1.4.6–7, 2.12.30, p. 458, n. a).

In short, to embrace commerce and the peculiar spirit of cosmopolitanism that it inspires is to embrace moral corruption and turn one's back on republican and Christian virtue alike; and Montesquieu has no compunctions whatsoever in either regard. He warns moralists tempted to "make laws which shock the *esprit général*" that they should attend to the unedifying fact that "not all political vices are moral vices & that not all moral vices are political vices" (3.19.11). As he later explains, "one can say that the laws of commerce perfect mores for the same reason that they destroy mores. Commerce corrupts pure mores: this is the subject of Plato's complaints; it polishes & softens barbarous mores, as we see all the days" of our lives (4.20.1).

In endorsing this paradox—that private vices can promote the public good and that the progress from barbarism to civilization is grounded in moral corruption—Montesquieu is following the lead of and even borrowing language from the Jansenist Pierre Nicole, the savant Pierre Bayle, and Bernard Mandeville (*MP* 1553), a Dutch immigrant to England whose book *The Fable of the Bees: or, Private Vices, Publick Benefits*—originally published in attenuated form as *The Grumbling Hive: or, Knaves Turn'd Honest* to no acclaim in 1705, and then reprinted in a much-expanded edition under its more familiar title in 1714—had suddenly and unexpectedly come to enjoy a *grand succés de scandale* when a Middlesex jury sought the suppression of a still-further-expanded edition on moral grounds in 1723, some five years before Montesquieu arrived on the scene. In this notorious and highly influential work, Mandeville not only defended vanity as a spur to commercial growth and to progress in the sciences and the arts; like Nicole and Bayle, he contended that "self-liking" is at the root of all the splendid, external qualities that men justly admire. To begin with, he stoutly denied that human beings are by nature "sociable"; the origins of human association he attributed to the fear of wild beasts. For the cooperative capacity of his contemporaries, he had a simple explanation: in the course of time, "by living together in Society," men underwent a process akin to the fermentation of grapes. Painful experience slowly taught them that it is in every man's interest to accommodate himself to his fellows, and "good Manners or Politeness came into the World" and even supplanted brutishness when the canniest human beings acquired the civilizing art of subterfuge and learned "to be proud of hiding their Pride." "The nearer we search into human Nature," the Dutch-born satirist argued, "the more we shall be convinced that the Moral Virtues are the Political Offspring which Flattery begot upon Pride." A careful study of history would reveal that "Luxury and Politeness ever grew up together."[16]

Montesquieu did not share Mandeville's doubts as to the existence of natural foundations for human sociability.[17] But he was persuaded, nonetheless, by the Dutchman's history of the progress of politeness and luxury, and he thought it particularly applicable to his native France,[18] where the *esprit général* inspired in the citizens a "taste for the world & for commerce with women above all else," and where it facilitated at the same time their possession of "a sociable humor, an openness of heart, a joy in living, a taste, a facility for communicating their thoughts." In France, Montesquieu writes, "one could restrain the women, make laws to correct their morals [*moeurs*], & limit their luxury, but who knows whether one would not lose, thereby, a certain taste which is the source of the nation's riches & a politeness that draws foreigners to it" (*EL* 3.19.5–6). That "the society of women spoils mores," Montesquieu readily admits. He merely insists, citing Mandeville as his authority, that it "forms taste" at the same time: "the desire [*envie*] to outdo others in pleasing establishes finery [*parures*]; the desire to please someone other than oneself establishes fashion [*les modes*]." The latter he takes to be "an important object" on which to reflect—for, "by dint of rendering one's *esprit* frivolous, one gives constant increase to the branches of commerce" (3.19.8).[19]

One reason that Montesquieu is inclined to embrace commerce is that, he believes, it leads "to peace." It is difficult, he explains, "for two nations which have business together [*negocient ensemble*]" to go to war given that the very process of exchange "renders them reciprocally dependent" so that "if one has an interest in buying, the other has an interest in selling." In short, "all these unions are founded on mutual needs." The full ramifications of this fact are visible when one contrasts agriculture as a mode of subsistence with commerce. Real estate, such as the land worked by cultivators of the soil, is national in character: as a "species of wealth," Montesquieu notes, it "belongs to each state in its particularity." The distinct territories that they farm distinguish the peoples of the earth, set them apart, and provide occasions for their wars. "The spirit of commerce" has the opposite effect: it "unites the nations" even though "it does not unite individuals at the same time." The ordinary objects of commerce, "movable effects, such as silver, bank notes, letters of exchange, company shares, ships, & every form of merchandise, belong to the entire world, which, in this respect, composes but a single state of which all the societies are members." Montesquieu acknowledges that "the people which possesses the movable effects of the universe in the greatest amount is the wealthiest." He knows that "some states," such as Holland and England, "have an immense quantity of these; they acquire them by their produce [*denrées*], by the labor of their workers, by their industry, by their discoveries, even by chance." But he insists that, although "the avarice of the nations disputes the movables of the entire universe," it generally does so in a fashion that reduces the likelihood of war (4.20.2, 23).[20]

Montesquieu devotes attention to commerce not only because, as a mode of subsistence, it promotes a species of cosmopolitanism tending to cure destructive prejudices, polish and soften barbarous mores, and reduce the likelihood of war. He is interested in it also because commerce is anything but static. It is "subject" to what he calls "great revolutions" (4.21.1), and he thought these of sufficient import that he devoted the second book of the fourth part of *The Spirit of Laws* to their study.[21] In this book, Montesquieu charts the course of international trade both ancient and modern. To this end, he focuses his attention on the history of technology and travel, surveying advances in ship design, examining the voyages of discovery undertaken in ancient times, assessing the importance of the invention of the compass, and cataloguing the modern voyages of discovery—which had eventuated in the colonization and development of the New World and in the establishment of a great overseas trade linking Europe not only with Africa and the Americas but with India and the Far East as well (4.21).[22] Montesquieu does not pretend to do this subject full justice. He leaves it to others, such as his Scottish admirers Adam Smith, Adam Ferguson, John Robertson, John Millar, Lord Kames, and Dugald Stewart, to explore this question more fully.[23] It is for his immediate purposes more than sufficient that he make straight the way.[24]

Montesquieu's point is merely to bring home to his readers the degree to which commercial dynamism has transformed—perhaps permanently[25]—the setting for politics. In his opinion, it is not sufficient that one acknowledge that commerce is always politically embedded; one must also recognize that in modern times the viability of polities has come to depend to a very considerable extent on the extent to which they can accommodate and even promote commerce. In this sense, if in no other, commerce has achieved a measure of autonomy. "I would like to drift along a tranquil river," Montesquieu writes when he first broaches commerce as a theme. "I am swept on by a torrent" (4.20.1).[26]

REVOLUTIONS IN COMMERCE

To one degree or another, in the epochs before Montesquieu's own age, political circumstances conspired to hamper commercial progress. "Sometimes destroyed by conquerors, sometimes obstructed by monarchs, commerce wanders the earth, flees from where it is oppressed, takes its repose where one lets it breath again: it reigns today where once one saw only deserts, seas, & rocks; there where it once reigned, there are only deserts now." If commerce has a "history," that history is indistinguishable from "that of the communication of peoples. Their various destructions & a certain ebb & flow of populations & devastations form its greatest events" (4.21.5). To the extent that, in modern times, commerce actually managed to surmount most of the obstacles cast in its path by the accidents of history, its advances were due to a late medieval invention that liberated it to a considerable degree from political control.

Pagan and Christian Rome seem to have symbolized for Montesquieu the greatest obstacles to the progress of commerce. The French philosophe was an unabashed admirer of the ancient Romans—so much so that he anticipated Edward Gibbon in devoting a separate treatise to the study of their rise and decline, as we have seen (I.2, above). They were, he asserts, among "the freest peoples who have ever existed on the earth" (*EL* 2.12.19). In one passage within *The Spirit of Laws*, Montesquieu remarks, "I find myself strengthened in my maxims when I have the Romans on my side" (1.6.15). In another, he exclaims, "Examine the

Romans! You will never find them so superior as in their choice of circumstances in which to do evil & good" (4.22.12). Of all "the people in the world," he considered the Romans the nation "which best understood how to fit their laws to their projects" (4.23.20). His admiration was not, however, unbounded.[27] "The Romans," he wrote, "conquered all in order to destroy all" (2.10.14);[28] and "in destroying all the peoples" that they conquered, "the Romans destroyed themselves" as well. "Unceasing in action, effort, & violence, they used themselves up like a weapon always in play" (4.23.20). They were impressive, he readily admits, when "their republic" flourished in the full "vigor [*force*] of its institution," and the regulations designed to augment the supply of Rome's citizens "had only to repair the losses that she had incurred as a consequence of her courage, her audacity, her firmness, her love of glory, & her virtue itself." Later, however, "not even the wisest laws could reestablish that which a dying republic, a general anarchy, a military government, a harsh empire, a proud despotism, a weak monarch, & a court stupid, idiotic, & superstitious had successively knocked down: one could say" of the Romans "that they conquered the world only to render it weak & to deliver it without defense to the barbarians" (4.23.23).

In Montesquieu's view, one of the chief reasons for Rome's decline was the antipathy of the Romans to commerce.[29] In this, to be sure, they were not alone. Athens was a maritime city with an "empire over the sea." It lacked the "singular institutions" which ruled out trade for Sparta and other cities. At one point, Montesquieu speaks of Athens as the "commercial republic" that it might have been (1.5.6); at another, he lists it among the devotees of what he calls "the commerce of economy" (4.20.4). Later, however, he acknowledges that this putatively "commercial nation" was "more attentive to extending its maritime empire than to using it," and he remarks that Athens was so "full of projects for glory" that she never "achieved the great commerce promised by the working of her mines, the multitude of her slaves, the number of her sailors, her authority over the Greek towns, &, more than all this, the fine institutions of Solon" (4.21.7). In short, in Athens, as in the other Greek cities "which had as their principal object war, all labor & all the professions conducive to monetary gain were regarded as unworthy of a free man." When Aristotle (*Pol.* 1277a37-b7) intimated that it was a sign of "corruption that in certain democracies artisans succeeded in becoming citizens," he was, according to Montesquieu, correct: for "among the Greeks all retail trade [*tout bas commerce*] was considered vile [*infâme*]" (*EL* 1.4.8).[30]

Rome was an even more extreme case than Athens. For a brief time, in her infancy, she possessed something like "singular institutions" of the sort that distinguished Sparta (3.19.16, n. a), but this cannot have lasted long, for these were incompatible with "the confusion, the negligence, the extended affairs of a great people" in command of an extensive empire (1.4.7). More pertinent is the fact that Rome was not a maritime city. She put her faith in "land forces" and looked down—as did, in fact, most of the Athenians' fellow Greeks—on the sly martial "practices of the peoples of the sea." Never, Montesquieu insists, did the Romans display any "jealousy with regard to commerce. . . . Their genius, their glory, their military education, the form of their government distanced them from commerce." Well into the Principate, it was a matter of public "policy" for the Romans "to separate themselves from all the nations which had not been subjugated: the fear that they would convey to these peoples the art of conquering made the Romans neglect the art of enriching themselves. They made laws preventing all commerce with the barbarians." If in later times Rome nonetheless established centers for trade on her frontiers, it was a sign of her growing weakness in the face of barbarian demands. "I know well," writes Montesquieu, "that people—full of these two ideas: first, that commerce is of all things in the world the one most useful to the state; &, second, that the Romans had the best policy in the world—have believed that the Romans very much encouraged & honored commerce. The truth is that they rarely thought about it" at all (4.21.13–15).[31]

One could, of course, argue that the commerce that eventually developed between Rome and southern Arabia and India "procured for the Romans a great carrying trade [*navigation*], which is to say a great power; that the new merchandise increased commerce within the empire [*commerce intérieur*]; that it favored the arts & encouraged industry; that the number of the citizens multiplied in proportion to the new means that they had for subsistence; that the new commerce produced luxury, which we have proven to be as favorable to the government of one alone as it is fatal to that of the many; that this establishment coincided in time with the fall of their republic; that luxury at Rome was necessary; & that a town which drew to it all the riches of the universe was obliged to send those riches back in exchange for luxury goods" (4.21.16). Never, however, does Montesquieu suggest that the Romans themselves ever advanced or even conceived of such an argument. It may have been in their interest to promote commerce, but the "right of nations" and the "civil law," as these were elaborated and practiced under the Roman emperors, were "no less hostile" to commerce than the "political constitution" of republican Rome (4.21.14).

The absence of an appreciation for the advantages of commerce, so visible in ancient Athens and Rome and so fatal to their prospects in the long run, was no less evident in the Latin Middle Ages. Rome's fall meant the virtual elimination of commerce from Europe. The warrior nobility that emerged in the wake of the barbarian conquest had no interest in it, and there was little in the laws and customs of the Germanic peoples to encourage its revival (4.21.18–19). Subsequently, the recovery of Aristotle's works and the adoption by the Schoolmen of his critique of lending at interest conspired to hamper trade. At this point, Montesquieu reports, "commerce passed to" the Jews, "a nation" much "toyed with from one century to another," which was

> then covered in infamy, & so commerce was no longer distinguished from the most horrid usury, from monopolies, from the levy of subsidies, & all dishonest means of acquiring silver. The Jews, enriched by their exactions, were then pillaged by the princes with the same tyranny. . . .
>
>   Nonetheless, one saw commerce emerge from the bosom of vexation & despair. The Jews, proscribed by each country in turn, found the means for saving their effects. By this they rendered their retreats forever fixed—since such a prince, who wanted very much to get rid of them, would not for all that be in a humor to be rid of their money as well.

These late medieval Jews managed to save their property by making it disappear. For the first time in human history, as a consequence of their invention of letters of exchange, "commerce was able to elude violence & to maintain itself everywhere," for "the richest trader had nothing but invisible goods, which could be conveyed everywhere & leave not a trace in any place." According to Montesquieu, this invention obliged theologians "to rein in their principles." As a result, "commerce, which had been linked by violence with bad faith, returned, so to speak, to the bosom of probity." The ruling order within Europe may have shared the Greek and the Roman predilection for conquest and war, the attendant contempt for trade, and a profound dislike for those who secured their livelihood in this fashion, but this mattered no longer. From the moment that the Jewish bankers introduced the letter of exchange, "it became necessary for princes to govern themselves with greater sagacity than they would themselves have thought possible—since, in the event, great acts of authority [*les grands coups d'autorité*] proved to be so maladroit that experience gave rise to the recognition that only good government [*la bonté du gouvernement*] brings prosperity." If scholastic speculation was responsible for "all the evils that accompanied the destruction of commerce," it was "to the avarice of princes" that Europe owed "the establishment of a thing which places commerce in a certain fashion beyond their power" (4.21.20).[32]

    Largely as a consequence of the liberation of commerce from political control, Montesquieu writes, trade gradually grew into a force capable of defeating "barbarism" in Europe (4.21.20). This development was due in considerable measure to the growing importance of state finance. Montesquieu was exceedingly sensitive to the relationship between economic prosperity and military power. He was born in the year in which William of Orange supplanted James II as king of England; his childhood coincided with the War of the League of Augsburg; and he came of age during the War of the Spanish Succession, as we have seen (I.1, above). Like many of his countrymen, he was surprised by William's ability to fight Louis XIV to a standstill, and he marveled at the military genius that enabled the duke of Marlborough to inflict on that formidable French monarch a series of crippling military defeats. Like them as well, he thought long and hard concerning the preconditions for the awesome marshaling of financial resources that enabled England and Holland to put together the requisite coalitions and keep the vast armies of William and of Marlborough constantly in the field.[33]

In 1734, as we have also seen (I.1, above), Montesquieu had occasion to compose a brief treatise exploring the reasons why no one, after the fall of the Roman empire, had managed to establish and sustain in Europe a universal monarchy. Initially intended to serve as the concluding chapter of his *Considerations on the Greatness of the Romans and their Decline* and ultimately destined to be pillaged for material to be inserted within his *Spirit of Laws*,[34] this work traced the failure of Europe's monarchs to the fact that, in modern times, "new discoveries" had transformed the very nature of war (*RMU* 1.1–6). The first of these had its origins, as we later learn (*EL* 2.10.1–4, 5.24.3), in the changes effected in Europe's moral climate by Christianity. In antiquity, conquest had been the principal means for achieving prosperity. In modern times, "the right of nations" had been reinterpreted in such a manner as to render war unprofitable by ruling out the enslavement of the conquered and the sale of their lands (*RMU* 1.8–19).

The remaining "discoveries" had taken place in the sphere of commerce and technology. Where power had once made wealth, "wealth" had come to "make power." In antiquity, "poverty was able to confer on a People great advantages." When "the Cities employed in their wars none but their own Citizens, Armies made up of those who were rich were composed of people lost in softness, indolence, & pleasures," and "they were often destroyed by those of their neighbors who, being accustomed to a life painful & harsh, were better suited to war & to the military exercises of that age." In modern times, the various states employed permanent, standing mercenary forces drawn from "the vilest part of all the Nations"; none of these were enervated by luxury more than the rest; and advances in military technology had made all capable of instruction in the military art. "At present," Montesquieu observed, "Europe conducts all the Carrying Trade & Commerce in the Universe"; and "in so far as a State takes more or less part in this Carrying Trade or in this Commerce, it is necessary that its power increase or diminish" relative to its rivals—for, to the degree that the projection of "power" has come to be synonymous with the deployment of sizable armies of well-equipped "regular troops," that power is "founded on Commerce & on industry" (1.19–2.64).

It is not surprising, then, that in the course of the discussion of commerce included within his *Spirit of Laws* Montesquieu paused to reflect on the fact that "Europe has arrived at so high a degree of power [*puissance*] that history offers nothing that compares with it if one considers the immensity of expenditure, the great scope of military engagements, the number of troops, & the continuity in their upkeep" (*EL* 4.21.21). This growth in military power was made possible by a vast augmentation in revenues, which was in turn a consequence of the enormous increase in trade. As Montesquieu observes, a dramatic "increase [*enflure*]" in imports and exports "will produce a thousand advantages for the state: there will be more consumption, more things on which the arts can be exercised, more men employed, more means of acquiring power." In modern times, rulers are forced to do everything in their power to promote commerce, and they find it essential to establish the rule of law and provide for the security of persons and property. It is in this context, that Montesquieu writes with evident delight, "We have begun to cure ourselves of Machiavellianism, & we will continue the cure all the days of our lives. There is greater need for moderation in councils. Those things which in other times one called *coups d'État* would today, apart from the horror, be acts of foolhardiness [*imprudences*]. Happy it is that men are in a situation in which, though their passions inspire them with the thought of being rogues, they have an interest in not being such" (4.20.23, 21.20, 22.13–14).

This observation should give us pause. Commerce on a grand scale was for the states of early modern Europe a *sine qua non*, since trade had come to provide the essential foundation for every projection of power. Polities incompatible with commerce, such as the Greek cities equipped with "singular institutions," could no longer be sustained. Imperial republics, such as Athens and Rome, which were forced to tolerate trade but were prevented by their guiding principle from ever fully embracing and giving it every encouragement, were no longer militarily viable. Despotism would no doubt survive. In many parts of the world, the climate and terrain appeared to rule out any alternative, and political liberty was in the best of circumstances an achievement. Everywhere, one could always say of despotism that it "jumps up, so to speak, before our eyes," that "it is uniform throughout," and that "as the passions alone are necessary for its establishment, the whole world is good enough for that" (1.5.14, p. 297). But, survive though it undoubtedly would, despotism's grip would inevitably be weakened.

Commerce depends on confidence. It is possible, Montesquieu remarks, for a "state to achieve prosperity" only "to the extent that, on the one hand, silver effectively [*bien*] represents all things &, on the other, all things effectively represent silver, & they are signs of one another—which is to say that, in proportion to their relative value, one can have one as soon as one has the other." "Never," he then adds, "is this ever achieved except in a moderate government." In a despotism, he insists, "it would be a prodigy if things represented their sign." The medium of "exchange" required by "commerce" simply cannot be sustained therein. Coinage will not circulate: it cannot "represent" things and function as "a sign of the value of all merchandise" in places where "tyranny & distrust cause everyone to bury his silver" (4.22.2, 14).[35]

This helps explain why Montesquieu contends that "it is pointless even to mention despotism" in a discussion of commerce. As we have had ample opportunity to note, in ordinary circumstances, such a polity is constitutionally incapable of sustaining the rule of law and of safeguarding persons and property. The absence of "confidence" and the prevalence of "uncertainty" as to the security of one's goods "naturalize usury there," and the government itself encourages "peculation" on the part of its agents. Because of the high rates of interest and the general insecurity, merchants "know not how to conduct commerce on a grand scale" and "live from one day to the next." In a nation reduced to "servitude," Montesquieu tells us, avarice inevitably trumps mercantile acquisitiveness: "one works to conserve more than to acquire" (1.5.15, 4.20.4). Nowhere in the world can a polity as economically stagnant as despotism manage to sustain itself against the forces brought to bear against it by technologically dynamic and commercially vibrant states of the sort that have appeared in western Europe.

The one crucial question, then, that remains to be addressed is that of the precise import of commerce for the moderate governments. To this end, we will have to re-examine the monarchies that existed on the European continent in Montesquieu's day—as well as the republic disguised as a monarchy, whose constitution took as its direct object the establishment of liberty, which lay just off shore.

Three

MONARCHY'S PLIGHT

We are approaching a state of crisis and a century of revolutions . . . I hold it to be impossible that the great monarchies of Europe have yet a long time to last. All have shined, and every state that shines is in decline. I have for my opinion reasons more particular than this maxim; but to speak them aloud would be inopportune, and everyone sees them only too well.

— *Jean-Jacques Rousseau*

On the face of it, the liberation of commerce from political control and the vast expansion afforded it by the discovery of the compass, the improvements in ship design, and the new trade routes to Africa, America, and Asia opened up by the great voyages of discovery should have been highly advantageous to Europe's monarchies. If commerce produced economic inequality, as assuredly it would, this would be all to the good. If it encouraged luxury, that, too, would be of advantage in a polity inclined to whimsy, insistent on hierarchy, and apt to give free rein to the frivolity of women. Montesquieu in no way shrinks from announcing the fact that, "in the government of one alone," commerce will "ordinarily be founded on luxury." Nor does it bother him in the least that such "a commerce of luxury" will have as its "principal object: procuring for the nation pursuing it everything which serves its pride, its delights, & its fantasies." In a polity distinguished by great disparities in wealth, it is the luxury of the rich that enables the poor to live (*EL* 1.7.4, 4.20.4). "Vanity" Montesquieu commends as a "good motive [*ressort*] for government." It produces "goods without number. From it," as his compatriots have shown, "are born luxury, industry, the arts, fashion, politeness, taste" (3.19.9). Without it, in fact, the French could not display the qualities that make them so attractive to all the world: "a sociable hu-

186

mor, an openness of heart, a joy in living, a taste, a facility for communicating their thoughts" (3.19.5–8).[1]

After reading Montesquieu, Parisians may well have been inclined to say things that, in his opinion, the ancient Romans had never even contemplated saying—that its new overseas commerce "procured" for their country "a great carrying trade, which is to say a great power; that the new merchandise" imported from distant parts "increased commerce within the country [*commerce intérieur*]; that it favored the arts & encouraged industry; that the number of the citizens multiplied in proportion to the new means that they had for subsistence; that the new commerce produced luxury, which" is "as favorable to the government of one alone as it is fatal to that of the many"; that, in the capital, such "luxury was necessary; & that a town which drew to it all the riches of the universe was obliged to send those riches back in exchange for luxury goods" (4.21.16).

By this time, the political system in France had itself come to rely on commerce. In a monarchy, Montesquieu insists, it is essential that distinctions be maintained and that the nobility be prohibited from engaging in trade (4.20.21).[2] But, in such a polity, it is no less advantageous that merchants be able to rise above their inherited station and buy their way into the nobility. Montesquieu does not expect his readers to applaud the fact that "the prize of virtue" is so often awarded to "wealth," but he does want them to recognize that this practice is "exceedingly useful" as a spur to industry and an incentive to national prosperity. As he puts it, the fact that they can acquire "nobility in exchange for silver [*à prix d'argent*] powerfully encourages the merchants to place themselves in a condition to succeed in doing so." While remaining merchants, "they have the hope of obtaining nobility—but without the actual inconvenience. They have no means of leaving their profession more certain than performing its functions well & with distinction [*avec honneur*], a thing ordinarily connected with the achievement of a competency [*suffisance*]."

Social mobility of this sort is also essential for the survival of the most significant element within the nobility, which is always in need of new recruits. In France, the "warrior nobility" is inclined to bankrupt itself on the presumption "that it is shameful to increase one's goods if one has not begun by dissipating them." This class accepts no pay: it "serves" the prince and the French nation "with the capital of its goods"; and "when it is ruined" thereby, thanks to the sordid but salutary traffic in offices and honors, it can gracefully "give place to another" part of the nation which is able and willing to "serve with its capital in turn" (4.20.22).

MONARCHY AND COMMERCIAL SOCIETY

Monarchy favors and is favored by a "commerce of luxury," but it is by no means clear that it can profit from a vast expansion of trade of the sort that characterized seventeenth- and eighteenth-century Europe.[3] To begin with, monarchy requires a set of practices regarding landed property which effectively rule out its treatment as a commodity. If the nobility is to be sustained, it must be hereditary and there must be primogeniture. For similar reasons, "noble lands will have privileges just as noble persons do," for, just as "one cannot separate the dignity of the monarch from that of his realm," so "one can hardly separate the dignity of the noble from that of his fief." This requires that there be "substitutions" designed to "preserve goods within families" and laws providing for "redemption" so that descendants can recover "for the family lands which the prodigality of a parent has alienated." These infringements on the exchange of landed property inevitably "do harm to commerce," and this recognition leads Montesquieu to argue that they not be extended in any unnecessary way. In monarchies, he contends, "it is necessary that the laws favor all the commerce that the constitution of this government is able to tolerate so that the subjects can, without perishing, satisfy the requirements, ever-recurring, of the prince & his court" (1.5.9).

To this, we can add that monarchical government fosters tastes that are not conducive to the conduct of what Montesquieu calls "the commerce of economy." Because this species of commerce "is founded," as the name suggests, on economizing, which is to say, "on the practice of gaining little & even of gaining less than any other nation, & of securing compensation for itself solely through gaining incessantly, it is hardly possible that it could be pursued by a people among whom luxury is established—who spend large sums & notice only objects that are grand." This would not much matter were it not for the fact that it is only in states practicing "the commerce of economy" as their mode of subsistence that one finds "the greatest enterprises," for the citizens "there possess an audacity [*hardiesse*] not to be found in monarchies." Their boldness arises from a natural process peculiar to "the commerce of economy," for, in a polity favorable to such trading practices, "one species of commerce leads to another, the small to the middling [*médiocre*], the middling to the grand"—so that "he who has had so great a desire to gain a little puts himself in a situation in which he has no less desire to gain a great deal." Moreover, despite their taste for grandeur, monarchies are unfriendly to "the great enterprises of commerce." These are "always necessarily mixed with public affairs," which, "in monarchies most of the time," are regarded as "suspect" by merchants uncertain as to the safety of "their property." Only where one is supremely confident "that what one has acquired is secure [*sûr*], does one dare expose it in order to acquire more," for in such a place "one runs a risk only with regard to the mode [*moyens*] of acquisition" (4.20.4).[4]

Trading companies illustrate the problem in one way; banks, in another. Associations of merchants, such as Britain's East India Company, cannot be introduced "into countries governed by one alone" because they "give to private wealth the strength of public wealth" and thereby threaten the power of the prince. Fiduciary institutions provide the "credit" necessary for "the commerce of economy." To suppose them compatible with monarchy, however, would be "to suppose silver on the one side & on the other power [*la puissance*]: which is to say, on the one side, the capacity [*faculté*] to possess everything without any power [*pouvoir*]; &, on the other, power [*le pouvoir*] without any such capacity at all." In such a polity, "no one but the prince has secured or been able to secure a treasure; & wherever there is a treasure, as soon as it seems excessive, right then it becomes the treasure of the prince" (4.20.10).[5] Monarchy may in most respects be a far cry from despotism, and in modern times its inclination to abuse power when tempted by riches may be checked in some measure by an awareness of the consequences attendant on the merchants' use of the letter of exchange, but it nonetheless requires a measure of hierarchy and subordination inconsistent with the massive concentration of movable wealth in private hands that is necessary if a nation is to take full advantage of the possibilities afforded commercial enterprise in a mercantile age.

Montesquieu was among the first to recognize and reflect on the institutional constraints dictating that, whenever the French monarchy made a wholehearted effort to project power within Europe and beyond, it courted insolvency and brought itself to the verge of bankruptcy—but he was by no means the last. Money really had become the sinews of war; and, in the wake of the War of the Spanish Succession, circumstances repeatedly conspired to bring this difficulty to the attention of those who governed France. To an astonishing degree, French political discourse in the second half of the eighteenth century revolved around the problem posed—within a world dominated by fiscal-military states—by the need to promote confidence and properly finance the public debt.[6]

In Montesquieu's opinion, the obstacles to the monarchy's solving this problem were insuperable.[7] He was arguably right.[8] If a monarchy were to confront and overcome the institutional logic that he had identified; if, in the interests of national prosperity and the military power made possible by such prosperity, it were somehow willing and able to curb its aversion to such concentrations of wealth; if it somehow managed to foster a "commerce of economy" supplementing the "commerce of luxury" natural to it; and if it also succeeded in establishing institutions and practices sufficient to instill in the world's merchants both the conviction that the riches that they acquired in grand commercial enterprises would be secure under its rule and the illusion that the public debt would eventually be paid, it is by no means clear that this monarchy would thereby gain in stability and strength. The fact that commerce fosters economic inequality in no way alters the fact that it promotes social equality at the same time. "Commerce is," as Montesquieu puts it, "the profession of equal people" (1.5.8). It brings human beings together within a sphere in which the transactions that occur presuppose the absence of any distinctions of status or rank worth noticing. To the extent that the spirit of commerce permeates a monarchical society and propagates within it the norms and expectations of the marketplace, it will subvert its principle. When Montesquieu remarks that "commerce cures destructive prejudices," he has more in mind than he is willing on this occasion to say (4.20.1). One is left wondering whether he is not intimating that, within what would later come to be called the *ancien régime*, commerce is not, in fact, a Trojan Horse.

Indeed, it is not even clear that "the commerce of luxury," when it extends itself to the fullest extent possible, is favorable to the monarchical principle—especially where, as in the case of France, it fosters the growth of large towns and of a great capital. "The more there are of men together," Montesquieu observes with an eye to Mandeville's *Fable of the Bees*, "the more vain they are & the more they sense the birth in themselves of the desire to draw attention to themselves in trivial ways [*par de petites choses*]. If they are so great in number that the majority are unknown to one another, the desire to distinguish oneself redoubles because there is more hope of success. Luxury gives this hope; each assumes the marks of the condition given precedence to his own. But as a consequence of the wish to distinguish themselves all become equal, & one distinguishes oneself no longer: where everyone wishes to make himself noticed, no one is noticed at all." From all of this, Montesquieu reports, there arises "a general discomfort [*une incommodité générale*]" rooted in a profound and inescapable disharmony "between needs & means"—for the citizens of the ancient Greek republics that were endowed with "singular institutions" were correct in their suspicion that, if they failed to proscribe "silver" and the commerce that coinage facilitates, these would "multiply infinitely their desires & supplant [*suppléer*] nature, which has given us very limited means for irritating our passions & for corrupting one another." As a consequence of the vanity which commerce favors and is favored by, men gathered together in cities and towns come to have "more desires, more needs, more fantasies." Commerce can never increase their means at a rate faster than vanity augments what they take to be needs. It is in "the nature of commerce," Montesquieu tells us, "to render superfluous things useful & useful things necessary" (1.4.6, 7.1, 4.20.23). The profound discomfort to which commercial civilization gives rise and the equality of condition associated with it can hardly have been favorable to the long-term prospects of continental Europe's great monarchies.

Montesquieu was aware of the problem well before he is likely even to have heard of *The Fable of the Bees*. The French whom Usbek describes in the *Persian Letters* are obsessed with honor, with glory, and rank (*LP* 87–88/89–90). But, in Paris, in the final days of Louis XIV, we learn that a different ethos sets the tone. In that city, Usbek finds that "liberty & equality reign." There, one may be distinguished by "Birth, Virtue, even merit displayed in war," but, "however brilliant" one's origins and attainments "may be," these "do not save a man from the crowd, in which he is confounded. Jealousy of rank is there unknown. It is said that in Paris the man who holds first place [*le premier de Paris*] is he who has the best horses for his Coach" (86.1–4/88). In consequence, among the Parisians, there appears an "ardor for work" and a "passion for self-enrichment" that "passes from condition to condition, all the way from the Artisans to the Great [*aux Grands*]," for "no one likes being poorer than the one he sees immediately below him." Paris presents itself as a city where "interest" is revealed as "the greatest Monarch on the earth." There, "you will see a man who has enough to live on until the day of judgment, who works without ceasing, & risks shortening his days, to amass, says he, enough on which to live" (103.45–60/106).[9] There, in short, you will see none but the bourgeois.

In Usbek's Paris, wealth has evidently become the sole determinant of a man's standing, and the passion for honor, glory, and rank has lost its purchase. That, under the influence of commerce, this should happen in the capital of what Montesquieu will later call "the most beautiful monarchy in the world" (*EL* 1.5.10) bodes ill for this form of government—especially if, as Montesquieu seems to have been persuaded, "it is a great capital, above all else, that fashions the general spirit of a nation" (*MP* 1903), especially if, as he also claims, "it is Paris that makes the French" (1581), especially if we can take at face value Usbek's claim that "the same Spirit is conquering [*gagne*] the Nation: one sees there nothing but work & industry" (*LP* 103.59–60/106). If the love of honor is the passion that serves as monarchy's *principe*, if it and it alone sets monarchy in motion, Paris was in Montesquieu's day a grave threat to the regime, for honor's eclipse presages monarchy's arrest.

These developments were of the greatest importance, but they would not have had quite as much disruptive potential had monarchy not come under siege for other reasons long before. Moreover, to make matters worse, as in due course we shall see, the commercial revolution underway in Montesquieu's age was seconded in nearly all its effects by another less tangible but no less dramatic and important shift in the circumstances within which eighteenth-century Europeans found themselves conducting their affairs: the onset of what Montesquieu himself called "enlightenment."

MONARCHY IN DECLINE

In discrete chapters hidden away within the second part of *The Spirit of Laws*, Montesquieu displays a keen sensitivity to the role played by historical contingency in setting limits to the range of political possibilities. The chapter immediately following his discussion of England's constitution he devotes to "the monarchies that we know" (*EL* 2.11.7). His purpose in using this phrase becomes clear in the next chapter, which seeks to explain "why the ancients had no very clear idea of monarchy" and opens with the claim that "the ancients had no knowledge at all of the government founded on a body of nobility & still less of the government founded on a legislative body formed by the representatives of a nation" (2.11.8). Aristotle was himself "visibly embarrassed" when he treated monarchy, Montesquieu insists. The peripatetic philosopher distinguished five species of monarchy and did so without regard to "the form of the constitution," emphasizing, instead, "matters accidental such as the virtues or the vices of the prince or matters external" such as "usurpation" and "the succession." Neither he nor any of "the ancients" knew anything of "the distribution of the three powers in the government of one alone," which explains why none of them was "able to fashion for himself a just idea of monarchy" (2.11.9). The only exception was the short-lived monarchy in early Rome (2.11.12), and it did not attract the attention of the ancient theorists.

The ignorance of the ancients in this particular stemmed from a lack of experience. That which they were inclined to call monarchy was either, as in the case of Sparta, a hereditary magistracy embedded within a republic or, as in the case of Persia, a despotism. They had no notion as to how one might distribute the three powers so as to temper the government of one alone (2.11.9–12). The moderns stumbled upon the requisite knowledge by accident. Prior to their conquest of the Roman empire, the Germanic peoples were free, as Tacitus makes clear. In Germany, they conducted their affairs by means of national assemblies; and, when this proved unworkable during and after the conquest, they opted to send "representatives" to such gatherings. Initially, because the lesser people were

slaves, the government that emerged was "a mixture of aristocracy & monarchy."
It underwent an evolution, however, as it became customary to issue "letters of
emancipation" to ordinary folk. "Soon, the civil liberty of the people, the prerogatives of the nobility & clergy, & the power of the kings found itself in such a concert," writes Montesquieu, "that I do not believe that there has ever been on the
earth a government so well tempered as was that in each part of Europe in the
time when it existed there." At the end of his discussion, he pauses to remark just
how "worthy of wonder [*admirable*]" it is "that the corruption of the government
of a conquering people should have formed the best species of government that
men have been able to imagine" (2.11.8).[10]

Apart from despotism, all forms of government would appear to be historically
contingent: all seem apt to strut and fret their hour upon the stage and then be
heard no more. This stricture evidently includes the monarchy that Montesquieu seemingly so much admires. That there will some day be what he pointedly refers to as a "dissolution of monarchies" he simply assumes (1.5.11). The
only matter in question is the timetable. That monarchy's demise is on the horizon Montesquieu does not expressly say. Instead, he intimates.

As we have seen, monarchy owed its existence to the peculiar history of Europe in the wake of the collapse of the Roman empire in the West, and the policies of Richelieu, Louis XIV, and their successors threatened to subvert and ultimately destroy its finest exemplar. It would be an error, however, to suppose that
Montesquieu's grave misgivings as to the tenor of royal policy in France ex-
hausted his fears. That which was attempted with considerable, if incomplete
success in France was pervasive on the European continent as a whole.[11]

When Montesquieu first introduces his peculiar account of monarchy's nature or structure, he notes, if only in passing, that in England "the prerogatives of
the lords, the clergy, the nobility, & the towns" have been abolished, and he then
later adds that "the English have removed all the intermediary powers that
formed their monarchy." In the intervening paragraphs, he adds that Spain and
Portugal have suffered a "loss of their laws," and he implies that both have already succumbed to despotism. In the same chapter, he deplores the attempts
made "in some states in Europe" to abolish seigneurial justice, and he takes that
bastion of monarchical liberty the French parlements to task for "ceaselessly
striking at the patrimonial jurisdiction of the lords & that of the ecclesiastics."
Even if it was a mistake to establish an independent ecclesiastical jurisdiction in
the first place, he intimates, once it has been established and has become an in-
tegral "part of the law of the land," it should be allowed to stand lest its elimination provide precedent for other, far more dangerous reforms. One must ask
"whether between two powers recognized as independent, conditions ought not

to be reciprocal, & whether it is not a matter of equal concern that a good subject defend the justice of the prince & that he defend the limits to that justice that have always been prescribed" (1.2.4).

Montesquieu does not dwell on the trends that he points out. Once in the past he had studied the process by which "Gothic Government became weaker little by little, either as a consequence of the necessary corruption of all Governments or because of the establishment of regular troops," and he had pondered the manner in which "Sovereign authority" had "insensibly replaced in Europe" its "Feudal" analogue (*RMU* 15.256–62). But, upon reflection, Montesquieu had judged it an imprudence on his part to publish the pertinent work; and so, as we have seen (I.1, above), he had instructed the printer to suppress his *Reflections on Universal Monarchy in Europe*. In *The Spirit of Laws*, when he discusses Europe's discovery of the principle of representation, he similarly refrains from remarking on the virtual disappearance of representative institutions from the European continent in the century and a half immediately preceding his own day. His silence was not a function of indifference. The subject was of great interest to him. He had given thought to the character of the Estates General and to the defects that had afflicted that institution (*MP* 160, 1184, 2257), and there is evidence suggesting that he was inclined to believe that "gothic government" of the sort he so admired (*EL* 2.11.8) "would have survived" in France had "the laws" stipulated early on, as they had in the Holy Roman Empire, that "an assembly of *seigneurs* and an assembly of deputies from the towns" be "joined with the assembly of Peers" (*MP* 1302, pp. 364–65). Moreover, in a brief essay that he drafted for the Regent soon after the death of Louis XIV, he had, in fact, suggested reviving provincial assemblies in the *pays d'élection* of France where they were in effect defunct.[12] If, in *The Spirit of Laws*, he does not speak at length regarding the recent history of these institutions, it is because he sees no necessity. Thanks to the controversy stirred up by Henri, comte de Boulainvilliers,[13] everyone in his day was aware of what had transpired. It was sufficient that he add to the praise that he lavished on the "concert" that had emerged in medieval Europe between "the civil liberty of the people, the prerogatives of the nobility & clergy, & the power of the kings" a passing word to the wise indicating his own awareness that this concert and the "well-tempered" government that attended it were no longer in place (*EL* 2.11.8).[14]

Precisely when this "well-tempered" government succumbed we are left to divine for ourselves. In his notebooks, Montesquieu wrote that "the death of Charles VII" on 22 July 1461 marked "the last day of French liberty." With the succession of Louis XI, he added, "one sees, in a moment, another king, another people, another politics, another species of forbearance [*patience*], and the passage from liberty to servitude was so great, so sudden [*prompt*], so rapid, the means so strange, so odious to a free nation—that one knows not how to regard this except as a fainting spell [*un esprit d'étourdissement*] that suddenly befell the kingdom" (MP 1302, pp. 366–67). Of course, this may be hyperbole. It appears in the collection entitled *Mes pensées*, as do further reflections of a similar nature on the same transition (195), on the growing attraction of the capital and court for the nobility in and after the reign of Francis I, on the manner in which urban and court society corrupted the morals of French women and subverted marriage (1272, 1340), on the role that came to be played by feminine intrigue in the distribution of honors and places at court (1254), and on the debasement (*avilissement*) that came to be associated with the achievement of high office (*dignités*) in France (1273)—and all of these may reflect a passing fancy on its author's part. Nonetheless, it does seem clear that monarchy in France was in trouble well before Richelieu came on the scene. If we had the *History of Louis XI* that Montesquieu is said to have composed and that a secretary mistakenly consigned to the flames, we would no doubt be better informed concerning Montesquieu's understanding of the details.[15]

Montesquieu's reticence on this subject in his published works deserves attention. In the years following the appearance of his *Persian Letters*, as we have seen (I.1, above), he had become profoundly sensitive to the role that censorship had come to play in modern monarchies. As he put it in his notebooks,

> Since the discovery of the printing press, there is no longer any true history. Before this, the princes were not attentive to it, and public administration [*la police*] was not mixed up with it. Today, all the books are submitted to the inquisition of the public administration [*cette police*], which has instituted rules of discretion. To violate these is an offense. One has learned in this fashion that princes take offense at what one says about them. In other times, they did not care; then, one spoke the truth. (MP 1462)

Over the years, Montesquieu had made himself expert in "the rules of discretion" established by what the French called *la police*, and he knew only too well what constituted "an offense."[16] He was perfectly aware that it would be dangerous for him openly to denounce as a despotism the absolute monarchy predominant in France in his own time, and he may even have come to think such an act counter-productive. It was principally with his own country in mind that Montesquieu prefaced his *Spirit of Laws* with the admonition: "One senses abuses long-standing, and one sees their correction; but one sees as well the abuses inherent in the correction itself. One allows the ill if one fears that which is worse" (*EL* Préf.). In the circumstances, it was not just safer, it was apt to do more good,

that he praise the French polity for the good qualities that it might still pretend to
possess. The best way to instill judiciousness is to display it.

It also made sense that Montesquieu simply describe in detail the species of
corruption to which monarchy is prone. In this fashion, he could leave it to those
among his compatriots who read his great book to consider at their own leisure
whether—in France, as in Spain and Portugal—the towns and the corporate
bodies constituted by the nobility and the clergy had been gradually losing their
privileges; whether the prince at Versailles ascribed "everything solely to himself" and summoned "the state to his capital, the capital to his court, & the court
to his person alone"; whether "pre-eminent [*les premières*] dignities" were in the
process of becoming "marks of a pre-eminent servitude," whereby "one deprives
the great of popular respect" and "renders them the vile instruments of arbitrary
power"; and whether "honor" was to an increasing degree "set in contradiction
with honors" so that "one is able to be covered at the same time with infamy &
with dignities" (1.8.6–7).[17] Alternatively, thoughtful readers could simply consider whether, in France, "the lucrative profession of tax-farmers" was in the
process of becoming "an honored profession" (2.13.20).

Montesquieu could also drop a hint. It can, for example, hardly be an accident that the only chapter title in his great book in which the word "danger" appears is a chapter which explores the consequences of "the corruption of the
principle of monarchical government" (1.8.8).[18] And if, upon consideration,
readers of *The Spirit of Laws* were still at a loss for answers to the questions that
Montesquieu posed, they could turn back to his *Persian Letters*, wherein Usbek
and Rica comment on the decline of the parlements (*LP* 89.13–23/92, 134/140)
and describe in unflattering terms the operation of court at Versailles (22/24, 35/
37, 122.20–30/127), depict the manner in which favor and the machinations of
adulterous women consistently trump merit in the making of royal appoint-
ments (cf. 35/37, 86.9–16/88, 104/107, with 87.42–49/89),[19] touch on the prominent status accorded tax farmers (46.33–45/48, 95/98), and ponder the moral
and political consequences of the speculation spawned by John Law's financial
legerdemain (126.9–23/132, 129.8–44/135, 132.1–2, 22–41/138, 136.43–105/142).
"In all hearts," writes Usbek, "I have seen suddenly born an insatiable thirst for
riches. In a moment, I have seen take form a detestable Conspiracy to enrich
oneself—not by honest work & generous industry but by the ruin of the Prince,
of the State, & of the Fellow-Citizens. . . . What greater crime can a Minister
commit than this—to corrupt the morals [*moeurs*] of an entire Nation, degrade
the most generous souls, tarnish the radiance of high office [*des dignitez*], obscure virtue itself, & confound those of highest birth in universal contempt?"
(138.28–31, 41–44/146).[20]

It is, tellingly, on this note—in describing the collapse of a financial system instigated by a radical proponent of *Étatisme* whose measures he will later, with considerable justification, describe as "lethal [*funeste*]," and whom he will denounce as "one of the greatest promoters of despotism that one has seen in Europe" (*EL* 1.2.4, 6.29.6)[21]—that Montesquieu brought his narrative of Usbek's observations in Paris to an end (*LP* 138/146).[22] That in subsequent letters he will go on to describe in detail the disintegration taking place within Usbek's harem in Ispahan at this very time and then recount the rebellion of his favorite wife, Roxane (139–50/147–61), is more telling yet—for, among other things, the harem is, as we have seen (I.3, above), a parody of the court at Versailles; and Roxane justifies her fierce assertion of her right to freedom on the basis of an appeal to the laws of nature of the very sort that will eventually be deployed in France against the monarchy itself (*LP* 150/161).

In *The Spirit of Laws,* for the reasons indicated, Montesquieu was less forthcoming. There seems also to have been another, perhaps more compelling reason that dictated in that work a measure of discretion on Montesquieu's part, as we shall soon see. "Sometimes," as he puts it, "silence expresses more than any discourse" (*EL* 2.12.12). Some things, he had learned in the years subsequent to his publication of the *Lettres persanes,* are best left unsaid.

THE PROSPECTS OF MONARCHY IN AN ENLIGHTENED AGE

In the eighteenth century, Europe was caught up in a shift in sensibility and outlook every bit as profound as that which marked Christianity's rise to predominance, and there was no greater proponent of this transformation than Montesquieu himself. Already in 1721, in his *Persian Letters,* he had had Rica make a mockery of the sacral character of the French monarchy (*LP* 22.24–42/24), as we have seen (I.3, above). In the same work, we find him using Usbek to announce and even celebrate the fact that Christianity has begun to lose its *élan.* As this fictional visitor from Persia puts it, "the Christians are beginning to rid themselves of the spirit of intolerance that animated them" in the past. The decision to expel the Jews from Spain is now, he asserts, recognized as a blunder, and "in France" the same can be said for Louis XIV's decision to harass the Huguenots for embracing a "faith that differed a little from that of the prince." To an increasing degree, he explains, Christians now recognize "that to love religion & be observant, one does not have to hate & persecute those who are nonobservant." They even "perceive," he tellingly adds, "that zeal for the advancement of Religion is different from the attachment to religion that one ought to have" (cf. *LP* 58.21–27/60 with *EL* 5.25.10).[23]

In 1748, in his *Spirit of Laws*, Montesquieu adopted the same self-protective literary trope. The sentiments expressed in the "remonstrance" directed at the inquisitors of Portugal and Spain that he put into the mouth of an unnamed Jew are clearly sentiments that he subscribed to himself. He, too, was pleased to "live in a century in which natural enlightenment [*la lumière naturelle*] is more alive than it has ever been, in which philosophy has enlightened human understanding [*éclairé les esprits*]," and "in which the respective rights of men with regard to one another & the empire that one conscience has over another are better understood" (5.25.13). In fact, Montesquieu's principal purpose in writing his magnum opus was to contribute to and encourage this salutary trend.[24]

Toward the end of his *Spirit of Laws*, in a chapter at one point intended to serve as the work's conclusion, Montesquieu accuses Plato, Aristotle, Machiavelli, Thomas More, James Harrington, and the various apologists for one-man rule of falling prey to their resentments, loves, and personal predilections. "In all times," he observes, "the laws come into contact with the passions & prejudices of the legislator. Sometimes they pass through & take on their color; sometimes they stop there & become incorporated with them" (6.29.19). From this propensity, he claims himself to be immune. "I have drawn my principles," he writes in the preface to his book, "not from my prejudices, but from the nature of things." Four paragraphs later, he spells out the practical import of his literary efforts. "It is not a matter indifferent that the people be enlightened [*éclairé*]," he asserts. "The prejudices of the magistrates had their beginning as the prejudices of the nation. . . . I would believe myself the happiest of mortals if I could act in such a manner as to make it possible for human beings to cure themselves of their prejudices" (Préf.)

When Montesquieu speaks of "prejudices," he has in mind "not that which causes one to be unaware of [*ce qui fait qu'on ignore de*] certain things but that which causes one to be unaware of oneself [*ce qui fait qu'on s'ignore soi-même*]." "Man" he describes as "that flexible being who accommodates himself in society to the thoughts & impressions of others." As such, he "is equally capable of knowing his own nature when one shows it to him & of losing even the sentiment of it when one conceals it from him" (Préf.). In Montesquieu's judgment, the task of the philosopher is to dispel human self-forgetfulness by bringing home to man just who and what he really is (1.1.1). From enlightenment in this regard, the French philosophe believes, a profound moral progress will ensue—for the "knowledge" produced by enlightenment is indistinguishable in its effects from the cosmopolitan spirit inspired by commerce. Just as "commerce cures destructive prejudices" and promotes "gentle mores [*moeurs douces*]" by causing a "knowledge of the mores of all the nations to penetrate everywhere" and by encouraging men to "compare" their own ways with those adopted else-where, so the "knowledge" produced by enlightenment will not only "enable human beings to cure themselves of their prejudices" but make them "gentle [*doux*]"—since "reason leads" men "to humanity," and "only prejudices cause them to renounce it" (Préf., 3.15.3, 4.20.1).

There are two reasons why this development is pertinent to an assessment of monarchy's long-term prospects. To begin with, European monarchy was sacral in its character,[25] and the species of enlightenment that Montesquieu champi-oned was, as he knew,[26] entirely incompatible with the requisite ethos of rever-ence and awe.[27] Moreover, even if one were to suppose that monarchy could somehow subsist in the absence of such a foundation on the strength of the pas-sion for honor alone, as Montesquieu may well have presumed, it matters a great deal that the honor which animates this polity is, "philosophically speaking, a false honor" (1.3.7)—utterly inconsistent with what one learns concerning the fundamental equality of man when one contemplates human beings in their natural state (1.1.2–3, 8.3, 3.15.7, 17.5). False, however, it certainly is (1.5.19, 5.24.6)—and, therefore, this honor is, as we have already seen (II.1, above), more consistent with "vanity" than with any justifiable "pride" (*EL* 3.19.9). It demands "preferences & distinctions" which have no foundation in nature at all. It is grounded, Montesquieu insists, in "the prejudice of each person & condition" (1.3.6–7). As such, it is constituted by a profound forgetting of self, and it is re-sponsible for "the miserable character of courtiers," who are distinguished by "ambition in idleness, baseness in pride, a desire to enrich oneself without work, an aversion for truth, flattery, treason, perfidy, the abandonment of all one's en-gagements, contempt for the duties of the citizen, fear of the virtue of the prince, hope looking to his weaknesses, & . . . the perpetual ridicule cast on virtue" (1.3.5).[28]

Of course, outside the court, this same "false honor" does cause those who are not "good men" to behave almost as if they were "good citizens" (1.3.6), and it has other salutary consequences as well. In the *Persian Letters*, as we have seen (II.3, above), Montesquieu describes "the desire for glory" to which it gives rise as a "fortunate fantasy"; and to this seemingly salutary species of self-forgetting, he at-tributes the astonishing cheerfulness with which French soldiers enter battle (*LP* 87.1–30/89).[29] In *The Spirit of Laws*, he suggests that "false honor" inspires a cer-tain politeness on the part of those in its grip, and he intimates that it makes men sociable, teaches them good taste, and inspires a certain joy in living (*EL* 1.4.2, 2.9.7, 3.19.5). At the same time, he contends, it limits the power of the monarch, prevents his exercise of power from becoming arbitrary, and gives rise to the tem-pering, the modifications, the accommodations, the terms, the equivalents, the

negotiations, the remonstrances, and the propensity to propose alternative policies which elicit from the prince and his court a species of enlightenment that
one would not otherwise find in the government of one alone (1.3.10, 5.10, 6.4).
Above all, as we have seen (II.1, above), it inspires the rule of law (*EL* 1.2.4, 5.10
6.1, 5–6, 9, 21, 2.11.11).

These are, however, consequences entirely unintended: they are rooted in
fantasy; they are grounded in self-forgetting; they reflect what, Montesquieu repeatedly emphasizes, is honor's whimsical (*bizarre*) character (1.3.8, 4.2, 5.19,
p. 303). Moreover, as he knew, these advantages are purchased at a very considerable price. For understandable reasons, when he addressed the question of
monarchy in his published works, Montesquieu was noticeably reticent with regard to its conformity with the demands of justice. In fact, nowhere therein did
he even raise the obvious and unavoidable question: whether a regime of artificial preferences and distinctions can be made compatible with what one can infer in this regard from the natural equality of man. In private, however, as one
would expect, he was more forthcoming. There, he was perfectly capable of
commenting on the "reasons why republics become more flourishing than
countries governed by one alone," and in his notebooks he was prepared to emphasize not only the "greater security" conferred within such governments on
"that which one has acquired," the fact that republics inspire "greater love for the
public good and the Fatherland" than do monarchies, and their propensity to offer "more means for succeeding by way of personal merit and fewer for succeeding by way of base behavior." He was also prepared to acknowledge as a highly
significant advantage the fact that republics provide "greater equality of condition and, in consequence, greater equality of fortune." If, he explained, one
wishes "to form a monarchical state," it is requisite to have "a rich nobility that
has authority and privileges vis-à-vis a people in poverty [*un peuple pauvre*]." The
unspoken truth of monarchical government is not just "luxury" and "expenditure in the Nobility." It is also "misery in the People" (*MP* 1760).[30]

It is in light of these observations that we should interpret the cryptic, carefully
worded claims that, some years before, Montesquieu had Usbek advance in the
Persian Letters: that "gentleness in Government contributes marvelously to the
propagation of the species"; that "all the Republics are a steady proof of this"; and
that "it is not the same in Countries subject to arbitrary power." For, in this context, when Usbek emphasizes that civic equality promotes "equality in fortunes"
and points to the concentration of property in the hands of "the Prince, the
Courtiers, & certain individuals" and "the extreme poverty" under which "all
others groan" where the government is arbitrary (*LP* 118/122), he is clearly speak-

ing in such a fashion as to remind Montesquieu's French readers of their own country, where the population was generally thought to be in decline. The polemical character of Montesquieu's remarks is even more obvious in the parallel chapter that would later appear in *The Spirit of Laws*—where, initially, he would emphasize the unfortunate demographic consequences that ensue when "the clergy, the prince, the towns, the great ones, certain leading citizens imperceptibly become proprietors of the entire country" and leave large parts of it "uncultivated," as was, he had no need to say, the case in France; and where he would then suggest that, in such a situation, the only way to promote population growth is to redistribute the land and to provide the citizens with the means for clearing and cultivating it (EL 4.23.28).[31]

Monarchy has other grave defects, apart from its propensity to promote inequality and injustice, and Montesquieu was especially sensitive to these. Where all are inclined to "judge men's actions not as good but as beautiful [*belles*], not as just but as grand, not as reasonable but as extraordinary" (1.4.2), honor's reign will have consequences, he intimates, that are neither good nor just nor reasonable. Because of the ethos of honor, monarchies take as their "object" the prince's "glory & that of the state" (2.11.5). In them, "men of war have no object other than glory, or at least honor or fortune" (1.5.19, p. 304); and though this "desire for glory" may well be a "fantasy," it is anything but "fortunate" (cf. LP 87.1–30/89). As a result of this particular desire's dominion over the imagination, "the spirit of monarchy is war & aggrandizement" (EL 2.9.2), and there is nothing salutary about this. "Above all," writes Montesquieu when he turns to the question of war, "let us not speak of the glory of the prince: his glory is his pride [*orgeuil*]." Indeed, wherever one derives "the right of war" from "the arbitrary principles of glory," there, in that very place, "streams of blood will inundate the earth" (2.10.2).

GLORY'S BITTER FRUITS

Montesquieu's misgivings in this last regard were nothing new. In the *Persian Letters*, by way of preparing an assault on the manner in which "the particular quarrels" and prickly honor of princes such as Louis XIV had been made a ground for going to war, he had had Usbek denounce "public Law [*Droit public*]" as it had come to be practiced under Machiavellian influence throughout Europe (LP 91–92/94–95). It would not be unfair to say, Usbek observed, "that the passions of the Princes, the patience of the Peoples, the flattery of the Writers have corrupted all of its principles." In consequence, he added, it has become "a

Science that teaches Princes just how far they can go in violating justice without upsetting their interests." It is a "design" forged by "the desire to reduce iniquity to a system for the sake of hardening their consciences" (91.1–14/94).

Montesquieu was not a willfully blind, unbending opponent of war.[32] He recognized that there are worse things, such as the loss of liberty and all of the provisions for personal security that accompany it. This he knew perfectly well. He recognized war's "necessity"; he contended that, when it is necessary, the decision for war is derived from "rigid justice" (*EL* 2.10.2). In the *Persian Letters*, he had been willing to have Usbek acknowledge that a people under attack could justly defend themselves and that they could come to the aid of an ally under assault (*LP* 92.12–13/95). In *The Spirit of Laws*, where he spoke in his own name and examined the question with much greater precision, he went considerably further. There, he discussed the conditions necessary for the justification of preventive war, and he hinted at the need to resist the quest for universal monarchy. In doing so, he adopted and restated an argument first articulated by François de Salignac de La Mothe-Fénelon, exiled archbishop of Cambrai, in the *Supplement* that his great nephew appended in 1734 to the *Examination of Conscience concerning the Duties of Royalty* that he had composed at some point prior to April 1711 for the edification of his former charge and prospective heir to the French throne, the duke of Burgundy.[33]

When Montesquieu considered what role was properly to be accorded to "offensive force" by the "law of nations," he took as his starting point a series of familiar suppositions—that "the life of states is like that of men"; that, just as human beings "have the right to kill in case of natural defense," so states "have the right to make war for their own preservation"; and that there is one crucial difference between the situation of human beings and that of states. Between citizens, he contends, "the right of natural defense" does not ordinarily eventuate in "the necessity for attack." They have as an alternative a recourse "to tribunals." They cannot justly have recourse to offensive force to defend themselves "except in brief, transitory circumstances [*les cas momentanés*] in which one would be lost if one waited for help from the laws." In short, in an emergency, citizens can resort not only to defensive force to fend off an attack in progress, but also to offensive force to pre-empt assault just before an attack in preparation has actually begun, but they cannot justly resort to offensive force as a preventive measure on the basis of a calculation with regard to their long-term security. When they can wait for help, this they must do.

States are, Montesquieu insisted, in a completely different situation, for there are no tribunals to which they can have recourse. "Between societies," he observed, "the right of natural defense sometimes carries with it [*entraîne*]" not just the right but "the necessity to attack, when a people sees that a longer peace would place another people in a position to destroy it & that attack at this moment is the only means for preventing its destruction." Here the focus is not on self-defense when attacked nor even on pre-emption in a dire emergency. In the absence of tribunals to which one can have effective recourse, prevention is sanctioned as well. If a statesman sees that a shift in the balance of power is taking place that would put the people whom he rules at a terrible and quite possibly fatal disadvantage should there later be war, he cannot delay. It would be irresponsible for him to spend an extended period in pondering the immediate intentions of his potential foe. These are arguably unknowable. In any case, over time intentions change and, when opportunity knocks, ambitions grow. Two facts are decisive: that "a longer peace would place another people in a position to destroy" the people for whose welfare he is responsible, and that, if he delays, "the moment" for effective, preventive action will pass. If the balance of power is about to be upset and there is a reasonable prospect that by war his people might prevent this from happening, he not only may attack: he must (*EL* 2.10.1–2).

Montesquieu understood the burdens of statesmanship. He came of age during the War of the Spanish Succession, as we have seen. He recognized that, in attempting to place his grandson on the throne of Spain, Louis XIV had deliberately sought to upset the balance of power and that, by this act, he had, in fact, initiated the war (*MP* 577). There is every reason to suppose that Montesquieu approved of the rationale underpinning the grand alliance that took shape between Britain, Holland, and Austria for the purpose of preventing Louis XIV from uniting in the hands of his prospective heir the crowns of France and Spain. Of course, it would have been exceedingly impolitic for a Frenchman to have publicly taken such a stand, and this Montesquieu understood. But, by tiptoeing around the subject in a manner sanctioned by Fénelon, he managed to hint at his opinion of the matter, and in his notebooks, for the information of future generations, he left a statement concerning the question that is dispositive, as we shall soon see.

In his *Spirit of Laws*, Montesquieu made no mention of the Spanish succession per se; and in what he published, he prudently confined himself in the abstract to domestic concerns, pertinent to any nation placed in the predicament once faced by Spain. When "the political law, which has established in a state a certain order of succession, becomes destructive of the political body for which it was made," he began, "there can be no doubt that another political law can alter that order." In fact, given that, when "a great state" becomes "an accessory to another state," it "is weakened" thereby, the new law of succession accords perfectly with the one it supplants, for the two are instrumental to a common end summed up by the principle: "the safety of the people is the supreme law." To be precise, Montesquieu adds, "if a great state has for an heir someone in possession of another great state, the first state can very well exclude him" from the throne; and, "with greater reason, it has the right to make him renounce" his claim. Moreover, by the same logic, the state in danger of being acquired and subordinated can stipulate in a marriage contract (as Spain, in fact, had) that "those contracting the marriage renounce on their own behalf & on behalf of their off-spring the rights that they would have had over it" (*EL* 5.26.23).

In the body of the pertinent chapter, Montesquieu speaks in permissive terms of what a political community may and may not do. In the title, however, he speaks, with greater candor, the language of necessity and self-preservation, and he indicates, moreover, that there are also occasions when the issue has to be settled under "the law of nations [*droit des gens*]" (5.26.23). With this last, cryptic gesture, Montesquieu points beyond what he actually published to an argument contained in what was originally intended to serve as the concluding paragraph of the chapter. This paragraph, he tells us in his notebooks, where he had it copied for future reference, he ultimately opted "for good reason [*pour rai-son*]"—no doubt, as in the case of his *Reflections on Universal Monarchy*, for fear that it would get him into real trouble—to excise from his *Spirit of Laws*. In it, he adds that, "if it happens that a state abandons itself and does not fashion a political law to preserve its independence or prevent its partition, and if such negligence can put other nations in peril, there can be no doubt that, in this case, it is necessary to regulate the succession not by the political Law but by the Right of nations [*Droit des gens*], which intends that the divers nations do all that they can to preserve themselves, and which does not suffer that their own ruin should depend on the negligence of a particular nation" (*MP* 1900). In short, given what was at stake, the decision to go to war for the purpose of insuring that there would never be a union of the French and the Spanish crowns, which was undertaken by England, Holland, and Austria in 1702, was not just predictable: it was morally necessary and entirely just.

Montesquieu was even prepared to argue that, had the French won the battle of Blenheim, the mere prospect that the balance of power in Europe was about to be overturned would have been sufficient to force the lesser powers to abandon their posture as free-riders and to join the war against France. They would not have tarried to ponder whether Louis XIV harbored hostile intentions in their regard. They would not have bothered to parse the fine distinction between pre-emptive and preventive war.[34] They would, he argued, have done what had become a moral necessity. "Germany," Montesquieu wrote in his *Reflections on Universal Monarchy in Europe*, "which had hardly entered the war except through the sale of soldiers, would have taken the lead: the North would have risen; the neutral powers would have taken sides, & his allies would have changed sides" (*RMU* 17.366–71).

Montesquieu was not an early modern Woodrow Wilson. He admired the speculative spirit of Charles-Irénée Castel, abbé de Saint-Pierre (*MP* 1295, 1940), to be sure, and he honored him for his character as well (1876)—especially, one must suspect, because of the remarkable stubbornness and courage that the man had displayed in defending the Regent's abortive experiment with *polysynodie*. But he also regarded as "chimerical" the onetime diplomat's revival of Henry IV's "Grand Design"—that great project for the establishment under French hegemony of a European federation which would be capable, by way of arbitration, of establishing perpetual peace on the continent; and he feared that, if implemented, this thinly disguised scheme for the establishment of universal monarchy might foster illusions and weakness of the sort to which Europe is subject today and thereby open the door to a new barbarian conquest (188). Like Fénelon, Montesquieu took balance-of-power politics as a given and even as a good, for he recognized that it and it alone stood between the likes of Charles V, Philip II, Louis XIV and the achievement of universal monarchy in Europe. Liberty on that continent would have been doomed had it not been for the wariness of the various powers, their commitment to sustaining the balance of power, and their propensity to anticipate and willingness to thwart imperial schemes—in extremis, if need be, by way of preventive war.[35] What Montesquieu objected to so strenuously was not balance-of-power politics: it was the policy personified by Louis XIV—the making of war on the basis of what he termed with evident disdain "the arbitrary principles of glory, of decorum [*bienséance*], of utility" (*EL* 2.10.2).

In a war justified solely on the basis of such arbitrary principles, Montesquieu subsequently observed, the fruits of victory rarely, if ever, justify the sacrifices made. "Ordinarily, in a monarchy which has long labored for conquest," Montesquieu reports, "the provinces of its original domain are thoroughly crushed [*très foulées*]. They have to suffer abuses both new & old, & often a vast capital, which engulfs everything, has deprived them of population." If the monarch were to treat his new provinces as he treated his old, "the state would be lost." The provinces that he had conquered would send taxes to the capital, and nothing would return; the frontiers would be ruined and would become weak; the peoples there would be disaffected; and the subsistence of his armies would be precarious. Such, then, is "the necessary condition of a conquering monarchy: a frightful luxury in the capital, destitution in the provinces at some distance, abundance at the extremities" (2.10.9).

If there is an element of passion and a sense of immediacy in these passages, it is because Montesquieu is here describing the France of Louis XIV into which he was born.[36] Moreover, the France of Louis XV, in which Montesquieu lived, persisted in embracing the "arbitrary principles" that had guided the Sun King's conduct, and it refused to acknowledge the fact, made evident during the War of the Spanish Succession, that, even when stretched to the limit, the French kingdom could not marshal the resources requisite for so ambitious a projection of power.[37] In 1740, France had joined Prussia in launching a war against Austria, aimed at placing a French nominee on the throne of the Holy Roman Emperor and at dismantling the Hapsburg empire. This war, in which France was to find itself locked in combat with Austria on the continent and with Great Britain in India, in the New World, and on the high seas, Montesquieu regarded as wholly unnecessary, profoundly unjust, and foolish in the extreme; and in the months in which he dispatched *The Spirit of Laws* in its various parts to his publisher in Geneva, he must have been in considerable distress, for the war, which had once again bankrupted France, was then still underway.[38]

Montesquieu's indictment of the spirit of monarchy was not, however, restricted to its consequences in time of war. Even in peacetime, he insists, this spirit wreaks havoc. When he first examines the question of taxation, he issues a warning against the propensity, especially prevalent in monarchies, to sacrifice "the real needs of the people" to "the imaginary needs of the state." These latter are pursued in consequence of "the passions & weaknesses of those who govern." They arise from "the charm of an extraordinary project, the sick envy of vainglory, & a certain powerlessness of the mind against its fantasies." All too often, Montesquieu observes, "those with an uneasy spirit [*esprit inquiet*]" have risen "under the prince to the head of affairs" and have confused "the needs of the state" with "the needs of their little souls" (2.13.1). In consequence of this, he later restates almost word for word the argument that he had advanced in his *Reflections on Universal Monarchy in Europe* (RMU 24.432–52):

> A new malady has extended itself across Europe: it has seized our princes & causes them to keep an inordinate number of troops. It has its redoublings & of necessity it becomes contagious: since, as soon as one state augments that which it calls its troops, the others immediately augment theirs in such a fashion that one gains nothing by this apart from the common ruin. Each monarch keeps on foot all the armies that it would be possible for him to have if his peoples were in danger of being exterminated; & one calls peace this condition in which all strive against all. In this fashion Europe is so ruined that individuals who were in the situation in which the three most opulent powers of this part of the world find themselves would have nothing on which to live. We are poor

with the wealth & commerce of the entire universe; & soon, as a consequence of having soldiers, we will have nothing but soldiers, & we shall be like the Tartars.

The ultimate result, Montesquieu explains, is "the perpetual augmentation of taxes [*tributs*]," and ruling out "remedies in the time to come" is the fact that "one no longer reckons on one's revenues" alone and that "one makes war with one's capital" as well (*EL* 2.13.17).

In the privacy of his notebooks, Montesquieu went even further, contemplating a prospect that was unthinkable. Alluding to the mutinies which had taken place within the French army among unpaid troops in the aftermath of the War of the Spanish Succession, he hinted at the likelihood that within Europe military despotism on the Roman model would in due course emerge. "So many troops," he mused. "Someday they will sense their strength" (*MP* 1345).[39]

There was, as Montesquieu recognized, a fatal contradiction at the heart of the ethos of honor that animated the monarchies of Europe in his day. On the one hand, by making impossible the development of a commerce of economy, this ethos diminished the resources that a state could command; and, at the same time, it promoted on the part of the ruling order within that state a profound longing for martial glory and an ambition for dominion which knew no bounds. Such a polity was bound to overreach and to fail—not just once, but over and over again—and sooner or later, as a consequence of insolvency and repeated humiliation, it would come apart. Bitter were the fruits of the monarchical principle.

A DEATH KNELL FOR THE OLD REGIME

In the long run, as Montesquieu surely understood, the indirect method that he had chosen for dispelling prejudice would also be likely to sound a death knell for the old monarchical order. It really is quite difficult to imagine how, in an increasingly commercial, communicative, cosmopolitan world, a "prejudice" rooted in artificial "preferences & distinctions," subject at all times to the dictates of "whimsicality," and associated with senseless aggrandizement, easily avoidable wars, and an intolerable tax burden can survive the quest to enlighten mankind and to remind men just who and what they really are. Although, in his *Spirit of Laws*, Montesquieu prudently refrained from spelling out in detail the implications of the vast expansion in commerce and that of the enlightenment project for the future of his native France, he had no need to exercise a similar self-restraint in the notebooks he kept.

There, in one entry, he acknowledged that "it appears that what one calls *heroic valor* is going to disappear [*va se perdre*] in Europe" (760). There, in another, he observed that "this spirit of glory and of valor is disappearing little by little among us"; and though he alluded to alterations in the *ius gentium*, to changes in the character of war, and to the manner in which monarchs rewarded their favorites at court and encouraged "idleness" on their part, he traced this development, first and foremost, to the fact that "philosophy has gained ground" and that "the ancient ideas of heroism and the new ones of chivalry have disappeared [*se sont perdues*]" (761). And there, in a third entry, he bluntly remarked that "philosophy and, I dare say, even a certain good sense has gained too much ground in this century for heroism to henceforth fare well." The pursuit of glory had come to seem vain and "just a bit ridiculous."

> Each century has its own particular genius: a spirit of disorder and independence was formed in Europe with the Gothic government; the monastic spirit infected the times of the successors of Charlemagne; thereafter the spirit of chivalry reigned; that of conquest appeared with regular troops; and it is the spirit of commerce that reigns today.
>
> This spirit of commerce causes one to calculate everything. But glory, when it is entirely alone, enters into the calculations of none but fools.

Glory of the sort that guided Alexander is, he insisted, "chimerical" and is subject "to the same revolutions as prejudice" (810). It can withstand anything — apart from ridicule (575), the only thing now feared in France (1491); and "that which in other times one called *glory, laurels, trophies, triumphs, crowns* is today paid out in cash" (1602).

In France, Montesquieu observed, the subversion of the ethos of honor accomplished by philosophy and commerce had also been powerfully reinforced by the peculiar species of "commerce with women" that had grown up in the shadow of the French court. Thanks to the influence that women exercise in and by means of the salon, he wrote, "all things in need of *esprit* have become ridiculous," and the French "have lost their taste" for the tragedies of Corneille and Racine. Moreover, as a consequence of the fact that women—who are incapable of attachment "to anything fixed"—now sit in judgment on men, vanity in France has lost the focus that transformed it into a passion for honor, glory, and renown, and contemporary Frenchmen no longer have a capacity for sustained and concentrated effort. "Men of war cannot endure war," and "men of affairs [*gens de cabinet*] cannot endure the conduct of public business [*cabinet*]." The serious particularities of ordinary political life have been drained of meaning and significance, and none but "general objects"—which, "in practice, come to nothing"—now receive acknowledgment. "In this fashion," Montesquieu ex plained, men in France have been deprived of their manliness. "There is now only one sex, and we are all women in *esprit*; and, if one night we were to change in appearance [*visage*], no one would perceive that there had been any other change. Even if women were to take up all of the responsibilities [*les emplois*] that Society confers and men were deprived of all those that Society can deny, neither sex would be discomfited" (1062).[40]

There is no doubt a case to be made for "gallantry" of the sort for which Montesquieu's compatriots were known, especially given the fact that women are, as he suggests in his *Spirit of Laws*, "quite enlightened judges with regard to a part of the things which constitute personal merit." But, as the very same passage implies, there are "things" constitutive of "personal merit" that, in his estimation, women do not judge well at all (*EL* 6.28.22). As he explains elsewhere in his great book, the "commerce of gallantry . . . produces laziness." It "causes the women to corrupt even before they have themselves been corrupted." It "gives to everything a price & lowers the value of what is important," and it "causes one to base one's conduct solely on the maxims of ridicule that women understand so well how to establish." In the end, as sexes, "the two sexes are spoiled: the one loses its distinctive and essential quality, as does the other; the arbitrary is introduced into that which was absolute" (1.7.7–8, 3.19.12).[41]

Of course, the most incendiary of the remarks found in Montesquieu's notebooks were left out of *The Spirit of Laws*, but they were excluded not because these ruminations were on their author's part mere passing thoughts. In this case, as we have just seen, what he dared not say openly in his great book, he found ways to insinuate; and, in his discussion of monarchical government, he made his misgivings clear—so clear, in fact, that he thought it expedient that he expressly deny that what he was writing was intended as a satire on that form of government (1.3.6). It is, then, in no way surprising that the depiction of monarchy in his magnum opus provoked a firestorm of criticism from intelligent readers (men and women alike), for—despite and, perhaps, even because of his disclaimers—it was easy to infer what Montesquieu had carefully left unsaid. Contemporary French churchmen, Jansenist and Jesuit alike, were hostile in the extreme, and *The Spirit of Laws* was soon condemned by the Sorbonne and placed on the Vatican's Index of Prohibited Books. It was clear to these ecclesiastics, as it should be clear to anyone who pauses to reflect on the implications of Montesquieu's insistent depiction of the principle of monarchy as "false honor," that one cannot dispel "prejudice" in the manner that he proposes without violating the principle and rendering ridiculous and therefore insupportable the whimsical passion that is supposed to set monarchy in motion (1.3.6–7, 5.19, 5.24.6).[42]

Had he lived to witness the French Revolution, Montesquieu would no doubt have recoiled in horror. Everything that he wrote in his magnum opus with regard to monarchy was aimed at instilling in those responsible for the conduct of policy a wisdom and a moderation sufficient to enable them to escape the pitfalls of despotism and so avoid the revolutionary consequences attendant on such foolishness.[43] We can be confident, however, that, had he lived to the end of the eighteenth century, Montesquieu would have been surprised no more by the course of events — once inherited institutions were abandoned, once things were fully set in motion, once the French nation's way of thinking had been shocked — than was his fervent admirer Edmund Burke, who once described the author of *The Spirit of Laws* as "the greatest genius which has enlightened this age."[44]

Montesquieu understood the dangers. He knew perfectly well that, in an age of enlightenment, commercial expansion, and rapid technological progress, in which educated women come to set the tone for society, the monarchical principle can only with great difficulty be sustained. Fortunately, in his opinion, there was another form of moderate government that was admirably suited to the new world then emerging. In the past, he wrote in his notebooks, France had displayed an "extreme facility" in recovering from "her losses, her maladies, her depopulations," and she had always found within herself the "resourcefulness" with which to "endure" and "even surmount the internal vices of her various governments" (*MP* 1302, p. 366). There was no reason that she should not do so again. Montesquieu recognized that, thanks to the role played by luxury, women, and fashion in France, mores and manners were there in flux,[45] and he evidently hoped that the intermediary powers still in existence there would, if properly reinvigorated, gradually, gently, and imperceptibly move the country in the proper direction. As the sixth part of his *Spirit of Laws* demonstrates, Montesquieu had immense respect for the capacity of the judicial power to effect a salutary transformation without shocking a nation's way of thinking—if endowed with wisdom and prudence, if inclined to the exercise of judgment, and if given time (*EL* 6.27–31).

One may doubt whether Montesquieu ever ceased to believe what he had Usbek say in his *Persian Letters* — that monarchy is "a violent state tending always to degenerate into a Despotism or a Republic," and that despotism is the more likely outcome (*LP* 99.9–16/102).[46] After all, as we have more than once noted, in his *Spirit of Laws*, he acknowledge that "the spirit of monarchy is war & aggrandizement" (*EL* 2.9.2), and he was perfectly prepared to draw the logical conclusion—that monarchies tend to outgrow the territorial limits that they can tolerate: so that just as "rivers run together into the sea, monarchies advance to lose themselves in despotism" (1.8.17).[47] Lest his readers fail to recognize the way developments in France had been tending, he repeatedly brought before their eyes as a warning the less than salutary example offered by Spain.[48]

The France that Usbek describes in the *Persian Letters* and that Montesquieu later depicts in his *Spirit of Laws* is not one: it is three, and they are profoundly at odds with one another. In the countryside, where the influence of the nobility of the sword is at its height, France presents itself as a monarchy governed by the code of honor. At Versailles, however, where obsequious priests and fawning courtiers hold the stage and women set the tone and rule the roost, the love of honor has degenerated into a degrading pursuit of royal favor, and France exhibits in embryo many of the attributes of despotic rule. And, in Paris—where liberty and equality reign, where jealousy of rank has disappeared, and honor has degenerated into mere vanity—money makes the man, and France has come to resemble England, a republic in the guise of a monarchy. A house so divided against itself cannot long stand, and Montesquieu knew it.[49]

If Montesquieu nonetheless harbored a modicum of hope, it must, then, have been due to the possibility that France might become a republic concealed under the form of a monarchy.[50] "The disadvantage" associated with a transformation from one form of government to another, Montesquieu wrote in his *Spirit of Laws*, "does not arise when a state passes from a moderate government to a moderate government, as from a republic to a monarchy or from a monarchy to a republic, but when it collapses & hurls itself from a moderate government into despotism" (1.8.8). In fact, he later added, "states often flourish more fully during the passage unfelt [*insensible*] from one constitution to another than they do under one constitution or the other. It is then that all the springs [*ressorts*] of the government are taut [*tendus*], that all the citizens lodge claims [*prétentions*]; that one is attacked or one is doted on [*qu'on se caresse*]; & that there is a noble emulation among those who defend the constitution in decline & those who advance the one that prevails." Rome had once followed such a trajectory (2.11.13), as we have seen (II.4, above), and, even more to the point, so had England, as Montesquieu was fully aware. Why not, he thought, why not, then, France?[51]

Four

DEMOCRACIES BASED ON COMMERCE

The Greek statesmen & political writers who lived under popular government knew of no force able to sustain them other than virtue. Those of today speak only of manufactures, of commerce, of finance, of wealth, & of luxury itself.

—*Charles-Louis de Secondat, baron de La Brède et de Montesquieu*

That Montesquieu doubted whether monarchy had a future was by no means evident to all of those who read *The Spirit of Laws* in its author's lifetime, and it is not universally recognized today. In the scholarly world, there have been many who have regarded him as a reactionary, writing in the interests of a declining feudal class;[1] and there are others, even now, who attempt to square the circle by depicting him as an aristocratic liberal, persuaded that the prospects for liberty were at least as good in France under what we now call the *ancien régime* as they were across the Channel in England, if not better.[2] He was, we are all too frequently reminded, a man of his time.

Claude Adrien Helvétius, who was a man of no mean intelligence, has often been cited as a witness by those intent on pressing this case. A letter attributed to him reports that, at some point in 1747, he had worked his way through the as-yet-unpublished manuscript of *The Spirit of Laws* not just once nor, in fact, twice but thrice. What he found therein left him appalled, or so the letter claims—and not just at what he regarded as an excessive and unjustified enthusiasm for the English form of government on the part of the book's author. In the judgment of the letter's author, the genius and erudition that Montesquieu had displayed in the work, though admirable, splendid, and beauteous, had been put to very bad use, and the letter, which is addressed to him, chides him for finding reason where nothing but folly reigns. "I see you," the letter begins in gentle mockery, "like the hero of Milton, floundering in the midst of chaos, and emerging victorious from the dark. Thanks to you, we are going to be thoroughly instructed concerning the spirit of the legislation of the Greeks, the Romans, the Vandals, & the Visigoths; we will be familiar with the tortuous maze through which the human spirit must crawl for the purpose of civilizing certain unfortunate peoples oppressed by tyrants or religious charlatans. You have told us: here is the world as it has been governed, & as it governs itself still. To it, you often attribute a reason & a wisdom belonging, in fact, only to you—for which, moreover, it will be very surprised to receive honors from you."

In the end, however, despite his jocular tone, the letter's author did not mince words. Where Montesquieu spied monarchy, he found only "despotism." He had only contempt for the "intermediary powers" so admired by the author of *The Spirit of Laws,* and he accused him of compromising with "prejudice" and of flattering the priests, the aristocrats, and other such despots. "This is the reproach that I have always advanced with regard to your principles [*principes*]," he wrote. That Montesquieu's *principes* might, in fact, "apply to the actual state of affairs," he readily conceded. But he argued that "a writer who wants to be useful to men should occupy himself more with true maxims in a better order of things to come than with consecrating those maxims which are dangerous, at the very moment when prejudice lays hold of them to put them to use and perpetuate itself." In his opinion, "to employ philosophy to give" to maxims of this sort "consequence is to cause the human spirit to take a retrograde step & to perpetuate the abuses that interest & bad faith are only too apt to promote."[3]

There are good reasons for doubting whether Helvétius wrote any such letter. No manuscript copy survives, and the letter is absent from the comprehensive edition of Helvétius's works ushered into print in 1781 by his widow and his disciple and literary executor Martin Lefebvre de La Roche. Moreover, the letter's tone is inconsistent with the tone of deference and deep admiration evident in Helvétius's epistolary intercourse with Montesquieu in the late 1740s and early 1750s, and the opinions expressed therein are contrary to those conveyed in the works that Helvétius published in the wake of Montesquieu's death. They are in complete and perfect harmony, however, with what we can discern of the political stance adopted by La Roche in 1789, the tumultuous year in which the letter was first published.[4]

For our purposes here, however, it matters not one whit that the letter attributed to Helvétius is a forgery. Whether it was composed by Helvétius upon reading *The Spirit of Laws* in 1747 or by La Roche in the heat of the political struggle that took place concerning the French constitution in 1789 is a matter of indifference. For the letter has this virtue: in the clearest possible fashion, it states a charge entertained by Anne-Robert-Jacques Turgot; subsequently taken up by his disciple Jean-Antoine-Nicolas de Caritat, marquis de Condorcet; elaborated by Antoine Louis Claude Destutt, comte de Tracy, in his *Commentary and Review of Montesquieu's Spirit of Laws*; and endorsed by Thomas Jefferson,[5] which is still being lodged against the author of *The Spirit of Laws* in our own time; and it articulates a political doctrine that can serve as a touchstone against which to test the character of Montesquieu's political teaching as applied to his native France.

THE SPIRIT OF MODERATION

At first blush, the author of the letter foisted on Helvétius would appear to be right. In the very first paragraph of the preface to his *Spirit of Laws*, Montesquieu issued an emphatic disclaimer: "I do not possess [*n'ai point*] by nature," he wrote, "a disapproving spirit [*l'esprit désapprobateur*]." He had no desire to offend, he insisted. Nothing at all had been placed in his book out of ill intent. With regard to the government of his country, his was a posture of filial piety and gratitude. "I do not write," he added a few paragraphs thereafter, "to censure that which is established in any country at all. Each nation will find here the reasons for its maxims, & from them one will naturally draw this conclusion [*conséquence*]: that it is appropriate that no changes be proposed except by those who are born with sufficient good fortune to be able to penetrate with a stroke of genius the entire constitution of a state." At this point, however, Montesquieu suddenly reversed course, or so it would seem, qualifying his disclaimer in a fashion that suggests that he had more in common with the letter's author than otherwise might appear to be the case. "It is not a matter indifferent," he observed, "that the people be enlightened [*éclairé*]. The prejudices of the magistrates had their beginning as the prejudices of the nation." And soon thereafter he intimated that he regarded it as his task to "make it possible for human beings to cure themselves of their prejudices" (*EL* Préf.).

Some of what Montesquieu wrote in his preface is obviously disingenuous. The author of the *Lettres persanes* had always been perfectly prepared to censure laws and practices rooted in harmful prejudices, and, as we have had ample opportunity to notice, in his *Spirit of Laws* he did so with some abandon—presumably because he regarded himself as someone with the good fortune "to be able to penetrate with a stroke of genius the entire constitution of a state." Montesquieu did not, however, share the conviction of the letter's author that there are only two forms of government—good and bad—and he did not relish the prospect in France of a sudden, abrupt change of regime.[6] In the preface to his

Spirit of Laws, immediately after endorsing popular enlightenment, he explained himself in a fashion that was in no way disingenuous: "In a time of ignorance, one harbors no doubt, even when one does the greatest evils; in a time of enlightenment [*lumière*], one trembles as well [*encore*] when one does the greatest goods. One senses the ancient abuses, one sees their correction; but one sees as well [*encore*] the abuses inherent in the correction itself. One leaves the evil if one fears that which is worse; one leaves the good if one is in doubt with regard to the better. One looks on the parts only to judge the whole as such [*du tout ensemble*]; one examines all the causes to see the results" (Préf.).[7] Given the predilection for prudence and caution evident in this passage, we should not be surprised to discover that, in the first book of *The Spirit of Laws*, Montesquieu expressly eschewed stating a general regime preference and insisted, instead, that the laws "ought to be such as to be appropriate for the people for which they are made" and that it would be "a very great accident if the laws of one nation" were "able to suit another" (1.1.3).

This is, in fact, one of the principal points that Montesquieu wished to drive home by means of his great work. If he endorsed a species of universalism by defining "law, in general," as "human reason, insofar as it governs all the peoples of the earth," he insisted at that same time on qualifying this claim. To "the political & civil laws of each nation," he attributed a measure of rationality. Despite their diversity, he said, these are "nothing other than the particular cases to which this human reason applies itself" (1.1.3). Or at least, as he put it in his notebooks, this is what one can reasonably expect; this is the presumption with which someone seeking the *esprit* of even a "whimsical [*bizarre*]" law should always begin (MP 1934).

Then, to explain why the laws of one nation are unlikely to suit another, Montesquieu outlined the overall argument of his work. First, and most important, he argued, one must consider the laws in relation "to the nature & to the principle of the government which is established, or which one wishes to establish," for that there be some such *rapport* is a matter of necessity: "either the laws form this government, as do the political laws, or they maintain it, as do the civil laws." Then, he added that one can also expect the laws to be related (*Elles doivent être relative*)

> to the country in its *physical aspect*; to the climate, whether it be icy, broiling, or temperate; to the quality of the terrain, to the country's situation, to its size [*grandeur*]; to the species of life adopted by the peoples, whether they be husbandmen [*laboreurs*], hunters, or herdsmen; they should be related [*elles doivent se rapporter*] to the degree of liberty that the constitution is able to tolerate [*souffrir*], to the religion of the inhabitants, to their inclinations, to the

riches they possess, to their number, their commerce, their mores, their manners. Finally, the laws have relations [*elles ont des rapports*] with one another; they have relations with their origin, with the object of the legislator, with the order of things on which they are established.

"It is," he concluded, "from all of these perspectives [*dans toutes ces vues*] that one must consider the laws" (*EL* 1.1.3).[8]

Long before, in his *Persian Letters*, as we have seen (II.1, above), Montesquieu had argued that the government "most in conformity with reason" and "most perfect" is "a Government gentle [*doux*]," free from unnecessary "severity," which "moves towards its end with minimal expense" by conducting "men in the manner that accords best with their propensities & inclinations" (*LP* 78.4–10/80). Now, in his magnum opus, Montesquieu contended that "the government most in conformity with nature is that government whose particular disposition best relates to the disposition of the people for whom it is established" (*EL* 1.1.3). In the interim, he had not changed his mind one whit. As he explained in the first chapter of what was until the last moment intended to be the concluding book of *The Spirit of Laws*, he had written that massive work, with its examination of the laws from an enormous variety of perspectives, "to prove" that "the spirit of moderation ought to be that of the legislator" (6.29.1). He wrote it, in sum, to alert lawgivers to the astonishing number of things that they had to take into consideration if they were to frame a government consistent with the particular disposition of the people for whom it was to be established.

In the penultimate chapter of the crucial twenty-ninth book of his *Spirit of Laws*, Montesquieu identified the principal obstacle standing in the way of the achievement of his aim. "There are," he observed, "certain ideas of uniformity, which sometimes lay hold of men of great spirit [*les grands esprits*]," such as Charlemagne, "& which infallibly strike small *esprits*, who find in it a species of perfection that they recognize because it is impossible that they not discover it: in public administration [*police*] the same weights, in commerce the same measures, in the State the same laws, in all parts the same religion." In sharp contrast with the author of the letter attributed to Helvétius, in contrast with those who would carry through the French Revolution and impose on France and its immediate neighbors the Napoleonic Code, Montesquieu doubted whether uniformity was "always without exception *à propos*"; and, by way of a rhetorical question, he insisted that "greatness of genius consists more in knowing in what case uniformity is needed & in what case differences are required" (6.29.18).[9]

If, at the very last moment, after the typesetting had begun, almost as an afterthought, Montesquieu transformed what had been a chapter into a book of one chapter (6.27) and, in a fury, composed three additional books (6.28, 30–31) so that he could conclude his *Spirit of Laws* with a series of studies on the evolution of Roman and French law,[10] and if he ultimately chose to situate in their midst the theoretical book originally intended as that massive work's conclusion (6.29), it was not simply and solely, or even primarily, because he hoped to correct the *thèse nobiliaire* advanced by Henri, comte de Boulainvilliers,[11] which he characterized as a "conspiracy against the Third Estate"; to refute the *thèse royale* advanced in response by the abbé Jean-Baptiste Dubos,[12] which he characterized as a "conspiracy against the nobility" (6.30.10); and to tone down, moderate, and redirect thereby the great political debate concerning the proper interpretation of the ancient constitution then raging in France.[13] It was above all—as he pointed out in his notebooks at the time (MP 1794–95, 1939), and as Jean Le Rond d'Alembert reaffirmed after his death[14]—because he wished to illustrate by example, as well as to describe in the abstract, "the manner in which laws are to be composed" (*EL* 6.29): the manner in which, under the pressure of developments, they decompose and are to be recomposed with an eye to the changing circumstances of the community they serve.

The examples that Montesquieu chose were particular and of special interest to his compatriots, and this was no accident. In introducing a book in which he discussed the relationship between the feudal law of the Franks and the establishment of their monarchy (6.30), and in preparing the way for a book in which he would trace the "revolutions" of that monarchy (6.31), he readily conceded that there would have been

> an imperfection in my work had I passed by in silence an event that took place once in the world and that may never again take place, had I not spoken of laws that one sees make their appearance in a single moment in all of Europe, without depending on those hitherto known, of laws which have produced good and ill without limit [*infinis*]; which have left behind rights when domain was ceded; which, in giving to many persons divers species of lordship over the same things or the same persons, have diminished the weight of lordship in its entirety; which have imposed divers limits on authorities [*empires*] overextended; which have produced rule and regularity [*la règle*] with a tendency to anarchy and anarchy with a tendency to order and to harmony. (6.30.1)

Montesquieu's interest in this subject was not, however, that of an antiquarian. Nor was his aim simply or even primarily parochial and polemical. In studying the origins and the evolution of the French monarchy in the past, he was also pondering the future development of monarchy in France and on the continent of Europe more generally. It is by no means fortuitous that—while the word *liberté* and its cognates appear forty-four times in Part One, one hundred thirty-three times in Part Two, ninety times in Part Three, twenty times in Part Four, and only twelve times in Part Five of *The Spirit of Laws*—they appear one hundred times in Part Six.[15]

Montesquieu was persuaded that gradual, piecemeal reform, especially when carried out prudently and unobtrusively by courts of law under the guise of legal interpretation, can be favorable to what he meant when he spoke of liberty. He was convinced that over time this approach is tolerably likely to produce a government whose particular disposition relates well to the disposition of the people for whom it has been established, and he very much doubted that a systematic uprooting and replacement of traditional customs and practices would eventuate in anything even remotely as apt.[16] Although he rejected the Aristotelian metaphysics that provided the common-law thinking of Englishmen such as Sir Edward Coke with its underpinning,[17] Montesquieu was thoroughly familiar with the species of artificial reasoning that the latter championed (*MP* 1645, p. 481), and he shared the predilections of those among Coke's successors, such as John Selden, who sought to justify the English jurist's mode of proceeding on the basis of the modern understanding of the role played by reason and passion in human life.[18] Like them, as we have had occasion to observe, Montesquieu believed that "reason has a natural" and even "a tyrannical empire." If, he observed, while discussing the evolution of the civil law in France, "one resists" reason, "this resistance" will nonetheless prove to be the foundation of reason's "triumph." "Just a little time," he writes, "& one is forced to return to her side" (*EL* 6.28.38). To reasoning as a process, Montesquieu was, in consequence, the greatest of friends, and this is why he thought it possible, on the basis of the *principes* that he had discovered on his travels abroad and that he had with great effort subsequently articulated in his book (Préf.), to specify the logic or *esprit* evident in laws produced in the course of time by the repeated application of "human reasoning" to "particular cases" (cf. 1.1.3 with 6.28.6).[19] But, by the same token, to rationalism left in politics unchecked, unbridled, and unobstructed, he was firmly, even fiercely opposed.

To understand fully the import of Montesquieu's rejection of rationalism in politics, and to grasp the significance of what he means by legislative moderation, one must attend to the fact that he was profoundly sensitive to the psychological impact of political change. This accounts for his warning lawgivers that an attempt on the part of "those who govern" to "establish" institutions or practices "that shock a nation's way of thinking" is bound to be counter-productive (3.19.3). There is in each nation, he believed, a "general spirit," an *esprit général* formed by "the climate, religion, the laws, the maxims of government, the example of things past, mores, & manners" (3.19.4), and, as we have seen (III.1, above), when he first deployed the crucial term in his *Considerations on the*

Causes of the Greatness of the Romans and their Decline, he did so with an eye to asserting that all government is limited in its scope. It was, he contended, on this *esprit général* that "power itself has its foundation," and "when power," even despotic power, "shocks this *esprit*, it shocks itself & brings itself of necessity to a halt" (*CR* 22.207–15).

Moreover, as we have also seen (II.2), Montesquieu believed that political liberty in its relation with the citizen is for the most part a state of mind. However well-meaning a reform might be, he observed, if it shocked "a nation's way of thinking," it would upset profoundly whatever tranquillity of mind was enjoyed by those within that nation, and it would instill in the governed the "opinion" that they lived under a "tyranny" (*EL* 3.19.3). In this context, with particular reference to the French nation—endowed as it was with "a sociable humor, an openness of heart, a joy in living, a taste, a facility for communicating their thoughts"—Montesquieu added that a legislator should "take care not to change the general spirit of a nation" for fear that, in attempting "to upset [*gêner*], by the laws, its manners," he would "upset its virtues" as well. It is, he insisted, essential that "the legislator follow the spirit of the nation when it is not contrary to the principles of the government, for we do nothing so well as that which we do freely while following our natural genius" (3.19.5). It is here that he asserted that, even for "the best laws, it is necessary that minds & spirits [*esprits*] be prepared" (3.19.2). Such was the argument that he directed at men like the author of the letter once attributed to his friend Helvétius.

THE TASTE FOR DOMINATION

The same set of convictions governed Montesquieu's attitude regarding the administration of territories conquered in war. As we have seen (I.2, II.2, III.3, above), he had no use for the *ius gentium* of the Greeks and the Romans, which eventuated, he contended, in the extermination of those conquered. Nor was he prepared to sanction eliminating a conquered society, dispersing its inhabitants, and selling its land. The first policy he thought contrary to "the law of nature, which arranges everything so that it tends towards the conservation of the species." Both policies he considered contrary to "the law of natural enlightenment, which wishes that we do unto others as we would have them do unto us." In this regard, Montesquieu preferred "the right of nations [*droit des gens*]" as it was practiced within Europe in his own time. The right to conquer derives, he insisted, from the right to go to war. Its aim is self-preservation. Moreover, he observed, conquest is a species of acquisition, "& the spirit of acquisition carries with it the spirit of conservation & of use, not that of destruction." The policy generally followed within Europe in his own day—a policy which dictated that the conquering power not shock the conquered nation's way of thinking but "continue to govern" the society conquered "according to its own laws & take for itself only the exercise of the political & civil government"—Montesquieu regarded as admirable. "It is necessary," he concluded, "to render homage to our modern times, to the species of reasoning dominant at present, to today's religion, to our philosophy, & our mores" as well (*EL* 2.10.2–3, 5.24.3).

It is also necessary, he believed, to admire Alexander the Great. After his "conquest" of Persia, Montesquieu tells us, Alexander "abandoned all of the prejudices that had served him in making it. He took up the mores of the Persians in order to avoid upsetting the Persians by making them take up the mores of the Greeks," and "to the peoples conquered" he left not only "their mores," but "their civil laws as well," and often he even left in place "the kings & governors that he had found" in authority when he had arrived. "He showed respect for ancient traditions and for all the monuments reflecting the glory or vanity of the peoples" conquered. In short, if "the Romans conquered all in order to destroy all, Alexander wanted to conquer all in order to preserve all; & with regard to whatever country he entered, his first ideas, his first designs, were always to do something capable of augmenting its prosperity & power" (2.10.13–14).[20] This he did chiefly through a systematic promotion of commerce (4.21.8–9).[21]

All of these reservations notwithstanding, there were circumstances in which Montesquieu was prepared to sanction a conquering power's administering a salutary shock to a nation's way of thinking. In certain circumstances, he favored its giving to a conquered society "a new political & civil government." On this matter, he spoke with caution: "A conquest can destroy harmful prejudices & place, if one dare speak in this fashion, a nation under a better genius" (2.10.3–4). Montesquieu did not sanction thereby what we sometimes now euphemistically call humanitarian intervention. In this sphere, above all others, he was suspicious of "arbitrary principles," whether they derived from a concern with glory, with decorum, or utility (2.10.2), and he was not inclined to multiply the justifications for going to war. Instead, he distinguished carefully between the right to go to war, which derived from the right of self-defense and sometimes justified conquest, and the dictates of the *droit des gens* with regard to peoples already conquered; and, tellingly, he cited the all-important "law of natural enlightenment" solely with regard to the latter (2.10.2–3).[22] In the appropriate circumstances, he explained, "it is up to the conqueror to make reparation [*reparer*] for a part of the evils that it has done." The right of conquest he defined as "a right necessary, legitimate, & unfortunate, which always leaves an immense debt to be paid if it is to settle its obligations to human nature" (2.10.4).

According to Montesquieu, the requisite circumstances, though extreme, arise with some frequency. "Ordinarily," he observes, conquered states lack "the strength [*force*]" that they possessed at "their institution." Time has passed; "corruption has been introduced; the laws have ceased to be executed; the government has become an oppressor." When "a government has arrived at the point where it is no longer able to reform itself," he asks, "what does it lose from being refounded?" Imagine, he suggests, "a people where, by a thousand ruses & artifices, the rich have exercised an infinity of means for usurpation" and have done so "*insensiblement*—in such a manner that it is not felt." Imagine a people "where the unfortunate, who groans as he sees what he believes to be abuses become laws, is subject to oppression & believes that he is wrong in feeling oppressed." A conqueror, he writes, "a conqueror, I say, is able to alter the direction in which everything is tending [*dérouter tout*]," and "the first thing to suffer violence" at this conqueror's hands should be what Montesquieu calls, in a poignant formulation, *la tyrannie sourde*—a tyranny that is deaf and indifferent, a tyranny that is muted, muffled, and well concealed (2.10.4).[23] The author of the *Persian Letters* was no friend to sacral polities grounded on the conviction that an individual is God's viceroy on earth or that an order of priests has divine sanction for rule;[24] and, as we have just seen (III.3, above), though exceedingly reticent in public, he was by no means oblivious to the fact that a polity based on "false honor," which demands artificial "preferences & distinctions" and is grounded in "the prejudice of each person & condition," is unjust and prone to serious abuse. There was less of a difference between Montesquieu and the author of the letter attributed to his friend Helvétius than one might imagine.

Nonetheless, in circumstances less extreme, where there has been no conquest—above all, where the existing government, though it may be considerably less than perfect, is not beyond redemption—Montesquieu was profoundly at odds with the author of the letter: for, in such circumstances, he really was prepared to compromise with prejudice and to flatter those predominant within the existing political order. This he no doubt did in his depiction of European monarchy—in part, presumably, with an eye to the manner in which his book would be received by the authorities in Paris who had ordered the arrest of Voltaire and the burning of his *Philosophical Letters*; in part, surely, in order to secure a hearing within the ruling order of his native land; and in part because he recognized that shocking French public opinion was likely to do far more harm than good. Flattery can be and, in his case, often was deployed as a mode of exhortation. He praised the English for the qualities that he wished them to have, and he did the same for the French. In any case, where circumstances were at all propitious, Montesquieu's aim was not to effect an immediate and violent purgation of prejudice himself. It was something rather more modest: he sought only to equip his readers in such a way as to "make it possible for human beings to cure themselves of their prejudices" (*EL* Préf.). In short, he sought to render men capable of self-government.

The real difference, then, between Montesquieu and the author of the letter attributed to Helvétius was not simply that the latter was in so great a hurry that he was prepared to run rough-shod over the sensibilities of his compatriots and that the former was not. Montesquieu thought that something more was at stake. In his judgment, moderation was requisite, for haste really would make waste. There are occasions, he firmly believed, in which a "wise legislator" will proceed "in a manner *sourde et insensible* — muted, muffled, well-concealed, & unfelt" (1.6.13, p. 323).

Montesquieu may have harbored another concern as well, for he had long been sensitive to the fact that tyrannical behavior is perfectly compatible with a pretense to and even a plausible presumption of enlightenment. When he composed his *Persian Letters*, he exploited the literary conceit at the heart of the book for two discrete purposes. One of these we have from time to time had occasion to note: by adopting the perspective of a foreign visitor, Montesquieu was able to lampoon with great abandon and an appearance of good humor the society in which he lived. The other we have barely mentioned. In Montesquieu's epistolary novel, there was also a parallel narrative, distinct from that of foreign travel, which was unfolding at the same time. While Usbek, his younger companion Rica, and their compatriot Rhedi are exploring France, Venice, and other parts of Europe, Usbek is in regular communication with the eunuchs back home who guard his harem and with his many wives. His trip abroad he initially represents as a philosophical adventure undertaken for the sake of enlightenment, enabling him to achieve a species of detachment and objectivity otherwise hard to obtain (*LP* 1.5–10). Although this turns out to be a pretext (8.1–25), it nonetheless accurately describes his actual pursuits in the West and, even more emphatically, those of his Persian friends Rica and Rhedi (8.13–14, 23/25, 46/48). In Usbek's depiction of France and of Europe more generally, understanding is what he in some measure arguably achieves, and this acute understanding and that of his fellow travelers is for the reader the principal attraction of the book.[25] But, in dealing with his slaves and wives, Usbek does not display similar enlightenment. He is perfectly capable of articulating a doctrine of radical personal autonomy: he asserts his right to withdraw from a society that has become burdensome to him; he even contends that he has a right to take his own life (74/76). He is thoroughly familiar with the doctrine of natural liberty that underpinned the radical Whig interpretation of England's Glorious Revolution articulated by John

Locke (101.4–16/104).[26] But, as becomes increasingly and in the end dramatically clear, it is as a despot, denying the natural liberty of his wives and slaves, that he actually lives,[27] and in his self-forgetfulness in this particular regard he personifies precisely and perfectly what Montesquieu means when he speaks of prejudice (*EL* Préf.).[28]

Montesquieu even intimates that philosophical detachment and prejudice of this very sort may be closely allied. In what constitutes on chronological, if not narrative, grounds the very first letter in his *Lettres persanes*, Zachi, one of Usbek's wives, writes to lament his departure, and in doing so, she reminds him of "that famous quarrel among your wives." Each of the women in Usbek's harem, she explains, claimed to be superior in beauty, and this occasioned a contest:

> We presented ourselves before you after having exhausted everything that the imagination is able to furnish in the way of finery [*parures*] & of ornament. You looked with pleasure on the miracles of our art: you marvelled at the lengths to which ardor had carried us in the quest to please you: but soon you caused these borrowed charms to give way to graces more natural: you destroyed our work: it was necessary that we strip off the ornaments, which you had come to think awkward and inconvenient [*incommodes*]: it was necessary to appear before your gaze [*vue*] in the simplicity of nature. I counted shame as nothing: I thought of my glory alone. Fortunate Usbek, what charms were laid out before your eyes: we watched you for a long time wander from enchantment to enchantment: your uncertain soul remained for a long time undecided [*sans se fixer*]: each new grace demanded from you tribute: in a moment we were all covered with your kisses: you carried your curious gaze [*curieux regards*] into the most secret places: you made us adopt for an instant a thousand different positions: always new commands, & always a new obedience. (*LP* 3.10–25)

Slowly, imperceptibly, what begins as a beauty contest turns into something else, as erotic desire, then curiosity gets the better of Usbek's humanity.[29] It is perhaps in this light that we should read Montesquieu's cryptic observation that "the speculative sciences [*les sciences de spéculation*] render men savage" (*EL* 1.4.8). In his estimation, for detachment and the spirit of contemplation, men pay a very high price (2.14.7; 4.23.21, pp. 705–7; 5.24.10–11).

In his *Spirit of Laws*, in the book preceding his extended discussion of "the manner in which to compose laws," Montesquieu pointed explicitly to the political dimension of the all-too-human propensity for self-forgetfulness. "By a misfortune attached to the human condition," he observed,

> great men who are moderate are rare; & as it is always easier to follow one's impulse [*force*] than to arrest it, within the class of superior people, one may per-

haps with greater facility find people extremely virtuous than men extremely wise.

The soul tastes so much delight in dominating other souls; even those who love the good love themselves so strongly that there is no one who is not so unfortunate as to still have reason to doubt his own good intentions: &, in truth, our actions depend on so many things that it is a thousand times easier to do good than to do it well. (6.28.41)

The consequences are all too easy to see. As Montesquieu observes in an early chapter devoted to punishment, "Often a lawgiver, who wishes to correct an evil, dreams of nothing but this correction; his eyes are open to this object and closed with regard to the inconveniences. Once the evil has been corrected, one sees only the harshness of the lawgiver; but there remains a vice in the State, which this harshness has produced: minds [*esprits*] are corrupted; they have become accustomed to despotism" (1.6.12).

If Montesquieu resisted the temptation posed by uniformity, if he preferred piecemeal reform, if he thought it essential that human beings be left to cure themselves of their own prejudices, it was presumably because he recognized that for others, convinced of their own enlightenment, to attempt to effect a cure on their behalf was likely to eventuate in tyranny. To grasp where piecemeal reform might ultimately lead in the case of France, one must consider Montesquieu's account of commercial republicanism, and one must ascertain what he surmised concerning the prospects of this particular form of government.

DEMOCRACIES BASED ON COMMERCE

Early in the second part of *The Spirit of Laws*, when Montesquieu remarks that "the spirit of monarchy is war & aggrandizement," he adds an assertion that, in context, must seem more than passing strange, contending that "the spirit of republics is peace & moderation" (2.9.2). As we have already seen (II.2, above), such a claim can hardly be advanced with regard to the virtuous republics that have been the primary focus of his attention up to that point. As Montesquieu later admits, "aggrandizement was the object of Rome; war, that of Lacedaemon" (*EL* 2.11.5). "It is necessary," he insists, "to regard the Greeks as a society of athletes & warriors." In fact, it is crucial to recognize that the "Greek towns" had as their "principal object war" (1.4.8). Although one might be tempted to think of Athens as a commercial polity and an exception to this rule, she was, in fact, "full of projects for glory" and, therefore, "more attentive to the extension of her maritime empire than to its enjoyment" (cf. 1.5.6, 4.20.4, with 4.21.7), as we have also seen (III.2, above). In keeping with this fact, the *ius gentium* governing Athenian conduct was no less "abominable" than the code of war honored in the other ancient cities, for she was no less inclined to destroy cities captured and to sell into slavery their inhabitants than they were (*EL* 6.29.14). In general, the spirit of Montesquieu's ancient republics was anything but "peace & moderation." They were no less oriented toward war and aggrandizement than were the monarchies peculiar to modern times.[30]

To begin to make sense of Montesquieu's odd claim regarding the republican propensity for peace and moderation, one must first recall to mind his suggestion that commerce is conducive "to peace" (4.20.2), and one must then attend closely to what he says earlier, in the midst of his discussion of the importance of frugality to democracy, for there he digresses briefly to allude to a puzzling phenomenon, an apparent contradiction in terms, not often mentioned in scholarly analyses of his account of republicanism, and even more rarely discussed at length.[31] "It is true," Montesquieu concedes in a brief digression, "that when democracy is based on commerce, it can very easily happen that particular individuals have great wealth & that the mores there are not corrupted." This odd and unforeseen result comes about, he explains, because "the spirit of commerce" quite often "carries with it a spirit of frugality, economy, moderation, industry, wisdom, tranquillity, orderliness, & regularity [*règle*]. In this fashion, as long as this spirit subsists, the wealth that it produces has no bad effect. The evil arrives when an excess of wealth destroys this spirit of commerce; suddenly one sees born the disorders of inequality, which had not yet made themselves felt" (1.5.6).

Montesquieu suggests that within such a republic one can best sustain "the spirit of commerce" if one makes arrangements to insure that "the principal citizens engage in commerce themselves," and he tellingly indicates that this works best where "this spirit reigns alone & is crossed by no other," where "the laws favor it," where "the same laws, by their dispositions, divide fortunes in proportion to their increase through commerce & thereby place each poor citizen in a condition of ease sufficient that he can work as others do & each rich citizen in a condition of mediocrity sufficient [*dans une telle médiocrité*] that he has need of work if he is to preserve what he has or acquire more." In "a commercial republic," Montesquieu concludes, the statute which "gives to all children an equal proportion in succession to their fathers" is "a very good law." Where partitive inheritance is the norm, it makes no difference "what fortune the father has made," since "his children, always less rich than he was" at the time of his death, "will be induced to flee luxury & to work as he did" (1.5.6).

Montesquieu does not dwell on this option, and in the pertinent passage he mentions no examples apart from Athens. In the first part of his work, he seems far less interested in exploring the nature of commercial republicanism than in examining the character of a species of "republic," governed by an entirely different, far more martial spirit, which is "based on virtue" and on that alone (1.5.19, p. 305); and to this end he focuses his attention first and foremost on polities endowed with "singular institutions," as we have seen (II.1, 4, III.1, above).

Nor does Montesquieu have much to say on the subject of commercial republicanism in Parts Two and Three of *The Spirit of Laws*. There, to the extent that he interests himself in what he thinks of as democratic republicanism, his attention is focused on Rome, the greatest and most successful of the ancient warrior republics. It is only in the fourth part of his work, where he makes commerce itself his theme, that he picks up the thread.

It is in this context that Montesquieu suggests that commerce has a "connection [*rapport*] with the constitution." If, in monarchies, "it is ordinarily founded on luxury," he explains, so "is it often founded on economy in the government of the many." In "republics" such as Tyre, Carthage, Corinth, Marseilles, Rhodes, Florence, Venice, and Holland, "the merchants eye all the nations of the earth & carry to one that which they take from another." It is in the "republic based on commerce," that merchants practice a "commerce of economy," making modest gains but never ceasing to profit, moving imperceptibly from trade on a small scale to commerce on a middling and even grand scale. It is here that, for the sake of sustaining their carrying trade, they are sometimes even willing to conduct a particular trade at a loss. It is in republics, where merchants possess "a greater certitude" with regard to the safety of "their property" and remain confident that what they acquire will be "secure," that they mount "the greatest enterprises" and display "an audacity not to be found" anywhere else. It is here, therefore, that one finds banks and sometimes great trading companies as well (*EL* 4.20.4, 6, 10, 17, 21.7).[32]

In the course of this discussion, without any sort of fanfare—merely by mentioning Florence, Venice, and Holland alongside Tyre, Carthage, Corinth, Marseilles, and Rhodes—Montesquieu also makes it clear that commercial republics have one highly important attribute that distinguishes them from republics of virtue: they still exist. This fact deserves close attention and careful investigation.

In *De l'Esprit des lois*, as in his *Considerations on the Romans* and his *Reflections on Universal Monarchy in Europe*, as we have seen (I.1–2, II.2, above), Montesquieu follows Machiavelli in insisting that a cultural chasm separates antiquity in Europe from modernity.[33] In the preface to his magnum opus, he makes a point of the fact that "antiquity" has its own peculiar "*esprit*," and he indicates that he has taken great care in his work "to capture its *esprit* in order not to look on as similar those cases that are genuinely different." Then, lest the importance of this crucial matter be neglected, he repeats precisely the same point, but in different words, indicating that his aim has been "not to miss the differences distinguishing cases that seem similar" (*EL* Préf.). Thereby, he tests his reader's capacity to discern the similarities in cases that seem different, and he playfully hints as well at the need to develop this capacity.[34] In the work's penultimate book, he will once again reiterate the point: "To transport back into centuries remote all the ideas of the century in which one lives—this is, of the sources of error, the one that is the most fertile. To those people who wish to render modern all the former centuries, I will say what the priests of Egypt said to Solon: 'O Athenians! You are nothing but children'" (6.30.14).

In the interim, as we have also seen (II.1–2, above), Montesquieu clarifies what he means by the *esprit* predominant in antiquity. "The better part of the ancient peoples lived in governments which had virtue for their principle," he explains, "& when this principle was in full force there, they did things which we no longer see today, & which astonish our little souls." Their advantage lay in the fact that "their education never suffered contradiction: Epaminondas, the last day of his life, said, heard, saw, & did the same things as in the age when he commenced instruction." In contrast, Montesquieu insists, "we today receive three educations different from & contrary to one another: that of our fathers that of our schoolmasters, that of the world. What we are told in the last overthrows the ideas imparted by the first two." The difference between our situation and that of Epaminondas is due, we are told, "in considerable part to the contrast existing in our day between the engagements that arise from religion & those that arise from the world—a contrast that the ancients knew nothing of" (*EL* 1.4.4). This is apparently why the moderns possess such "little souls," and it explains why in modern times republics of virtue no longer exist.[35]

Of course, in a republic where "the spirit of commerce" inspires "work" rather than luxury and idleness, it may co-exist with "virtue" of a sort (1.7.2): as Pierre Nicole, Pierre Bayle, and Bernard Mandeville had pointed out (II.3, above), the market rewards diligence, frugality, and civility, and the commercial spirit is conducive to a species of self-discipline. But it is fair to say that democracies based on commerce are not ordinarily founded on political virtue as such.[36] When Montesquieu attributes to their citizens "a spirit of frugality, economy, moderation, industry, wisdom, tranquillity, orderliness, & regularity" (*EL* 1.5.6), he makes no mention whatsoever of "the principle" or "human passions" that are supposed to "set" democratic republics "in motion." He is silent as to their citizens' "love of the laws & the fatherland"; he nowhere attributes to these citizens a spirit of self-renunciation; he does not contend that the merchants within a commercial republic will prefer the public interest to their own; and if he emphasizes their frugality, he nowhere suggests that, in these polities, the economic inequality produced by commerce is in any way tempered by "a love of equality." Montesquieu is silent in all of these regards because he knows perfectly well that "commerce corrupts pure mores" and that the spirit of commerce and communication is incompatible with republican virtue (cf. 1.5.6 with 1.3.1, 4.5, 5.3–5, and see 1.4.6, 4.20.1). Although commercial republics were evidently marginal in antiquity, they survived Christianity's victory over paganism for the same reason that despotism did: they are founded on a phenomenon no less cosmopolitan and no less alien to the spirit of particularism required by virtuous republics than is Christianity itself. While "the Greek statesmen & political writers [*les politiques grecs*] who lived under popular government knew of no force able to sustain them other than virtue," their counterparts in the republics of Montesquieu's day "speak only of manufactures, of commerce, of finance, of wealth, & of luxury itself" (1.3.3). So the French philosophe insists.[37]

If, in antiquity, commercial republics were an aberration, even then they had a raison d'être. If they were able to turn their backs on the spirit of war and aggrandizement that typified the ancient republics, it was nearly always because they had to do so—because they were ill positioned for the cultivation of crops and for expansion by land. Generally, in fact, as Montesquieu tells us, these republics were a product of necessity. Marseilles was typical. It was well situated for commerce. Montesquieu calls it a "necessary retreat in the midst of a tempestuous sea," where "the winds, the shoals of the sea, the disposition of the coasts" ordained that "the peoples of the sea" touch shore. It lacked alternatives: "the sterility of its territory destined its citizens to the commerce of economy." And the situation of its inhabitants encouraged the virtues that Montesquieu elsewhere associates with the spirit of commerce. "It was necessary," he contends, that the people of Marseilles "be industrious to supply [*suppléer*] that which nature refused; just in order to live among barbarous nations from whom they had to derive their prosperity; moderate so that their government could be always tranquil; &, finally, frugal in their mores in order to be able to live from a commerce which they would the more securely preserve the less advantageous it was." In general, Montesquieu argues, it is "violence & vexation" that give "birth to the commerce of economy, when men are constrained to find refuge in the marshes, in the islands, in the shallows of the sea, & even on perilous reefs." Such also were the origins of Tyre, Venice, and the towns of Holland. "Fugitives found their security there. It was necessary to subsist; they drew their subsistence from the universe as a whole" (1.5.6, 4.20.5).[38]

It is with the demise of virtuous republicanism in mind that one should, then, read the cryptic claim that Montesquieu advances in the crucial chapter that he devotes to the "danger" associated with "the corruption of the principle of monarchical government." When he suggests that "the disadvantage" associated with a transformation from one form of government to another "does not arise when a state passes from a moderate government to a moderate government, as from a republic to a monarchy or from a monarchy to a republic" (1.8.8), he can only have in mind the commercial republic with its "spirit . . . of moderation" (1.5.6)—for, apart from aristocracies of the sort found in Italy, which tend toward despotism and are anything but moderate, no other species of republic is coeval with monarchy, which is a distinctive feature of modern Europe and was, with the exception of very early Rome (2.11.12), entirely unknown in classical antiquity (2.11.8, 6.30.1).

THE GREATEST OF THE COMMERCIAL REPUBLICS

When Montesquieu first indicates that "democracy" can be "based on commerce," he lists as an example Athens alone (1.5.6). When he first introduces the notion of a "commerce of economy," he mentions Athens among its practitioners (4.20.4). Much later, when he once again singles out Athens with an eye to her commercial character, he places great emphasis on her possession of an "empire over the sea"—an empire imperfect in one particular, which was identified by the author of *The Constitution of the Athenians* attributed to Xenophon. Because "Attica belongs to the mainland [*tient à la terre*]," Montesquieu quotes from this tract, Athens' "enemies ravage" her territory when "she makes expeditions abroad." Her leading men then "let their farms [*terres*] be destroyed & place their goods in security on some isle. The people, who have no farms, live without uneasiness [*inquiétude*]." If only, the tract's author wistfully adds, "the Athenians inhabited an island &, besides this, possessed an empire over the sea, so long as they remained masters of the sea, they would have the power to injure others without being subject to injury themselves." At this juncture, Montesquieu feels compelled to chime in, "You could say that Xenophon wanted to speak of England" (cf. 4.21.7 with Xen. *Ath. Pol.* 2.14–16).

Here is a case in which Montesquieu expects his more attentive readers to recall to mind the substance of his claim that "antiquity" has its own peculiar "*esprit*" and to take care lest they "miss the differences distinguishing cases that seem similar" (*EL* Préf.). For, from his perspective, modern England was everything that ancient Athens might have been and was not. The Athenians Montesquieu describes as a "commercial nation," but, as we have more than once had occasion to note, he quickly concedes that they succumbed to the spirit of war and aggrandizement: as he puts it, they were "more attentive to extending their maritime empire than to using it." Athens was, in fact, so "full of projects for glory" that she never "achieved the great commerce promised by the working of her mines, the multitude of her slaves, the number of her sailors, her authority over the Greek towns, &, more than all this, the fine institutions of Solon." In effect, then, she sacrificed economic to political and imperial concerns (4.21.7). England, though far better situated for war and aggrandizement, tended to do the opposite. England really was a democracy based on commerce, and, as such, it exemplified the spirit of peace and moderation.[39]

England was, in fact, everyone's ideal trading partner. It was, as Montesquieu puts it, "a nation which demands little & which the requirements of commerce render to some degree dependent; a nation which, as a consequence of the breadth of its vision & the extent of its business, knows where to place all superfluous merchandise." England was "rich & able to take on much in the way of produce [*denrées*]." It tended "to pay for this promptly." It had, "so to speak, a need to be faithful." It was "pacific on principle" and inclined to "seek gain & not conquest" (4.20.8).

One consequence is that, in modern times, the English tended not to be a threat to the territorial integrity of the nearby states on the European continent. "Politics" Montesquieu describes as "a dull file": it "achieves its end slowly by wearing away." The English lack the patience for this. They "would be unable to endure the delays, the details, the cold-bloodedness [*sang-froid*] of negotiations; in these they would often be less successful than every other nation; & they would lose, by their treaties, that which they had obtained by their arms." Their inability to attend to high politics may have had another root as well. While "other nations made the interests of commerce give way to political interests," Montesquieu tells us, England "always made its political interests give way to the interests of its commerce" (3.14.13, 4.20.7).

To suppose, however, that their commercial orientation was somehow damaging to the English would be a considerable blunder. "This is the people in the world," Montesquieu emphasizes, "who have known best how to take advantage of these three great things at the same time: religion, commerce, & liberty" (4.20.7). Montesquieu does not trace in any detail the evolution by which the English came to be in this fortunate condition, but his passing remarks do suggest that they came by these three advantages by proceeding along a single path.

To begin with, the English were not forced to become commercial. They were blessed with an abundance of food—sufficient "to nourish" not only "those who cultivate the earth & those who provide clothing" but those who devote their attention to "the frivolous arts" (1.7.6). It helped, no doubt, that Magna

Carta protected foreign merchants from having their wares confiscated in time of war (4.20.14). It was undoubtedly significant that in England the nobility was not barred from engaging in trade (4.20.21). But the crucial event appears to have taken place when Henry VIII set out to reform the Church of England. In Montesquieu's judgment, the turning point came when he "destroyed the monks, a nation indolent in itself which sustained the indolence of others—for, while these practiced hospitality, an infinity of idle folk, gentlemen & bourgeois both, passed their lives running from convent to convent." Henry "shut down as well the alms houses [*hospitaux*] where the lower orders found subsistence, just as the gentlemen found theirs in the monasteries." It was only after "these changes," Montesquieu contends, that "the spirit of commerce & of industry established itself in England" (4.23.29).

Henry VIII's reign seems to have been a turning point in more than one way. In *The Spirit of Laws*, Montesquieu does little to trace England's political evolution, though he does make it clear that Henry governed as a despot, and he specifies that his rule marked "the point of extreme servitude" separating the age—brought to a violent end at Bosworth's Field by Henry's father Henry VII—when England's "nobles" had exercised "an immoderate power," and the time when "the people had begun to sense its power."[40]

In his *Considerations on the Romans*, in his notebooks, and in works that he left unpublished, Montesquieu was more forthcoming. There is reason to suspect that he had read Sir Francis Bacon's *History of Henry VII* (S 561), and he was certainly familiar with the argument advanced by James Harrington in *Oceana* (EL 2.11.6, p. 407; 6.29.19).[41] It comes, then, as no surprise that he attended closely to the changes that had taken place in English land tenure under the early Tudors. In his *Considerations on the Romans*, as we have seen (I.3, above), he compared Henry VII with Rome's Servius Tullius, arguing that the former had "augmented the power of the Commons in order to degrade [*avilir*] the Great" and that, thereby, he had unwittingly prepared the way for a dissolution of the monarchy (CR 1.42–45). Elsewhere, he indicated his awareness that the English king had "allowed the great nobles [*seigneurs*] to alienate their land." He knew that "the people" had then "acquired it," and he observed that if, under Henry VII, the people had managed to secure "the property of the nobility," under his son, Henry VIII, "the nobility" had come into possession of "the property of the clergy." That the entire process had abased the nobility and "elevated the commons," he was also very much aware (NA 882).

Elsewhere, Montesquieu described Henry's daughter Elizabeth as "the last monarch of England," arguing that James I "succeeded" to her "estates" but "not to her authority" and that he had "the dignity without the force, a great name without power"—which left him in "the saddest condition that there is in the world." The demise of the monarchy Montesquieu traced to three sources —first, to Elizabeth's decision to put Mary Stuart on trial, which "weakened in the mind of the English the idea of sovereign grandeur" and served as a precedent for Oliver Cromwell's engineering of the execution of Charles I; then, to her father's decision to make himself "chief of the church," which liberated "the minds" of his countrymen, which were "hitherto repressed," and gave them over to a "fanaticism and enthusiasm" that caused them "no longer to recognize power and to be indignant against the laws themselves"; and, finally, to Charles I's "incapacity for governing." The three children of the "tyrant" Henry VIII, who had ruled "in the time when the power of the nobility had come to be abolished and the people had just begun to take up that power," may have sustained "in some small measure a remnant of the ancient style," he observed, but James I inherited nothing but "a phantom of royalty," and his son was an incompetent, who deserved comparison with Henry III of France.[42]

These two princes, destined for destruction, were alike in being "weak and superstitious, always embarrassed in their personal endeavors, full of prejudices [*préventions*] in their hates and their loves, equally ready to undertake and to concede everything, always bold or timid at the wrong time, having a certain concern for making themselves loved by their courtiers, and none for rendering themselves agreeable to their subjects." Princes of this sort might have gotten by during "the prosperity of a monarchy," when "the strength [*force*] of the government compensates for the weakness of the one who governs," and "a prince can with impunity incur contempt." But, as Montesquieu observed, "when the State is in decline [*dans sa décadence*], there is nothing that can compensate for the weakness of the laws apart from a respect for the person of the prince, and, at such a time, his imperfections and vices are real wounds for the State." Whatever vestiges of England's ancient monarchy survived the Tudor dynasty appear to have been eliminated in the 1640s—when, having blundered into a situation in which it seemed inevitable that he would be "cast down in a trice, without any conspiracy against his person, without an effusion of blood, without combat, and solely by the civil power," Charles I managed to put up a fight and instigate a civil war,[43] at the end of which "the English nobility were interred" beside him "under the debris of the throne" (*EL* 1.8.9).

In Montesquieu's opinion, the Tudor monarchs had a great deal to answer for. They could not be accused of weakness and superstition, of fecklessness and incompetence. They had mastered the political art, and they blundered, nonetheless. The crushing of England's feudal nobility, the closing down of her monasteries and alms houses, the subjection of her church to the secular power, and the solemn execution of a foreign queen—these were despotic deeds, which, when seconded by the attendant changes in land tenure, had consequences unforeseen by their perpetrators. By this means, the Tudors destroyed England's ancient monarchy, shocked the nation's *esprit général*, subverted deference to traditional authority, and threw men back on their own devices. Inadvertently, they opened the way for the development among the English of an ethos of "independence" and self-reliance that favored commercial enterprise, popular government, religious dissent, and even free-thinking—and that was favored by each of these in turn.[44]

The Englishmen that Montesquieu encountered when he sojourned in Great Britain from November 1729 to May 1731 struck him as more like "kings" than subjects. In their dealings with one another, they comported themselves as "confederates rather than fellow citizens." They were "haughty [*fière*]," and they were "proud [*superbe*]." But, unlike their neighbors the French, they were neither sociable nor "vain." In England, there were "many people" who cared not a whit "to please anyone" and who abandoned "themselves to their own humors" (3.19.5, 9, 27, pp. 582–83). If the English lacked the "greatness of soul" sometimes elicited from its nobility by monarchy, they possessed in its place a profound "independence" of both spirit and mind. One might describe them as "*recueillis*"—collected within themselves, contemplative, and even withdrawn—but, in their customary state of "retirement [*retraite*]" from "society," they could be relied on to "do their thinking each & every one entirely on his own" (1.5.12, 3.19.27, pp. 575, 583).

The citizens of a polity like the one in England would be, as Montesquieu puts it, "at all times independent." Each would have "his own will" and value "his independence according to his pleasure." Each would follow "his caprices & his fantasies" in matters public as well as private. The laws of the English would favor no individual in preference to another; no citizen there would fear another citizen; and none would depend on any other. In Montesquieu's England, since the enjoyment and preservation of liberty would require freedom of the press, everyone would be able to say what he thought—to "say & write everything that the laws did not expressly prohibit his saying & writing"—and this everyone would do. It goes almost without saying that every citizen within such a state would also be inclined to make much more of "his own liberty than of the glory belonging to a few citizens or one" (3.19.27, pp. 575, 577).[45]

"With regard to religion," Montesquieu tells us that the same spirit of fierce independence was apt to reign. "Since, within the state, each citizen would possess his own will & would in consequence be conducted by his own illumination [*lumières*] or fantasies, it would come to pass that" many "would display a great indifference with regard to every sort of religion of whatever type," and the clergy would be given "so little credit that the other citizens would have more." The clergy would be mindful of this fact and, instead of forming a separate order, its members would prefer to "bear the same burdens as the laity." In an attempt "to attract respect from the people, they would distinguish themselves by a retired life, by conduct more reserved, & mores more pure." Aware that they had not the means with which to constrain and that they could neither protect religion nor expect that it would protect them, they would opt for persuasion, take up the pen, and produce "works" of genuine merit "proving revelation & the providence" of God (3.19.27, pp. 580–81).

As a consequence of the reigning indifference,[46] Montesquieu notes, nearly everyone would be "inclined to embrace the dominant religion"—though, of course, some in their capriciousness would be "zealous for religion in general," and "the sects would multiply." It would not be "impossible," he adds in an especially revealing aside, "that there would be in this nation people who had no religion & who would nevertheless be unwilling to endure being obliged to change the religion that they would have had if they had had one," for the sort of men formed by a species of government which takes political liberty as its direct object "would sense right away that their lives & property were no more theirs than their manner of thinking & that he who is able to rob them of the one would be better able yet to deprive them of the other" (3.19.27, p. 580).

Those who governed in the England that Montesquieu constructed on the basis of observation and reflection were dependent on public opinion. Theirs would be "a power which is replenished [*se remonte*], so to speak, & remade every day." They would tend, therefore, to pay "greater regard to those who were useful than to those who might divert them." There would be in evidence, Montesquieu adds, "fewer courtiers, flatterers, pleasers" and fewer of "the types who draw advantage from the emptiness of spirit" that afflicts "the great." Precisely because they would be so unlike their neighbors the French, the English would be "emancipated from destructive prejudices." They would judge men simply as men: hardly at all with reference to "their frivolous talents & attributes," and almost solely in terms of their "real qualities"—their "personal merit" and their "wealth" (3.19.27, pp. 578, 581).[47]

Montesquieu's Englishmen were to be "always preoccupied with their interests." In consequence, they would lack "that politeness that is founded on idleness [*oisiveté*]," for they "really would not have the time." This species of politeness he associated with "the establishment of arbitrary power," arguing that "absolute government produces idleness" and that "idleness causes the birth of politeness." Nonetheless, the very fact that the populace in England would be sizable and that men would "need to do business [*d'avoir des ménagements*] with one another & not displease" meant that among the English "there would be politeness" of a sort (3.19.27, pp. 581–82). There was, Montesquieu intimated, much to be said for this particular species of *politesse*. The politeness nourished in monarchies was a politeness of manners rooted in rivalry (1.4.2, p. 263), and, as a consequence, it was a mode of conduct wholly external, which "flatters the vices of others" (3.19.16). In their solitude, the English might be relatively insensitive to "ridicule" of the sort that flourished within royal courts, but they were in no way oblivious to or tolerant of genuine "vice," and the politeness that they would be most likely to display was, he implied, a "politeness of morals [*moeurs*]," a species of conduct genuine and internal, rooted in a sense of obligation. "That which ought to distinguish us from barbarous peoples," he explained, is more closely bound up with "the politeness of morals than with the politeness of manners" (cf. 3.19.16, 27, pp. 582–83, with 1.3.5).[48]

Largely because of their lack of pretensions, the English would possess "a solid luxury," which would be founded on "real needs" and "not on the refinements of vanity." Many would enjoy "a great superfluity" and, since "frivolous things" would, in effect, be "proscribed," they would have "more wealth than occasion for expense" (3.19.27, p. 581). If England was exceptionally prosperous, Montesquieu explains, it seems to have been mainly due to the peculiar fashion in which "mores" there followed "the laws" (3.19.26). In part, we can surmise, as a consequence of what Henry VIII had done in suppressing the monasteries and alms houses and in reining in the church, the laws of Montesquieu's England left "all the passions" there "free." The consequences were everywhere to be seen. "Hatred, envy," and "jealousy" appeared "in their full extent," and these all seem to have found expression in "the ardor to enrich & distinguish oneself" (3.19.27, p. 575).

The manner in which that ardor expressed itself was determined by circumstances. England was an island. It was not necessary that it conquer its neighbors in order to see to its own defense: territorial acquisition would only have weakened it. England was also blessed with abundant good land. It had no need to resort to "war in order to enrich itself." Provided, as it was, then, with "peace & liberty" and "emancipated," as we have seen, "from destructive prejudices," this nation was "inclined to become commercial," and it engaged in trade on an exceptionally "grand" scale. It set up industries for the production of high-priced finished goods made from the produce of its land. Situated in the North, blessed by nature with "a great number of superfluous products [*denrées*]," and by its climate denied a similarly "great number of species of merchandise [*marchandises*]," it engaged in a commerce "with the peoples of the South" that was as "necessary" to it as it was "grand," and it negotiated "reciprocally useful" commercial agreements with the states that it favored with this "advantageous commerce" (3.19.27, pp. 577–79).

It would be a mistake to trace the character of the English to their commerce, for Montesquieu makes it clear that this commerce was largely due to the character that was already theirs. There can, however, be no doubt that the commercial spirit reinforced important propensities that the English already possessed. It provided, as we have seen (II.4, above), a material underpinning for the independence that enabled England's "middle class" to exercise its characteristic "virtue" and sustain thereby her separation of powers. It promised to cure any "destructive prejudices" to which the English might in the future be inclined to fall prey (*EL* 4.20.1). And it no doubt contributed to the process by which a people, once inclined to "fanaticism & enthusiasm," who had become "indignant against the laws themselves," eventually settled into a mood of religious indifference. Montesquieu has the experience of the English in mind when he observes that penal laws aimed at the suppression of religious dissent are generally counterproductive, and he is obviously alluding to the effects of England's turn to commerce when he then adds that "as a general rule invitations contribute more forcefully to changing religion than do penalties" and remarks that it is a surer strategy "to attack religion by favor, by the conveniences [*commodités*] of life, by the hope of fortune; not by that which warns one of one's mortality but by that which makes one forget it; not by that which provokes indignation but by that which casts one into a disposition lukewarm [*quit jette dans la tiédeur*] so that other passions act on our souls & those which religion inspires fall silent" (5.25.12). Such are the effects of "solid luxury" among a commercial people "always occupied with their own interests" (3.19.27, p. 581).

By now it should be obvious that, in certain crucial regards, England was better suited to the enlightened, commercial world order emerging in the eighteenth century than were the ancient monarchies of the European continent. It favored and was in no way threatened by commerce. Its political institutions and its social order were, in fact, sustained by what Montesquieu calls the commerce of economy.[49] England encouraged the establishment of banks and trading companies. It subordinated its political to its economic interests, and it engaged in trade on an unprecedented scale. The equality promoted by commerce the English embraced. They spurned the "false honor" engendered by monarchy, rejected artificial "preferences & distinctions," and judged men by their merits and their wealth. They emancipated themselves from "destructive prejudices" of every sort and embraced religious toleration. They were in no way enamored with "the arbitrary principles of glory." Rarely, if ever did they sacrifice "the real needs of the people" to "the imaginary needs of the state." For they preferred "gain" to "conquest" and "peace" to "war & aggrandizement."

The fact that the English were "pacific on principle" was a source of strength, not weakness. After all, they lived on an island and maintained an "empire of the sea." They might think it essential to their security that Scotland be absorbed and Ireland kept in thrall. Otherwise, however, they had no territorial ambitions and, therefore, no great need for "strongholds, fortresses, & armies on land." Even when they sent out colonies, they did so "more for the purpose of extending their commerce than for domination." They were, in consequence, free from the "new malady" that had "extended itself across Europe," for they had no need to maintain "an inordinate number of troops" in peacetime and did not suffer a "perpetual augmentation of taxes" therefrom. "Poor with the wealth & commerce of the entire universe" the English were certainly not (2.13.17; 3.19.27, pp. 578–79; 4.20.8).

Of course, England did have "need of an army at sea" to protect its commerce and "guarantee it against invasions," and it maintained "every sort of facility" to sustain its "forces at sea." But it was relatively easy for the English to field "a navy superior to that of all the other powers," for the latter "had need to employ their finances for war on land" and "had not enough for war on the sea" as well. This left the English in the position that Xenophon had imagined for his fellow Athenians: blessed with "the power to injure others without being subject to injury themselves"; and they displayed "a haughtiness [*fierté*] natural" in men who are "capable of giving insult everywhere" and who believe "that their power has no more limits than the ocean" itself (3.19.27, pp. 578–79, 4.21.7). In his *Persian Letters*, as we have seen, Montesquieu had had Rica single out as a wonder England, which as "Mistress of the Sea (a thing hitherto unheard of), mixed Commerce with Empire" (LP 130.30–34/136). A few years after that work's appearance, he told an Irish visitor that the English were the only nation that had managed such a combination.[50]

As we can now see, England was quite unlike Athens. Nowhere does Montesquieu say that it was "full of projects for glory." Nowhere does he tell us that it was "more attentive to extending its maritime empire than to enjoying it," and he positively denies that by means of aggression it followed Athens, which "increased jealousy instead of augmenting its influence." He insists, instead, that England's capacity to project power at sea gave it "a great influence in the affairs of its neighbors." The fact that it generally "did not employ its power for conquest," he explains, caused those neighbors to "seek out its friendship" all the more and to "fear its hatred more than the inconstancy of its government & its internal agitation would seem to promise it." Moreover, he adds, if it was "the destiny of its executive power" to be "almost always uneasy at home [*inquiétée au dedans*]," it was nonetheless "respected abroad," and with some frequency England found itself at "the center of negotiations in Europe," to which it brought "a greater measure of probity & good faith than the other" participants" since "its ministers" were so "often obliged to justify their conduct before a popular council." The simple fact that they would be held "responsible [*garants*] for events" produced by "circuitous conduct [*une conduite detournée*]" on their part instilled in them the conviction that "it would be safest for them to take the straightest path" (cf. *EL* 3.19.27, pp. 579–80, with 4.21.7).

In short, no state was better situated to cope with the new situation created within the world by the vast expansion of commerce then underway. If, within Europe, monarchy's future was in question, the same could certainly not be said with regard to the republic disguised as a monarchy that had so recently taken shape just offshore. It is no wonder that Montesquieu suggested to William Domville that "in Europe the last sigh of liberty will be heaved by an Englishman" and that its policy was such that it was likely to "slow down the velocity [*promptitude*]" with which "other nations," such as France, made their way to "total collapse [*chute entière*]."[51] It is no wonder that he seriously considered dedicating his *Spirit of Laws* to Frederick, prince of Wales (*MP* 1860).

AFTERWARDS

I would like to imagine with what new traits despotism could be produced in the world. I see an innumerable multitude of men, alike and equal, who turn about without repose in order to procure for themselves petty and vulgar pleasures with which they fill their souls. . . . Over these is elevated an immense, tutelary power, which takes sole charge of assuring their enjoyment and of watching over their fate. It is absolute, attentive to detail, regular, provident, and gentle. It would resemble the paternal power if, like it, it had as its object to prepare men for manhood, but it seeks, to the contrary, to keep them irrevocably fixed in childhood. . . . It does not break wills; it softens them, bends them, and directs them; rarely does it force one to act, but it constantly opposes itself to one's acting on one's own; it does not destroy; it prevents things from being born; it does not tyrannize, it gets in the way, it curtails, it enervates, it extinguishes, it stupefies, and finally it reduces each nation to nothing more than a herd of timid and industrious animals, of which the government is the shepherd.

—*Alexis de Tocqueville*

If Montesquieu is right, modern republics possessing the advantages that he attributed to Great Britain enjoy an economic and moral superiority that virtually guarantees their survival when pitted against traditional monarchies and old-fashioned despotic states. Our own experience in more recent times would suggest that they profit from a similar, if perhaps less decisive, superiority when pitted against the populist tyrannies and the totalitarian regimes that emerged in late modernity. Over the last three hundred years, though they may at times have stumbled, they did endure.

None of this, however, can alter the force of Montesquieu's disturbing claim that, "just as all human things come to an end, so the state of which we speak will lose its liberty; it will perish. Rome, Lacedaemon, & Carthage have in fact perished. This state will perish when the legislative will be more corrupt than the executive power." None of it can change the fact that the modern republic condemns its citizens to *inquiétude* and thereby denies them the tranquillity of spirit that constitutes political liberty in its relation with the citizen. None of it can prevent us from seeing just how fragile the ethos of vigilance and jealous distrust to which this *inquiétude* gives rise really is. None of this can stop us from wondering just how long political liberty in its relation with the constitution can be sustained.

For those who live in modern commercial polities modeled to one degree or another on "the republic disguised as a monarchy" that Montesquieu discovered on his visit to England, there is, after all, a great deal at stake. One must keep always in mind the twofold warning issued by the author of *The Spirit of Laws* on the very first occasion in which he mentioned the English form of government. "Abolish in a monarchy," he began, "the prerogatives of the lords, the clergy, the nobility & the towns," as "did Parliament in England," and "you will soon have a popular state—or, indeed, a state despotic." And to this he soon added, "The English, in order to favor liberty, have eliminated all the intermediary powers which formed their monarchy. They have good reason to conserve this liberty"—for, "if they should come to lose it, they would be one of the most fully enslaved peoples on the earth."

One must keep Montesquieu's warning in mind in part because the enlightenment experiment was tried, and in time there was in Europe a "dissolution of monarchies"—as, he supposed, there would be. Eventually, all of the states on the continent abandoned "harmful prejudices" and jettisoned "false honor," embraced the natural equality of man, and abolished "the prerogatives of the lords, the clergy, the nobility & the towns." In the process, they eliminated "the intermediary powers" which had formed their monarchies; and, for periods of varying length, these polities became popular states on the English model. But, in the last century, they failed to conserve their liberty, and, after inventing and propagating species of populist despotism more fully tyrannical than any hitherto known to man, the peoples of Montesquieu's Europe became—as, he feared, they might—"the most fully enslaved peoples on the earth."

Above all, however, one must keep Montesquieu's warning in mind because we now live in a world in which there are no virtuous republics and there are no monarchies of the sort that he had in mind. His "intermediary powers" are a thing of the past. No prerogatives are left to "the lords, the clergy, the nobility & the towns." In our world, there are states popular, and there are states despotic, and, more often than not, thanks to the advantages afforded to rulers by modern communications and technology, those who reside in the latter are quite fully enslaved. Moreover, in principle, there is no reason to suppose that states of the former sort cannot become states of the latter sort. After all, they have done so with some frequency in the past, and more than once Montesquieu's prediction to Domville that "in Europe the last sigh of liberty will be heaved by an Englishman" and that England will stand in the way of "the total collapse of other nations" was proven prescient.

It should, then, be obvious that further rumination is required. It should be evident that the future of mankind depends on the well-being of the modern republic and that we need to know more about the peculiar species of corruption to which it is prone. Fortunately, as we shall see in this work's companion volume, *Soft Despotism, Democracy's Drift*, Montesquieu was by no means the last to consider the crucial questions that he was the first to raise, and those, such as Jean-Jacques Rousseau and Alexis de Tocqueville, who followed in his footsteps in this particular regard were hardly less illustrious and insightful than was he.

NOTES

INTRODUCTION

1. In this connection, see Alan Charles Kors, "Can There Be an 'After Socialism'?" *Social Philosophy & Policy* 20:1 (Winter 2003): 1–17.

2. See Francis Fukuyama, "The End of History?" *National Interest* 16 (Summer 1989): 3–18, and *The End of History and the Last Man* (New York: Free Press, 1992). Note also *After History? Francis Fukuyama and His Critics*, ed. Timothy Burns (Lanham, MD: Rowman & Littlefield, 1994).

3. Cf. Samuel P. Huntington, "The Clash of Civilizations," *Foreign Affairs* 72:3 (Summer 1993): 22–49, and "The West: Unique, Not Universal," *Foreign Affairs* 75:6 (November/December 1996): 28–46, as well as *The Clash of Civilizations and the Remaking of the World Order* (New York: Simon and Schuster, 1996), with Neil McInnes, "The Great Doomsayer (Oswald Spengler's *The Decline of the West*)," *National Interest* 47 (Summer 1997): 65–77.

4. Richard Ned Lebow and Janice Gross Stein, *We All Lost the Cold War* (Princeton, NJ: Princeton University Press, 1994). Cf. John Lewis Gaddis, *We Now Know: Rethinking Cold War History* (Oxford, UK: Oxford University Press, 1997).

5. See Tony Judt, "A Story Still to Be Told," *New York Review of Books* 53:5 (23 March 2006): 11–13, reviewing John Lewis Gaddis, *The Cold War: A New History* (New York: Penguin Press, 2005).

6. The utopian vision underpinning the criticism directed at Gaddis is made manifest in Tony Judt, *Postwar: A History of Europe since 1945* (New York: Penguin, 2005).

7. See, for example, Ernest Gellner, *Conditions of Liberty: Civil Society and Its Rivals* (New York: Penguin, 1994); *Democratization in Eastern Europe: Domestic and International Perspectives*, ed. Geoffrey Pridham and Tatu Vanhanen (London: Routledge, 1994); Marina Ottaway, *Democratization and Ethnic Nationalism: African and Eastern European Experiences* (Washington, DC: Overseas Development Council, 1994); Christopher McMahon, *Authority and Democracy: A General Theory of Government and Management* (Princeton, NJ: Princeton University Press, 1994); *Developing*

Democracy, ed. Ian Budge and David McKay (London: Sage, 1994); *The Politics of Democratization: Generalizing East Asian Experiences*, ed. Edward Friedman (Boulder, CO: Westview, 1994); Joan M. Nelson et al., *Intricate Links: Democratization and Market Reforms in Latin America and Eastern Europe* (New Brunswick, NJ: Transaction, 1994); *Politics, Society, and Democracy: Comparative Studies*, ed. H. E. Chehabi and Alfred Stepan (Boulder, CO: Westview, 1995); *Political Culture and Constitutionalism: A Comparative Approach*, ed. Daniel P. Franklin and Michael J. Baun (Armonk, NY: M. E. Sharpe, 1995); Robert Amerson, *How Democracy Triumphed over Dictatorship: Public Diplomacy in Venezuela* (Washington, DC: American University Press, 1995); Robert Strausz-Hupé, *Democracy and American Foreign Policy: Reflections on the Legacy of Alexis de Tocqueville* (New Brunswick, NJ: Transaction, 1995). Many more could be listed.

8. See Matthew Continetti, "The Peace Party vs. the Power Party: The Real Divide in American Politics," *Weekly Standard* 12:16 (1–8 January 2007): 17–19, 22–24.

9. See Robin Abcarian, "Michelle Obama in Spotlight's Glare," *Los Angeles Times*, 21 February 2008, and Lauren Collins, "The Other Obama," *New Yorker*, 10 March 2008.

10. "Circular to the Governors of the States," 8 June 1783, in *The Writings of George Washington*, ed. John C. Fitzpatrick (Washington, DC: U.S. Government Printing Office, 1931–1944), XXVI 485–86.

11. In compiling the bibliographical data, Cecil Patrick Courtney has done yeoman work: on the *Persian Letters*, see Courtney, "Bibliographie II. Editions," in VF I 84–131, which should be read in conjunction with Edgar Mass, *Literatur und Zensur in der frühen Aufklärung: Produktion, Distribution und Rezeption der Lettres persanes* (Frankfurt am Main: Vittorio Klostermann, 1981), 139–271; and on Montesquieu's other two works, see Courtney, "Introduction à *Considérations sur les causes de la grandeur des Romains et de leur décadence* VI. Manuscrits et éditions," in VF II 48–85, and Courtney, "*L'Esprit des lois* dans la perspective de l'histoire du livre (1748–1800)," in *Le Temps de Montesquieu: Actes du colloque international de Genève (28–31 octobre 1998)*, ed. Michel Porret and Catherine Volpilhac-Auger (Geneva: Droz, 2002), 66–96.

12. Note Frank T. H. Fletcher, *Montesquieu and English Politics, 1750–1800* (London: E. Arnold, 1939), and William Stewart, "Montesquieu vu par les Anglais depuis deux siècles," in *Actes du congrès Montesquieu réuni à Bordeaux du 23 au 26 mai 1955* (Bordeaux: Imprimèries Delmas, 1956), 339–48; then see Cecil Patrick Courtney, *Montesquieu and Burke* (Oxford, UK: Blackwell, 1963); Paul O. Carrese, *The Cloaking of Power: Montesquieu, Blackstone, and the Rise of Judicial Activism* (Chicago: University of Chicago Press, 2003); and the secondary literatured cited in III.2, note 23, below.

13. Note Paul Merrill Spurlin, *Montesquieu in America, 1760–1801* (Baton Rouge: Louisiana State University Press, 1940), and see James W. Muller, "The American Framers' Debt to Montesquieu," in *The Revival of Constitutionalism*, ed. James W. Muller (Lincoln: University of Nebraska Press, 1988), 87–102; Anne M. Cohler, *Montesquieu's Comparative Politics and the Spirit of American Constitutionalism* (Lawrence: University Press of Kansas, 1988); Matthew P. Bergman, "Montesquieu's Theory of Government and the Framing of the American Constitution," *Pepperdine*

Law Review 18:1 (1990): 1–42; Rahe, *RAM* II.iii.4, III.Prologue, i.3–7, ii.2, iii.4–5, iv.3–5, 7, 9, v.3, 6; and the secondary literature cited in II.2, note 27, below.

14. See Catherine Larrère, "Droit de punir et qualification des crimes de Montesquieu à Beccaria," in *Beccaria et la culture juridique des lumières*, ed. Michel Porret (Geneva: Droz, 1997), 89–108, and David W. Carrithers, "Montesquieu's Philosophy of Punishment," *History of Political Thought* 19:2 (Summer 1998): 213–40.

15. See Michael A. Mosher, "The Particulars of a Universal Politics: Hegel's Adaptation of Montesquieu's Typology," *American Political Science Review* 78:1 (March 1984): 179–88, and Yoshie Kawade, "La Liberté civile contre la théorie réformiste de l'État souverain: Le Combat de Montesquieu," in *Le Travail des lumières: Pour Georges Benrekassa*, ed. Caroline Jacot Grapa, Nicole Jacques-Lefèvre, Yannick Séité, and Carine Trevisan (Paris: Honoré Champion, 2002), 203–23.

16. See Roberto Romani, "All Montesquieu's Sons: The Place of *Esprit Général, Caractère National*, and *Mœurs* in French Political Philosophy, 1748–1789," *Studies on Voltaire and the Eighteenth Century* 362 (1998): 189–235, whose reading of Montesquieu and of his critics and heirs nonetheless leaves something to be desired. The case of Denis Diderot is of special interest: see Arthur M. Wilson, "The Concept of *Mœurs* in Diderot's Social and Political Thought," in *The Age of the Enlightenment: Studies Presented to Theodore Besterman*, ed. W. H. Barber et al. (Edinburgh: Oliver & Boyd, 1967), 188–99. Note also Jacob T. Levy, "Montesquieu's Constitutional Legacies," in *Montesquieu and His Legacy*, ed. Rebecca E. Kingston (Albany: State University of New York Press, 2008), 115–37.

17. In this connection, see the essays collected in the two-volume study *Montesquieu e i suoi interpreti*, ed Domenico Felice (Pisa: Edizioni ETS, 2005). Note also Catherine Volpilhac-Auger, "*L'Esprit des lois*, une lecture *ad usum Delphini?*" in *Le Travail des lumières*, 137–71.

18. See Alexander Hamilton, John Jay, and James Madison, *The Federalist*, ed. Jacob E. Cooke (Middletown, CT: Wesleyan University Press, 1961) no. 47, p. 324; no. 78, p. 523n.

19. See Donald S. Lutz, "The Relative Influence of European Writers on Late Eighteenth-Century American Political Thought," *American Political Science Review* 78:1 (March 1984): 189–97.

20. *The Federalist* no. 47, pp. 324–25. See also Edmund Burke, *An Appeal from the New to the Old Whigs* (1791), in *The Writings and Speeches of the Right Honourable Edmund Burke* (Boston: Little, Brown, 1901), IV 211–12.

21. See James Madison, "Helvidius, No. 1," 24 August 1793, in *The Papers of James Madison*, ed. William T. Hutchinson, William M. E. Rachal, et al. (Chicago: University of Chicago Press, 1962–1977; Charlottesville: University Press of Virginia, 1977–1991), XV 68.

BOOK ONE, PREFACE

1. See Franz Bosbach, *Monarchia Universalis: Ein politischer Leitbegriff der frühen Neuzeit* (Göttingen: Vandenhoeck & Ruprecht, 1988), 107–21, and Steven C. A. Pin-

cus, "The English Debate over Universal Monarchy," in *A Union for Empire: Political Thought and the Union of* 1707, ed. John Robertson (Cambridge, UK: Cambridge University Press, 1995), 37–62. Note, in this connection, John Robertson, "Universal Monarchy and the Liberties of Europe: David Hume's Critique of an English Whig Doctrine," in *Political Discourse in Early Modern Britain*, ed. Nicholas Phillipson and Quentin Skinner (Cambridge, UK: Cambridge University Press, 1993), 349–73.

2. For the details, see Winston S. Churchill, *Marlborough: His Life and Times* (Chicago: University of Chicago, 2002), I 711–868. For a discussion of the battle's treatment in the press and of the disinformation campaign mounted by the French court, see Pierre Rétat, "Battailles," in *La Suite à l'ordinaire prochain: La Représentation du monde dans les gazettes* (Lyon: Presses Universitaires de Lyon, 1999), 111–22.

3. See Catherine Betty Abigail Behrens, *The Ancien Régime* (New York: Harcourt, Brace, & World, 1967), 138–62; Theda Skocpol, *States and Social Revolutions: A Comparative Analysis of France, Russia, and China* (Cambridge, UK: Cambridge University Press, 1979), 51–67; and Bailey Stone, *The Genesis of the French Revolution: A Global-Historical Interpretation* (Cambridge, UK: Cambridge University Press, 1994), 20–63, 111–47, and *Reinterpreting the French Revolution: A Global-Historical Perspective* (Cambridge, UK: Cambridge University Press, 2002), 1–61.

4. See Vivant de Mésagues, "Caractères moraux et politiques du présent Roi d'Angleterre, du Duc d'York son frere, du Duc de Cumberland son oncle, du Duc de Newcastle Ex-Ministre, &c &c &c &c.," 8 October 1763, Affaires étrangères, Mémoires et Documents, Angleterre, 48, f.113–24, extract printed under the title "Bilan de la politique de William Pitt," in Edmond Dziembowski, *Un nouveau Patriotisme français, 1750–1770: La France face à la puissance anglais à l'époque de la guerre de Sept Ans* (Oxford, UK: Voltaire Foundation, 1998), 499–507 (at 502).

5. See Churchill, *Marlborough: His Life and Times*, II 95–627.

6. A recent survey found that, among the 1070 full-time members of the top twenty-five history departments that *US News and World Report* ranked as having the best graduate programs, fewer than 2 percent listed military history or even a particular war as their specialty. Moreover, between 1975 and 1993, the number of dissertations dealing with diplomatic history that were written at leading universities dropped from .08 percent to .01 percent of the total; and, between 1985 and 1995, the *American Historical Review*— the flagship publication within the history profession in the United States—published not one article in diplomatic history. See Joyce Lee Malcolm, "Political Scientists to the Rescue of Diplomatic and Military History," *Historically Speaking* 5:6 (July–August 2004): 40–41, and note David A. Bell, "Military History Bites the Dust: Casualty of War," *New Republic* 236:15 (7 May 2007): 16–17.

7. Churchill, *Marlborough: His Life and Times*, II 381.

BOOK ONE, CHAPTER ONE. AFTER THE FALL

1. Nowhere was the shift in sentiment as profound and sudden as it was in France: see Pierre Nora, "Gaullists and Communists," in *Realms of Memory: Rethinking the French*

Past I: Conflicts and Divisions, ed. Pierre Nora, tr. Arthur Goldhammer (New York: Columbia University Press, 1996), 205–39.

2. For a recent description, see Colin Jones, *The Great Nation: France from Louis XV to Napoleon* (New York: Columbia University Press, 2002), 1–35, 52–59.

3. Toward the end of Louis's reign, even Bossuet was inclined to temper his enthusiasm for absolute rule: see Nannerl O. Keohane, *Philosophy and the State in France: The Renaissance to the Enlightenment* (Princeton, NJ: Princeton University Press, 1980), 251–58.

4. Note Montesquieu, *MP* 1613; and, for an overview of the Regency, see Henri Leclercq, *Histoire de la Régence pendant la minorité de Louis XV* (Paris: Champion, 1921–1922).

5. In this connection, see Ragnhild Hatton, "Louis et l'Europe: Éléments d'une révision historiographique," *XVIIe Siècle* 123 (1979): 109–35; Jeremy Black, *The Rise of the European Powers, 1679–1793* (London: Arnold, 1990), 28–30; and John A. Lynn, "A Quest for Glory: The Formation of Strategy under Louis XIV, 1661–1715," in *The Making of Strategy: Rulers, States, and War*, ed. Williamson Murray, MacGregor Knox, and Alvin Bernstein (Cambridge, UK: Cambridge University Press, 1994), 178–204, and *The Wars of Louis XIV, 1667–1714* (London: Longman, 1999). Note, however, Paul Sonnino, *Louis XIV and the Origins of the Dutch War* (Cambridge, UK: Cambridge University Press, 1988).

6. See Franz Bosbach, "Eine französische Universalmonarchie? Deutsche Reaktionen auf die europäische Politik Ludwigs XIV," in *Vermittlungen: Aspekte der deutsche französischen Beziehungen vom 17. Jahrhundert bis zur Gegenwart*, ed. Jochen Schlobach (Berne: Peter Lang, 1992), 53–68.

7. See Montesquieu, *MP* 1302, p. 389.

8. See Antoine Aubery, *Des justes Prétensions du Roy sur l'empire* (Paris: Antoine Bertier, 1667), 159.

9. See Bosbach, "Eine französische Universalmonarchie? Deutsche Reaktionen auf die europäische Politik Ludwigs XIV," 53–68 (esp. 56–59).

10. The book would not have been published with the *privilège du roi* had it not met with Louis's approval: see Joseph Klaits, *Printed Propaganda under Louis XIV* (Princeton, NJ: Princeton University Press, 1976). In this connection, see also Peter Burke, *The Fabrication of Louis XIV* (New Haven, CT: Yale University Press, 1992).

11. See Anthony Pagden, "Instruments of Empire: Tommaso Campanella and the Universal Monarchy of Spain," in Pagden, *Spanish Imperialism and the Political Imagination* (New Haven, CT: Yale University Press, 1990), 37–63. Note also Pagden, *Lords of All the World: Ideologies of Empire in Spain, Britain, and France, c. 1500–1800* (New Haven, CT: Yale University Press, 1995), 29–62.

12. In this connection see John M. Headley, "The Demise of Universal Monarchy as a Meaningful Political Idea," in *Imperium/Empire/Reich: Ein Konzept politischer Herrschaft im deutsch-britischen Vergleich/An Anglo-German Comparison of a Concept of Rule*, ed. Franz Bosbach and Hermann Hiery (Munich: K. G. Saur, 1999), 41–58.

13. See Lionel Rothkrug, *Opposition to Louis XIV: The Political and Social Origins of the French Enlightenment* (Princeton, NJ: Princeton University Press, 1965), 76–79.

14. See Rothkrug, *Opposition to Louis XIV*, 116–30.

15. Louis-Augustin Alemand, *Nouvelles Observations, ou Guerre civile des françois sur la langue* (Paris: Langlois, 1688) Epistre.

16. François de Salignac de La Mothe-Fénelon, *Supplément à l'Examen de conscience sur les devoirs de la royauté*, in Fénelon, *Œuvres*, ed. Jacques Le Brun (Paris: Bibliothèque de la Pléiade, 1983–1997), II 1003–9, which was penned at some point prior to Fénelon's death in 1715 and published long thereafter. For further discussion, see III.3, note 33, and its context, below. With regard to the ambitions of Fénelon, see Sanford B. Kanter, "Archbishop Fénelon's Political Activity: The Focal Point of Power in Dynasticism," *French Historical Studies* 4:3 (Spring 1966): 320–34.

17. One consequence of the absence of of such a vision was that, after a hiatus sufficient to enable the country to recover from the state of exhaustion in which the Sun King had left it, France resumed its quest for primacy on the continent of Europe and beyond: see Bailey Stone, *The Genesis of the French Revolution: A Global-Historical Interpretation* (Cambridge, UK: Cambridge University Press, 1994), 20–63, 111–47.

18. See J. H. Shennan, *Philippe, Duke of Orléans, Regent of France, 1715–1723* (London: Thames and Hudson, 1979), and Christine Pevitt, *Philippe, Duc d'Orléans, Regent of France* (New York: Atlantic Monthly Press, 1997), and consider the judgment that Montesquieu at one point thought of including in his *Lettres persanes: MP* 1613. Note also 173 and *Lettres de Xénocrate à Phérès* (1724), ed. Sheila Mason, in VF VIII 299–305, where, respectively, the descriptions of Pisistratus and Alcaméne are portraits of the Regent recently deceased.

19. See Antoin E. Murphy, *John Law: Economic Theorist and Policy-Maker* (Oxford, UK: Clarendon Press, 1997), and Henry C. Clark, *Compass of Society: Commerce and Absolutism in Old Regime France* (Lanham, MD: Lexington Books, 2007), 78–81. More generally, see Jones, *The Great Nation*, 61–73.

20. See François de Salignac de La Mothe-Fénelon, *Les Aventures de Télémaque* (ca. 1693–94), in Fénelon, *Œuvres*, II 1–326. The book's publication in 1699, an event of considerable political consequence (especially for Fénelon), appears to have been brought about by an unfaithful copyist.

21. In this connection, see Robert Shackleton, "The Death of Louis XIV and the New Freedom," in Shackleton, *Essays on Montesquieu and on the Enlightenment*, ed. David Gilson and Martin Smith (Oxford, UK: Voltaire Foundation, 1988), 487–98. The classic work charting the background to this sudden and dramatic shift in focus is Paul Hazard, *La Crise de la conscience européenne (1680–1715)* (Paris: Boivin, 1935). On the significance of the Regency, note also Ira O. Wade, *The Structure and Form of the French Enlightenment* (Princeton, NJ: Princeton University Press, 1977) I: *Esprit Philosophique*, 87–119.

22. See Cecil Patrick Courtney, "Montesquieu and English Liberty," in *Montesquieu's Science of Politics: Essays on The Spirit of Laws (1748)*, ed. David W. Carrithers, Michael A. Mosher, and Paul A. Rahe (Lanham, MD: Rowman & Littlefield, 2001), 273–90 (at 273).

23. See Georges Ascoli, *La Grande-Bretagne devant l'opinion française au XVIIe siècle* (Paris: Gamber, 1930), passim (esp. I 255–513, II 1–173).

24. See Louis-Sébastien Mercier, *Tableau de Paris*, new ed. (Amsterdam: s.n., 1783–1789), XI 127–28.

25. See Gabriel Bonno, *La Culture et la civilisation britannique devant l'opinion française de la Paix d'Utrecht aux "Lettres philosophiques" (1713–1734)* (Philadelphia: American Philosophical Society, 1948), *Transactions of the American Philosophical Society*, n.s. 38, no. 1 (1948).

26. See Ira O. Wade, *The Intellectual Development of Voltaire* (Princeton, NJ: Princeton University Press, 1969), 147–250. On the character and significance for the French Enlightenment of the interest that the French developed in the English at this time, see Wade, *The Structure and Form of the French Enlightenment*, I 120–71. For a brief discussion of Voltaire's predecessors, who were for the most part Huguenots, see Edmond Dziembowski, *Un nouveau Patriotisme français, 1750–1770: La France face à la puissance anglais à l'époque de la guerre de Sept Ans* (Oxford, UK: Voltaire Foundation, 1998), 19–20.

27. See Peter Gay, *Voltaire's Politics: The Poet as Realist* (New York: Vintage Books, 1965), 33–48; Theodore Besterman, *Voltaire*, 3rd ed. (Chicago: University of Chicago Press, 1976), 113–28; and René Pomeau, *D'Arouet à Voltaire, 1694–1734* (Oxford, UK: Voltaire Foundation, 1985), 203–56. For an earlier, more circumstantial, and ultimately less reliable account, see J. Churton Collins, *Voltaire, Montesquieu and Rousseau in England* (London: Eveleigh Nash, 1908), 1–116.

28. J. Patrick Lee, "The Unexamined Premise: Voltaire, John Lockman and the Myth of the *English Letters*," *Studies on Voltaire and the Eighteenth Century* 2001:08 (2001): 240–70, has disproven the claim that Voltaire wrote something like half of the letters in English.

29. See Voltaire, *Lettres philosophiques*, ed. Gustave Lanson,3rd ed. (Paris: Société des Textes Français Modernes, 1924), II 184–226, esp. 185 (XXV). For an eighteenth-century English translation of this chapter, see Voltaire, *Letters concerning the English Nation*, ed. Nicholas Cronk (Oxford, UK: Oxford University Press, 1994), 124–50. On the importance of this discussion, see Jean Mesnard, "Voltaire et Pascal," *French Studies in Southern Africa* 8 (1979): 2–12, which is reprinted in Mesnard, *La Culture du XVIIe siècle* (Paris: Presses Universitaires de France, 1992), 589–99; Arnoux Straudo, *La Fortune de Pascal en France au dix-huitième siècle* (Oxford, UK: Voltaire Foundation, 1997), 77–104; and Mark Hulliung, "Rousseau, Voltaire, and the Revenge of Pascal," in *The Cambridge Companion to Rousseau*, ed. Patrick Riley (Cambridge, UK: Cambridge University Press, 2001), 57–77. Note also Straudo, *La Fortune de Pascal en France au dix-huitieme siècle*, 179–88, 227–39, 301–29, 362–70.

30. See Pomeau, *D'Arouet à Voltaire*, 318–35 (esp. 330–31).

31. That, as he worked, Voltaire had his English, as well as his French, readership in mind seems clear: see Nicholas Cronk, "The *Letters concerning the English Nation* as an English Work: Reconsidering the Harcourt Brown Thesis," *Studies on Voltaire and the Eighteenth Century* 2001:08 (2001): 226–39.

32. See Gustave Lanson, *Voltaire* (Paris: Librairie Hachette, 1906), 52.

33. Jean-Antoine-Nicolas de Caritat, marquis de Condorcet, *Vie de Voltaire* (1791), in

François-Marie Arouet de Voltaire, *Œuvres complètes de Voltaire* (Paris: Th. Desoer, 1817–1819), I 13–15 (esp. 14).

34. See Besterman, *Voltaire*, 125.

35. See Voltaire, *Lettres philosophiques*, I 1–87 (I–VII). In the passage quoted here and in those that will be quoted hereafter, I have attempted to improve on Lockman's translation only where it departs significantly from the version published in French by Voltaire in Rouen. See Voltaire, *Letters concerning the English Nation*, 9–32.

36. Cf. Voltaire, *Lettres philosophiques*, I 74 (VI), with *Letters concerning the English Nation*, 30.

37. Cf. Voltaire, *Lettres philosophiques*, I 88–92 (VIII), with *Letters concerning the English Nation*, 33–34, and see Fénelon, *Les Aventures de Télémaque* V, in Fénelon, *Œuvres*, II 59, and Jones, *The Great Nation*, 38. In this connection, note Jean Garagnon, "Voltaire et Fénelon: Sur une Source de la *Lettre philosophique* no. 8, 'Sur le Parlement'," *French Studies* 43 (1989): 140–44.

38. Cf. Voltaire, *Lettres philosophiques*, I 120–22, II 195–96, 221 (X, XXV), with *Letters concerning the English Nation*, 42–43, 130, 147.

39. Letter from l'abbé Jean-Bernard Le Blanc to Jean Brouhier on 15 April 1734 (D718), in Voltaire, *Correspondence and Related Documents*, ed. Theodore Besterman (Geneva: Institut et Musée Voltaire, 1968–71; Banbury: Voltaire Foundation, 1970–76; Oxford, UK: Voltaire Foundation, 1977), II 460–62 (at 461–62), and in *The Complete Works of Voltaire*, ed. Theodore Besterman et al. (Geneva: Institut et Musée Voltaire, 1968–), LXXXVI 460–62 (at 461–62).

40. For a recent assessment of Cardinal Fleury's administration that is more sympathetic than was the judgment reached by Montesquieu, see Peter R. Campbell, *Power and Politics in Old Regime France, 1720–1743* (London: Routledge, 1996). Cf. Montesquieu, *MP* 1595.

41. For the particular context, see B. Robert Kreiser, *Miracles, Convulsions, and Ecclesiastical Politics in Early Eighteenth-Century Paris* (Princeton, NJ: Princeton University Press, 1978), passim (esp. 54–242); Catherine-Laurence Maire, *Les Convulsionnaires de Saint-Médard: Miracles, convulsions et prophéties à Paris au XVIIIe siècle*, Collection Archives (Paris: Gallimard/Julliard, 1985); Daniel Vidal, *Miracles et convulsions jansénistes au XVIIIe siècle: Le Mal et sa connaissance* (Paris: Presses Universitaires de France, 1987). See also Dale K. Van Kley, *The Religious Origins of the French Revolution: From Calvin to the Civil Constitution, 1560–1791* (New Haven, CT: Yale University Press, 1996), 75–134 (esp. 97–100).

42. See Gay, *Voltaire's Politics*, 66–67. The passage of time did not alter the hostility of Jansenist magistrates to the Enlightenment: see John Rogister, "Louis-Adrien Lepaige and the Attacks on *De l'Esprit* and the *Encyclopédie* in 1759," *English Historical Review* 92 (1977): 522–39.

43. He was by no means blind to the risk he was incurring: see the Letter from Voltaire to Pierre Robert Le Cornier de Cideville on 26 July 1733 (D636), in Voltaire, *Correspondence and Related Documents*, II 365, and in *The Complete Works of Voltaire*, LXXXVI 365.

44. See Gay, *Voltaire's Politics*, 67–68.

45. In this connection, see Robert Shackleton, "Allies and Enemies: Voltaire and Montesquieu," in Shackleton, *Essays on Montesquieu and on the Enlightenment*, 153–69, and Jean Ehrard, "Le Ver et la cochenille," in Ehrard, *L'Esprit des mots: Montesquieu en lui-même et parmi les siens* (Geneva: Droz, 1998), 195–211. Note also Domenico Felice, "Voltaire lettore e critico dell'*Esprit des lois*," in Felice, *Oppressione e libertà* (Pisa: ETS, 2000), 219–53. For the setting within which the two men operated, see also Shackleton, "When Did the French *Philosophes* Become a Party?" in Shackleton, *Essays on Montesquieu and on the Enlightenment*, 447–60.

46. Consider Montesquieu, *Mémoire concernant les moyens d'acquiter les dettes de l'état* (1715), ed. Jean Ehrard, in VF VIII 55–64, in light of Jean Ehrard, "À la Découverte des finances publiques: Le *Mémoire sur les dettes de l'état*," in *Montesquieu: Les Années de formation (1689–1720)*, ed. Catherine Volpilhac-Auger (Oxford, UK: Voltaire Foundation, 1999), 127–42, and David W. Carrithers, "Montesquieu and the Spirit of French Finance: An Analysis of His *Mémoire sur les dettes de l'état* (1715)," in *Montesquieu and the Spirit of Modernity*, ed. David W. Carrithers and Patrick Coleman (Oxford, UK: Voltaire Foundation, 2002), 159–90. In this connection, note Montesquieu, *MP* 274, 301, 341.

47. For the law of censorship and its practice, see Robert Shackleton, "Censure and Censorship: Impediments to Free Publication in the Age of Enlightenment," *Library Chronicle of the University of Texas at Austin* n.s. 6 (December 1973): 25–41, which is reprinted in Shackleton, *Essays on Montesquieu and on the Enlightenment*, 405–20; William Hanley, "The Policing of Thought: Censorship in Eighteenth-Century France," *Studies on Voltaire and the Eighteenth Century* 183 (1980): 265–95; and Edgar Mass, *Literatur und Zensur in der frühen Aufklärung: Produktion, Distribution und Rezeption der Lettres persanes* (Frankfurt am Main: Vittorio Klostermann, 1981), 5–68, 139–205.

48. Voltaire's philosophical letters appear to have been intended as a reply to those of Montesquieu: see Nicholas Cronk, "Introduction: Voltaire, an Augustan Author," in Voltaire, *Letters concerning the English Nation*, xxii, n. 26.

49. The best introduction to this important work is Diana J. Schaub, *Erotic Liberalism: Women and Revolution in Montesquieu's Persian Letters* (Lanham, MD: Rowman & Littlefield, 1995). See also Schaub, "Montesquieu on 'The Woman Problem'," in *Finding a New Feminism: Rethinking the Woman Question for Liberal Democracy*, ed. Pamela Grande Jensen (Lanham, MD: Rowman & Littlefield, 1996), 39–66. For Montesquieu's opinion regarding the controversy concerning Jansenism, see *MP* 426.

50. See Letter from Voltaire to Pierre Robert Le Cornier de Cideville on 26 July 1733 (D636), in Voltaire, *Correspondence and Related Documents*, II 365, and in *The Complete Works of Voltaire*, LXXXVI 365.

51. Cf. [Jean Le Rond d'Alembert], "Éloge de M. le President de Montesquieu," in *Encyclopédie, ou Dictionnaire raisonné des sciences, des arts, et des métiers*, ed. Denis Diderot and Jean Le Rond d'Alembert (Paris: Briasson, 1751–1772; Neufchastel: S. Faulche & Compagnie, 1765; Amsterdam: M. M. Rey, 1776–1777; Paris: Panckoucke, 1777–1780), V iii–xviii (at vii), with Montesquieu, *MP* 1079, 1586.

52. That Montesquieu closely studied the statesmanship of Marlborough is evident: *MP* 2162.

53. See Robert Shackleton, *Montesquieu: A Critical Biography* (Oxford, UK: Oxford University Press, 1961), 91, 122–23, 154. In this connection, see also Montesquieu, *MP* 1466, and Anton Vantuch, *"Réflexions sur la monarchie universelle:* Montesquieu et ses velléités de carrière diplomatique," *Acta Universitatis XVII. Novembris Pragensis. Bulletin* (1974): 177–221.

54. For the significance of this distinction, see Franklin L. Ford, *Robe and Sword: The Regrouping of the French Aristocracy after Louis XIV* (Cambridge, MA: Harvard University Press, 1953).

55. See the Letter from Montesquieu to Lady Hervey on 28 September 1733, in Nagel III 954–56 (at 955).

56. See Shackleton, *Montesquieu,* 91–145. For an earlier, still useful, if occasionally erroneous account, see Churton Collins, *Voltaire, Montesquieu and Rousseau in England,* 117–81. Note also Wade, *The Structure and Form of the French Enlightenment,* I 148–60. Note Montesquieu, *MP* 1132.

57. On the book's appearance, cf. the Letter from l'abbé Jean-Bernard Le Blanc to Jean Bouhier on 15 April 1734, in Hélène Monod-Cassidy, *Un Voyageur-philosophe au XVIIe siècle, l'abbé Jean-Bernard Le Blanc* (Cambridge, MA: Harvard University Press, 1941), 197–205 (at 203), with the Letter from Le Père Louis-Bertrand Castel to Montesquieu on 23 April 1734, in Nagel III 962–63; then see the Letter from l'abbé Jean-Bernard Le Blanc to Jean Bouhier on 3 June 1734, in Monod-Cassidy, *Un Voyageur-philosophe au XVIIIe siècle,* 209–11 (at 210), and the Letter from Le Père Louis-Bertrand Castel to Montesquieu in July, 1734, in Nagel III 969. The book was evidently printed well before it was released for sale to the general public.

58. See Michel Baridon, "Rome et l'Angleterre dans les *Considérations,"* in *Storia e ragione: Le Considérations sur les causes de la grandeur des Romains et de leur décadence di Montesquieu nel 250° della publicazione,* ed. Alberto Postigliola (Naples: Liguori, 1987), 293–309.

59. At one point, as we shall see, Montesquieu started to draft a preface, but he soon abandoned the enterprise and left the draft incomplete. See "Project de préface," in VF II 315–16.

60. See, for example, Shackleton, *Montesquieu,* 157–70; Judith N. Shklar, *Montesquieu* (Oxford, UK: Oxford University Press, 1987), 49–66; and Simone Goyard-Fabre, *Montesquieu: La Nature, les lois, la liberté* (Paris: Presses Universitaires de France, 1993), 24–44.

61. This helps explain why scholars have given it such short shrift: see, for example, Peter Gay, *The Enlightenment: An Interpretation* (New York: Alfred A. Knopf, 1966–1969) I: *The Rise of Modern Paganism,* 50, and Keohane, *Philosophy and the State in France,* 393, 396.

62. It was first published in *Deux Opuscules de Montesquieu,* ed. Charles de Montesquieu (Bordeaux: G. Gounouilhou, 1891), 11–42.

63. For an overview, see Michel Porret, "Introduction," in Montesquieu, *Réflexions sur la monarchie universelle en Europe,* ed. Michel Porret (Geneva: Droz, 2000), 7–68.

64. For the dating of the various hands, see Robert Shackleton, "Les Secrétaires de Montesquieu," in Shackleton, *Essays on Montesquieu and on the Enlightenment*, 65–72, which originally appeared in *French Studies* 8 (1954): 17–27 and was reprinted in Nagel II xxxv–xliii. In connection with the period in which the pertinent amanuensis was in service, see also Shackleton, "La Genèse de *l'Esprit des lois*" and "*L'Esprit des lois*: Le Manuscrit de la Bibliothèque nationale," in Shackleton, *Essays on Montesquieu and on the Enlightenment*, 49–63, 85–92, which originally appeared, respectively, in *Revue d'histoire littéraire de la France* 52 (1952): 425–38 and in Nagel III 567–75; then note Georges Benrekassa, "La Version manuscrite," in Charles-Louis de Secondat, baron de la Brède et de Montesquieu, *De l'Esprit des lois: Livres I et XIII (imprimé et manuscrit)* (Oxford, UK: Voltaire Foundation, 1998), xxv–xxxv (at xxviii n. 10, xxxii), and see Rolando Minuti, "Introduction à *Spicilège*," in VF XIII 3–80 (esp. 52–53, 68), and Georges Benrekassa, *Les Manuscrits de Montesquieu: Secrétaires, ecritures, datations* (Oxford, UK: Voltaire Foundation, 2004), 42–57. The case made by Catherine Volpilhac-Auger, "Une nouvelle 'Chaîne secrète' de *L'Esprit des lois*: L'Histoire de texte," in *Montesquieu en 2005*, ed. Catherine Volpilhac-Auger (Oxford, UK: Voltaire Foundation, 2005), 85–216 (esp. 103–51, 200–216), and "Introduction" and "Annexes A" in VF III xi–ccli (esp. xxxi–lxxviii, clxiv–clxviii), for a revision of Shackleton's scheme does not affect the dating here.

65. Cf. Montesquieu, *MP* 271 and 300, with particular attention to the attendant notes in Montesquieu, *Pensées, Le Spicilège*, ed. Louis Desgraves (Paris: Laffont, 1991), with Montesquieu, *RMU* 5–6, 20–22, and see Patrick Andrivet and Catherine Volpilhac-Auger, "Introduction à *Considérations sur les causes de la grandeur des Romains et de leur décadence*," and Catherine Larrère and Françoise Weil, "Introduction à *Réflexions sur la monarchie universelle en Europe*," in VF II 3–86 (esp. 6, 41–42), 321–37 (esp. 321–24). Scholars have been aware of the Bodmer manuscript for some time: see Henri Auguste Barckhausen, "Avant-Propos" and "Appendice des *Considérations*," in Montesquieu, *Considérations sur les causes de la grandeur des Romains et de leur décadence*, ed. Henri Auguste Barckhausen (Paris: Imprimerie nationale, 1900), iii–xix (esp. xvii), 165–85 (at 181–85), the first of which is reprinted in Barckhausen, *Montesquieu: Ses Idées et ses œuvres d'après les papiers de La Brède* (Paris: Librarie Hachette, 1907), 183–208 (esp. 192).

66. See "Catalogue des manuscripts envoyés à mon cousin en Angleterre," in Nagel III 1575–82 (at 1575) and in VF I lxxv–lxxx (at lxxv), which should be read in light of André Masson, "Introduction: I. Les Recueils de Notes de Montesquieu," in Nagel II ix–xxxiii (esp. xiii–xxi), and Shackleton, *Montesquieu*, 117–18.

67. See *EL* 1.8.17, 19, 21, p. 367, 2.9.6–7, 13.17, 3.17.6, 4.21.21, p. 642, 22, pp. 645–47, where Montesquieu lifts entire passages from *RMU* 8, 10, 15–17, 19–22, 24, and consider, more generally, *EL* 1.8.17–21, 2.9.6, 9–10.16, 11.19, 13.18, 3.17.3–4, 6, where Montesquieu elaborates on themes first developed in *RMU* 1–8, 14, 18–22, 25. In this connection, see Porret, "Introduction," 40–42.

68. In this connection, see Marco Platania, "Guerre ed equilibrio europeo in Montesquieu," *Studi settecenteschi* 22 (2002): 175–206, and Paul A. Rahe, "The Book That

Never Was: Montesquieu's *Considerations on the Romans* in Historical Context," *History of Political Thought* 26:1 (Spring 2005): 43–89.

69. Cf. Niccolò Machiavelli, *Dell'arte della guerra* 2.302–9, in Machiavelli, *Tutte le opere*, ed. Mario Martelli (Florence: G. C. Sansoni, 1971), 332–33, with Machiavelli, *Dell'arte della guerra* 5.93–104, in ibid., 359–60, and see *Istorie fiorentine* 5.1 and 6.1, in ibid., 738–39, 765–66; note Machiavelli, *Discorsi sopra la prima deca di Tito Livio* 2.6, in ibid., 155–56, and then consider the contrast that Machiavelli draws between the liberality of Cyrus, Caesar, and Alexander and the parsimony practiced in his own day by Pope Julius II, Louis XII of France, and Ferdinand of Spain: see *Il principe* 16, in ibid., 280–81. For a discussion of the place of this particular argument within Machiavelli's overall analysis of modern politics, see Rahe, *ATA* 56–100 (esp. 83–100).

70. Note, in this connection, *MP* 207.

71. Cf. *MP* 731, where Montesquieu echoes Machiavelli, and *EL* 2.10.3, where he restates the point made in the passage quoted. In the seventeenth century, though the "tax" levied on those overrun was severe, it was insufficient to cover the costs: see John A. Lynn, "How War Fed War: The Tax of Violence and Contributions during the *Grand Siècle*," *Journal of Modern History* 65:2 (June 1993): 286–310.

72. That this third argument is an afterthought is evident from the fact that Montesquieu reserves it for the second chapter of *RMU* and from the fact that, when he restates his argument in *The Spirit of Laws* (*EL* 2.10.1–3, which should be read with 5.24.3–4), he mentions it not at all: cf. Clark, *Compass of Society*, 89–95, 105 n. 58, with Rahe, "The Book That Never Was," 43–89.

73. Cf. Machiavelli, *Discorsi sopra la prima deca de Tito Livio* 2.10 and *Dell'arte della guerra* 7.178–79, in *Tutte le opere*, 159–60, 386. In the passage in his notebooks on which Montesquieu drew in formulating this argument, he singled out France, England, and Holland as Europe's commercial powers, arguing that in this capacity they "have been the three tyrants of Europe & of the world," and citing as evidence "the efforts so prodigious" mounted by "these three powers" during the War of the Spanish Succession. See *MP* 568. For the meaning of the French word *navigation* as deployed by Montesquieu, see *EL* 4.20.6.

74. Cf. *MP* 555, and 562. Note also *MP* 617, where Montesquieu contends that Louis XIV's desire "to see his grandson on the throne of Spain weakened" his "power." See as well *MP* 239, 375, 557, 645.

75. Cf. *MP* 252–61, and note *EL* 2.13.17, 4.21.21, pp. 644–45. In this connection, see John A. Lynn, "The Growth of the French Army during the Seventeenth Century," *Armed Forces and Society* 6 (1980): 568–85; "The *Trace Italienne* and the Growth of Armies: The French Case," *Journal of Military History* 55 (1991): 297–330; "Recalculating French Army Growth during the *Grand Siècle*, 1610–1715," *French Historical Studies* 18 (1994): 881–906; and "Forging the Western Army in Seventeenth-Century France," in *The Dynamics of Military Revolution, 1300–2050*, ed. Williamson Murray and McGregor Knox (Cambridge, UK: Cambridge University Press, 2001), 35–56, along with *Giant of the Grand Siècle: The French Army, 1610–1715* (Cambridge, UK: Cambridge University Press, 1998), and Guy Rowlands, *The Dynastic State and the Army under Louis XIV* (Cambridge, UK: Cambridge University Press, 2002). More generally, see Brian

M. Downing, *The Military Revolution and Political Change: Origins of Democracy and Autocracy in Early Modern Europe* (Princeton, NJ: Princeton University Press, 1992).

76. See Porret, "Introduction," 11–16, 23–38.

BOOK ONE, CHAPTER TWO. ROME ECLIPSED

1. Note Charles-Jacques Beyer, "Le Rôle de l'idée de postérité chez Montesquieu," in *La Fortune de Montesquieu: Montesquieu écrivain*, ed. Louis Desgraves (Bordeaux: Bibliothèque Municipale, 1995), 65–72 (at 66–67, 71–72); John Robertson, "Gibbon's Roman Empire as a Universal Monarchy: The *Decline and Fall* and the Imperial Idea in Early Modern Europe," in *Edward Gibbon and Empire*, ed. Rosamond McKitterich and Roland E. Quinault (Cambridge, UK: Cambridge University Press, 1997), 247–70 (at 256–70); and Patrick Andrivet and Catherine Volpilhac-Auger, "Introduction à *Considérations sur les causes de la grandeur des Romains et de leur décadence*," and Catherine Larrère and Françoise Weil, "Introduction à *Réflexions sur la monarchie universelle en Europe*," in VF II 3–86, 321–37, and see Marco Platania, "Guerre ed equilibrio europeo in Montesquieu," *Studi settecenteschi* 22 (2002): 175–206, and Paul A. Rahe, "The Book That Never Was: Montesquieu's *Considerations on the Romans* in Historical Context," *History of Political Thought* 26:1 (Spring 2005): 43–89, as well as Henry C. Clark, *Compass of Society: Commerce and Absolutism in Old Regime France* (Lanham, MD: Lexington Books, 2007), 89–95; and Michael Sonenscher, *Before the Deluge: Public Debt, Inequality, and the Intellectual Origins of the French Revolution* (Princeton, NJ: Princeton University Press, 2007), 100–102.

2. See J. S. Richardson, "*Imperium Romanum*: Empire and the Language of Power," *Journal of Roman Studies* 81 (1991): 1–9.

3. See Franz Bosbach, *Monarchia Universalis: Ein politischer Leitbegriff der frühen Neuzeit* (Göttingen: Vandenhoeck & Ruprecht, 1988), 20–124, and John Robertson, "Empire and Union: Two Concepts of the Early Modern European Political Order," in *A Union for Empire: Political Thought and the Union of 1707*, ed. John Robertson (Cambridge, UK: Cambridge University Press, 1995), 3–36 (esp. 6–22). Note, in this connection, John M. Headley, "The Hapsburg World Empire and the Revival of Ghibellinism," *Medieval and Renaissance Studies* 7 (1978): 93–127, and "Gattinara, Erasmus, and the Imperial Configurations of Humanism," *Archiv für Reformationsgeschichte* 71 (1980): 64–98, which should be read in conjunction with Karl Brandi, "Dantes Monarchia und die Italienpolitik Mercurino Gattinaras," *Deutsches Dante-Jahrbuch* 24 (1942): 1–19, and see Anthony Pagden, "Instruments of Empire: Tommaso Campanella and the Universal Monarchy of Spain," in Pagden, *Spanish Imperialism and the Political Imagination* (New Haven, CT: Yale University Press, 1990), 37–63. Note also Pagden, *Lords of All the World: Ideologies of Empire in Spain, Britain, and France, c. 1500–1800* (New Haven, CT: Yale University Press, 1995), 11–62. In this connection, see also John Robertson, "Universal Monarchy and the Liberties of Europe: David Hume's Critique of an English Whig Doctrine," in *Political Discourse in Early Modern Britain*, ed. Nicholas Phillipson and Quentin Skinner (Cambridge, UK: Cambridge University Press, 1993), 349–73, and "Gibbon's Roman Empire as a Universal

Monarchy," 247–70, as well as C. A. Pincus, "The English Debate over Universal Monarchy," in _A Union for Empire_, 37–62.

4. The _Historia romana_ once in the library at La Brède is arguably a relic from these years: consider _Historia romana_ (ca. 1700), ed. Catherine Volpilhac-Auger, in VF VIII 7–41, in light of Catherine Volpilhac-Auger, "Introduction," in ibid., 3–6.

5. Consider Montesquieu, _Dissertation sur la politique des Romains dans la religion_ (1716), ed. Lorenzo Bianchi, in VF VIII 83–98, in light of Lorenzo Bianchi, "Nécessité de la religion et de la tolérance chez Montesquieu: La _Dissertation sur la politique des Romains dans la religion_," in _Lectures de Montesquieu: Actes du Colloque de Wolfenbüttel (26–28 octobre 1989)_, ed. Edgar Mass and Alberto Postigliola (Oxford, UK: Voltaire Foundation, 1993), 25–39. See also Salvatore Rotta, "Montesquieu et le paganisme ancien," in ibid., 151–75.

6. See Montesquieu, _Discours sur Cicéron_ (ca. 1717), ed. Pierre Rétat, in VF VIII 125–31, which should be read in light of Pierre Rétat, "Introduction," in ibid., 119–24. For an English translation, see Montesquieu, "Discourse on Cicero," tr. David Fott, _Political Theory_ 30:5 (October 2002): 733–37.

7. Consider Montesquieu, _MP_ 221 and 1268, esp. p. 348, with an eye to the implications of the dating scheme advanced by Robert Shackleton, "La Genèse de _l'Esprit des lois_," in Shackleton, _Essays on Montesquieu and on the Enlightenment_, ed. David Gilson and Martin Smith (Oxford, UK: Voltaire Foundation, 1988), 49–63, which originally appeared in _Revue d'histoire littéraire de la France_ 52 (1952): 425–38. This essay should be read in conjunction with Shackleton, "Les Secrétaires de Montesquieu," in Shackleton, _Essays on Montesquieu and on the Enlightenment_, 65–72, which originally appeared in _French Studies_ 8 (1954): 17–27 and was reprinted in Nagel II xxxv–xliii; with Rolando Minuti, "Introduction à _Spicilège_," in VF XIII 3–80; and with Georges Benrekassa, _Les Manuscrits de Montesquieu: Secrétaires, ecritures, datations_ (Oxford, UK: Voltaire Foundation, 2004). The case made by Catherine Volpilhac-Auger, "Une nouvelle 'Chaîne secrète' de _L'Esprit des lois_: L'Histoire de texte," in _Montesquieu en 2005_, ed. Catherine Volpilhac-Auger (Oxford, UK: Voltaire Foundation, 2005), 85–216 (esp. 103–51, 200–216), and "Introduction" and "Annexes A," in VF III xi–ccli (esp. xxxi–lxxviii, clxiv–clxviii), for a revision of Shackleton's scheme does not affect the dating here.

8. See Letter to Antoine-Maurice de Solar, Commander of the Order of Malta, on 7 March 1749, in Nagel III 1199–1201 (at 1199).

9. There is a bilingual edition: see Dante, _Monarchia_, ed. and tr. Prue Shaw (Cambridge, UK: Cambridge University Press, 1995). See Charles T. Davis, _Dante and the Idea of Rome_ (Oxford, UK: Clarendon Press, 1957); Ernst H. Kantorowicz, _The King's Two Bodies: A Study in Mediaeval Political Theology_ (Princeton, NJ: Princeton University Press, 1957), 451–95; Larry Peterman, "An Introduction to Dante's _De Monarchia_," _Interpretation: A Journal of Political Philosophy_ 3 (1973): 169–90, and "Dante's _Monarchia_ and Aristotle's Political Thought," _Studies in Medieval and Renaissance History_ 10 (1973): 3–38; and Joel L. Kraemer, "Averroes, Dante, and the Dawn of European Enlightenment," in _Enlightening Revolutions: Essays in Honor of Ralph Lerner_, ed. Svetozar Minkov, with Stéphane Douard (Lanham, MD: Lexington Books, 2006), 57–75.

10. These passages come alive only when read in conjunction with the *Universal Monarchy*: see *CR* 1.108–13, 3.1–15, 4.108–13, 128–63, 5.168–77, 6.133–37.

11. See Michel Porret, "Introduction," in Montesquieu, *Réflexions sur la monarchie universelle en Europe*, ed. Michel Porret (Geneva: Droz, 2000), 7–68 (esp. 11–16, 23–38) — with particular attention to the notes.

12. See Louis-Bertrand Castel, *L'Homme moral opposé à l'homme physique* (Toulouse: [s.n.], 1756), 101–2, and consider the Letters from Le Père Castel to Montesquieu in March, April, and May, 1734, in Nagel III 960–67. The last of these letters is especially revealing with regard to the fears of both men. For further evidence, see Jean Ehrard, "Une Amitié de trente ans: Castel et Montesquieu," in *Autour du Père Castel et du clavecin oculaire, Études sur le XVIIIe siècle*, XXIII, ed. Roland Mortier and Hervé Hasquin (Brussels: Éditions de l'Université de Bruxelles, 1995), 69–81, reprinted in Ehrard, *L'Esprit des mots: Montesquieu en lui-même et parmi les siens* (Geneva: Droz, 1998), 213–30, and Andrivet and Volpilhac-Auger, "Introduction à *Considérations sur les causes de la grandeur des Romains et de leur décadence*," 36–37.

13. For the details, see Cecil Patrick Courtney, "Les Éditions des *Considérations sur les causes de la grandeur des Romains et de leur décadence*, 1734–1758," *Revue française d'histoire du livre* 102–3 (1999): 57–78 (esp. 57–60), and Andrivet and Volpilhac-Auger, "Introduction à *Considérations sur les causes de la grandeur des Romains et de leur décadence*," 37–40, 50–55.

14. At [Montesquieu], *Reflections on the Causes of the Grandeur and Declension of the Romans* (London: W. Innys and R. Manby, 1734), 99 and 190, note c, the translation accords with what is found in the uncorrected first impression: see *CR* 11.15, note c; 18.19, note c. But, at [Montesquieu], *Reflections on the Causes of the Grandeur and Declension of the Romans*, 11, note i, the translator makes use of the corrected text: see *CR* 1.143, note i. The evidence available concerning the translator's identity is not dispositive and suggests confusion in this regard even on the part of Montesquieu: see Robert Shackleton, "Les *Considérations sur les Romains* de Montesquieu: Étude bibliographique," in *Storia e ragione: Le Considérations sur les causes de la grandeur des Romains et de leur décadence di Montesquieu nel 250° della publicazione*, ed. Alberto Postigliola (Naples: Liguori, 1987), 13–19.

15. See the Letter from Le Père Louis-Bertrand Castel to Montesquieu in July 1734, in Nagel III 969 (with note d, which indicates that approval came on 14 July 1734), and the Letter from l'abbé Jean-Bernard Le Blanc to Jean Brouhier on 20 July 1734, in Hélène Monod-Cassidy, *Un Voyageur-philosophe au XVIIIe siècle, l'abbé Jean-Bernard Le Blanc* (Cambridge, MA: Harvard University Press, 1941), 211–13 (at 213), which suggests that the book went on sale in Paris immediately, or almost immediately, thereafter. We get an indication of the trouble that Montesquieu took to secure the *privilège du roi* from his exchange of letters with Madame de Tencin in May 1734, in Nagel III 968–69, and from the Letter from l'abbé Jean-Bernard Le Blanc to Jean Bouhier on 3 June 1734, in Monod-Cassidy, *Un Voyageur-philosophe au XVIIIe siècle*, 209–11 (at 210).

16. See Letter from Montesquieu to Sir Hans Sloane on 4 August 1734 in Nagel III 970.

17. As Ursula Haskins Gonthier has pointed out to me, the English translation was advertised that month in *Gentleman's Magazine* 4 (1734): 456.

18. Cf. [Montesquieu], *Reflections on the Causes of the Grandeur and Declension of the Romans*, 153, 194.

19. Nor should one regard the latter as an afterthought. The *Universal Monarchy* may well have been composed prior to the essay whose argument it was designed to supplement: it was almost certainly thought through beforehand. Parts of it were, in fact, written in the 1720s, prior to Montesquieu's travels in Germany, Italy, and England. Thus, for example, *RMU* 16.275–359, is drawn from *Considérations sur les richesses de l'Espagne* (ca. 1727), ed. Pierre Rétat, in VF VIII 595–623, as is *EL* 4.21.22—to which Montesquieu added a note in 1749 (p. 645, n. b), specifying that the brief unpublished work from which it was derived was written "more than twenty years before." The material evidence confirms this claim: two versions of the *Considérations sur les richesses de l'Espagne* survive in manuscript—one in Montesquieu's hand, the other partly in his hand and partly in that of the amanuensis who penned *MP* 300, part of which appears in *RMU* 6.86–97. This individual, l'abbé Bottereau-Duval, is known to have been employed by Montesquieu from 1721 to 1728 and possibly also for a time after his return from England in 1731 and early 1732: see Andrivet and Volpilhac-Auger, "Introduction à *Considérations sur les causes de la grandeur des Romains et de leur décadence*," 6 n. 11, and Catherine Larrère, "Introduction à *Considérations sur les richesses de l'Espagne*," in VF VIII 583–94 (esp. 583), which should be read in light of Shackleton, "Les Secrétaires de Montesquieu," 65–72 (esp. 67, 69); Minuti, "Introduction à *Spicilège*," 3–80 (esp. 35–36, 50–51, 68); and Benrekassa, *Les Manuscrits de Montesquieu*, 23–217 (esp. 34–41). Note, in this connection, Robert Shackleton, "La Genèse de *l'Esprit des lois*," 49–63 (esp. 51–53). The case made by Volpilhac-Auger, "Une nouvelle 'Chaîne secrète' de *L'Esprit des lois*," 85–216 (esp. 103–51, 200–216), and "Introduction" and "Annexes A," in VF III xi–ccli (esp. xxxi–lxxviii, clxiv–clxviii), for a revision of Shackleton's scheme does not affect the dating here. Note also Catherine Volpilhac-Auger, "Annexe B.5. Emprunts de *L'Esprit des lois* aux *Réflexions sur la monarchie universelle* et aux *Considérations sur les richesses de l'Espagne*," in VF IV 921–22.

20. See Letter to Louis de Kergorlay on 15 December 1850, in Alexis de Tocqueville, *Œuvres, papiers et correspondances*, ed. J.-P. Mayer et al. (Paris: Gallimard, 1951–), XIII:2 229–34 (esp. the paragraph at 232–33 whence comes the epigraph for this chapter), and in Alexis de Tocqueville, *Lettres choisies, Souvenirs*, ed. Françoise Mélonio and Laurence Guellec (Paris: Gallimard, 2003), 700–705. Note also Letter to Pierre Freslon on 20 September 1856, in ibid., 1212–16 (at 1213–14), and see David W. Carrithers, "Montesquieu and Tocqueville as Philosophical Historians: Liberty, Determinism, and the Prospects for Freedom," in *Montesquieu and His Legacy*, ed. Rebecca E. Kingston (Albany: State University of New York Press, 2008), 149–77.

21. One should read Montesquieu, "Project de préface," in VF II 315–16, in light of Andrivet and Volpilhac-Auger, "Introduction à *Considérations sur les causes de la grandeur des Romains et de leur décadence*," 6–9, 48; note Montesquieu, *MP* 1483; and then see Bosbach, *Monarchia Universalis*, 1–19: as the context makes clear, when Montesquieu speaks of *la monarchie*—like Dante, the Ghibellines, and the Guelfs of an earlier age—he has in mind empire, not a particular form of government.

22. See Jean Ehrard, "'Rome enfin que je hais . . . ' ?" in *Storia e ragione*, 23–32, which is reprinted in Ehrard, *L'Esprit des mots*, 55–65.

23. Robert Shackleton, *Montesquieu: A Critical Biography* (Oxford, UK: Oxford University Press, 1961), 157–70, rightly emphasizes Montesquieu's silence in this regard: cf. Jacques-Bénigne Bossuet, *Discours sur l'histoire universelle* (1681) (Paris: Flammarion, 1926), 59–108, 353–94 (1.9–11, 3.6–8). There is, of course, more to this than immediately meets the eye: see Mark Hulliung, *Montesquieu and the Old Regime* (Berkeley: University of California Press, 1976), 167–72; Richard Myers, "Christianity and Politics in Montesquieu's *Greatness and Decline of the Romans*," *Interpretation: A Journal of Political Philosophy* 17 (1989–1990): 223–38; and Douglas Kries, "The Displacement of Christian Historiography in Montesquieu's Book on the Romans," in Kries, *Piety and Humanity: Essays on Religion and Early Modern Political Philosophy* (Lanham, MD: Rowman & Littlefield, 1997), 233–58.

24. As Etorre Levi-Malvano, *Montesquieu and Machiavelli*, tr. A. J. Pansini (Kopperl, TX: Greenvale Press, 1992), demonstrated in 1912, Montesquieu borrowed heavily from the *Discourses on Livy* for the *Dissertation sur la politique des Romains dans la religion* that he read to the Academy of Bordeaux in 1716 and returned to the same source when he composed his *Considerations on the Romans*. For further evidence, see André Bertière, "Montesquieu, lecteur de Machiavel," in *Actes du Congrès Montesquieu réuni à Bordeaux du 23 au 26 mai 1955* (Bordeaux: Impriméries Delmas, 1956), 141–58, and Robert Shackleton, "Montesquieu and Machiavelli: A Reappraisal," in Shackleton, *Essays on Montesquieu and on the Enlightenment*, 117–31, which first appeared in *Comparative Literature Studies* 1 (1964): 1–13 and was reprinted in *Comparative Literature: Matter and Method*, ed. A. Owen Aldridge (Urbana: University of Illinois Press, 1969), 283–95. See also Francesco Gentile, "De Machiavel à Montesquieu," *Notiziario culturale italiano* 11:1 (1970): 1–13; Corrado Rosso, *Montesquieu moraliste: Des Lois au bonheur* (Bordeaux: Ducros, 1971), 317–26; Henri Drei, *La Vertu politique: Machiavel et Montesquieu* (Paris: Harmattan, 1998); and Paul Carrese, "The Machiavellian Spirit of Montesquieu's Liberal Republic," in *Machiavelli's Liberal Republican Legacy*, ed. Paul A. Rahe (New York: Cambridge University Press, 2006), 121–42 (esp. 121–30). There is reason to think that Montesquieu re-read the *Discourses on Livy*, this time in Italian, shortly after his return to France from England: note S 561 (with particular attention to n. 5).

25. This passage should arguably be read, as both Machiavelli and Montesquieu may have read it, in light of Verg. *Aen.* 6. 893–901. For a provocative treatment of this passage in light of the book as a whole, see Eve Adler, *Vergil's Empire: Political Thought in the Aeneid* (Lanham, MD: Rowman & Littlefield, 2003). In this connection, note also Sergio Bertelli, "Noterelle Machiavelliane: Un codice di Lucrezio et di Terenzio," *Rivista storica italiana* 73:3 (September 1961): 544–53, and Paul A. Rahe, "In the Shadow of Lucretius: The Epicurean Foundations of Machiavelli's Political Thought," *History of Political Thought* 28:1 (Spring 2007): 30–55, and ATA 22–55.

26. Niccolò Machiavelli, *Il principe* 15, in Machiavelli, *Tutte le opere*, ed. Mario Martelli (Florence: G. C. Sansoni, 1971), 280.

27. Consider the Letter from Montesquieu to Lady Hervey on 28 September 1733, in Nagel III 954–56 (at 955), in light of Andrivet and Volpilhac-Auger, "Introduction à *Considérations sur les causes de la grandeur des Romains et de leur décadence*," 40.

28. See Hulliung, *Montesquieu and the Old Regime*, 140–67, who rightly sees in the *Considerations on the Romans* not just an appropriation of Machiavelli but also a thoroughgoing critique.

29. This passage was dropped from the edition published in 1748 and was not restored in subsequent editions. Montesquieu had been thinking about the relationship between communication and policy since the early 1720s, if not before: note *MP* 8–9, and see Shackleton, "La Genèse de *l'Esprit des lois*," 49–63 (esp. 51–52). For the significance given the word *police* at this time, see Peter France, "Polish, police, *polis*," in France, *Politeness and Its Discontents: Problems in French Classical Culture* (Cambridge, UK: Cambridge University Press, 1992), 53–73, and Daniel Gordon, *Citizens without Sovereignty: Equality and Sociability in French Thought, 1670–1789* (Princeton, NJ: Princeton University Press, 1994), 18–23.

30. Since the publication of Hannah Arendt, *The Human Condition* (Chicago: University of Chicago Press, 1958), and the appearance of its sequel, Jürgen Habermas, *Strukturwandel der Öffentlichkeit: Untersuchungen zu einer Kategorie der bürgerlichen Gesellschaft* (Neuwied: Hermann Luchterhand Verlag, 1962), now available in translation as Habermas, *The Structural Transformation of the Public Sphere: An Inquiry into a Category of Bourgeois Society*, tr. Thomas Burger (Cambridge, MA: MIT Press, 1989), the role played by public opinion in eighteenth-century France (and in Europe more generally) has received considerable scrutiny: see Keith Michael Baker, "Politics and Public Opinion under the Old Regime: Some Reflections," in *Press and Politics in Pre-Revolutionary France*, ed. Jack R. Censer and Jeremy D. Popkin (Berkeley: University of California Press, 1987), 204–46, which is revised, expanded, and reprinted as Baker, "Public Opinion as a Political Invention," in Baker, *Inventing the French Revolution* (Cambridge, UK: Cambridge University Press, 1990), 167–99, along with Mona Ozouf, "L'Opinion public," in *The French Revolution and the Creation of Modern Political Culture*, ed. Keith Michael Baker et al. (Oxford, UK: Pergamon Press, 1987–1994) I: *The Political Culture of the Old Regime*, 419–34; Gordon, *Citizens without Sovereignty*, passim; Arlette Farge, *Subversive Words: Public Opinion in Eighteenth-Century France*, tr. Rosemary Morris (University Park: Pennsylvania State University Press, 1995); and James Van Horn Melton, *The Rise of the Public in Enlightenment Europe* (Cambridge, UK: Cambridge University Press, 2001). For a much earlier study, which remains valuable, see J. A. W. Gunn, *Queen of the World: Opinion in the Public Life of France from the Renaissance to the Revolution* (Oxford, UK: Voltaire Foundation, 1955).

31. The significance of what had happened was already visible at the time of the Regency: see Thomas Kaiser, "The Abbé de Saint-Pierre, Public Opinion, and the Reconstruction of the French Monarchy," *Journal of Modern History* 55:4 (December 1983): 618–43, and "Money, Despotism, and Public Opinion in Early Eighteenth-Century France: John Law and the Debate on Royal Credit," *Journal of Modern History* 63:1 (March 1991): 1–28.

32. Cf. Gabriel Naudé, *Considérations politiques sur les coups d'État* (1639) (Paris: Éditions

de Paris, 1988), 116–17. Montesquieu came to this conclusion concerning the import of the invention of letters of exchange quite early on: consider *MP* 77 and 280, in light of Shackleton, "La Genèse de *l'Esprit des lois*," 49–63 (esp. 51–52). Regarding Montesquieu's understanding of Machiavelli, see also *MP* 207.

33. See Walter Kuhfuss, "La Notion de modération dans les *Considérations* de Montesquieu," in *Storia e ragione*, 277–92.

34. Cf., however, J. H. Whitfield, *Machiavelli* (New York: Russell & Russell, 1947), 114, who contends that it is "in Montesquieu's account that we first find an exposé of Roman conduct that might easily have served for a copybook for Hitler, with treaties meant to be violated, the yielding of an adversary at one point merely an earnest for a series of yieldings, tribute imposed to make rulers unpopular, and so forth. Montesquieu thus systematized a new view of the Romans which Machiavelli in his simplicity never dreamt of."

35. Cf. Machiavelli, *Discorsi sopra la prima deca di Tito Livio* 1.18.3, 3.8, 16.1–2, 24 (esp. 3.24), which should be read in light of 1.17.1, 35, 37, 40, 46, 53, 60, 2.20, 3.1, 6.19, 28, 31.4, 34, 49, all in *Tutte le opere*, 101–4, 117–20, 123–25, 128–29, 134–36, 143–44, 176, 195–97, 209–13, 222–23, 231, 234–35, 239, 241–43, 253–54. For a meditation on Machiavelli's account of the republic's fall and that of the empire as well, see J. G. A. Pocock, *Barbarism and Religion* (Cambridge, UK: Cambridge University Press, 1999–) III: *The First Decline and Fall*, 208–32.

36. Some of Montesquieu's early readers were shocked by the vehemence of his attack on Rome: see Shackleton, *Montesquieu*, 156–57.

37. See Letter from Claude Adrien Helvétius in 1747, in Nagel III 1102–5 (esp. 1104). For a translation, see the appendix to [Antoine Louis Claude Destutt, comte de Tracy], *A Commentary and Review of Montesquieu's Spirit of Laws*, [tr. Thomas Jefferson] (Philadelphia: William Duane, 1811), 285–89.

38. See Frances Acomb, *Anglophobia in France, 1763–1789: An Essay in the History of Constitutionalism and Nationalism* (Durham, NC: Duke University Press, 1950), 124–28, and Robert Koebner, "The Authenticity of the Letters on the *Esprit des lois* Attributed to Helvetius," *Bulletin of the Institute of Historical Research* 24:69 (May 1951): 19–43, who argue persuasively that the letter is a forgery produced in 1789 by Martin Lefebvre de La Roche, who edited the philosophe's complete works at the end of the eighteenth century. In this connection, see also Marie-Thérèse Inguenaud and David Smith, "Un Disciple d'Helvétius: Martin Lefebvre de La Roche (1738–1806)," *Studies on Voltaire and the Eighteenth Century* 374 (1999): 29–52.

39. See Alexander Hamilton, James Madison, and John Jay, *The Federalist*, ed. Jacob E. Cooke (Middletown, CT: Wesleyan University Press, 1961) no. 47, pp. 324–25, whence comes the epigraph to II.Pref., below. See also Edmund Burke, *An Appeal from the New to the Old Whigs* (1791), in *The Writings and Speeches of the Right Honourable Edmund Burke* (Boston: Little, Brown, 1901), IV 211–12, whence comes the epigraph to this volume.

40. In Montesquieu's published works, there was not a great deal to go on: see *LP* 101/104, 130.30–33/136, and consider *CR* 8.101–6, which is discussed at length in I.3, below.

41. See Charles de Secondat, "Mémoire pour servir a l'éloge historique de M. de Mon-

tesquieu," in Louis Vian, *Histoire de Montesquieu: Sa Vie et ses œuvres* (Geneva: Slatkine Reprints, 1970), 396–407 (at 401).

42. Bibliothèque Nationale de France (Paris) n.a.fr. 12832–12836. In this connection, see Georges Benrekassa, "La Version manuscrite," in Charles-Louis de Secondat, baron de la Brède et de Montesquieu, *De l'Esprit des lois: Livres I et XIII (imprimé et manuscrit)* (Oxford, UK: Voltaire Foundation, 1998), xxv–xxxv; Georges Benrekassa, "La Fabrique de la pensée: L'Étude, la connaissance et l'usage du manuscrit dans *L'Esprit des lois* de Montesquieu," in *Écrire aux XVIIe et XVIIIe siècles: Genèse de textes littéraires et philosophiques*, ed. Jean-Louis Lebrave and Almuth Grésillon (Paris: CNRS Editions, 2000), 105–35; Volpilhac-Auger, "Une nouvelle 'Chaîne secrète' de *L'Esprit des lois*," 85–216 (esp. 85–102, 152–94), and "Introduction," "Annexes A," and "Annexe B.5. Emprunts de *L'Esprit des lois* aux *Réflexions sur la monarchie universelle* et aux *Considérations sur les richesses de l'Espagne*," in VF III xi–ccli (esp. xiii–xxx, lxxix–cxxiv, cxliii–clvi, clxxvii–ccli), IV 921–22.

43. Cf. Shackleton, "Les Secrétaires de Montesquieu," 65–72; Minuti, "Introduction à *Spicilège*," 3–80; and Benrekassa, *Les Manuscrits de Montesquieu*, 23–217, who are in accord, with Volpilhac-Auger, "Une nouvelle 'Chaîne secrète' de *L'Esprit des lois*," 103–51, 200–216, and "Introduction III. De la Main à la plume. Les Secrétaires de Montesquieu," "Annexe A.4. Tableau chronologique partiel de la correspondance manuscrite subsistante de Montesquieu (1734–1754)," and "Annexe A.6. Tableau des 'mains' et des papiers et concordance du manuscrit et de l'imprimé (1748)—Manuscrit de *L'Esprit des lois*, Manuscrit 2506," in VF III xxxi–cxxiv, clxiv–clxviii, clxxvii–ccxxvi, who argues for a somewhat different scheme.

44. See Shackleton, "La Genèse de *l'Esprit des lois*," 49–63, along with Shackleton, "*L'Esprit des lois*: Le Manuscrit de la Bibliothèque nationale," in Shackleton, *Essays on Montesquieu and on the Enlightenment*, 85–92, which originally appeared in Nagel III 567–75; note Shackleton, *Montesquieu*, 285; then see Volpilhac-Auger, "Une nouvelle 'Chaîne secrète' de *L'Esprit des lois*," 85–184 (esp. 117–19, 152–54, 158–60), and "Introduction III. De la Main à la plume. Les Secrétaires de Montesquieu," "Introduction IV. Genèse de *L'Esprit des lois*," "Annexe A.4. Tableau chronologique partiel de la correspondance manuscrite subsistante de Montesquieu (1734–1754)," "Annexe A.6. Tableau des 'mains' et des papiers et concordance du manuscrit et de l'imprimé (1748) —Manuscrit de *L'Esprit des lois*," and "Annexe B.5. Emprunts de *L'Esprit des lois* aux *Réflexions sur la monarchie universelle* et aux *Considérations sur les richesses de l'Espagne*," in VF III xxxi–cxxiv (esp. xlvi–xlviii, lxxix–lxxxiii, lxxxix–xciii), clxiv–clxviii, clxxvii–ccxxxvi (esp. cxci–cxcii, ccv), IV 921–22, who is in agreement with Shackleton on this particular point. From the chapter of his *Universal Monarchy* cited in the text, Montesquieu later had copied out as well the paragraph (*RMU* 8.113–18) that constitutes *EL* 1.8.19: see *MS* 173 with Volpilhac-Auger, "Annexe A.4. Tableau chronologique partiel de la correspondance manuscrite subsistante de Montesquieu (1734–1754)" "Annexe A.6. Tableau des 'mains' et des papiers et concordance du manuscrit et de l'imprimé (1748)—Manuscrit de *L'Esprit des lois*," and "Annexe B.5. Emprunts de *L'Esprit des lois* aux *Réflexions sur la monarchie universelle* et aux *Considérations sur les richesses de l'Espagne*," in VF III clxiv–clxviii, clxxxviii, IV 921–22. In general, where

Montesquieu revised the text of his original draft of a chapter, he did so by substituting a fresh page for the one on which the material needing revision had appeared. It is quite likely that the version of *EL* 2.11.6 he ultimately published differed little from the one originally drafted.

45. See Larrère and Weil, "Introduction à *Réflexions sur la monarchie universelle en Europe*," 321–24.

BOOK ONE, CHAPTER THREE. CARTHAGE ASCENDANT

1. Note *MP* 657.
2. As one would expect, this policy merely systematized what had been from the time of the Wars of Religion the general drift of affairs: see Michel Antoine, "La Monarchie absolue," and Ralph Giesey, "The King Imagined," in *The French Revolution and the Creation of Modern Political Culture*, ed. Keith Michael Baker et al. (Oxford, UK: Pergamon Press, 1987–1994) I: *The Political Culture of the Old Regime*, 3–24, 41–59.
3. With the portrait provided by Montesquieu, one should compare Jacques-Bénigne Bossuet, *Discours sur l'histoire universelle* (1681) (Paris: Flammarion, 1926), 68–70 (1.9 at the end and 1.10 at the beginning), which should be read in light of Jean Ehrard, "'Rome enfin que je hais . . . ' ?" in *Storia e ragione: Le Considérations sur les causes de la grandeur des Romains et de leur décadence di Montesquieu nel 250° della pubblicazione*, ed. Alberto Postigliola (Naples: Liguori, 1987), 23–26, and in Ehrard, *L'Esprit des mots: Montesquieu en lui-même et parmi les siens* (Geneva: Droz, 1998), 55–58. Then note Vittorio de Caprariis, "I *Romani* di Saint-Évremond," *Rivista storica italiana* 67:1 (March 1955): 5–30, 67:2 (June 1955): 148–81; consider Patrick Andrivet, "L'Auguste de Saint-Évremond et l'*Octave* de Montesquieu," in *Storia e ragione*, 139–58, which should be read in conjunction with Andrivet, *Saint-Évremond et l'histoire romaine* (Orléans: Paradigme, 1998); and see Ursula Haskins Gonthier, "Montesquieu and England: Enlightened Exchanges in the Public Sphere (1689–1755)," doctoral thesis, University of Oxford, 2006, 109–53, who cites Charles Perrault, *Le Siècle de Louis le Grand* (Paris: Jean Baptiste Coignard, 1687), 3. Note also Catherine Volpilhac-Auger, "L'Image d'Auguste dans les *Considérations*," in *Storia e ragione*, 159–67.
4. See Letter from Voltaire to Pierre Robert Le Cornier de Cideville on 26 July 1733 (D636), in Voltaire, *Correspondence and Related Documents*, ed. Theodore Besterman (Geneva: Institut et Musée Voltaire, 1968–71; Banbury: Voltaire Foundation, 1970–76; Oxford, UK: Voltaire Foundation, 1977), II 365, and in *The Complete Works of Voltaire*, ed. Theodore Besterman et al. (Geneva: Institut et Musée Voltaire, 1968–), LXXXVI 365.
5. See Denis Diderot, *Lettre adressée à un magistrat sur le commerce de la librairie*, 2nd ed., ed. Bernard Grasset (Paris: B. Grasset, 1937), 143.
6. See Letter to l'abbé Ottaviano, comte di Guasco, on 4 October 1752 in Nagel III 1438–42 (at 1441), with particular reference to ibid., 1441, n. d, which was added by Guasco —on whom, see Robert Shackleton, "L'Abbé de Guasco, ami et traducteur de Montesquieu," in *Actes de l'Académie nationale des sciences, belles-lettres et arts de Bourdeaux*, 4th ser., 15 (1958): 49–60, which is reprinted in Shackleton, *Essays on Mon-*

tesquieu and on the Enlightenment, ed. David Gilson and Martin Smith (Oxford, UK: Voltaire Foundation, 1988), 217–29.

7. In this connection, see Pauline Kra, "La Défense des *Lettres persanes*," and Jean-Paul Schneider, "Les *Lettres persanes*, trente ans après," in *Montesquieu, Œuvre ouverte? (1748–1755): Actes du Colloque de Bordeaux (6–8 décembre 2001, Bordeaux, bibliothèque municipale)*, ed. Catherine Larrère (Oxford, UK: Voltaire Foundation, 2005), 18–49.

8. It is noteworthy that, in sketching out a preface for the revised edition, at one point Montesquieu considered saying not only that the work had been "abandoned by its author at birth" but that he had played no part thereafter "except in regretting that he had composed it [*que par le repentir de l'avoir fait*]." See *MP* 2033 (esp. p. 629, n. c), which is reprinted in VF I 611–13 (where the pertinent material can be found in the *apparatus criticus* at the very end).

9. There is more to this claim than one might think: see David D. Bien, "Manufacturing Nobles: The *Chancellerie* in France to 1789," *Journal of Modern History* 61:3 (September 1989): 639–52, and "Aristocracy," in *A Critical Dictionary of the French Revolution*, ed. François Furet and Mona Ozouf, tr. Arthur Goldhammer (Cambridge, MA: Belknap Press, 1989), 616–28.

10. Montesquieu, who took a dim view of Louis XIV, considered writing a history of his reign: *MP* 1038, 1111, 1122–23, 1145, 1183.

11. In this connection, see Peter Burke, *The Fabrication of Louis XIV* (New Haven, CT: Yale University Press, 1992), 1–133 (esp. 125–33); then consider Jeffrey W. Merrick, *The Desacralization of the French Monarchy in the Eighteenth Century* (Baton Rouge: Louisiana State University Press, 1990); and note Montesquieu, *MP* 1265 in conjunction with 1252, 1983.

12. See Louis Desgraves, "Montesquieu et l'Académie française" (1957), in Desgraves, *Montesquieu: L'Œuvre et la vie* (Paris: L'Esprit du Temps, 1994), 39–60; Robert Shackleton, *Montesquieu: A Critical Biography* (Oxford, UK: Oxford University Press, 1961), 85–89, and Edgar Mass, *Literatur und Zensur in der frühen Aufklärung: Produktion, Distribution und Rezeption der Lettres persanes* (Frankfurt am Main: Vittorio Klostermann, 1981), 156–62.

13. Note Fernand Baldensperger, "Un Jugement diplomatique inédit sur Montesquieu en Angleterre," *Revue de littérature comparée* 9 (1929): 348–50, and see Mass, *Literatur und Zensur in der frühen Aufklärung*, 161. In this connection, note also Anton Vantuch, "*Réflexions sur la monarchie universelle*: Montesquieu et ses velléités de carrière diplomatique," *Acta Universitatis XVII. Novembris Pragensis. Bulletin* (1974): 177–221.

14. In the posthumous edition of 1758, Usbek is made to seem slightly less pessimistic.

15. Note the depiction of priests in general as eunuchs in *LP* 113/117 and the suggestion that their castration would be appropriate in 80.1–3/82; then consider 2–4, 6–7, 9, 19–20/20–21, 24–25/26–27, 39–41/41–43, 45/47, 51/53, 60/62, 62–63/64–65, 68–69/70–71, 77/79, 93/96, 139–48/147–56, 149/159, 150/161 in light of 35.10–25/37, 86.5–16/88, and 104/107. The posthumous edition 1758 edition includes a number of additional letters pertinent to the narrative of the harem: see Montesquieu, *Lettres persanes* 15, 22, 157–

58, 160, in Pléiade I 154, 163, 369–70, 372. It was in the first of these that Montesquieu distinguished the servitude of obedience from the servitude of command. In this connection, see Pauline Kra, "Religion in Montesquieu's *Lettres persanes*," *Studies on Voltaire and the Eighteenth Century* 72 (1970): 11–224 (esp. 187–204); Diana J. Schaub, *Erotic Liberalism: Women and Revolution in Montesquieu's Persian Letters* (Lanham, MD: Rowman & Littlefield, 1995), passim (esp. 16–54, 71–92); and Céline Spector, *Montesquieu, Les Lettres persanes: De l'Anthropologie à la politique* (Paris: Presses Universitaires de France, 1997), 75–78.

16. See Orest Ranum, "Personality and Politics in the *Persian Letters*," *Political Science Quarterly* 84:4 (December 1969): 606–27, who is quite right to emphasize *S* 465, where Montesquieu suggests that Dubois had the Regent read Hobbes. For a useful exposition of the logic of fear and collaboration underpinning despotism as depicted in the *Lettres persanes*, see Corey Robin, "Reflections on Fear: Montesquieu in Retrieval," *American Political Science Review* 94:2 (June 2000): 347–60, who neglects the secondary literature highlighting the elements in the harem narrative suggesting a burlesque of the religious orders and of Christianity more generally, which is cited in note 19, this chapter; and who therefore errs in taking at face value Usbek's predilection for passing off despotic command as holy law. For a brief discussion clarifying the difference between the two, see Bernard Manin, "Montesquieu, la république et le commerce," *Archives Européennes de Sociologie* 42:3 (2001): 573–602 (at 577–82).

17. See Letter from Denis Dodart on 11 August 1723, in VF XVIII 51–52 (at 51). In this connection, note *MP* 739, 783.

18. Consider Mass, *Literatur und Zensur in der frühen Aufklärung*, 172–74, in light of ibid., 5–68.

19. The various references to eunuchs and wives being "consecrated" and that to the provision of a "holy education within the [harem's] Sacred walls," which can be found in *LP* 39.4/41, 40.15/42, 60.4–8/62 and also in *Lettres persanes* 22, in Pléiade I 163, which reprints the posthumous edition of 1758, and the depiction of Roman Catholic priests as eunuchs in *LP* 113/117 should be read with an eye to Kra, "Religion in Montesquieu's *Lettres persanes*," 187–204, and to Schaub, *Erotic Liberalism*, 16–54, 71–92, who argue, quite plausibly, that Montesquieu also intends that the harem be interpreted as an image of a convent, on the one hand, and of the Roman Catholic Church, on the other.

20. See Mass, *Literatur und Zensur in der frühen Aufklärung*, 139–271. The impressive critique laid out by Jean Baptiste Gaultier, *Les Lettres persannes convaincues d'impiété* (Paris: n.p., 1751), deserves special attention.

21. See Laurence Macé, "*Les Lettres persanes* devant l'Index: Une Censure 'posthume'," in *Montesquieu en 2005*, ed. Catherine Volpilhac-Auger (Oxford, UK: Voltaire Foundation, 2005), 48–59.

22. See Robin Briggs, "The Catholic Puritans: Jansenists and Rigorists in France," in Briggs, *Communities of Belief: Cultural and Social Tension in Early Modern France* (Oxford: Clarendon Press, 1989), 339–63, and Catherine-Laurence Maire, "Port-Royal: The Jansenist Schism," in *Realms of Memory: Rethinking the French Past I: Conflicts and Divisions*, ed. Pierre Nora, tr. Arthur Goldhammer (New York: Columbia Univer-

sity Press, 1996), 301–51. For a brief history of Jansenism more recent yet, see William Doyle, *Jansenism: Catholic Resistance to Authority from the Reformation to the French Revolution* (London: Macmillan, 2000).

23. See Lucien Ceyssens and Joseph A. G. Tans, *Autour de l'Unigenitus: Recherches sur la genèse de la Constitution* (Louvain: Leuven University Press, 1987).

24. Montesquieu thought Fleury's handling of the problem a great success: *MP* 914, 1226.

25. This material should be read in light of what Montesquieu intimates elsewhere in this work regarding the defects of Christianity in general and Roman Catholicism in particular: see *LP* 27/29, 44/46, 46–47/48–49, 55/57, 80/82, 110/114, 112–13/116–17, 128/134, 137/143. From the outset, Montesquieu was an admirer of the tolerant policy pursued by the ancient pagans: consider Montesquieu, *Dissertation sur la politique des Romains dans la religion* (1716), ed. Lorenzo Bianchi, 186–92, in VF VIII 83–98 (at 92), in light of Lorenzo Bianchi, "Religione e tolleranza in Montesquieu," *Rivista di storia della filosofia* 49:1 (January–March 1994): 49–71, as well as Lorenzo Bianchi, "Nécessité de la religion et de la tolérance chez Montesquieu: La *Dissertation sur la politique des Romains dans la religion*," in *Lectures de Montesquieu: Actes du Colloque de Wolfenbüttel (26–28 octobre 1989)*, ed. Edgar Mass and Alberto Postigliola (Oxford, UK: Voltaire Foundation, 1993), 25–39. See also Salvatore Rotta, "Montesquieu et le paganisme ancien," in ibid., 151–75.

26. Note also the letter on this subject added to the posthumous edition: *Lettres persanes* 124, in Pléiade I 315–16; and, in this context, consider *LP* 107/110 and *MP* 1254.

27. For the details, see the lively, analytical account produced by Paul Langford, *The Excise Crisis: Society and Politics in the Age of Walpole* (Oxford, UK: Clarendon Press, 1975). For an overview focused on the role played by popular opinion in British politics in the eighteenth century, see James Van Horn Melton, *The Rise of the Public in Enlightenment Europe* (Cambridge, UK: Cambridge University Press, 2001), 19–44 (esp. 27–28). In general, students of this subject have paid insufficient attention to developments much earlier, under the early Stuarts and during the interregnum: see Joad Raymond, "The Newspaper, Public Opinion, and the Public Sphere in the Seventeenth Century," in *News, Newspapers, and Society in Early Modern Britain*, ed. Joad Raymond (London: Frank Cass, 1999), 109–40, and Rahe, *ATA* 179–83.

28. Note François Furet and Mona Ozouf, "Deux légitimations historiques de la société française au XVIIIe siècle: Mably et Boulainvilliers," *Annales ÉSC* 34 (1979): 438–50, and see Harold A. Ellis, *Boulainvilliers and the French Monarchy: Aristocratic Politics in Early Eighteenth-Century France* (Ithaca, NY: Cornell University Press, 1988), and Diego Venturino, *Le ragioni della tradizione, nobiltà e mondo moderno in Boulainvilliers (1685–1722)* (Turin: Casa editrice Le Lettere, 1993).

29. See Élie Carcassonne, *Montesquieu et le problème de la constitution française au XVIIIe siècle* (Paris: Presses Universitaires de France, 1927), esp. 25–38, 261–96; Dale Van Kley, *The Damiens Affair and the Unraveling of the Old Regime, 1750–1770* (Princeton, NJ: Princeton University Press, 1984), 166–225; and Ran Halévi, "The Illusion of 'Honor': Nobility and Monarchical Construction in the Eighteenth Century," tr. Mary Schwartz, in *Tocqueville and Beyond: Essays on the Old Regime in Honor of*

David D. Bien, ed. Robert M. Schwartz and Robert A. Schneider (Newark: University of Delaware Press, 2003), 71–85.

30. For a lucid account of the ambiguous role that the parlements played, see John J. Hurt, *Louis XIV and the Parlements: The Assertion of Royal Authority* (Manchester, UK: Manchester University Press, 2002), 1–16.

31. See William Doyle, "The Parlements," in *The Political Culture of the Old Regime*, 157–67, and David A. Bell, *Lawyers and Citizens: The Formation of a Political Elite in Old Regime France* (New York: Oxford University Press, 1994), 21–66.

32. Note Montesquieu, *MP* 2266, and see Rebecca E. Kingston, *Montesquieu and the Parlement of Bordeaux* (Geneva: Librairie Droz, 1996), and Jacob T. Levy, "Montesquieu's Constitutional Legacies," in *Montesquieu and His Legacy*, ed. Rebecca E. Kingston (Albany: State University of New York Press, 2008), 115–37.

33. See Jean Starobinski, "Exile, Satire, Tyranny: Montesquieu's *Persian Letters*," in Starobinski, *Blessings in Disguise; or, The Morality of Evil*, tr. Arthur Goldhammer (Cambridge, MA: Harvard University Press, 1993), 60–83 (at 71–73); then reflect on what can be discerned concerning the general drift of affairs in France: see Antoine, "La Monarchie absolue," 3–24, and Giesey, "The King Imagined," 41–59; and consider Sarah Hanley, *The Lit de Justice of the Kings of France: Constitutional Ideology in Legend, Ritual, and Discourse* (Princeton, NJ: Princeton University Press, 1983). In this connection, note also William F. Church, "The Decline of the French Jurists as Political Theorists, 1660–1789," *French Historical Studies* 5:1 (Spring 1967): 1–40, and Colin Kaiser, "The Deflation in the Volume of Litigation at Paris in the Eighteenth Century and the Waning of the Old Judicial Order," *European Studies Review* 10 (1980): 309–36.

34. See A. Lloyd Moote, *The Revolt of the Judges: The Parlement of Paris and the Fronde, 1648–1652* (Princeton, NJ: Princeton University Press, 1971), and note Paul Alexandre R. Janet, *Histoire de la science politique dans ses rapports avec la morale*, 4th ed. rev. (Paris: Félix Alcan, 1913), 361–65.

35. See Hurt, *Louis XIV and the Parlements*, 17–199.

36. After taking note of David A. Bell, "Des Stratégies d'opposition sous Louis XV: L'Affaire des avocats, 1730–31," *Histoire, économie et société* 9:4 (1990): 567–90, and *Lawyers and Citizens*, 62–112, consider the exemplary analytical account provided by Peter R. Campbell, *Power and Politics in Old Regime France, 1720–1743* (London: Routledge, 1996), 193–274. Then see Melton, *The Rise of the Public in Enlightenment Europe*, 45–77 (esp. 48–55). Note also Farge, *Subversive Words*, 7–48, 59–98, 109–21.

37. In the aftermath, consistent with his worries concerning the vulnerability of the parlements, Montesquieu came to be persuaded that raising the issue again would be an act of great imprudence on their part: after reading *MP* 690, 1226, note 2158, 2168, 2176, 2247; see the Letter of Montesquieu to Jean Baptiste François Durey de Meinières on 9 July 1753, in Nagel III 1465–69; and consider Montesquieu's *Mémoire sur le silence à imposer sur la Constitution*, 1754 (Bordeaux, BM, MS 2103), which was originally published in *Mélanges inédits de Montesquieu*, ed. Le Baron de Montesquieu (Bordeaux: G. Gounoilhou, 1892), 227–34 and has now been reprinted in VF IX 529–35. See also Bordeaux, BM, MS 2506/1 f. 4, which is published in Catherine Volpilhac-Auger,

L'Atelier de Montesquieu: Manuscrits inédits de La Brède (Oxford, UK: Voltaire Foundation, 2001), 152–53.

38. See Gonthier, "Montesquieu and England," 109–53.

39. From Montesquieu's exchange of letters with Madame de Tencin in May, 1734, in Nagel III 968–69, and from the Letter from l'abbé Jean-Bernard Le Blanc to Jean Bouhier on 3 June 1734, in Hélène Monod-Cassidy, *Un Voyageur-philosophe au XVIIIe siècle, l'abbé Jean-Bernard Le Blanc* (Cambridge, MA: Harvard University Press, 1941), 209–11 (at 210), we get an indication of the difficulties that Montesquieu faced when he sought the *privilège du roi.*

40. To the copies already published in Amsterdam and slated for distribution in France, Montesquieu added a sheet of errata reflecting the change. Subsequent editions printed in France incorporated the change; editions published abroad followed the language of the original edition: see the notes to CR 8.101–2. As one would expect, the work's original English translator followed the version found in the unexpurgated first impression: see [Montesquieu], *Reflections on the Causes of the Grandeur and Declension of the Romans* (London: W. Innys and R. Manby, 1734), 84.

41. Note *MP* 650.

42. See [Charles-Louis de Secondat, baron de la Brède et de Montesquieu], *De l'Esprit des loix* (Geneva: Barrillot & Fils, [1748]), I 499–522.

43. In this connection, see Guillaume Barrera, "Montesquieu et la mer," *Revue Montesquieu* 2 (1998): 7–44 (esp. 36–44).

44. At least in part, the second essay was already in existence when secretary "H," who appears to have worked for Montesquieu from the spring of 1741 to the fall of 1742, produced a clean copy of the more or less fully articulated manuscript of *The Spirit of Laws.* It is possible that the second essay was originally drafted before 1734; if so, it was thoroughly revised not only before this particular clean copy was produced, but again thereafter at some point before secretary "O" completed his work in the autumn of 1746. Given Montesquieu's eagerness in 1733 to discuss English affairs, it is highly likely that, if the original draft postdates the *Considerations on the Romans,* it was produced not long after that work's appearance. Cf. Robert Shackleton, *L'Esprit des lois:* Le Manuscrit de la Bibliothèque nationale," in Shackleton, *Essays on Montesquieu and on the Enlightenment,* 85–92 (esp. 92), which originally appeared in Nagel III 567–75, with Shackleton, *Montesquieu,* 295–96, and see Catherine Volpilhac-Auger, "Une nouvelle 'Chaîne secrète' de *L'Esprit des lois:* L'Histoire de texte," in *Montesquieu en 2005,* ed. Catherine Volpilhac-Auger (Oxford, UK: Voltaire Foundation, 2005), 85–216 (esp. 119–25, 152–63), and "Introduction III. De la Main à la plume. Les Secrétaires de Montesquieu," "Annexe A.4. Tableau chronologique partiel de la correspondance manuscrite subsistante de Montesquieu (1734–1754)," and "Annexe A.6. Tableau des 'mains' et des papiers et concordance du manuscrit et de l'imprimé (1748)—Manuscrit de *L'Esprit des lois,* Manuscrit 2506," in VF III xxxi–cxxiv, clxiv–clxviii, clxxvii–ccli (esp. xlviii–lv, lxxix–xcvi, ccviii–ccix), whose redating of the tenure of some of Montesquieu's secretaries seems justified.

45. Consider [Montesquieu], *Two Chapters of a celebrated French work, intitled De l'Esprit des loix, translated into English. One, treating of the constitution of England; another of*

the character and manners which result from this constitution (Edinburgh: Hamilton and Balfour, 1750), in light of Ernest Campbell Mossner, *The Life of David Hume*, 2nd ed. (Oxford, UK: Clarendon Press, 1980), 229, 232, and Warren McDougall, "Gaven Hamilton, Bookseller in Edinburgh," *British Journal for Eighteenth-Century Studies* 1 (1978): 1–19, and see Cecil Patrick Courtney, "Morals and Manners in Montesquieu's Analysis of the British System of Liberty," in *Montesquieu and His Legacy*, 31–48, who draws attention to evidence proving that this little pamphlet was published some months before the release of Thomas Nugent's comprehensive English translation of *L'Esprit des lois*.

46. In this connection, see Keith Michael Baker, "Politics and Public Opinion under the Old Regime: Some Reflections," in *Press and Politics in Pre-Revolutionary France*, ed. Jack R. Censer and Jeremy D. Popkin (Berkeley: University of California Press, 1987), 204–46 (at 214–21), which is revised, expanded, and reprinted as Baker, "Public Opinion as a Political Invention," in Baker, *Inventing the French Revolution* (Cambridge, UK: Cambridge University Press, 1990), 167–99 (at 173–78). There can be little doubt that Montesquieu's rhetorical strategy in *EL* 3.19.27 is deliberate. In this chapter, at some point after 1741/42, one of Montesquieu's secretaries systematically substituted the conditional for the future tense: consider Montesquieu, *MS* 483–91 in light of Volpilhac-Auger, "Annexe A.4. Tableau chronologique partiel de la correspondance manuscrite subsistante de Montesquieu (1734–1754)," and "Annexe A.6. Tableau des 'mains' et des papiers et concordance du manuscrit et de l'imprimé (1748)—Manuscrit de *L'Esprit des lois*," in VF III clxiv–clxviii, ccviii–ccix.

47. For a detailed discussion, with full citation of the secondary literature, see II.2–4, III.4, below.

48. An exception to the rule is John Robertson, "Universal Monarchy and the Liberties of Europe: David Hume's Critique of an English Whig Doctrine," in *Political Discourse in Early Modern Britain*, ed. Nicholas Phillipson and Quentin Skinner (Cambridge, UK: Cambridge University Press, 1993), 349–73 (at 364–68), who notices as well the connection between Montesquieu's *Universal Monarchy* and the discussion of English foreign policy in this chapter of *The Spirit of Laws*.

49. Cf. Montesquieu, *MP* 36.

50. Note Montesquieu, *CR* 3.1–31, which should be read in conjunction with *MP* 557, 639, and 746, and *RMU* 24.432–52, which should be read in light of *MP* 252, 645, and 1345. Then see *EL* 2.13.17, 4.20.4–5, 10. For a more recent discussion of this question, see Roland Mousnier, "L'Évolution des finances publiques en France et en Angleterre pendant les guerres de la Ligue d'Augsbourg et de la Succession d'Espagne," *Revue historique* 205 (1951): 1–23.

51. This passage should be read in light of Montesquieu, *EL* 4.22.17–18. Montesquieu had not always thought England's propensity for borrowing an advantage: cf. *MP* 154. Nor was he always persuaded that England could manage its debt: see 17, 252, 259–61. To its significance and to the measures taken for its management, he remained at all times sensitive: 1640, 1649–50, 2258. In his final judgment, however, Montesquieu was far more sanguine than was David Hume, and he was remarkably perceptive as well: after perusing Istvan Hont, "The Rhapsody of Public Debt: David Hume and Voluntary

State Bankruptcy," in *Political Discourse in Early Modern Britain*, 321–48, which is reprinted in Hont, *Jealousy of Trade: International Competition and the Nation-State in Historical Perspective* (Cambridge, MA: Harvard University Press, 2005), 325–53, note Melton, *The Rise of the Public in Enlightenment Europe*, 61–75 (esp. 72–75); see P. G. M. Dickson, *The Financial Revolution in England: A Study in the Development of Public Credit, 1688–1756* (London: Macmillan, 1967); Douglas North and Barry Weingast, "Constitutions and Commitment: Evolution of the Institutions Governing Public Choice in Seventeenth Century England," *Journal of Economic History* 49 (1989): 803–32; and Bruce Carruthers, *City of Capital: Politics and Markets in the English Financial Revolution* (Princeton, NJ: Princeton University Press, 1996); then consider John Brewer, *The Sinews of Power: War, Money, and the English State, 1688–1783* (New York: Knopf, 1989). England's financial revolution was modeled on that achieved by the Dutch in the sixteenth century: see James D. Tracy, *A Financial Revolution in the Netherlands* (Berkeley: University of California Press, 1985), and *A Financial History of the Netherlands*, ed. Marjolein 't Hart, Joost Jonker, and Jan Luiten Van Zanden (Cambridge, UK: Cambridge University Press, 1997).

52. Cf., for example, Roger L'Estrange's claim, advanced on the eve of the Restoration, that "our former Government, eminently, included all the perfections of a Free-State, and was the Kernel, as it were, of a Common-wealth, in the shell of Monarchy." See [L'Estrange], *A Plea for Limited Monarchy, As it Was Established in this Nation, Before the Late War* (1660), in *The Struggle for Sovereignty: Seventeenth-Century English Political Tracts*, ed. Joyce Lee Malcolm (Indianapolis, IN: Liberty Press, 1999), I 495–504 (at 499). Consider also Sir Robert Walpole's remark that Britain's government "was in reality a popular government that only bore the name of monarchy," as reported by his friend, and Montesquieu's friend and correspondant, John, Lord Hervey, *Some Materials towards Memoirs of the Reign of King George II*, ed. Romney Sedgwick (London: Eyre & Spottiswoode, 1931), 128–29. This sort of claim was frequently heard from the late Tudor period on: see Patrick Collinson, "The Monarchical Republic of Queen Elizabeth I," *Bulletin of the John Rylands Library of Manchester* 69 (1987): 394–424. Note also David Hume, "Of the Liberty of the Press" (1741), "Of the Independency of Parliament" (1741), and "Of the Parties of Great Britain" (1741), in Hume, *Essays Moral, Political, and Literary*, rev. ed., ed. Eugene F. Miller (Indianapolis, IN: Liberty Classics, 1985), 9–13, 44–53, 64–72.

53. That, in deploying this phrase, Montesquieu had England in mind was perfectly evident to readers at the time: see Letter from David Hume to Montesquieu on 10 April 1749, in Nagel III 1217–22 (at 1218, with n. c) and in *Letters of David Hume*, ed. J. Y. T. Greig (Oxford: Clarendon Press, 1932), I 133–38 (at 134, with n. 5).

54. To grasp what Montesquieu has in mind when he speaks of *préjugés destructeurs*, one must reflect on *EL* Préf., 2.10.4, 4.20.1–2, 7; 5.25.12–13, and consider Diana J. Schaub, "Of Believers and Barbarians: Montesquieu's Enlightened Toleration," in *Early Modern Skepticism and the Origins of Toleration*, ed. Alan Levine (Lanham, MD: Lexington Books, 1999), 225–47. Note also Montesquieu, "Discours sur les motifs qui doivent nous encourager au sciences," 15 November 1725, ed. Sheila Mason, in VF VIII 495–502 (esp. 495–98), and *MP* 1252, 1265, 1268, 1983.

55. This should be read in conjunction with *EL* 4.20.12.

56. Already, in the early 1720s, Montesquieu was persuaded that England alone had managed to combine empire with commerce: note *LP* 130.30–34/136; then see Shackleton, *Montesquieu*, 77–78.

57. Cf. Niccolò Machiavelli, *Istorie fiorentine* 1.29, in Machiavelli, *Tutte le opere*, ed. Mario Martelli (Florence: G. C. Sansoni, 1971), 652–53.

58. While on his visit to England, Montesquieu wrote that "if any nation is to be abandoned by its colonies, this will commence with the English nation." See *NA* 883.

59. This should be read in conjunction with *EL* 4.20.8; 21.7, p. 611. Cf. *MP* 428, where Montesquieu suggests that it should be a "great maxim for France to force England always to have a land army" since the fact that it would "cost it a great deal of money" would "diminish to that degree its funds for the navy." Note also 645, 2082.

60. After consulting I.1, note 67, above, see Montesquieu, *EL* 2.11.5–20.

61. In this connection, see Georges Ascoli, *La Grande-Bretagne devant l'opinion française au XVIIe siècle* (Paris: Gamber, 1930), and Josephine Grieder, *Anglomania in France, 1740–1789: Fact, Fiction, and Political Discourse* (Geneva: Librairie Droz, 1985).

62. After digesting Catherine Betty Abigail Behrens, "Nobles, Privileges, and Taxes in France at the End of the Ancien Régime," *Economic History Review*, 2nd ser. 15:3 (April 1963): 451–75; Peter Mathias and Patrick O'Brien, "Taxation in Britain and France, 1715–1810: A Comparison of the Social and Economic Incidence of Taxes Collected for the Central Government," *Journal of European Economic History* 5 (1976): 601–50; David Bien, "Offices, Corps, and a System of State Credit: The Uses of Privilege under the Ancien Régime," in *The Political Culture of the Old Regime*, ed. Keith M. Baker (Oxford, UK: Pergamon Press, 1987), 87–114; Michael Kwass, *Privilege and the Politics of Taxation in Eighteenth-Century France: Liberté, Egalité, Fiscalité* (Cambridge, UK: Cambridge University Press, 2000); and Gail Bossenga, "The Patrimonial State, Markets, and the Origins of the French Revolution," *1650–1850: Ideas, Aesthetics, and Inquiries in the Early Modern Era* 11 (2005): 443–509, consider Michael Sonenscher, "The Nation's Debt and the Birth of the Modern Republic: The French Fiscal Deficit and the Politics of the Revolution of 1789," *History of Political Thought* 18:1 (Spring 1997): 64–103 and 18:2 (Summer 1997): 267–325, and *Before the Deluge: Public Debt, Inequality, and the Intellectual Origins of the French Revolution* (Princeton, NJ: Princeton University Press, 2007). In this connection, note David Stasavage, *Public Debt and the Birth of the Democratic State: France and Great Britain, 1688–1789* (Cambridge, UK: Cambridge University Press, 2003).

63. See Catherine Betty Abigail Behrens, *The Ancien Régime* (New York: Harcourt, Brace, & World, 1967), 138–62; Theda Skocpol, *States and Social Revolutions: A Comparative Analysis of France, Russia, and China* (Cambridge, UK: Cambridge University Press, 1979), 51–67; and Bailey Stone, *The Genesis of the French Revolution: A Global-Historical Interpretation* (Cambridge, UK: Cambridge University Press, 1994), and *Reinterpreting the French Revolution: A Global-Historical Perspective* (Cambridge, UK: Cambridge University Press, 2002), 1–61. In this connection, note also Catherine Betty Abigail Behrens, *Society, Government, and the Enlightenment: The Experiences of Eighteenth-Century France and Prussia* (New York: Harper & Row, 1985).

64. In this connection, see James C. Riley, *The Seven Years War and the Old Regime in France: The Economic and Financial Toll* (Princeton, NJ: Princeton University Press, 1987). Note, however, David R. Weir, "Tontines, Public Finance, and Revolution in France and England, 1688–1789," *Journal of Economic History* 49 (1989): 95–124.

65. See John F. Bosher, *French Finances, 1770–1795: From Business to Bureaucracy* (Cambridge, UK: Cambridge University Press, 1970), who traces the incapacity of France in this regard to the character of the regime; Jean Egret, *Necker: Ministre de Louis XVI, 1775–1790* (Paris: Champion, 1975); Robert D. Harris, *Necker: Reform Statesman of the Ancien Régime* (Berkeley: University of California Press, 1979), and *Necker and the Revolution of 1789* (Lanham, MD: University Press of America, 1986); and Eugene N. White, "Was There a Solution to the Ancien Régime's Financial Dilemma?" *Journal of Economic History* 49 (1989): 545–68.

66. See Frances Acomb, *Anglophobia in France, 1763–1789: An Essay in the History of Constitutionalism and Nationalism* (Durham, NC: Duke University Press, 1950).

67. See Henry C. Clark, *Compass of Society: Commerce and Absolutism in Old Regime France* (Lanham, MD: Lexington Books, 2007), 153–91. With regard to Physiocratic doctrine more generally, see Michael Sonenscher, "Physiocracy as Theodicy," *History of Political Thought* 23:2 (Summer 2002): 326–39, and *Before the Deluge*, 199–222.

68. See [Abbé Séran de la Tour], *Parallèle de la conduite des Carthaginois, à l'égard des Romains, dans la seconde guerre punique avec la conduite de l'Angleterre, à l'égard de la France, dans la guerre déclarée par ces deux puissances en 1756, où l'on voit l'origine, les motifs, les moyens & les suites de cette guerre jusqu'au mois de décembre 1756* (s.l.: s.n., 1757), passim (esp. 170, whence comes the epigraph for this chapter).

69. See Edmond Dziembowski, *Un nouveau Patriotisme français, 1750–1770: La France face à la puissance anglais à l'époque de la guerre de Sept Ans* (Oxford, UK: Voltaire Foundation, 1998), along with Clarence D. Brenner, *L'Histoire nationale dans la tragédie française du dix-huitième siècle* (Berkeley: University of California Press, 1929), 243–66; Charles Gevaert Salas, "Punic Wars in France and Britain," Ph.D. diss., Claremont Graduate School, 1996; and Nicholas Rowe, "Romans and Carthaginians in the Eighteenth Century: Imperial Ideology and National Identity in Britain and France during the Seven Years War," Ph.D. diss., Boston College, 1997; then see Norman Hampson, *The Perfidy of Albion: French Perceptions of England during the French Revolution* (London: St. Martin's Press, 1998).

70. See Stone, *Reinterpreting the French Revolution*, 62–268.

71. See Paul A. Rahe, *Soft Despotism, Democracy's Drift: Montesquieu, Rousseau, Tocqueville, and the Modern Prospect* (New Haven, CT: Yale University Press, 2009) II. By the 1770s, Rousseau's argument was beginning to have a political impact: see Roger Barny, *Prélude idéologique à la Révolution française: Le Rousseauisme avant 1789* (Paris: Belles Lettres, 1985).

72. Consider Harold T. Parker, *The Cult of Antiquity and the French Revolutionaries: A Study in the Development of the Revolutionary Spirit* (Chicago: University of Chicago Press, 1937), and Claude Mossé, *L'Antiquité dans la Révolution française* (Paris: Albin Michel, 1989), in conjunction with Denise Leduc-Fayette, *Jean-Jacques Rousseau et le mythe de l'antiquité* (Paris: J. Vrin, 1974).

73. In this connection, see David A. Bell, *The Cult of the Nation in France: Inventing Nationalism, 1680–1800* (Cambridge, MA: Harvard University Press, 2001).

74. See Dominique de Villepin, *Les Cent Jours, ou L'Esprit de sacrifice* (Paris: Librairie Académique Perrin, 2001).

75. He had reached this conclusion by 1914, if not before: see Fraser J. Harbutt, *The Iron Curtain: Churchill, America, and the Origins of the Cold War* (New York: Oxford University Press, 1986), 8–9.

76. For recent attempts to articulate the peculiar logic underpinning the conduct of foreign policy in the United States, see Walter Russell Mead, *Special Providence: American Foreign Policy and How It Changed the World* (New York: Routledge, 2002), and Robert Kagan, *Dangerous Nation* (New York: Knopf, 2006).

77. See Leo Strauss, *What Is Political Philosophy? and Other Studies* (New York: Free Press, 1959), 49–50, and Charles-Jacques Beyer, "Le Rôle de l'idée de postérité chez Montesquieu," in *La Fortune de Montesquieu: Montesquieu écrivain*, ed. Louis Desgraves (Bordeaux: Bibliothèque Municipale, 1995), 65–72.

BOOK TWO, PREFACE

1. We do not know for sure whether he began to write in 1734, but he was undoubtedly doing so by 1739: see Robert Shackleton, *Montesquieu: A Critical Biography* (Oxford, UK: Oxford University Press, 1961), 225–43, and Catherine Volpilhac-Auger, "La Biographie, un miroir déformant," in VF III clxix–clxxvi.

2. These two passages should be read in light of *EL* 6.28.41, 29.19.

3. See Letter to Antoine-Maurice de Solar, Commander of the Order of Malta, on 7 March 1749, in Nagel III 1199–1201 (at 1200). Here and in the preface to *The Spirit of Laws*, Montesquieu is employing the plural term *principes* in the loose, non-technical sense in which he uses it in the title of *EL* 3.19 and with some frequency elsewhere (1.4.2, p. 264, and 8; 5.9; 8.14; 2.11.5; 3.17.7, 19.5, 16–17, 27, p. 574; 6.28.6). As is suggested by Montesquieu's choice of words in 1.5.18, 8.11–12, 2.11.13, 16, the plural term as used in these passages quite often includes what he has in mind when he uses the singular term in its technical sense.

4. Consider [Jean Le Rond d'Alembert], "Éloge de M. le President de Montesquieu," in *Encyclopédie, ou Dictionnaire raisonné des sciences, des arts, et des métiers*, ed. Denis Diderot and Jean Le Rond d'Alembert (Paris: Briasson, 1751–1772; Neufchastel: S. Faulche & Compagnie, 1765; Amsterdam: M. M. Rey, 1776–1777; Paris: Panckoucke, 1777–1780), V iii–xviii (at vii–viii) in light of Plut. *Lyc.* 4 (with 12 and 31) and Montesquieu, *EL* 1.4.6. In this connection, see Louis Desgraves, "Les Voyages et la pensée constitutionnelle de Montesquieu" (1989), in Desgraves, *Montesquieu: L'Œuvre et la vie* (Paris: L'Esprit du Temps, 1994), 123–42.

5. In this connection, see Charles-Jacques Beyer, "Le Rôle de l'idée de postérité chez Montesquieu," in *La Fortune de Montesquieu: Montesquieu écrivain*, ed. Louis Desgraves (Bordeaux: Bibliothèque Municipale, 1995), 65–72.

BOOK TWO, CHAPTER ONE. PRINCIPLES

1. Note Blaise Pascal, *Pensées sur la religion et sur quelques autres sujets, qui ont esté trouvées après sa mort parmy ses papiers*, 3rd ed., ed. Étienne Périer (Paris: Guillaume Desprez, 1671), 184–86 (XXV.4–6, in the expanded edition published in 1678 and frequently republished thereafter), where the epigraph to this chapter is to be found.

2. Consider Cecil Patrick Courtney, "Montesquieu and the Problem of 'La Diversité'," in *Enlightenment Essays in Memory of Robert Shackleton*, ed. Giles Barber and C. P. Courtney (Oxford, UK: Voltaire Foundation, 1988), 61–81, and "Montesquieu and Natural Law," in *Montesquieu's Science of Politics: Essays on the Spirit of Laws (1748)*, ed. David W. Carrithers, Michael A. Mosher, and Paul A. Rahe (Lanham, MD: Rowman & Littlefield, 2001), 41–67, along with Jacob T. Levy, "Montesquieu's Constitutional Legacies," and Catherine Larrère, "Montesquieu and Liberalism: The Question of Pluralism," in *Montesquieu and His Legacy*, ed. Rebecca E. Kingston (Albany: State University of New York Press, 2008), 115–37, 279–301, in light of Bertrand Binoche, *Introduction à De l'Esprit des lois de Montesquieu* (Paris: Presses Universitaires de France, 1998), 153–96, and Michael Zuckert, "Natural Law, Natural Rights, and Classical Liberalism: On Montesquieu's Critique of Hobbes," *Social Philosophy & Policy* 18:1 (2001), 227–51. In a passage specifying the "idea of this book," which he composed for his *Spirit of Laws* and excised in due course, Montesquieu observed, "One should not regard this as a treatise on jurisprudence: it is rather a particular method [*une espèce de méthode*] for studying jurisprudence: it is not the body of laws that I seek but their soul." See Montesquieu, *MS* 735, and "Rejets de *L'Esprit des lois* conservés dans les dossiers de La Brède," in Nagel III 599–642 (at 625–26).

3. See Marcel Prélot, "Montesquieu et les formes de gouvernement," in *La Pensée politique et constitutionnelle de Montesquieu: Bicentenaire de L'Esprit des lois, 1748–1948* (Paris: Recueil Sirey, 1952), 110–32; Simone Goyard-Fabre, "La Typologie des gouvernements selon Montesquieu," *L'École des lettres* (28 April 1973): 39–43; Thomas L. Pangle, *Montesquieu's Philosophy of Liberalism: A Commentary on The Spirit of the Laws* (Chicago: University of Chicago Press, 1973), 48–52, 70–71; Paul Vernière, *Montesquieu et "L'Esprit des lois," ou La Raison impure* (Paris: Société d'édition d'enseignement supérieur, 1977); Catherine Larrère, "Les Typologies des gouvernements chez Montesquieu," in *Études sur le XVIIIe siècle*, ed. Jean Ehrhard (Clermont-Ferrand: Association des publications de la Faculté des Lettres, 1979), 87–103, which appears in revised form under the same title in *Cahiers Montesquieu* 5 (2001): 157–72; Tzvetan Todorov, "Droit naturel et formes de gouvernement dans L'Esprit des lois," *Esprit* n.s. 75 (March 1983): 35–48; Paul A. Rahe, "Forms of Government: Structure, Principle, Object, and Aim," in *Montesquieu's Science of Politics*, 69–108, whence comes much of what follows; and Diana J. Schaub, "The Regime and Montesquieu's Principles of Education," in *Montesquieu and the Spirit of Modernity*, ed. David W. Carrithers and Patrick Coleman (Oxford, UK: Voltaire Foundation, 2002), 77–100. Note also Michael A. Mosher, "The Particulars of a Universal Politics: Hegel's Adaptation of Montesquieu's Typology," *American Political Science Review* 78:1 (March 1984): 179–88.

4. For a penetrating, if not in all respects persuasive, discussion of this propensity on Mon-

tesquieu's part, see Louis Althusser, *Politics and History: Montesquieu, Rousseau, Hegel, and Marx*, tr. Ben Brewster (London: NLB, 1972), 17–42.

5. Cf. Polyb. 6.3.5–10.14 with Xen. *Mem.* 4.6.12, *Oec.* 21.9–12; Pl. *Pol.* 291d–303b, *Leg.* 3.689e–702d, 4.712c–715d, 8.832b–d; Arist. *Eth. Nic.* 1160a31–1161b10, *Pol.* 1278b30–1280a5, 1284b35–1285b33, 1295a7–24, *Rh.* 1365b21–1366a22, and see Pl. *Leg.* 6.756e–758a, Arist. *Pol.* 1281b22–38 (esp. 28–31), 1295a25–1297a12 (esp. 1296b14–16), 1297b1–27, 1329a2–17, 1332b12–41. Note, in this connection, Pind. *Pyth.* 2.86–88, Hdt. 3.80–83, and Thuc. 8.97.2. In Montesquieu's day, with the exception of a few fragments, the pertinent passages of Cicero's *Republic* (1.20.33–2.44.70, 3.13.23, 25.37–35.48) were as yet undiscovered.

6. Although he is perfectly aware of the possibility that an aristocracy will degenerate into a "despotism of the few" and a democracy into a "despotism of the people," Montesquieu seems to have been persuaded that these are unstable and will quickly enough collapse into a "despotism of one alone": consider "Dossier de *L'Esprit des lois*," no. 235, in Pléiade II 1048, and *MP* 1893, in light of Larrère, "Les Typologies des gouvernements chez Montesquieu," 87–103. Note, however, Montesquieu's willingness to describe as an "oligarchy" a nobility that has become "hereditary" and, because of this structural change, prone to "extreme corruption" (*EL* 1.8.5).

7. See Thomas Hobbes, *The Elements of Law Natural and Politic*, 2nd ed., ed. Ferdinand Tönnies (London: Frank Cass, 1969) II.i.3; *De Cive: The Latin Version*, ed. Howard Warrender (Oxford, UK: Clarendon Press, 1983) II.vii.1–17, x.2; and *Leviathan*, ed. Edwin Curley (Indianapolis, IN: Hackett, 1994) II.xix.1–2.

8. The pertinent passage was initially included in and eventually excised from *EL* 1.3.9: see Montesquieu, *MS* 37, and "Dossier de *L'Esprit des lois*," in Pléiade II 996.

9. For the most part, Machiavelli is content to juxtapose republics with principalities: consider *Il principe* 1 with an eye to the implications of ibid. 15–19, in Machiavelli, *Tutte le opere*, ed. Mario Martelli (Florence: G. C. Sansoni, 1971), 258, 280–89. He makes it clear, however, that in the end even this distinction is illusory: cf. *Discorsi sopra la prima deca de Tito Livio* 1.20 with *Il principe* 9, in *Tutte le opere*, 105, 271–72; see Harvey C. Mansfield, Jr., "Machiavelli and the Modern Executive," in *Understanding the Political Spirit: Philosophical Investigations from Socrates to Nietzsche*, ed. Catherine H. Zuckert (New Haven, CT: Yale University Press, 1988), 88–110 (esp. 97–102), and Mansfield, *Taming the Prince: The Ambivalence of Modern Executive Power* (New York: Free Press, 1989), 1–149. And yet, in his discussion of Ottoman Turkey and of France, he insists on the crucial importance of the very features that are determinative for Montesquieu's denial that monarchy and despotism are one and the same: see *Il principe* 4 and 19, in *Tutte le opere*, 262–63, 284–89. Consider, more generally, Machiavelli, *Discorsi sopra la prima deca de Tito Livio* 1.2–8, 16, 19, 55, 58, 3.1, in *Tutte le opere*, 78–90, 99–101, 104–5, 136–42, 195–97, in light of Mansfield, *Machiavelli's New Modes and Orders: A Study of the Discourses on Livy* (Ithaca, NY: Cornell University Press, 1979), 32–62, 79–83, 88–90, 160–64, 168–74, 299–305 (esp. 304–5); note Elena Fasano Guarini, "Machiavelli and the Crisis of the Italian Republics," in *Machiavelli and Republicanism*, ed. Gisela Bock, Quentin Skinner, and Maurizio Viroli (Cambridge, UK: Cambridge University Press, 1990), 17–40; and see Rahe, *RAM* II.v.12, n. 173, and Paul

Carrese, "The Machiavellian Spirit of Montesquieu's Liberal Republic," in *Machiavelli's Liberal Republican Legacy*, ed. Paul A. Rahe (New York: Cambridge University Press, 2006), 121–42 (esp. 137–40). Note Robert Shackleton, "Montesquieu and Machiavelli: A Reappraisal," in Shackleton, *Essays on Montesquieu and on the Enlightenment*, ed. David Gilson and Martin Smith (Oxford, UK: Voltaire Foundation, 1988), 117–31. For an overview, see Etorre Levi-Malvano, *Montesquieu and Machiavelli*, tr. A. J. Pansini (Kopperl, TX: Greenvale Press, 1992), 13–87 (esp. 33). David Hume, who draws a distinction quite similar to the one deployed by Montesquieu, traces it to Machiavelli: see David Hume, "That Politics May be Reduced to a Science" (1741), in Hume, *Essays Moral, Political, and Literary*, rev. ed., ed. Eugene F. Miller (Indianapolis, IN: Liberty Fund, 1985), 21–24.

10. In this connection, see David Bien, "Old Regime Origins of Democratic Liberty," in *The French Idea of Freedom: The Old Regime and the Declaration of Rights of 1789*, ed. Dale K. Van Kley (Stanford, CA: Stanford University Press, 1994), 23–71, and Gail Bossenga, "Status, *Corps*, and Monarchy: Roots of Modern Citizenship in the Old Regime," in *Tocqueville and Beyond: Essays on the Old Regime in Honor of David D. Bien*, ed. Robert M. Schwartz and Robert A. Schneider (Newark: University of Delaware Press, 2003), 127–54.

11. Precisely because he distinguished monarchy from despotism and did so in this fashion, historians, especially in France, have tended to treat *The Spirit of Laws* as a partisan tract written in defense of the order into which Montesquieu was himself born. Some take him to be a reactionary aristocrat: see III.4, note 1, below. Others treat him as an aristocratic liberal: see III.4, note 2, below. In their eagerness to make of Montesquieu a man of his own time, however, very few scholars are inclined even to contemplate the possibility that he wrote *The Spirit of Laws*, as he said that he had, with an eye to being "useful" to people "seven or eight centuries" after his own time: Montesquieu, *MP* 1940 and "Dossier de *L'Esprit des lois*" no. 198, in Pléiade II 1039–40.

12. In this connection, see Robert Koebner, "Despot and Despotism: Vicissitudes of a Political Term," *Journal of the Warburg and Courtauld Institutes* 14 (1951): 275–302; Melvin Richter, "Despotism," in *Dictionary of the History of Ideas*, ed. Philip P. Wiener (New York: Scribners, 1973–1974), II 1–18; Franco Venturi, "Oriental Despotism," *Journal of the History of Ideas* 24 (1963): 133–42; Lucette Valensi, *The Birth of the Despot: Venice and the Sublime Port*, tr. Arthur Denner (Ithaca, NY: Cornell University Press, 1993); and the essays published in *Dispotismo: Genesi e sviluppi di un concetto filosofico-politico*, ed. Domenico Felice (Naples: Liguori, 2001–2002). Then see Françoise Weil, "Montesquieu et le despotisme," in *Actes du Congrès Montesquieu réuni à Bordeaux du 23 au 26 mai 1955* (Bordeaux: Impriméries Delmas, 1956), 191–215; Badreddine Kassem, *Décadence et absolutisme dans l'œuvre de Montesquieu* (Paris: Librairie Minard, 1960); David B. Young, "Montesquieu's View of Despotism and His Use of Travel Literature," *Review of Politics* 40 (1978): 392–405; Roger Boesche, "Fearing Monarchs and Merchants: Montesquieu's Two Theories of Despotism," *Western Political Quarterly* 43 (1990): 741–61; Melvin Richter, "Montesquieu's Comparative Analysis of Europe and Asia: Intended and Unintended Consequences," in *L'Europe de Montesquieu: Actes du colloque de Gênes (26–29 mai 1993)*, ed. Alberto Postigliola and Maria Grazia Bottaro

Palumbo (Oxford, UK: Voltaire Foundation, 1995), 329–48; Binoche, *Introduction à De l'Esprit des lois de Montesquieu*, 199–242; Domenico Felice, "Una forma naturale e monstruosa di governo: Il dispotismo nell'*Esprit des lois,*" in *Leggere l'Esprit des lois: Stato, società, e storia nel pensiero di Montesquieu*, ed. Domenico Felice (Naples: Liguori, 1998), 9–102, which appears in revised form as "Una filosofia del dispotismo: Forma naturale e mostruosa di governo," in Felice, *Oppressione e libertà: Filosofia e anatomia del dispotismo nel pensiero di Montesquieu* (Pisa: ETS, 2000), 19–117, and "Dispotismo e libertà nell'*Esprit des lois* di Montesquieu," in *Dispotismo*, 189–255, which appears in revised form as "Dispotismo e libertà," in Felice, *Per una scienza universale dei sistemi politico-sociali: Dispotismo, autonomia della giustizia e carattere delle nazioni nell'Esprit des lois di Montesquieu* (Florence: Leo S. Olschki, 2005), 1–71; and Sharon R. Krause, "Despotism in *The Spirit of Laws,*" in *Montesquieu's Science of Politics*, 231–71. In this connection, see also Paul Vernière, "Montesquieu et le monde musulman, d'après *L'Esprit des lois,*" in *Actes du Congrès Montesquieu*, 175–90; Thomas E. Kaiser, "The Evil Empire? The Debate on Turkish Despotism in Eighteenth-Century French Political Culture," *Journal of Modern History* 72:1 (March 2000): 6–34; and Frederick G. Whelan, "Oriental Despotism: Anquetil-Duperron's Response to Montesquieu," *History of Political Thought* 22:4 (Winter 2001): 619–47. Note Corey Robin, "Reflections on Fear: Montesquieu in Retrieval," *American Political Science Review* 94:2 (June 2000): 347–60, with an eye to I.3, note 16, above.

13. Bernard Manin, "Montesquieu et la politique moderne," in *Cahiers de philosophie politique* 2–3 (Reims: Université de Reims, 1985), 157–229 (esp. 182–229), which is reprinted in *Lectures de L'Esprit des lois*, ed. Céline Spector and Thierry Hoquet (Bordeaux: Presses Universitaires de Bordeaux, 2004), 171–231 (esp. 192–231) , and Catherine Larrère, "Montesquieu and Liberalism," 279–301, do much to clarify what it is that links Montesquieu with Aristotle and distinguishes these two exponents of political prudence from Plato, Hobbes, Rousseau, and the like—but they err in suggesting that both are somehow pluralists with regard to political ends. Their discussion of Plato and Aristotle should be contrasted with that to be found in Arlene W. Saxonhouse, *Fear of Diversity: The Birth of Political Science in Ancient Greek Thought* (Chicago: University of Chicago Press, 1992). As will become clear in the course of this extended essay, Montesquieu's appreciation for political and cultural diversity derives from the emphasis he gives to a unitary principle of political psychology. For further exploration of the links between Montesquieu and Aristotle, see Judith N. Shklar, "Virtue in a Bad Climate: Good Men and Good Citizens in Montesquieu's *L'Esprit des lois,*" in *Enlightenment Studies in Honour of Lester G. Crocker*, ed. Alfred J. Bingham and Virgil W. Topazio (Oxford, UK: Voltaire Foundation, 1979), 315–28, and Simone Goyard-Fabre, *Montesquieu: La Nature, les lois, la liberté* (Paris: Presses Universitaires de France, 1993). That Montesquieu is best read as a sociologist I am persuaded neither by Émile Durkheim, "Montesquieu's Contribution to the Rise of Social Science," *Montesquieu and Rousseau: Forerunners of Sociology*, tr. Ralph Manheim (Ann Arbor: University of Michigan Press, 1965), 1–64, nor by Pierre Manent, *The City of Man*, tr. Marc A. LePain (Princeton, NJ: Princeton University Press, 1998), 11–85 (esp. 50–85). As Tzvetan Todorov, *On Human Diversity: Nationalism, Racism, and Exoticism in French Thought*,

tr. Catherine Porter (Cambridge, MA: Harvard University Press, 1993), 353–83, demonstrates, in Montesquieu political analysis is inseparable from moral reflection. In this connection, see also Raymond Aron, *Main Currents of Sociological Thought*, tr. Richard Howard and Helen Weaver (New York: Basic Books, 1965–1967) I: *Montesquieu, Comte, Marx, Tocqueville, the Sociologists and the Revolution of 1848*, 11–56.

14. See Althusser, *Politics and History*, 43–60. Unfortunately, Althusser's heavy-handed and clumsy attempt to depict Montesquieu as a partisan of his own class (26–29, 96–106) mars his otherwise perceptive discussion of the latter's analysis of republicanism, monarchy, and despotism (61–86).

15. For an extended meditation on the significance of this unexpected shift, see Manent, *The City of Man*, 11–85 (esp. 11–49, 82–85).

16. See Montesquieu, "Réponses et explications données à la faculté de théologie," in Pléiade II 1174–95 (at 1181).

17. In Britain, this understanding of the English constitution was the common sense of the matter: see I.3, notes 52–53, above.

18. It is not fortuitous that, in every draft of the title for this chapter, apart from the last, the term *principes* figured prominently: note Montesquieu, *MS* 228, and see Catherine Volpilhac-Auger, "The Art of the Chapter Heading in Montesquieu, or 'De la Constitution d'Angleterre'," *Journal of Legal History* 25:2 (August 2004): 169–79. That he has discussed "the principles" of England's "constitution" in *EL* 2.11.6 Montesquieu specifies at 3.19.27, p. 574. In 2.11.5, at 3.19.27, p. 574, and in the titles for 2.11.6 that Montesquieu considered but ultimately rejected, he is evidently employing the plural term *principes* in the loose, non-technical sense in which he uses it in the preface to his book (Préf.), in the title of 3.19, and with some frequency elsewhere: see the II.Pref., note 3, above.

19. See Pangle, *Montesquieu's Philosophy of Liberalism*, 1–19. Note also Anne M. Cohler, "Montesquieu's Perception of His Audience for the *Spirit of Laws*," *Interpretation* 11:3 (September 1983): 317–32.

20. As Sharon Krause, "The Spirit of Separate Powers in Montesquieu," *Review of Politics* 62 (2000): 231–65 (at 236 n. 11) points out, this conclusion is reinforced by Montesquieu's claim (2.11.6, p. 407) that the English republican James Harrington erred in failing to recognize that the liberty which he sought when he composed the elaborate constitutional provisions of his *Oceana* had been fully established in England under the ancient constitution. There is reason to believe that Montesquieu had long contemplated this possibility: in his *Persian Letters*, which were published more than a quarter of a century before the appearance of his *Spirit of Laws*, he had mentioned "England" in tandem with "the Republics of Holland" and "Venice" in such a manner as to imply that the government of England was also somehow republican: see *LP* 78/80.

21. For an argument along these lines, see Mark Hulliung, *Montesquieu and the Old Regime* (Berkeley: University of California Press, 1976), 1–3, 14, 212–21. See also D. J. Fletcher, "Montesquieu's Concept of Patriotism," *Studies on Voltaire and the Eighteenth Century* 56 (1976): 541–55. Cf., however, Giuseppe Cambiano, "Montesquieu e le repubbliche greche," *Rivista di filosofia* 45 (1974): 93–144. In this connection, see also Cambiano, *Polis: Histoire d'un modèle politique*, tr. Sophie Fermigier (Paris: Aubier,

2003), 297–354. For a useful survey of the secondary literature dealing with Montesquieu's understanding of and attitude toward republicanism, see Marco Platania, "Repubbliche e repubblicanesimo in Montesquieu: Percorsi bibliografici, problemi e prospettive di ricerca," *Annali della Fondazione Luigi Einaudi* 35 (2001): 147–92. Note also Thomas Casadei, "Modelli repubblicani nell'*Esprit des lois*: Un 'ponte' tra passato e futuro," in *Libertà, necessità e storia: Percorsi dell'Esprit des lois di Montesquieu*, ed. Domenico Felice (Naples: Bibliopolis, 2003), 13–74, and Marco Platania, *Montesquieu e la virtù: Rappresentazioni della Francia di Ancien Régime e dei governi repubblicani* (Turin: UTET, 2007).

22. In this connection, see also Montesquieu, *MP* 918, 1203. Note also 655.

23. Cf. *MP* 655, where Montesquieu suggests that "the English would be less free if there were no king in England" and cites as proof the putative fact that the Dutch are less free when they lack a stadholder. Note also 751, 884.

24. I first set out much of the pertinent evidence in Paul A. Rahe, "The Primacy of Politics in Classical Greece," *American Historical Review* 89:2 (April 1984): 265–93; I restate and amplify my argument and then explore its consequences for our understanding of classical civilization in Rahe, *RAM* I.

25. See Paul A. Rahe "Situating Machiavelli," in *Renaissance Civic Humanism: Reappraisals and Reflections*, ed. James Hankins (Cambridge, UK: Cambridge University Press, 2000), 270–308; "In the Shadow of Lucretius: The Epicurean Foundations of Machiavelli's Political Thought," *History of Political Thought* 28:1 (Spring 2007): 30–55; and *ATA* 19–55.

26. Cf. Pl. *Rep.* 443d–e, Rom. 6:17–18, and Thomas Aquinas, *Summa theologiae*, ed. Thomas Gilby, O.P., et al. (New York: McGraw Hill, 1964–1976) Ia q.77 a.4.

27. See Pangle, *Montesquieu's Philosophy of Liberalism*, 50–70, who juxtaposes Aristotle's exploration of the character of political virtue, its defects, and the manner in which it points beyond itself to moral and philosophical virtue with Montesquieu's quite different account. See also Manent, *The City of Man*, 12–49 (esp. 12–34).

28. Consider Arist. *Eth. Nic.* 1103a4–b25 in light of 1097b28–1098a18, 1098b22–99a21.

29. In this connection, see Schaub, "The Regime and Montesquieu's Principles of Education," 88–96.

30. Montesquieu's elaborate comparison of republican Sparta, despotic China, and early Rome in this regard deserves attention: consider *EL* 3.19.16–21 with an eye to 1.5.19, p. 306; note 1.6.9 (esp. n. a), 7.6–7, and 8.21; and see II.3–4, below.

31. Note also Montesquieu, *LP* 112/116.

32. See Montesquieu, *MP* 210, where "the greater part of the republics of Greece" are included as well.

33. For further evidence suggesting the depth of Montesquieu's admiration for the ancients, see *MP* 110, 221, 1253, 1607.

34. Elsewhere (*EL* 1.6.15, 4.22.12, 23.20), Montesquieu is lavish in the praise that he accords ancient Rome.

35. See Pangle, *Montesquieu's Philosophy of Liberalism*, 52–106 (esp. 72–106), 112–13; Bernard Yack, *The Longing for Total Revolution: Philosophic Sources of Social Discontent from Rousseau to Marx and Nietzsche* (Princeton, NJ: Princeton University Press,

1986), 36–48; Alain Pons, "Amour des lois et amour de la liberté chez Montesquieu," in *L'Amour des lois: La Crise de la loi moderne dans les sociétés démocratiques* (Montreal: Les Presses de l'Université Laval, 1996), 187–95; Elena Russo, "The Youth of Moral Life: The Virtue of the Ancients from Montesquieu to Nietzsche," in *Montesquieu and the Spirit of Modernity*, 101–23; and Sharon R. Krause, *Liberalism with Honor* (Cambridge, MA: Harvard University Press, 2002), 32–43. In this connection, see also Roger B. Oake, "Montesquieu's Analysis of Roman History," *Journal of the History of Ideas* 16 (1955): 44–59; David Lowenthal, "Montesquieu and the Classics: Republican Government in *The Spirit of Laws*," in *Ancients and Moderns: Essays on the Tradition of Political Philosophy in Honor of Leo Strauss*, ed. Joseph Cropsey. (New York: Basic Books, 1964), 258–87; and David W. Carrithers, "Democratic and Aristocratic Republics Ancient and Modern," in *Montesquieu's Science of Politics*, 109–58.

36. Note the similar discussion of republicanism at *EL* 1.7.2. Montesquieu was friendly neither to monasticism nor to clerical celibacy nor to the contemplative and speculative spirit: consider the cryptic comments concerning speculation and monks in 1.4.8, 6.9, and see 2.14.7, 4.23.21, pp. 705–7, 29, 5.24.10–12, 25.4–6. Note also *LP* 113/117.

37. One cure for this disease is provided by commerce: see Manent, *The City of Man*, 36–49, 80–85.

38. Consider Montesquieu, *EL* 4.21.20, pp. 640–41, in light of Vickie B. Sullivan, "Against the Despotism of a Republic: Montesquieu's Correction of Machiavelli in the Name of the Security of the Individual," *History of Political Thought* 27:2 (Summer 2006): 263–88.

39. Consider Montaigne, "De la Cruauté" and "De la Vertu," in *Les Essais de Michel de Montaigne*, ed. Pierre Villey and V.-L. Saulnier (Paris: Presses Universitaires de France, 1978) 2.11, 29, in light of Rahe, *RAM* II.i.3–4.

40. Because Montesquieu's discussion of classical republicanism is so vigorous, so exciting, and so replete with admiration, the severity of his criticism of this form of government was lost on many of his early readers—who took him for a partisan: see Robert Shackleton, *Montesquieu: A Critical Biography* (Oxford, UK: Oxford University Press, 1961), 276–77; Wyger R. E. Velema, "Republican Readings of Montesquieu: *The Spirit of Laws* in the Dutch Republic," *History of Political Thought* 18:1 (Spring 1997): 43–63; *Poteri, democrazia, virtù: Montesquieu nei movimenti repubblicani all'epoca della Rivoluzione francese*, ed. Domenico Felice (Milan: Franco Angeli, 2000); Catherine Larrère, "Montesquieu républicain? De l'Interprétation universitaire pendant la IIIe République," *XVIIIe siècle* 21 (1989): 150–62, and "Montesquieu and the Modern Republic: The Republican Heritage in Nineteenth-Century France," in *Montesquieu and the Spirit of Modernity*, 235–49; and Paul A. Rahe, *Soft Despotism, Democracy's Drift: Montesquieu, Rousseau, Tocqueville, and the Modern Prospect* (New Haven, CT: Yale University Press, 2009) II.Pref. This propensity is still very much evident in the scholarship: see, for example, Nannerl O. Keohane, "Virtuous Republics and Glorious Monarchies: Two Models in Montesquieu's Political Thought," *Political Studies* 20 (1972): 383–96; "The President's English: Montesquieu in America, 1976," *Political Science Reviewer* 6 (1976): 355–87; and *Philosophy and the State in France: The Renaissance to the Enlightenment* (Princeton, NJ: Princeton University Press, 1980), 392–419

(esp. 408–19); and, more recently, Eric Nelson, *The Greek Tradition in Republican Thought* (Cambridge, UK: Cambridge University Press, 2004), 127–94. Some try to reconcile Montesquieu's admiration with his criticism of classical republicanism by suggesting that his book reflects an evolution in his thought from an enthusiasm for the ancients to a hostility to them: see Joseph Dedieu, *Montesquieu et la tradition politique anglaise en France: Les Sources anglaises de l'Esprit des lois* (Paris: Gabalda, 1909), 131–39, and Robert Shackleton, "La Genèse de *L'Esprit des lois*," in Shackleton, *Essays on Montesquieu and on the Enlightenment*, 49–63, which originally appeared in *Revue d'histoire littéraire de la France* 52 (1952): 425–38. Few appreciate the degree to which his assessment of each of the non-despotic polities is similarly balanced and nuanced.

41. Toward the end of the first part of his great work, Montesquieu prepares his readers for his subsequent discussion of the English constitution and way of life (*EL* 2.11.6, 3.19.27) with a series of tantalizing references suggestive of the English polity's moderation: see II.2, below.

42. In this connection, see Manin, "Montesquieu et la politique moderne," 182–229, which is reprinted in *Lectures de L'Esprit des lois*, 192–231, and Anne M. Cohler, *Montesquieu's Comparative Politics and the Spirit of American Constitutionalism* (Lawrence: University Press of Kansas, 1988), 66–97. Note also Walter Kuhfuss, *Mässigung und Politik: Studien zur politischen Sprache und Theorie Montesquieus* (Munich: Wilhelm Fink Verlag, 1975), 94–229. The argument advanced by Donald A. Desserud, "Virtue, Commerce, and Moderation in the 'Tale of the Troglodytes': Montesquieu's *Persian Letters*," *History of Political Thought* 12:4 (Winter 1991): 605–26, though intriguing, is not justified by the textual evidence on which it is putatively based.

43. On Montesquieu's choice of metaphors, see Denis de Casabianca, "Dérèglements mécaniques et dynamique des fluides dans *L'Esprit des lois*," *Revue Montesquieu* 4 (2000): 43–70.

44. The same can be said for his younger contemporary David Hume: see Hume, "That Politics May be Reduced to a Science" (1741), "Whether the British Government Inclines More to Absolute Monarchy, or to a Republic" (1741), "Of Civil Liberty" (1741), and "Of the Coalition of Parties" (1758), in Hume, *Essays Moral, Political, and Literary*, 15, 26–31, 53, 94, 493–94, 500.

45. See also *EL* 1.3.10, 2.12.29, 5.26.2

46. See Keohane, *Philosophy and the State in France*, 392–415; Cohler, *Montesquieu's Comparative Politics and the Spirit of American Constitutionalism*, 85–94; and Michael A. Mosher, "Monarchy's Paradox: Honor in the Face of Sovereign Power," in *Montesquieu's Science of Politics*, 159–229. Cf. Pangle, *Montesquieu's Philosophy of Liberalism*, 64–69, 98–100, 102–3, 113–14, 151–53, 212–39, 301–3, who is so intent on situating Montesquieu within the tradition of modern natural right (20–47) and on making of him a partisan of the English polity (104–60, 197–200, 219–39) that he fails to do justice to Montesquieu's appreciation of the advantages that monarchy has to offer, with Manin, "Montesquieu et la politique moderne," 157–229, which is reprinted in *Lectures de L'Esprit des lois*, 171–231, who goes too far in the opposite direction by failing to give due emphasis to the unitary principle of political psychology that underpins Montesquieu's subtle analysis of the defects and advantages associated with the diverse polit-

ical and cultural forms. In contrast with Pangle, Pierre Manent emphasizes Montesquieu's rejection of doctrinaire politics—but he then follows Pangle in devoting his attention almost solely to the opposition between classical republicanism and the commercial polity established in England: *The City of Man*, 11–85. To get a sense of the obstacles that stand in the way of reducing Montesquieu's argument to a straightforward endorsement of liberal democracy, one should consider the critique of Montesquieu advanced from that point of view by Antoine Louis Claude Destutt, comte de Tracy: see [Tracy], *A Commentary and Review of Montesquieu's Spirit of Laws*, [tr. Thomas Jefferson] (Philadelphia: William Duane, 1811).

47. The distaste that Montesquieu came to feel for Venice and the other Italian republics of his own day first evidences itself in the remarks that he jotted down while visiting Venice and traveling elsewhere in Italy: see Montesquieu, *Voyage de Gratz à La Haye*, in Pléiade I 544–84 (esp. 545–49, 552–54, 557, 559), 715.

48. Consider Montesquieu's failure to discuss the aristocratic republic in *EL* 1.4 in light of the first paragraph of 1.5.8.

49. See David W. Carrithers, "Not So Virtuous Republics: Montesquieu, Venice, and the Theory of Aristocratic Republicanism," *Journal of the History of Ideas* 52 (1991): 245–68. Note also David Wootton, "Ulysses Bound? Venice and the Idea of Liberty from Howell to Hume," in *Republicanism, Liberty, and Commercial Society: 1649–1776*, ed. David Wootton (Stanford, CA: Stanford University Press, 1994), 341–67, and see Domenico Felice, "Il quasi dispotismo delle repubbliche italiane," in *Oppressione e libertà*, 151–67.

50. Cf. Johnson Kent Wright, "A Rhetoric of Aristocratic Reaction? Nobility in *De l'Esprit des lois*," in *The French Nobility in the Eighteenth Century: Reassessments and New Approaches*, ed. Jay M. Smith (University Park: Pennsylvania State University Press, 2006), 227–51 (esp. 238–41), who fails to distinguish moderation as a principle or passion that sets a specific form of government in motion from moderation as a description of the way in which a particular government performs.

51. Note Montesquieu, *MP* 1062, 1422, 1491.

52. For an extended commentary on the foundations of this claim, see Céline Spector, *Montesquieu: Pouvoirs, richesses et sociétés* (Paris: Presses Universitaires de France, 2004), 37–143, 202–17.

53. As Binoche, *Introduction à De l'Esprit des lois de Montesquieu*, 125, points out, in these passages Montesquieu is alluding to Bossuet, who had juxtaposed the "false honor" arising from an ambition for the things of this world with the true honor sought by Christians.

54. Cf. Sir Isaac Newton, *Philosophiæ naturalis principia mathematica* (London: Joseph Streater, 1687) 1.23.

55. Cf. Adam Smith, *The Theory of Moral Sentiments* IV.i.10 and *An Inquiry into the Nature and Causes of the Wealth of Nations* IV.ii.9, with "The History of Astronomy" III.2, in *Essays on Philosophical Subjects*—all to be found in *The Glasgow Edition of the Works and Correspondence of Adam Smith* (Oxford, UK: Oxford University Press, 1976). Smith may be indebted to Montesquieu for the outlines of his argument, or the similarity in what they have to say may be due to a debt they both owe Pierre Nicole and Bernard

Mandeville. In this connection, note Pierre Rétat, "De Mandeville à Montesquieu: Honneur, luxe et dépense noble dans *L'Esprit des lois,*" *Studi francesci* 50 (May–August 1973): 238–49, and Céline Spector, "Vices privés, vertus publiques: De la *Fable des abeilles* à *L'Esprit des lois,*" in *Montesquieu and the Spirit of Modernity*, 127–57, and see II.3, below.

56. Note, in this connection, *EL* 1.5.19, p. 304. For an extended meditation on the passage cited in the text, see Catherine Larrère, "Montesquieu, noblesse et commerce. Ordre social et pensée économique," in *Il pensiero gerarchico in Europea, XVII–XIX secolo,* ed. Antonella Alimento and Cristina Cassina (Florence: Olschki, 2002), 31–48.

57. Everyone who read *The Character of a Trimmer* (ca. 1684–85) understood that Lord Halifax was referring to the example set for James II of England by Louis XIV of France: see *The Works of George Savile, Marquis of Halifax,* ed. Mark N. Brown (Oxford, UK: Clarendon Press, 1989), I 195–96. For the opinion of France prevalent in England in the 1720s, see [John Trenchard and Thomas Gordon], *Cato's Letters* (1720–23), ed. Ronald Hamowy (Indianapolis, IN: Liberty Press, 1995), I 11, 15, 59–60, 234–35, 308–9, 395, II 525–44 (esp. 539–43), 661–69, 888–89, 910–18. Cf. *A Character of King Charles II* (ca. 1686–95), ed. Alexander Pope, in *The Works of George Savile,* II 484–505 (esp. 504). In England, on all sides, it had long been taken for granted that the French monarchy was absolute, oppressive, and even tyrannical: see Sir John Fortescue, *The Governance of England* (1471), in Fortescue, *On the Laws and Governance of England,* ed. Shelley Lockwood (Cambridge, UK: Cambridge University Press, 1997), 87–92, 108–9; [Henry Parker], *The Case of Shipmony Briefly Discoursed* (1640); [Charles Herle], *A Fuller Answer to a Treatise Written by Doctor Ferne* (1642); *The Peoples Right Briefly Asserted* (1649); [Roger L'Estrange], *A Plea for Limited Monarchy, As it Was Established in this Nation, Before the Late War* (1660); [William Cavendish, Duke of Devonshire], *Reasons for His Majesties Passing the Bill of Exclusion* (1681), and [John Wildman], *Some Remarks Upon Government* (1689), in *The Struggle for Sovereignty: Seventeenth-Century English Political Tracts,* ed. Joyce Lee Malcolm (Indianapolis, IN: Liberty Press, 1999), I 93–125 (at 100, 122–23), 223–60 (at 254 and 256), 359–68 (at 362), 495–504 (at 498), II 720–28 (at 725), 865–901 (at 883); [Henry Parker], *Observations upon Some of his Majesties Late Answers and Expresses* (London: s.n., 1642), 2; Thomas May, *The History of the Parliament of England* (London: George Thomason, 1647), 18; John Milton, *The Tenure of Kings and Magistrates* (1649), in *Complete Prose Works of John Milton,* ed. Don M. Wolfe (New Haven, CT: Yale University Press, 1953–1982), III 200; Marchamont Nedham, *The Case of the Commonwealth of England, Stated* (1650), ed. Philip A. Knachel (Charlottesville: University Press of Virginia, 1969), 23–24, 112, *The Excellencie of a Free State* (1656), ed. Richard Baron (London: A. Millar and T. Cadell, 1767), 49–50, 152–53, and *Christianissimus Christianandus* (London: Jonathan Edwin, 1678), 3; *James Harrington's Oceana* (1656), ed. S. B. Liljegren (Heidelberg: C. Winter, 1924), 47–48; James Harrington, *A System of Politics* (n.d.) 5.21, in *The Political Works of James Harrington,* ed. J. G. A. Pocock (Cambridge, UK: Cambridge University Press, 1977), 842; James Tyrrell, *Patriarcha Non Monarcha* (London: Richard Janeway, 1681), 122; Algernon Sidney, *Discourses concerning Government* (ca. 1683), ed. Thomas G. West (Indianapolis, IN: Liberty Classics, 1990), 58, 287; and An-

thony Ashley Cooper, third earl of Shaftesbury, *Soliloquy: Or, Advice to An Author* (1710) II.1, in Shaftesbury, *Charakteristicks of Men, Manners, Opinions, Times*, ed. Philip Ayres (Oxford, UK: Clarendon Press, 1999), I 115–16.

58. For a brief but subtle discussion of the problem which gives rise to this dispute, see Pierre Manent, "Les Théoriciens de la monarchie: Bodin et Montesquieu," in *Les Monarchies*, ed. Emmanuel Le Roy Ladurie (Paris: Presses Universitaires de Frances, 1986), 91–99. For a further development of this analysis, see Ran Halévi, "La Modération à l'épreuve de l'absolutisme: De l'Ancien Régime à la Révolution française," *Le Debat* 109 (March–April 2000): 73–98. Cf. Hulliung, *Montesquieu and the Old Regime*, 15–107 (esp. 15–53), 173–230, who presents Montesquieu as a radical critic of monarchy inclined to see it as an ugly and unstable polity destined to become ever more despotic if it does not evolve in the direction taken by England, with Mosher, "Monarchy's Paradox," 159–229, who argues, to the contrary, that Montesquieu follows Jean Bodin both in drawing a sharp distinction between *pouvoir absolu* and *pouvoir arbitraire* and in supposing that the French monarchy is somehow absolute without being arbitrary as well. It is difficult to square Mosher's thesis, which owes much to Manent, with *EL* 3.19.27, p. 580, where Montesquieu juxtaposes *un gouvernement absolu* with *un gouvernement libre* — seemingly, on the basis that the former presupposes what the latter rules out: *un pouvoir arbitraire*. Note also 3.19.27, p. 581—where he treats *le pouvoir arbitraire* and *le gouvernement absolu* as equivalents. David Hume fits Mosher's description better than does Montesquieu, for he treats France as an "absolute monarchy" and yet insists that one can affirm of France and of Europe's "civilized monarchies" more generally that which "was formerly said in praise of republics alone, *that they are a government of Laws, not of Men.*" See Hume, "Of the Liberty of the Press" (1741), "Of Civil Liberty" (1741), and "Of the Rise and Progress of the Arts and Sciences" (1742), in Hume, *Essays Moral, Political, and Literary*, 10, 90–95, 118, 124–27.

59. In this connection, see Pierre Manent, *An Intellectual History of Liberalism*, tr. Rebecca Balinski (Princeton, NJ: Princeton University Press, 1994), 53–64; Jean Ehrard, "Actualité d'un demi-silence: Montesquieu et l'idée de souveraineté," *Rivista di storia della filosofia* 49:1 (January–March 1994): 9–20, which is reprinted as "La Souveraineté," in Ehrard, *L'Esprit des mots: Montesquieu en lui-même et parmi les siens* (Geneva: Droz, 1998), 147–60; Catherine Larrère, "Montesquieu: L'Éclipse de la souveraineté," in *Penser la souveraineté à l'époque moderne et contemporaine*, ed. Gian Mario Cazzaniga and Yves Charles Zarka (Paris: Vrin, 2001), 199–214; and Yoshie Kawade, "La Liberté civile contre la théorie réformiste de l'État souverain: Le Combat de Montesquieu," in *Le Travail des lumières: Pour Georges Benrekassa*, ed. Caroline Jacot Grapa, Nicole Jacques-Lefèvre, Yannick Séité, and Carine Trevisan (Paris: Honoré Champion, 2002), 203–23.

60. For an extended and valuable meditation on this important passage, see Sharon R. Krause, "The Politics of Distinction and Disobedience: Honor and the Defense of Liberty in Montesquieu," *Polity* 31:3 (Spring 1999): 469–99, along with Krause, *Liberalism with Honor*, 32–66.

61. See Manent, "Les Théoriciens de la monarchie: Bodin et Montesquieu," 91–99 (esp. 95–99).

62. See Élie Carcassonne, *Montesquieu et le problème de la constitution française au XVIIIe siècle* (Paris: Presses Universitaires de France, 1927), 81.

63. See Catherine Maire, "L'Église et la nation: Du Dépôt de la vérité au dépôt des lois, La Trajéctoire janséniste au XVIIIe siècle," *Annales ÉSC* 46:5 (September–October 1991): 1177–1205, and David A. Bell, *Lawyers and Citizens: The Formation of a Political Elite in Old Regime France* (New York: Oxford University Press, 1994), 79.

64. See also Montesquieu, *MP* 589, 2266.

65. Cf. *EL* 1.6.5 with Niccolò Machiavelli, *Discorsi sopra la prima deca di Tito Livio* 1.7, in *Tutte le opere*, 87–88.

66. See also *EL* 2.12.25.

67. See Melvin Richter, "Comparative Political Analysis in Montesquieu and Tocqueville," *Comparative Politics* 1:2 (January 1969): 129–60 (at 158–59). Cf., however, Melvin Richter, "The Uses of Theory: Tocqueville's Adaptation of Montesquieu," in *Essays in Theory and History: An Approach to the Social Sciences*, ed. Melvin Richter (Cambridge, MA: Harvard University Press, 1970), 74–102 (at 84–85).

68. In the first of these two passages, when Montesquieu refers to the fact that, toward the middle of the reign of Louis XIV, Scotland and England did not form, as they later would, *un corps de monarchie*, he may be using the term *monarchie* merely to refer to the two realms having come to form a single *imperium*, in much the same fashion as he had used the noun in the uncensored version of his *Considerations on the Causes of the Greatness of the Romans and their Decline* in speaking of the Roman republic as having achieved "universal Monarchy." Consider [Montesquieu], *Reflections on the Causes of the Grandeur and Declension of the Romans* (London: W. Innys and R. Manby, 1734), 153, 194, in light of I.2, above.

69. See Kenneth Minogue, *Citizenship and Monarchy: A Hidden Fault Line in Our Civilisation* (London: Institute of United States Studies, 1998). Nowhere, however, does Montesquieu resort to the traditional language and refer to England's polity as "a mixed monarchy [*monarchie mixte*]." But, in his notebooks, he does refer to it on one occasion as a "monarchy blended [*mêlée*]," and he elsewhere describes it as a "government" that has been "moderated": see *MP* 918, 1744, and "Dossier de *L'Esprit des lois*," no. 238, in Pléiade II 1048–49. Montesquieu's allusion to England as "a republic concealed under the form of a monarchy" was apparently a very late addition to the manuscript of *The Spirit of Laws*: consider Montesquieu, *MS* 87, in light of Catherine Volpilhac-Auger, "Annexe A.4. Tableau chronologique partiel de la correspondance manuscrite subsistante de Montesquieu (1734–1754)," and "Annexe A.6. Tableau des 'mains' et des papiers et concordance du manuscrit et de l'imprimé (1748) — Manuscrit de *L'Esprit des lois*," in VF III clxiv–clxviii, clxxxiii, and see Keohane, "Virtuous Republics and Glorious Monarchies," 393 n. 3, with Shackleton, *Montesquieu*, 236.

70. In this connection, see Mosher, "Monarchy's Paradox," 159–229.

71. David Hume, whose comments on *The Spirit of Laws* Montesquieu thought "full of enlightenment & of good sense," regarded this observation as not only apt but "novel and striking": see Letter from David Hume to Montesquieu on 10 April 1749, in Nagel III 1217–22 (at 1217–18, with nn. a and c) and in *Letters of David Hume*, ed. J. Y. T. Greig (Oxford: Clarendon Press, 1932), I 133–38 (at 133–34, with 133 n. 1, 134 n. 1).

72. In his published works, Montesquieu nowhere specifies precisely when England ceased to be monarchical. In his notebooks, however, he was more forthcoming: see III.4, below.

73. In his notebooks, Montesquieu remarks that "money is" in England "accorded sovereign esteem" while "honor and virtue" are accorded but "little." See NA 878. On the contrast between England and France, see Spector, *Montesquieu: Pouvoirs, richesses et sociétés*, 182–220.

74. See Hulliung, *Montesquieu and the Old Regime*, 46–48. See also ibid., 14, 85–88, 208–11.

75. Cf. Louis Althusser, "Despote et monarque chez Montesquieu," *Esprit* 267 (November 1958): 595–614, and *Politics and History*, 65–95—who is so eager to fit Montesquieu into the procrustean bed of Marxist historical analysis and therefore to make of him a simple partisan of the class from which he hailed (26–29, 96–106) that he allows his own partisanship to blind him to the manner in which the latter's discussion of England is revealing of far deeper concerns which cannot be explained in terms of the interests of the French nobility—with Judith N. Shklar, "Montesquieu and the New Republicanism," in *Machiavelli and Republicanism*, 265–79, and see Georg Wilhelm Friedrich Hegel, *The Philosophy of Right*, tr. T. M. Knox (Oxford, UK: Oxford University Press, 1942), 177–78 (no. 273), and Manent, *The City of Man*, 11–49 (esp. 12–17).

BOOK TWO, CHAPTER TWO. UNEASINESS

1. Cf., however, Gustave Lanson, "L'Influence de la philosophie Cartésienne sur la littérature française," *Revue de métaphysique et de morale* 4 (1896): 517–50 (at 538–46), which is reprinted in Lanson, *Études d'histoire littéraire* (Paris: Librairie Ancienne Honoré Champion, 1929), 58–96 (at 84–90), and Henri Auguste Barckhausen, "Le Désordre de *L'Esprit des lois*," *Revue du droit public et de la science politique en France et à l'étranger* 12 (1898): 31–40, reprinted in Barckhausen, *Montesquieu: Ses Idées et ses œuvres d'après les papiers de La Brède* (Paris: Librarie Hachette, 1907), 253–66, from whose observations one can, nonetheless, learn a great deal, with Jean Ehrard, "La 'Chaîne' de *L'Esprit des lois*," in Ehrard, *L'Esprit des mots: Montesquieu en lui-même et parmi les siens* (Geneva: Droz, 1998), 179–92.

2. See [Jean Le Rond d'Alembert], "Éloge de M. le President de Montesquieu," in *Encyclopédie, ou Dictionnaire raisonné des sciences, des arts, et des métiers*, ed. Denis Diderot and Jean Le Rond d'Alembert (Paris: Briasson, 1751–1772; Neufchastel: S. Faulche & Compagnie, 1765; Amsterdam: M. M. Rey, 1776–1777; Paris: Panckoucke, 1777–1780), V iii–xviii (at viii–ix).

3. Letter to Pierre-Jean Grosley on 8 April 1750, in Nagel III 1293–97 (at 1294–95).

4. See Joseph de La Porte, *Observations sur l'Esprit des lois, ou L'Art de lire ce livre, et de l'entendre et d'en juger* (Amsterdam: Pierre Mortier, 1751).

5. On Montesquieu's mode of composition, see Thomas L. Pangle, *Montesquieu's Philosophy of Liberalism: A Commentary on the Spirit of the Laws* (Chicago: University of Chicago Press, 1973), 11–19, and Bertrand Binoche, *Introduction à De l'Esprit des lois de*

Montesquieu (Paris: Presses Universitaires de France, 1998), 8–27, which should be read with an eye to the secondary literature cited in I.1, note 47, above.

6. See [d'Alembert], "Éloge de M. le President de Montesquieu," x–xiii.

7. Had Melvin Richter, "The Uses of Theory: Tocqueville's Adaptation of Montesquieu," in *Essays in Theory and History: An Approach to the Social Sciences*, ed. Melvin Richter (Cambridge, MA: Harvard University Press, 1970), 74–102, taken to heart what d'Alembert and Montesquieu said in the passages cited above, he would not have been so quick to cite Montesquieu's treatment of England as an indication of intellectual "carelessness" on his part.

8. There are good reasons for rejecting the long-dominant scholarly presumption that the posthumous edition best reflects the intentions of the author: see Albert Postigliola, "Editer *L'Esprit des lois*," in *Editer Montesquieu, Publicare Montesquieu*, ed. Alberto Postigliola (Naples: Liguori Editore, 1998), 65–77.

9. See Letters to l'abbé Ottaviano, comte di Guasco, on 30 January 1747, to Monsignor Gaspare Cerati on 31 March 1747, and to l'abbé Ottaviano, comte di Guasco, on 4 May 1747, in Nagel III 1079, 1081–84. The date of 30 February 1747 found in the manuscript of the first of these three letters is obviously wrong; the date of 20 February 1747 assigned by the editor is off by three weeks.

10. See Letters from Jacob Vernet in July/August, 1748 and on 4 September 1748, in Nagel III 1121–22, 1130–32 (at 1130), where the evidence allows one to infer that Vernet bore responsibility for the omission of the parts.

11. See Charles-Louis de Secondat, baron de la Brède et de Montesquieu, *De l'Esprit des loix*, nouvelle édition (Geneva: Barrillot et Fils, 1750). For the circumstances in which this and its predecessor in 1749 were produced: see Letter from Pierre Michel Huart at the beginning of March 1749, in Nagel III 1198–99, which should be read in light of François Furet, "La *Librairie* du royaume de France au 18e siècle," in *Livre et société dans la France du XVIIIe siècle*, ed. Geneviève Bollème et al. (Paris: Mouton, 1965–1970), I 3–32, which is reprinted in translation as "Book Licensing and Book Production in the Kingdom of France in the Eighteenth Century," in Furet, *In the Workshop of History*, tr. Jonathan Mandelbaum (Chicago: University of Chicago Press, 1984), 99–124. As Roger Caillois points out, this division corresponds nicely with the five parts of the work under Montesquieu's original plan and the supplement that he composed in part while the type was being set: see Pléiade II 1497.

12. See Letter to Pierre-Jean Grosley on 8 April 1750, in Nagel III 1293–97 (at 1297).

13. For the suggestion that the work's division into six parts is an element within an elaborate numerological scheme, see Robert McMahon, "The Numerological Structure of *The Spirit of the Laws*," *Interpretation: A Journal of Political Philosophy* 30:3 (Summer 2003): 251–64.

14. For the means by which one can decode this phrase, see I.3, notes 52–53, above.

15. For a thoughtful discussion of the import of this analysis, see Michael A. Mosher, "The Particulars of a Universal Politics: Hegel's Adaptation of Montesquieu's Typology," *American Political Science Review* 78:1 (March 1984): 179–88.

16. Note also Montesquieu, *EL* 6.29.14.

17. In her discussion of Montesquieu's scheme, Ana Samuel, "The Design of Montesquieu's *The Spirit of the Laws*: The Triumph of Freedom over Determinism," forthcoming in *American Political Science Review*, rightly lays considerable emphasis on Montesquieu's ostentatious failure to mention territorial constraints in his various discussions of the English form of government.

18. Cf. Montesquieu, *MP* 51, which speaks of there being three discordant tribunals: "that of the laws, that of honor, and that of Religion," and see Diana J. Schaub, "The Regime and Montesquieu's Principles of Education," in *Montesquieu and the Spirit of Modernity*, ed. David W. Carrithers and Patrick Coleman (Oxford, UK: Voltaire Foundation, 2002), 77–100 (esp. 80–88); then consider *MP* 1552.

19. See Letter to Leonhard Usteri on 30 April 1763 (no. 2662), in *Correspondance complète de Jean-Jacques Rousseau*, ed. Ralph A. Leigh (Oxford, UK: Voltaire Foundation, 1965–1998), XVI 127–28.

20. After considering Niccolò Machiavelli, *Discorsi sopra la prima deca di Tito Livio* 1 Proemio and 3.27.2, 43, in Machiavelli *Tutte le opere*, ed. Mario Martelli (Florence: G. C. Sansoni, 1971), 76, 233–34, 250, in conjunction with Machiavelli, *Discorsi* 2.2.2, 3.1.4, in ibid., 149–50, 250–51, see Vickie B. Sullivan, *Machiavelli's Three Romes: Religion, Human Liberty, and Politics Reformed* (Dekalb: Northern Illinois University Press, 1996), passim (esp. 15–59, 119–90), and Rahe, *ATA* 56–100.

21. For a passage deleted from Montesquieu's discussion of the *ius gentium* in this work: see *MP* 1814.

22. See also Montesquieu, *MP* 478, 551, 1296.

23. Montesquieu devotes most of the last part of his magnum opus to an examination of the convoluted internal logic governing the evolution over a period of centuries of the monarchical constitution and law in his native land: consider *EL* 6.28, 30–31, in light of the passage cited. See Iris Cox, *Montesquieu and the History of French Laws* (Oxford, UK: Voltaire Foundation, 1983), and "Montesquieu and the History of Laws," in *Montesquieu's Science of Politics: Essays on The Spirit of Laws (1748)*, ed. David W. Carrithers, Michael A. Mosher, and Paul A. Rahe (Lanham, MD: Rowman & Littlefield, 2001), 409–29. For a discussion of the corruption to which the Gothic government was itself in turn subjected, see Montesquieu, *RMU* 15.256–74. Note also *MP* 699, 1645.

24. Cf. Arist. *Eth. Nic.* 1138a5–7 with Thomas Hobbes, *Leviathan*, ed. Edwin Curley (Indianapolis, IN: Hackett, 1994) II.xxi.1–18, and *A Dialogue between a Philosopher and a Student of the Common Laws of England*, ed. Joseph Cropsey (Chicago: University of Chicago Press, 1971), 73. For an example of the confusion to which Montesquieu's discussion of liberty has given rise, see David Spitz, "Montesquieu's Theory of Freedom," *Essays in the Liberal Ideal of Freedom* (Tucson: University of Arizona Press, 1964), 28–35. Cf. Pierre Manent, *An Intellectual History of Liberalism*, tr. Rebecca Balinski (Princeton, NJ: Princeton University Press, 1994), 53–54 (esp. 60–63).

25. For a further exploration of this point, see *EL* 5.26.15, 20. Cf. 5.24.2.

26. In this discussion (*EL* 2.11.3–4), Montesquieu appears to be following John Locke: see the latter's *Two Treatises of Government: A Critical Edition with an Introduction and Apparatus Criticus*, 2nd ed., ed. Peter Laslett (Cambridge, UK: Cambridge University Press, 1970) II.iv.22, vi.57, ix.123.

27. See M. C. J. Vile, *Constitutionalism and the Separation of Powers* (Oxford, UK: Clarendon Press, 1967). That Montesquieu is discussing the separation of powers without employing the phrase is evident, as James Madison had occasion to observe, both from his inclination to criticize polities in which two or more of the powers are "united" or "joined" and from his insistence that "the power of judging" be "separated" from both "the executive" and "the legislative power." Consider *EL* 2.11.6, pp. 396–97, in light of Alexander Hamilton, James Madison, and John Jay, *The Federalist*, ed. Jacob E. Cooke (Middletown, CT: Wesleyan University Press, 1961) no. 47 (esp. pp. 324–27). Cf., however, Charles Eisenmann, "L'*Esprit des lois* et la séparation des pouvoirs," *Mélanges R. Carré de Malberg* (Paris: Librairie du Recueil Sirey, 1933), 163–92, and "La Pensées constitutionnelle de Montesquieu," in *Recueil Sirey du bicentenaire de l'Esprit des lois* (Paris: Librairie du Recueil Sirey, 1952), 133–60, and in *Lectures de L'Esprit des lois*, ed. Céline Spector and Thierry Hoquet (Bordeaux: Presses Universitaires de Bordeaux, 2004), 145–70, which are both reprinted along with Michel Troper, "Charles Eisenmann contre le mythe de la séparation des pouvoirs," in *Cahiers de philosophie politique* 2–3 (Reims: Université de Reims, 1985), 3–79. As one would expect, Montesquieu owed his terminology, in part, to the 1691 French translation of John Locke's *Second Treatise of Civil Government:* see Robert Shackleton, *Montesquieu: A Critical Biography* (Oxford, UK: Oxford University Press, 1961), 286. Note also Alberto Postigliola, "Sur quelques Interprétations de la 'séparation des pouvoirs' chez Montesquieu," *Studies on Voltaire and the Eighteenth Century* 154 (1976): 1759–75; and Bernard Manin, "Checks, Balances and Boundaries: The Separation of Powers in the Constitutional Debate of 1787," in *The Invention of the Modern Republic* (Cambridge, UK: Cambridge University Press, 1994), 27–62.
28. On this, see Pangle, *Montesquieu's Philosophy of Liberalism*, 117–38; Manent, *An Intellectual History of Liberalism*, 53–64; and Harvey C. Mansfield, *Taming the Prince: The Ambivalence of Modern Executive Power* (New York: Free Press, 1989), 213–46.
29. "Liberty," Montesquieu writes in his notebooks, "is that good which makes it possible to enjoy the other goods." It can be found in "well-regulated monarchies" and wherever one finds "good laws" functioning in the manner of "large nets" in which "the subjects" are like fish who "believe themselves free" because they do not "sense that they have been caught." For the pleasures associated with political participation, Montesquieu has little esteem: "I count," he writes, "as a very small thing the happiness of disputing furiously over the affairs of state and not ever saying one hundred words without pronouncing the word *liberty* as well as the privilege of hating half of the citizens." See *MP* 32, 434, 597, 828, 874, 943, 1574. If Montesquieu considers England "the freest country that there is in the world"—freer than "any republic"—it is not because there are elections in that country and debates in its Parliament but because "a man in England" can have "as many enemies as he has hairs on his head" and yet "nothing" will "on this account befall him." This last observation Montesquieu glosses with the remark that "this fact matters much because the health of the soul is as necessary as that of the body." See *NA* 884.
30. See Vickie B. Sullivan, "Against the Despotism of a Republic: Montesquieu's Correc-

tion of Machiavelli in the Name of the Security of the Individual," *History of Political Thought* 27:2 (Summer 2006): 263–88.

31. The remaining chapters of the eleventh book analyze in much greater detail the various polities with an eye to the separation of powers: consider *EL* 2.11.7–19 in light of 2.11.20.

32. Shackleton, *Montesquieu*, 288, took note of this fact but failed to detect its import (ibid., 288–301); Judith N. Shklar, *Montesquieu* (Oxford, UK: Oxford University Press, 1987), 86–88, was, characteristically, more perceptive. See also Mark Hulliung, *Montesquieu and the Old Regime* (Berkeley: University of California Press, 1976), 214–15.

33. Montesquieu quite often uses the verb *jouir* and its cognates to indicate mere possession rather than the delight that sometimes arises from possession: note, for example, *EL* 2.11.2, 20; 3.19.27, pp. 577–78, and see Sharon Krause, "The Spirit of Separate Powers in Montesquieu," *Review of Politics* 62 (2000): 231–65 (at 238–39, with nn. 14–15).

34. For an extended commentary on this chapter, see Jean-Jacques Granpré Molière, *La Théorie de la constitution anglaise chez Montesquieu* (Leyden: Presse Universitaire de Leyde, 1972), esp. 271–313. See also Alberto Postigliola, "En relisant le Chapitre sur la constitution d'Angleterre," *Cahiers de philosophie politique et juridique de l'Université de Caen* 7 (1985): 9–28, and note Sergio Cotta, "Montesquieu e la libertà politica," in *Leggere l'Esprit des lois: Stato, società, e storia nel pensiero di Montesquieu*, ed. Domenico Felice (Naples: Liguori, 1998), 103–35.

35. On the latter point, see also *EL* 2.11.18.

36. See Pangle, *Montesquieu's Philosophy of Liberalism*, 139–42.

37. See David W. Carrithers, "Montesquieu and the Liberal Philosophy of Jurisprudence," in *Montesquieu's Science of Politics*, 291–334.

38. See Pangle, *Montesquieu's Philosophy of Liberalism*, 142–45.

39. To assimilate Montesquieu's thinking on the question of liberty to that of Rousseau and Kant, one must assume, as does Sheila Mason, that, when the author of *The Spirit of Laws* defines "liberty in its relation with the citizen" solely in terms of the citizen's "security" and "tranquillity of mind," he could not possibly mean what he actually says. Cf. Mason, "Montesquieu on English Constitutionalism Revisited: A Government of Potentiality and Paradoxes," *Studies on Voltaire and the Eighteenth Century* 278 (Oxford, UK: Voltaire Foundation, 1990), 105–46 (esp. 116–20); then consider, in addition to the evidence to the contrary presented in the text of this essay, that cited in notes 29 and 40, this chapter. In pursuit of this assimilation, Mason (ibid., 116–28) also ignores Montesquieu's remarks justifying the restriction of the suffrage in England to men with tangible property (*EL* 2.11.6, p. 400); and then, by neglecting the all-important difference between "is thought to have" and "has," she misconstrues as a call for universal suffrage and an assertion of the rational dignity of the autonomous individual Montesquieu's rather more prosaic observation (2.11.6, p. 399) that the logic of the legal order in "a free state" dictates that "every man who is thought to have a free soul ought to be governed by himself."

40. Cf. Nannerl O. Keohane, "Virtuous Republics and Glorious Monarchies: Two Models in Montesquieu's Political Thought," *Political Studies* 20 (1972): 383–96 (at 393), who describes the English government as "a political bumblebee which, according to [Montesquieu's] principles, was not supposed to fly," and who suggests that "it might

best be regarded as a fourth type of regime, in which not virtue, honour or fear, but liberty, was the motive principle," with Donald Desserud, "Commerce and Political Participation in Montesquieu's Letter to Domville," *History of European Ideas* 25 (1999): 135–51 (at 140–41), who contends that "commerce" is England's "principle," the "motivation for political behaviour" allowing "this new system to work"; note Pangle, *Montesquieu's Philosophy of Liberalism*, 116–17, who argues that, where liberty reigns and "there is the least 'modification' of man's soul, it is the course of nature for the selfish passions for security to become dominant"; see Diana J. Schaub, "The Regime and Montesquieu's Principles of Education," in *Montesquieu and the Spirit of Modernity*, ed. David W. Carrithers and Patrick Coleman (Oxford, UK: Voltaire Foundation, 2002), 77–100 (at 99–100, esp. n. 33), who denies that England has "a particular passion as its principle"; and then consider the brief but penetrating discussion buried within Keith Michael Baker, "Politics and Public Opinion under the Old Regime: Some Reflections," in *Press and Politics in Pre-Revolutionary France*, ed. Jack R. Censer and Jeremy D. Popkin (Berkeley: University of California Press, 1987), 204–46 (at 214–21), which is revised, expanded, and reprinted as Baker, "Public Opinion as a Political Invention," in Baker, *Inventing the French Revolution* (Cambridge, UK: Cambridge University Press, 1990), 167–99 (at 173–78), and see Paul A. Rahe, "Forms of Government: Structure, Principle, Object, and Aim," in *Montesquieu's Science of Politics*, 69–108. There is a Hegelian flavor, alien to Montesquieu, in the suggestion of Alan Gilbert, "'Internal Restlessness': Individuality and Community in Montesquieu," *Political Theory* 22 (1994): 45–70 (esp. 54–66), that the principle of the English polity is "*individuality*—the passion of each to live a life of her own"—and that the species of individuality which he found in England was also somehow at the same time "*liberal*" and "*communitarian.*" For yet another view opposed to my own, see Cecil Patrick Courtney, "L'Image d'Angleterre dans *L'Esprit des lois*," in *Actes du colloque international tenu à Bordeaux, du 3 au 6 décembre 1998*, ed. Louis Desgraves (Bordeaux: Académie de Bordeaux, 1999), 243–53, and "Montesquieu and English Liberty," in *Montesquieu's Science of Politics*, 273–90. In his most recent contribution, however, Courtney has come around to a view akin to my own: see Cecil Patrick Courtney, "Morals and Manners in Montesquieu's Analysis of the British System of Liberty," in *Montesquieu and His Legacy*, 31–48.

41. Note François Duverger Véron de Forbonnais, *Un Extrait chapitre par chapitre du livre de l'Esprit des Lois: Des Observations sur quelques endroits particuliers de ce livre, & une idée de toutes les critiques qui en ont été faites, avec quelques remarques de l'éditeur* (Amsterdam: Arkstée and Merkus, 1753), 173–212 (at 182), and see Eluggero Pii, "Montesquieu e Véron de Forbonnais: Appunti sul dibattito settecentesco in tema di commercio," *Il pensiero politico* 10:3 (1977): 362–89.

42. After considering *EL* 2.11.6 and 2.12.1–2 with an eye to 1.5.6 and 4.20.5, see 1.5.14, 8.21, 2.11.5, 3.16.9, 18.1, 19.16, 19–20, 5.25.15, 6.29.18.

43. In his notebooks (*MP* 5), Montesquieu remarks that "the political world sustains itself by the internal, uneasy [*inquiet*] desire that each has to depart from the location in which he is placed. It is in vain that an austere morality should wish to efface the traits which the greatest of all the workers has impressed on our souls."

44. Note Paul A. Rahe, "In the Shadow of Lucretius: The Epicurean Foundations of Machiavelli's Political Thought," *History of Political Thought* 28:1 (Spring 2007): 30–55, and *ATA* 22–55, and see Paul Carrese, "The Machiavellian Spirit of Montesquieu's Liberal Republic," in *Machiavelli's Liberal Republican Legacy*, ed. Paul A. Rahe (New York: Cambridge University Press, 2006), 121–42 (esp. 131–41).

45. Cf. Machiavelli, *Discorsi sopra la prima deca di Tito Livio* 1.6, 37, 2 Proemio, in Machiavelli, *Tutte le opere*, 84–87, 119–20, 144–46, with Hobbes, *Leviathan* I.iii.3–5, viii.14–16, and with David Hume, *A Treatise of Human Nature*, ed. L. A. Selby-Bigge (Oxford, UK: Clarendon Press, 1888) II.iii.

46. Perhaps because he attributes to commerce what Montesquieu attributes to England's "laws" and explicitly associates with that country's "liberty," Pangle, *Montesquieu's Philosophy of Liberalism*, 146–60, fails to discern the degree to which *EL* 3.19.27 expresses grave reservations on Montesquieu's part with regard to the English form of government. Note, in this connection, ibid., 104–6, 197–200, 219–39, and see Pierre Manent, *The City of Man*, tr. Marc A. LePain (Princeton, NJ: Princeton University Press, 1998), 11–85 (esp. 46–49). Cf. Baker, "Politics and Public Opinion under the Old Regime: Some Reflections," 214–21.

47. Consider *EL* 1.1.2, 5.12, 2.11.3, 5.24.5, 26.15 with an eye to 5.24.2, and then see Manent, *An Intellectual History of Liberalism*, 60–63.

48. See also *EL* 5.24.2, 5, and *MP* 1625.

BOOK TWO, CHAPTER THREE. PARTISANSHIP

1. The first of these copies (Bibliothèque nationale MS 9203) provides the basis for the various editions published by Louis Lafuma, and the second (Bibliothèque nationale MS 12449) provides the basis for the editions published by Philippe Sellier. Both versions remain in print. I cite Blaise Pascal, *Pensées*, ed. Louis Lafuma (Paris: Seuil, 1978), and Blaise Pascal, *Pensées: Édition établie d'après la copie référence de Gilberte Pascal*, ed. Philippe Sellier (Paris: Classiques Garnier, 1999).

2. In this connection, see Jean Mesnard, *Pascal*, 4th ed. (Paris: Hatier, 1962), 126–54.

3. With regard to the *libertins érudits*, see Rahe, *ATA* 155–68, 297–312.

4. Cf. Pascal, *Pensées: Édition établie d'après la copie référence de Gilberte Pascal* nos. 1–414, which reproduces the material found in the twenty-seven bundles given titles, with Michel de Montaigne, "De la Vanité," *Essais* 3.9, in Montaigne, *Œuvres complètes*, ed. Albert Thibaudet and Maurice Rat (Paris: Bibliothèque de la Pléiade, 1962), 922–80 (esp. 966), and see August. *Conf.* 1.1. For an overview, see Karl Löwith, "Man between Infinites" and "Skepticism and Faith," in Löwith, *Nature, History, and Existentialism*, ed. Arnold Levison (Evanston, IL: Northwestern University Press, 1966), 102–30.

5. For a penetrating discussion of the corrosive element that was omitted, see Erich Auerbach, "On the Political Theory of Pascal," in *Blaise Pascal: Modern Critical Views*, ed. Harold Bloom (New York: Chelsea House, 1989), 17–35.

6. See Mara Miriam Varnos, "Pascal's *Pensées* and the Enlightenment: The Roots of a Misunderstanding," *Studies on Voltaire and the Enlightenment* 97 (1972): 17–145; Antony McKenna, *De Pascal à Voltaire: Le Rôle des Pensées de Pascal dans l'histoire des*

idées entre 1670–1734 (Oxford, UK: Voltaire Foundation, 1990), I 5–159; and Arnoux Straudo, *La Fortune de Pascal en France au dix-huitième siècle* (Oxford, UK: Voltaire Foundation, 1997); then, consider note 1, this chapter.

7. Cf. Varnos, "Pascal's *Pensées* and the Enlightenment," 17–145, who asserts that Pascal was generally misunderstood and unappreciated when he was not ignored, with McKenna, *De Pascal à Voltaire*, I 160–502, II 503–730, and Straudo, *La Fortune de Pascal en France au dix-huitième siècle*, passim, who chart in detail the debates that the *Pensées* inspired.

8. Forty-one fragments were added: see McKenna, *De Pascal à Voltaire*, I 328–49. Note the concordances provided in ibid., II 949–92, where the passages added are marked with a plus sign. Of the passages added, only seven cast light on Pascal's account of the human condition: these can most easily be found in Pascal, *Pensées*, ed. Lafuma, nos. 198, 434, 525, 551–52, 685, 688.

9. Consider Voltaire, *Lettres philosophiques*, ed. Gustave Lanson, 3rd ed. (Paris: Société des Textes Français Modernes, 1924), II 184–226, esp. 184–85 (XXV), in light of McKenna, *De Pascal à Voltaire*, II 733–915, and Straudo, *La Fortune de Pascal en France au dix-huitième siècle*, 77–104. For an English translation, see Voltaire, *Letters concerning the English Nation*, ed. Nicholas Cronk (Oxford, UK: Oxford University Press, 1994), 124–50.

10. See McKenna, *De Pascal à Voltaire*, I 186–229. For a discussion of this neglected figure, see Edward Donald James, *Pierre Nicole, Jansenist and Humanist: A Study of His Thought* (The Hague: Martinus Nijhoff, 1972).

11. See Maurice Cranston, *John Locke* (New York: Arno, 1979), 160–83.

12. See Rahe, *RAM* II.ii.1–6, vi.1–vii.10. In this connection, see *The Library of John Locke*, 2nd ed., ed. John R. Harrison and Peter Laslett (Oxford, UK: Clarendon Press, 1971) nos. 166, 168, 1465, 1848a, 1850, 1852, 2029, 2029a. Note also ibid. nos. 162, 169–70, 177–78a, 1849, 1851, 1853–56.

13. See John Locke, *Drafts for the Essay concerning Human Understanding, and Other Writings* I: *Drafts A and B*, ed. Peter H. Nidditch and G. A. J. Rogers (Oxford, UK: Clarendon Press, 1990).

14. After reading John Lough, "Locke's Reading during His Stay in France, 1675–79," *The Library*, 5th ser., 8 (1953): 229–58, and Cranston, *John Locke*, 140–41, 158–83 (esp. 158–64, 172–77), see Gabriel Dominique Bonno, *Les Relations intellectuelles de Locke avec la France (d'après des documents inédits)* (Berkeley: University of California Press, 1955), 49–63 (esp. 59–62), 74, 101, 103–4, 210, 224–26, 244–49, 251–52, who emphasizes Locke's interest in Pascal; John Marshall, *John Locke: Resistance, Religion, and Responsibility* (Cambridge, UK: Cambridge University Press, 1994), 89–90, 313–37, 151–52, 157, 168, 178–86, 188–97, who pays close attention to the first and the third of the three essays of Nicole that he translated; and McKenna, *De Pascal à Voltaire*, I 450–502, who discusses, among other matters, the themes treated here. Note also Straudo, *La Fortune de Pascal en France au dix-huitième siècle*, 312–16. For a bilingual edition of the three essays of Nicole translated by Locke—with Nicole's original on one side of the page and Locke's translation on the other—see *John Locke as Translator: Three of the Essais of Pierre Nicole in French and English*, ed. Jean S. Yolton (Oxford, UK: Voltaire

Foundation, 2000). In this connection, see *The Library of John Locke* nos. 2040–40b, 2222–23. Note also ibid. nos. 586, 1803, 1803a, 2085a.

15. See John Locke, *An Essay concerning Human Understanding*, ed. Peter H. Nidditch (Oxford, UK: Clarendon Press, 1979) II.x.9.

16. Cf. Locke, *An Essay concerning Human Understanding* II.xxi.55, with Thomas Hobbes, *Leviathan*, ed. Edwin Curley (Indianapolis, IN: Hackett, 1994) I.xi.1.

17. For a discussion of at least some of the ways in which this could be done, see Matthew W. Maguire, *The Conversion of Imagination: From Pascal through Rousseau to Tocqueville* (Cambridge, MA: Harvard University Press, 2006).

18. Cf. Locke, *An Essay concerning Human Understanding* II.vii.1–2, xx.6, 15, xxi.29–71, with Blaise Pascal, *Pensées sur la religion et sur quelques autres sujets, qui ont esté trouvées après sa mort parmy ses papiers*, 3rd ed., ed. Étienne Périer (Paris: Guillaume Desprez, 1671), 62, 159–64, 179–81 (where this chapter's epigraph is to be found), 192–210, 242–46, 266–72, 275–76 (VIII.1, XXI.1–4, XXIV.12, XXVI.1–4, XXVIII.35–36, XXIX.11, 18, 23, 29, 39, in the expanded edition published in 1678 and frequently republished thereafter), and with Pierre Nicole, "Traité de la faiblesse de l'homme" XI.48, XII.52, in *John Locke as Translator*, 90–93, 96–99, and see McKenna, *De Pascal à Voltaire*, I 464–77.

19. John Locke, *Essai philosophique concernant l'entendement humain: où l'on montre quelle est l'étendue de nos connoissances certaines, et la manière dont nous y parvenons*, tr. Pierre Coste (The Hague: Pierre Husson, 1714), 267n. This edition was originally published in 1700.

20. See Jean Deprun, *La Philosophie de l'inquiétude en France au XVIIIe siècle* (Paris: Librairie philosophique J. Vrin, 1979). Note in this connection the response of Leibniz, who defended Coste's use of *inquiétude* to convey what Locke had in mind when he spoke of man's characteristic *uneasiness*: see Gottfried Wilhelm Leibniz, *Nouveaux Essais sur l'entendement humain*, ed. André Robinet and Heinrich Schepers, in *Sämtliche Schriften und Briefe*, VI:6 (Berlin: Akademie-Verlag, 1962), 162–212 (esp. 163–66).

21. See *Catalogue de la bibliothèque de Montesquieu à La Brède*, ed. Louis Desgraves and Catherine Volpilhac-Auger (Oxford, UK: Voltaire Foundation, 1999) no. 1489.

22. Hegel appears to have recognized that, in these two particulars, Montesquieu's argument was intended as a corrective to Locke: see Georg Wilhelm Friedrich Hegel, *Natural Law*, tr. T. M. Knox (Philadelphia: University of Pennsylvania Press, 1975), 59–70, 128–29.

23. Note also Montesquieu, *MP* 1182.

24. See *Catalogue de la bibliothèque de Montesquieu à La Brède* no. 415.

25. See Montesquieu, S 374, 383, and MP 420, 1533.

26. See Pascal, *Pensées sur la religion et sur quelques autres sujets*, 294–95 (XXX.3, in the expanded edition published in 1678 and frequently republished thereafter). Note also the reference to *libido sentiendi, libido sciendi, libido dominandi* in ibid., 254–55 (XXVIII.55, in the expanded edition published in 1678 and frequently republished thereafter). For a survey of the seventeenth-century literature discussing *amour propre*, see Nannerl O. Keohane, *Philosophy and the State in France: The Renaissance to the*

Enlightenment (Princeton, NJ: Princeton University Press, 1980), 183–97, 262–82, 286–311. See, in particular, note 35, this chapter.

27. See Pascal, *Pensées: Édition établie d'après la copie référence de Gilberte Pascal* nos. 150, 243–44.

28. In this connection, note James, *Pierre Nicole*, 148–61, and Nannerl O. Keohane, "Noncomformist Absolutism in Louis XIV's France: Pierre Nicole and Denis Veiras," *Journal of the History of Ideas* 35:4 (October–December 1974): 579–96, and see Hans-Jürgen Fuchs, *Entfremdung und Narzissmus: Semantische Untersuchungen zur Geschichte der 'Selbstbezogenheit' als Vorgeschichte von französisch 'amour-propre'* (Stuttgart: J. B. Metzler, 1977), along with Dale Van Kley, "Pierre Nicole, Jansenism, and the Morality of Enlightened Self-Interest," in *Anticipations of the Enlightenment*, ed. Alan C. Kors and Paul Korshin (Philadelphia: University of Pennsylvania Press, 1987), 69–85; McKenna, *De Pascal à Voltaire*, I 225–27; and Johan Heilbron, "French Moralists and the Anthropology of the Modern Era: On the Genesis of the Notions of 'Interest' and 'Commercial Society'," in *The Rise of the Social Sciences and the Formation of Modernity: Conceptual Change in Context, 1750–1850*, ed. Johan Heilbron, Lars Magnusson, and Björn Wittrock (Dordrecht: Kluwer, 1998), 77–106.

29. See August. *In epistolam Joannis ad Parthos tractatus decem* 8.9.

30. See Pierre Nicole, "De la charité et de l'amour-propre," in Nicole, *Essais de morale*, ed. Laurent Thirounin (Paris: Presses Universitaires de France, 1999), 381–415 (esp. 406–7, where the passage from Augustine is cited and paraphrased). The same theme is developed in Nicole, "De la grandeur," in ibid., 197–243 (at 212–17). In this connection, see Keohane, *Philosophy and the State in France*, 293–303.

31. See Dale K. Van Kley, "The French Estates-General as Ecumenical Council," *Journal of Modern History* 61:1 (March 1989): 1–52, and Monique Cottret, "Les Jansénistes juges de Jean-Jacques," in *Jansénisme et Révolution*, ed. Catherine-Laurence Maire (Paris: Bibliothèque Mazarine, 1990), 81–102.

32. Note Edmond Préclin, *Les Jansénistes du XVIIIe siècle et la Constitution civile du clergé: Le Développement du richérisme, sa propagation dans le bas-clergé, 1713–1791* (Paris: J. Gamber, 1929), and consider Timothy Tackett, *Religion, Revolution, and Regional Culture in Eighteenth-Century France: The Ecclesiastical Oath of 1791* (Princeton, NJ: Princeton University Press, 1986), and Yann Fauchois, "Les Jansénistes et la Constitution civile du clergé," in *Jansénisme et Révolution*, 195–209, in light of Dale K. Van Kley, "Du parti janséniste au parti patriote (1770–1775)," in ibid., 115–30, and *The Religious Origins of the French Revolution* (New Haven, CT: Yale University Press, 1996), 353–60, as well as Catherine-Laurence Maire, "Agonie religieuse et transfiguration politique du jansénisme," in *Jansénisme et Révolution*, 103–14, and *De la Cause de Dieu à la cause de la Nation: Le Jansénisme au XVIIIe siècle* (Paris: Gallimard, 1998).

33. See David Hume, "Of Superstition and Enthusiasm" (1741), in Hume, *Essays Moral, Political, and Literary*, rev. ed., ed. Eugene F. Miller (Indianapolis, IN: Liberty Fund, 1985), 73–79 (esp. 78–79).

34. See Dale K. Van Kley, "The Jansenist Constitutional Legacy in the French Pre-Revolution," *Historical Reflections/Réflexions historiques* 13 (Summer–Fall 1986): 393–453,

which is reprinted in abbreviated form in *The Political Culture of the Old Regime*, ed. Keith M. Baker (Oxford, UK: Pergamon Press, 1987), 169–201; "The French Estates-General as Ecumenical Council," 1–52; and *The Religious Origins of the French Revolution*, passim.

35. This book, which has as its epigraph the claim that "our virtues are most often only vices disguised," is now available in a fine bilingual edition: consider La Rochefoucauld, *Maxims*, ed. and tr. Stuart D. Warner and Stéphane Douard (South Bend, IN: St. Augustine's Press, 2001), passim, in light of ibid. no. W1, which, though later suppressed, was the initial entry in the original edition of 1665, and nos. 1–4, 39–40, 46, 83, 88, 150, 171–72, 182, 187, 200, 213, 236, 245–47, 253–54, W14, W28, W32–34, P21, P26, P28. There is, of course, reason to wonder whether La Rochefoucauld's ultimate purpose was not identical with that of Pascal: note ibid. P22, which was not included in any of the editions published in the former's lifetime, and see Jean Starobinski, "La Rochefoucauld et les morales substitutives," *La nouvelle Revue française* 163 (July 1966): 16–35, 164 (August 1966): 211–29, and Philippe Sellier, "La Rochefoucauld, Pascal, St. Augustin," *Revue d'histoire littéraire de la France* 69 (1969): 551–75, as well as Keohane, *Philosophy and the State in France*, 289–93.

36. See Pierre Bayle, *Pensées diverses sur la comète* (1682), ed. A. Prat and Pierre Rétat (Paris: Société des Textes Français Modernes, 1994), passim, (esp. §§ 102–93, 239–63), who praises Pierre Nicole's *Essais de morale* as a "masterpiece" in ibid. §84. For a translation with an interpretive essay, see Pierre Bayle, *Various Thoughts on the Occasion of a Comet*, ed. and tr. Robert C. Bartlett (Albany: State University of New York Press, 2000).

37. See Robert Shackleton, "Bayle and Montesquieu," in *Pierre Bayle, le philosophe de Rotterdam: Études et documents*, ed. Paul Dibon (Amsterdam and Paris: Vrin, 1959), 142–49.

38. Consider Bernard Mandeville, *The Fable of the Bees: or, Private Vices, Publick Benefits*, ed. F. B. Kaye (Oxford, UK: Clarendon Press, 1924), which first appeared in highly attenuated form under the title *The Grumbling Hive: or Knaves Turn'd Honest* in 1705, and which was subsequently republished in ever-expanding editions in 1714, 1723, 1724, 1728, and 1733, and ultimately translated into French in 1740, in light of Marcel Raymond, "Du Jansénisme à la morale de l'intérêt," *Mercure de France* (June 1957): 238–55, and see Laurence Dickey, "Pride, Hypocrisy, and Civility in Mandeville's Social and Historical Theory," *Critical Review* 4:3 (Summer 1990): 387–431; E. J. Hundert, *The Enlightenment's Fable: Bernard Mandeville and the Discovery of Society* (Cambridge, UK: Cambridge University Press, 1994); and Pierre Force, *Self-Interest before Adam Smith: A Genealogy of Economic Science* (Cambridge, UK: Cambridge University Press, 2003), who draw attention to the strange kinship linking the peculiarly modern Epicureanism championed by Hobbes, Bayle, and Mandeville with the Jansenism of Pascal, Nicole, and La Rochefoucauld. In this last connection, note Joseph-Marie, comte de Maistre, *L'Église gallicane* (1821) 1.3–12, in *Œuvres du comte J. de Maistre*, ed. L'Abbé Migne (Paris: J.-P. Migne, 1862), 510–46.

39. Consider Adam Smith, *The Wealth of Nations*, in *The Glasgow Edition of the Works and Correspondence of Adam Smith* (Oxford, UK: Oxford University Press, 1976), with an

eye to Jacob Viner, *The Role of Providence in the Social Order: An Essay in Intellectual History* (Philadelphia: American Philosophical Society, 1972), 55–85, and Force, *Self-Interest before Adam Smith*, passim.

40. See II.1, above, and consider Keith Michael Baker, "Enlightenment and the Institution of Society: Notes for a Conceptual History," in *Main Trends in Cultural History: Ten Essays*, ed. Willem Melching and Wyger Velema (Amsterdam: Rodopi, 1994), 95–120.

41. See Pascal, *Pensées sur la religion et sur quelques autres sujets*, 176 (XXIV.1, in the expanded edition published in 1678 and frequently republished thereafter).

42. Suicide was for Montesquieu an abiding concern, to which he returned in each of his major works: see Jean-Marie Goulemot, "Montesquieu: Du Suicide légitimé à l'apologie du suicide héroïque," in *Gilbert Romme (1750–1795) et son temps*, ed. Jean Ehrard and Albert Soboul (Paris: Presses Universitaires de France, 1966), 163–74.

43. Note [Jean Le Rond d'Alembert], "Éloge de M. le President de Montesquieu," in *Encyclopédie, ou Dictionnaire raisonné des sciences, des arts, et des métiers*, ed. Denis Diderot and Jean Le Rond d'Alembert (Paris: Briasson, 1751–1772; Neufchastel: S. Faulche & Compagnie, 1765; Amsterdam: M. M. Rey, 1776–1777; Paris: Panckoucke, 1777–1780), V iii–xviii (at vii), and consider the argument advanced in Michael A. Mosher, "Monarchy's Paradox: Honor in the Face of Sovereign Power," in *Montesquieu's Science of Politics: Essays on The Spirit of Laws (1748)*, ed. David W. Carrithers, Michael A. Mosher, and Paul A. Rahe (Lanham, MD: Rowman & Littlefield, 2001), 159–229.

44. This fact explains why Locke speaks of "uneasiness" in *An Essay concerning Human Understanding* and not in his *Two Treatises of Government*: see Pierre Manent, *The City of Man*, tr. Marc A. LePain (Princeton, NJ: Princeton University Press, 1998), 111–55.

45. See Pierre Manent, *An Intellectual History of Liberalism*, tr. Rebecca Balinski (Princeton, NJ: Princeton University Press, 1994), 53–64 (esp. 58–63).

46. Consider David Hume, "Of the Independency of Parliament" (1741), "Whether the British Government Inclines more to Absolute Monarchy or to a Republic" (1741), and "Of Parties in General" (1741), in Hume, *Essays Moral, Political, and Literary*, rev. ed., ed. Eugene F. Miller (Indianapolis, IN: Liberty Fund, 1985), 42–63, in light of Hume, "Of the Liberty of the Press" (1741) and "Of the Parties of Great Britain" (1741), in ibid., 9–13, 64–72. It is not known whether, before drafting or substantially redrafting *EL* 3.19.27, Montesquieu read these essays. If, in fact, Montesquieu's analysis did owe something to that of Hume, it would help explain his decision to send a copy of his magnum opus to a relatively unknown Scot with whom at the time he was personally unacquainted: see the last paragraph of Letter from David Hume to Montesquieu on 10 April 1749, in Nagel III 1217–22 (at 1222) and in *Letters of David Hume*, ed. J. Y. T. Greig (Oxford: Clarendon Press, 1932), I 133–38 (at 138). There is reason to suppose that Montesquieu first drafted *EL* 3.19.27 at some point prior to 1741/42 and that, after considerable redrafting in the intervening years, he had a clean copy of the first three-quarters of the chapter made in 1745/46: consider Montesquieu, *MS* 483–91, in light of Catherine Volpilhac-Auger, "Annexe A.4. Tableau chronologique partiel de la correspondance manuscrite subsistante de Montesquieu (1734–1754)," and "Annexe A.6. Tableau des 'mains' et des papiers et concordance du manuscrit et de l'imprimé (1748)—Manuscrit

de *L'Esprit des lois*," in VF III clxiv–clxviii, ccviii–ccix. These revisions might have
been prompted by his having read Hume. The fact that neither the 1741 nor the 1742 edition of Hume's essays appears in the catalogue of Montesquieu's library is not dispositive. The various volumes of his work that Hume later sent to Montesquieu are missing
as well: note Letter from Montesquieu to David Hume on 3 September 1749, Letter
from David Hume to Montesquieu on 26 June 1753, and Letter from Montesquieu to
David Hume on 13 July 1753, in Nagel III 1255–56, 1460–65, 1470–71, the second of
which can be found also in *Letters of David Hume*, I 176–78; and then survey *Catalogue de la bibliothèque de Montesquieu à La Brède*. It is also quite possible that Montesquieu dispatched his magnum opus to Hume after reading the latter's essay "Of National Characters" (1748), now accessible in *Essays Moral, Political, and Literary*, 197–
215, which was first published in the third edition of Hume's essays within a month of
the appearance of *De l'Esprit des lois*. In this connection, see III.1, note 31, below.
47. Note Montesquieu, *MP* 1161.
48. Cf. Niccolò Machiavelli, *Discorsi sopra la prima deca di Tito Livio* 1.4, in Machiavelli,
Tutte le opere, ed. Mario Martelli (Florence: G. C. Sansoni, 1971), 82–83.
49. See Neal Wood, "The Value of Asocial Sociability: Contributions of Machiavelli, Sidney, and Montesquieu," in *Machiavelli and the Nature of Political Thought*, ed. Martin
Fleisher (New York: Athenaeum, 1972), 282–307 (esp. 298–305), and Paul Carrese,
"The Machiavellian Spirit of Montesquieu's Liberal Republic," in *Machiavelli's Liberal Republican Legacy*, ed. Paul A. Rahe (New York: Cambridge University Press,
2006), 121–42 (esp. 124–37). Note also Montesquieu, *MP* 814, 1252.

BOOK TWO, CHAPTER FOUR. CORRUPTION

1. A failure to appreciate this can lead to considerable confusion—especially when it is
seconded by an inclination to interpret Montesquieu's masterpiece in light of passing
remarks jotted down in his notebooks, observations made in works penned prior to his
discovery of his "principles" (Préf.), and passages wrenched out of their context in his
later writings: witness Roger Boesche, "Fearing Monarchs and Merchants: Montesquieu's Two Theories of Despotism," *Western Political Quarterly* 43 (1990): 741–61.
2. In this connection, note Badreddine Kassem, *Décadence et absolutisme dans l'œuvre de
Montesquieu* (Paris: Librairie Minard, 1960), and see Sharon Krause, "The Uncertain
Inevitability of Decline in Montesquieu," *Political Theory* 30 (2002): 702–27, along with
Jean-Patrice Courtois, "Temps, corruption et histoire dans *L'Esprit des lois*," in *Le
Temps de Montesquieu: Actes du colloque international de Genève (28–31 octobre 1998)*,
ed. Michel Porret and Catherine Volpilhac-Auger (Geneva: Droz, 2002), 305–17.
3. In this connection, note Montesquieu, *LP* 61/63, 96–97/99–100; see *EL* 3.16.11–12,
19.5–6, 8–9, 12, 14–15, 6.28.22. Note also Montesquieu, *MP* 1062, 1491, 1625, and see
III.1, 3, below.
4. In *EL* 1.8.2–3, Montesquieu draws heavily on the classical Greek descriptions of democratic Athens as it existed in the late fifth and fourth centuries: for the evidence, see
Rahe, *RAM* I.vii.2 (with the attendant notes).

5. Cf. Arist. *Eth. Nic.* 1160a31–1161b10, *Pol.* 1278b30–1280a5, *Rh.* 1365b21–1366a22. Note also Arist. *Pol.* 1295a25–1297a12.

6. Note *EL* 1.5.11, 2.12.7–8, and 6.29.16 (p. 877); then consider *MP* 927, 1302 (esp. pp. 385–86, 388–90), 1306, and Montesquieu, "Réflexions sur le caractère de quelques princes et sur quelques événements de leur vie" (ca. 1731–33), ed. Sheila Mason, VI, in VF IX 51–65 (at 60), in light of *LP* 22/24, 35/37. Note *MP* 857, and consider 1962 in light of Catherine Volpilhac-Auger, "Annexe B.2. Le *Testament politique* attribué au cardinal de Richelieu," in VF IV 899–901.

7. Note, in this connection, *EL* 1.5.19, p. 304.

8. For a detailed analysis of the corruption intrinsic to despotic regimes, see Sharon Krause, "Despotism in *The Spirit of Laws*," in *Montesquieu's Science of Politics: Essays on the Spirit of Laws (1748)*, ed. David W. Carrithers, Michael A. Mosher, and Paul A. Rahe (Lanham, MD: Rowman & Littlefield, 2001), 231–71.

9. In this connection, see Élie Carcassonne, "La Chine dans *L'Esprit des lois*," *Revue d'histoire littéraire de la France* 24 (1924): 198–205; Rolando Minuti, "Ambiente naturale e dinamica delle società politiche: Aspetti e tensioni di un tema di Montesquieu," in *Leggere l'Esprit des lois: Stato, società, e storia nel pensiero di Montesquieu*, ed. Domenico Felice (Naples: Liguori, 1998), 137–63 (esp. 148–63), which is reprinted in French as "Milieu naturel et sociétés: Réflexions sur un thème de Montesquieu," in *Le Temps de Montesquieu*, 223–44 (esp. 233–44); Jean-Patrice Courtois, *Inflexions de la rationalité dans L'Esprit des lois* (Paris: Presses Universitaires de France, 1999), 83–90; and Catherine Volpilhac-Auger, "On the Proper Use of the Stick: *The Spirit of Laws* and the Chinese Empire," in *Montesquieu and His Legacy*, ed. Rebecca E. Kingston (Albany: State University of New York Press, 2008), 81–95. Note also Jonathan D. Spence, *The Chan's Great Continent: China in Western Minds* (New York: Norton, 1998), 87–95, 213–14. As Spence points out (ibid., 87–92), Montesquieu was already displaying an intense curiosity regarding China in 1713—when, as a young man of twenty-four, he leapt at the chance to interview at length a visitor from China.

10. Note also Montesquieu, *MP* 1880.

11. Cf. David Hume, "Of the Rise and Progress of the Arts and Sciences" (1742), in Hume, *Essays Moral, Political, and Literary*, rev. ed., ed. Eugene F. Miller (Indianapolis, IN: Liberty Classics, 1985), 122 (esp. n. 13).

12. Regarding Montesquieu's choice of metaphors, see Denis de Casabianca, "Dérèglements mécaniques et dynamique des fluides dans *L'Esprit des lois*," *Revue Montesquieu* 4 (2000): 43–70.

13. See David B. Young, "Libertarian Demography: Montesquieu's Essay on Depopulation in the *Lettres persanes*," *Journal of the History of Ideas* 36:4 (October, 1975): 669–82.

14. Cf. Karl August Wittfogel, *Oriental Despotism: A Comparative Study of Total Power* (New Haven, CT: Yale University Press, 1957).

15. Montesquieu's account of the cycle to which despotic government in China is prone bears a striking resemblance to the account given of the ordinary course of affairs within the Islamic world by Ibn Khaldūn, *The Muqadimmah: An Introduction to History*, 2nd ed., tr. Franz Rosenthal (Princeton, NJ: Princeton University Press, 1967).

16. Note Montesquieu, *MP* 1271.

17. See Montesquieu, *EL* 1.2.2–3, 3.3, 5.3, 6–8, 15, 17–19, 6.3–5, 8, 11, 15, 17, 7.2, 4, 10–14, 8.5, 7, 11–14. Note also 2.9.1, 8, 10.3, 6, 14, 16–17.

18. See Niccolò Machiavelli, *Discorsi sopra la prima deca di Tito Livio* 1.4–5, in Machiavelli, *Tutte le opere*, ed. Mario Martelli (Florence: G. C. Sansoni, 1971), 82–83.

19. Cf. *MP* 212, where Montesquieu attributes a "fury for liberty" to the classical Greeks.

20. On the eve of the American Revolution, when English corruption became a theme in colonial discourse, the pertinent passage came to receive ample attention: note Bernard Bailyn, *The Ideological Origins of the American Revolution* (Cambridge, MA: Harvard University Press, 1967), 55–143; then see Donald S. Lutz, "The Relative Influence of European Writers on Late Eighteenth-Century American Political Thought," *American Political Science Review* 78:1 (March 1984): 189–97, who draws attention to the fact that, in the years leading up to 1776, Montesquieu was cited by the colonists more often than anyone other than John Locke. It was also at this time that the passage began to figure prominently in British discussions of their own trajectory: see Michael Sonenscher, *Before the Deluge: Public Debt, Inequality, and the Intellectual Origins of the French Revolution* (Princeton, NJ: Princeton University Press, 2007), 41–45 (esp. 44, n. 63).

21. See Letters from François, comte de Bulkeley, to Montesquieu on 21 January, 24 February, 17 March, and 5 May 1749 as well as on 17 September 1750; Letters from Montesquieu to William Domville on 4 March and 22 July 1749; Letter from William Domville to Montesquieu on 4 June 1749; and Letter from Montesquieu to Thomas Nugent on 18 October 1750, in Nagel III 1168–70, 1191–93, 1195–96, 1207–9, 1228–30, 1235–37, 1244–45, 1322, 1333–which should be read in light of of Robert Shackleton, "John Nourse and the London Edition of *L'Esprit des Lois*," in *Studies in the French Eighteenth Century Presented to John Lough*, ed. D. J. Mossop, G. E. Rodmell, and D. B. Wilson (Durham, UK: University of Durham, 1978), 248–59, and Cecil Patrick Courtney, "Montesquieu et ses relations anglaises: Autour de sa correspondance des années 1749–1750 sur deux éditions britanniques et deux traductions de *L'Esprit des lois*," in *Montesquieu, Œuvre ouverte? (1748–1755): Actes du Colloque de Bordeaux (6–8 décembre 2001, Bordeaux, bibliothèque municipale)*, ed. Catherine Larrère (Oxford, UK: Voltaire Foundation, 2005), 147–62.

22. Letter from William Domville to Montesquieu on 4 June 1749, in Nagel III 1235–37.

23. The remainder of this chapter is adapted from Paul A. Rahe, "Forms of Government: Structure, Principle, Object, and Aim," in *Montesquieu's Science of Politics*, 69–108 (at 94–97). For other recent discussions, in part along almost identical lines, see Bernard Manin, "Montesquieu, la république et le commerce," *Archives Européennes de Sociologie* 42:3 (2001): 573–602 (at 595–602), and Céline Spector, *Montesquieu: Pouvoirs, richesses et sociétés* (Paris: Presses Universitaires de France, 2004), 194–202.

24. Note, in this connection, *LP* 99/102.

25. See Letter from Montesquieu to William Domville on 22 July 1749, in Nagel III 1244–45. Cf. Sonenscher, *Before the Deluge*, 41–52, 56, 95–172, who neglects the missive actually dispatched to Domville and wrongly attributes to Montesquieu a conviction that the English form of government is exceedingly fragile and far more vulnerable to col-

lapse than the French monarchy. For a partial corrective with regard to the species of commerce practiced on opposite shores of the English Channel, see Henry C. Clark, *Compass of Society: Commerce and Absolutism in Old Regime France* (Lanham, MD: Lexington Books, 2007), 111–14, 121–29.

26. For extended discussions of this fragment, see Lando Landi, *L'Inghilterra e il pensiero politico di Montesquieu* (Padua: CEDAM, 1981), 244–369, and Donald Desserud, "Commerce and Political Participation in Montesquieu's Letter to Domville," *History of European Ideas* 25 (1999): 135–51. See also Cecil Patrick Courtney, "Montesquieu and English Liberty," in *Montesquieu's Science of Politics*, 273–90. Cf. Annelien de Dijn, *French Political Thought from Montesquieu to Tocqueville: Liberty in a Levelled Society?* (Cambridge, UK: Cambridge University Press, 2008), 24–25, who overlooks the exchange with Domville and the pertinent entry in Montesquieu's *Pensées* and argues that, in Montesquieu's estimation, "the "remarkable absence of intermediary powers" rendered English "liberty highly fragile."

27. There is no reason to suppose, as Desserud does, "Commerce and Political Participation in Montesquieu's Letter to Domville," 135, that the material under consideration comes from a second "letter" sent to Domville and then "recopied in Montesquieu's *Pensées.*"

28. Cf., for example, Mark Hulliung, *Montesquieu and the Old Regime* (Berkeley: University of California Press, 1976); Nannerl O. Keohane, *Philosophy and the State in France: The Renaissance to the Enlightenment* (Princeton, NJ: Princeton University Press, 1980), 392–419; Judith N. Shklar, *Montesquieu* (Oxford, UK: Oxford University Press, 1987); Manin, "Montesquieu, la république et le commerce," 573–602 (at 581–82); and, most recently, Spector, *Montesquieu: Pouvoirs, richesses et sociétés*, passim.

29. For an English translation of the letter in its entirety, see Desserud, "Commerce and Political Participation in Montesquieu's Letter to Domville," 145–49.

30. After reading II.1, note 73, above, see II.3 note 49, in context, above, cf. Clark, *Compass of Society*, 122.

31. In his aversion to classical virtue, understood as heroic self-sacrifice, and in his preference for this more modest form of virtue, understood as a spirited assertion of the long-term self-interest of a commercial people, Montesquieu was in the Whig mainstream: see Paul A. Rahe, "Antiquity Surpassed: The Repudiation of Classical Republicanism," in *Republicanism, Liberty, and Commercial Society: 1649–1776*, ed. David Wootton (Stanford, CA: Stanford University Press, 1994), 233–69.

32. In consequence, it would be completely inappropriate for an admirer of English liberty to share the disdain that, in his guise as a Roman republican, Cicero quite rightly expressed for "men of commerce . . . for whom all governments are equal as long as they are tranquil": note Cic. *Att.* 7.7–8, and cf. Montesquieu, *EL* 2.18.1 with *MP* 1960 (À Monsieur Domville), p. 600.

33. Montesquieu touches on the question of executive patronage in *EL* 3.19.27, p. 575.

34. See *EL* 3.19.27, pp. 576–77.

35. Elsewhere in his discussion of England Montesquieu treats elections as an antidote to corruption: *EL* 2.11.6, p. 402.

36. Cf. Sharon Krause, "The Spirit of Separate Powers in Montesquieu," *Review of Politics* 62 (2000): 231–65, who ignores the letter that Montesquieu wrote to William Domville and the notes that he penned in preparation for composing it and then argues that Montesquieu's worries concerning the long-term prospects for liberty in England arose from a conviction that the commercial spirit would gradually subvert the separation of powers: first, by eroding the residual distinction between peer and commoner needed to underpin it; second, by undercutting the inclination of the English to treat the person of their prince as sacred; and, third, by undermining their willingness to make sacrifices for the sake of retaining their liberty. There is warrant within *The Spirit of Laws* for supposing that commerce will promote social equality but none for attributing to Montesquieu the fear that a diminution in aristocratic deference would seriously threaten the separation of powers. Instead, as we have seen, he was persuaded that England's monarchical executive would eventually find the means with which to corrupt the legislative power. Krause's third claim has even less to recommend it. As should be evident from what was said in the last section of II.3, above, it runs counter to the tenor of Montesquieu, *EL* 3.19.27—which describes the English as a commercial people fervently involved in partisan politics, ferociously vigilant in defense of its liberties, and more than willing to "sacrifice its well-being, its ease, its interests" to defend its "freedom." Her third claim is similarly inconsistent, as we have now seen, with the observations elicited from Montesquieu by Domville's question—which suggest on his part an exceedingly sanguine assessment of commerce's role. In his quite similar attempt to read into *The Spirit of Laws* a deep suspicion of commerce, Roger Boesche cites the notes that Montesquieu wrote in preparation for responding to Domville in a fashion that misrepresents altogether the thrust of what Montesquieu has to say: see Boesche, "Fearing Monarchs and Merchants: Montesquieu's Two Theories of Despotism," 749–61 (esp. 754).

37. See Paul Langford, *The Excise Crisis: Society and Politics in the Age of Walpole* (Oxford, UK: Clarendon Press, 1975), who places particular emphasis on the pressure brought to bear on Parliament from out-of-doors by men engaged in trade (ibid., 44–61, 101–23, 151–71).

38. See also *EL* 1.8.6, and cf. Montesquieu, *CR* 15.100–103. For an extended meditation on the significance of this observation for Montesquieu and for his admirers after the French Revolution, see Dijn, *French Political Thought from Montesquieu to Tocqueville*.

39. Note Letter from David Hume to Montesquieu on 10 April 1749, in Nagel III 1217–22 (at 1217–18, with n. c) and in *Letters of David Hume*, ed. J. Y. T. Greig (Oxford: Clarendon Press, 1932), I 133–38 (at 134, with n. 1), and see David Hume, *The History of England from the Invasion of Julius Caesar to the Revolution in 1688* (Indianapolis, IN: Liberty Fund, 1983), IV 370. Hume's blunt warning, in the latter passage, that the people of England "are not secured by any middle power, or independent powerful nobility, interposed between them and the monarch" first appeared in the edition published in 1778. See Duncan Forbes, *Hume's Philosophical Politics* (Cambridge, UK: Cambridge University Press, 1975), 178–80.

40. See Letter from Montesquieu to William Domville on 22 July 1749, in Nagel III 1244–45.

BOOK THREE, PREFACE

1. See Oliver Wendell Holmes, "Montesquieu," *Collected Legal Papers* (New York: Peter Smith, 1952), 250–65 (at 262), who, like many readers, hardly ventured beyond the first part of *The Spirit of Laws.* See also David W. Carrithers, "Introduction," in Montesquieu, *The Spirit of Laws: A Compendium of the First English Edition,* ed. David W. Carrithers (Berkeley: University of California Press, 1977), 1–88 (at 30), who accuses Montesquieu of neglecting "the overall problem of historical development embodying evolutionary change," and Elena Russo, "The Youth of Moral Life: The Virtue of the Ancients from Montesquieu to Nietzsche," in *Montesquieu and the Spirit of Modernity,* ed. David W. Carrithers and Patrick Coleman (Oxford, UK: Voltaire Foundation, 2002), 101–23 (at 115), who asserts that, since "Montesquieu had no general model of evolutionary history," his interpretive categories "remained for him categories within a scheme of comparative sociology, the product of specific cultural, social and political contexts."

2. See David W. Carrithers, "Montesquieu's Philosophy of History," *Journal of the History of Ideas* 47:1 (January–March 1986): 61–80, who, in reaching this assessment, fails to take into consideration the one set of arguments that might be cited to the contrary: the history of commerce provided by Montesquieu in *EL* 4.21.

3. Consider Montesquieu, *Voyage de Gratz à La Haye,* in Pléiade I 575, in light of Robert Shackleton, *Montesquieu: A Critical Biography* (Oxford, UK: Oxford University Press, 1961), 114–16.

4. See Letter to l'abbé Ottaviano, comte di Guasco, on 6 December 1746, in Nagel III 1074.

5. See Charles-Louis de Secondat, baron de la Brède et de Montesquieu, *De l'Esprit des loix,* nouvelle édition (Geneva: Barrillot et Fils, 1750). With regard to this edition and its predecessor in 1749, which were actually published under a false imprint by Huart in Paris, see Letter from Pierre Michel Huart at the beginning of March 1749, and Letter to Pierre-Jean Grosley on 8 April 1750, in Nagel III 1198–99, 1293–97 (at 1297).

BOOK THREE, CHAPTER ONE. NATURE'S DOMINION

1. Cf. Aesch. *Pers.* 50, 74–75, 234, 241–42, 402–4, 584–97; Hdt. 7.101–4, 135–36; and Eur. *Hel.* 276, *Iph. Aul.* 1400–1401 with Isoc. 4.131–32, 150–52, 181–82, 5.107, 120–24, *Ep.* 3.5, 9.19; Pl. *Resp.* 4.435e–436a, *Tim.* 24c4–d2; Arist. *Pol.* 1285a15–29, 1313a34–b10, 1327b23–36. See also Hippocr. *Airs, Waters, and Places* 12, 16. Note Cic. *Rep.* 1.33.50.

2. Cf. Roger Mercier, "La Théorie des climats des *Réflexions critiques* à *L'Esprit des lois,*" *Revue d'histoire littéraire de la France* 53 (1953): 17–37, 159–74, and Robert Shackleton, "The Evolution of Montesquieu's Theory of Climate," *Revue internationale de philosophie* 33–34 (1955): 317–29, and *Montesquieu: A Critical Biography* (Oxford, UK: Oxford University Press, 1961), 302–19, with Catherine Volpilhac-Auger, "Annexe B.3. Sur quelques sources prétendues du livre XIV," in VF IV 902–16, who rightly draws attention to Montesquieu's research in the medical literature. In this connection, see also

Jean Ehrard, *L'Idée de nature en France dans la première moitié du XVIIIe siècle* (Paris: SEVPEN, 1963), II 691–737.

3. For a recent attempt to come to grips with this problem, see Sharon R. Krause, "History and the Human Soul in Montesquieu," *History of Political Thought* 24:2 (Summer 2003): 235–61 (at 235–52), and "Laws, Passion, and the Attractions of Right Action in Montesquieu," *Philosophy & Social Criticism* 32:2 (2006): 211–30.

4. See Désiré André, "Sur les Écrits scientifiques de Montesquieu," *Correspondant* 84:5 (1880): 1054–81; Shackleton, *Montesquieu*, 20–28, 59–60, 73–74; and Lorenzo Bianchi, "Montesquieu naturaliste," in *Montesquieu: Les Années de formation (1689–1720)*, ed. Catherine Volpilhac-Auger (Oxford, UK: Voltaire Foundation, 1999), 109–24.

5. See Denis de Casabianca, "Dérèglements mécaniques et dynamique des fluides dans *L'Esprit des lois*," *Revue Montesquieu* 4 (2000): 43–70.

6. See Letter to Denis Dodart in September 1725, in VF XVIII 173–75 (at 174). Montesquieu argued that, by unmasking paganism, Epicureanism paved the way for Christianity: *MP* 21.

7. After alluding to Pascal's wager and suggesting that it was better calculated to produce "fear" than "faith," Montesquieu mentions Epicurus' wish "to deliver men from the yoke of religion" and then pointedly adds that "the pagan religion was in no way a yoke": see *MP* 420.

8. See *MP* 112, 224; *LP* 73/75; and *S* 399. Spinoza's *Ethics* remained on Montesquieu's mind: consider the first sentence of *EL* 2.12.2, and see *MP* 2167. For a recent study, see Steven B. Smith, *Spinoza's Book of Life: Freedom and Redemption in the Ethics* (New Haven, CT: Yale University Press, 2003). In this connection, see also Smith, "What Kind of Democrat Was Spinoza?" *Political Theory* 33:1 (February 2005): 6–27.

9. Consider *"Traité du devoirs,"* 1 May 1725, ed. Sheila Mason, in VF VIII 437–39, and Letter to Monsignor de Fitz-James, bishop of Soissons, on 8 October 1750, in Nagel III 1327–29 (at 1327–28), in light of Shackleton, *Montesquieu*, 68–76.

10. See Simone Goyard-Fabre, *Montesquieu, adversaire de Hobbes* (Paris: Lettres Modernes, 1980).

11. See Georges Benrekassa, "L'Intelligence de l'historique: Constitution, théorie, et mise en œuvre de la notion de causalité historique dans les *Considérations sur les causes de la grandeur des Romains et de leur décadence*," in Benrekassa, *La Politique et sa mémoire: Le Politique et l'historique dans le pensée des lumières* (Paris: Payot, 1983), 37–89; Simone Goyard-Fabre, "Le Destin de Rome et la nature des choses," and Carlo Borghero, "Dal *génie* all'*esprit*: Fisico e morale nelle *Considérations sur les Romains* di Montesquieu," in *Storia e ragione: Le Considérations sur les causes de la grandeur des Romains et de leur décadence di Montesquieu nel 250° della publicazione*, ed. Alberto Postigliola (Naples: Liguori, 1987), 113–38, 251–76.

12. In this connection, see Pierre Rétat, "Introduction," in VF IX 205–17, who draws attention to the fact that the work was reproduced as a fair copy at some point between 1734 and 1739, and who suggests that it was composed in the mid-1730s, soon after the *Considerations on the Romans* and the *Universal Monarchy*. Note also Melvin Richter, "An Introduction to Montesquieu's 'An Essay on the Causes that May Affect Men's Minds and Characters'," *Political Theory* 4:2 (May 1976): 132–38, and see Catherine Volpilhac-

Auger, "La Dissertation *sur la différence des génies:* Essai de reconstitution," *Revue Montesquieu* 4 (2000): 226–37, who discusses a fragmentary work, begun in 1717, that was a precursor.

13. Cf. Heraclitus F67a (Diels-Kranz) ap. Schol. Chalcid. *In Tim.* 220 and Chrysippus ap. Chalcid. *In Tim.* 220 (SVF II 879), whence Montesquieu, who had long been interested in the Stoics, may have drawn this image. In this connection, see Catherine Larrère, "Le Stoïcisme dans les œuvres de jeunesse de Montesquieu," in *Montesquieu: Les Années de formation (1689–1720)*, 163–83, who drew my attention to the classical sources.

14. In this connection, see Montesquieu, *Défense de L'Esprit des lois*, in Pléiade II 1121–66 (at 1134–36).

15. It would be difficult to exaggerate the extent of Montesquieu's admiration for Descartes: note S 390, 565, 591, and see *MP* 50, 775, 1445, 1946, p. 585, along with "Essai d'observations sur l'histoire naturelle," 20 November 1721, ed. Lorenzo Bianchi, in VF VIII 195–223 (esp. 213, 223), and *LP* 94/97. In this connection, note Gustave Lanson, "L'Influence de la philosophie Cartésienne sur la littérature française," *Revue de métaphysique et de morale* 4 (1896): 517–50 (esp. 538–46), which is reprinted in Lanson, *Études d'histoire littéraire* (Paris: Librairie Ancienne Honoré Champion, 1929), 58–96 (esp. 84–90); Charles-Jacques Beyer, "Montesquieu et l'esprit cartésien," in *Actes du Congrès Montesquieu réuni à Bordeaux du 23 au 26 mai 1955* (Bordeaux: Impriméries Delmas, 1956), 159–73; Mark H. Waddicor, *Montesquieu and the Philosophy of Natural Law* (The Hague: Martinus Nijhoff, 1970), 22–31; Robert Alun Jones, "Ambivalent Cartesians: Durkheim, Montesquieu, and Method," *American Journal of Sociology* 100:1 (July 1994): 1–39; Alberto Postigliola, "Montesquieu entre Descartes et Newton," in *Montesquieu: Les Années de formation (1689–1720)*, 91–108, and Bianchi, "Montesquieu naturaliste," 109–24; as well as Denis de Casabianca, "Des Objections sans réponses? À Propos de la 'Tentation' matérialiste de Montesquieu dans les *Pensées*," *Revue Montesquieu* 7 (2003–4): 135–56.

16. See Montesquieu, "Discours sur les motifs qui doivent nous encourager au sciences," 15 November 1725, ed. Sheila Mason, in VF VIII 495–502 (esp. 495–98), and *MP* 1265. With regard to *préjugés destructeurs*, see also I.3, note 54, above. Note, in this connection, *MP* 1983, 1252.

17. Cf. Montesquieu, *MP* 2035, with René Descartes, *Les Passions de l'âme* 1.1–50, in Descartes, *Œuvres et lettres*, ed. André Bridoux (Paris: Bibliothèque de la Pléiade, 1953), 695–722. A similar outlook seems to inform Montesquieu, "Essai sur le goût" (ca. 1753–55), ed. Pierre Rétat, in VF IX 487–517. For an argument that Montesquieu was much closer in outlook to Spinoza than he was willing to admit, cf. Michael A. Mosher, "Was Montesquieu French? Reflections on the Passage from Nation to Humanity in Enlightenment Thought," Paper Delivered at the American Political Science Association Annual Meeting, Sheraton Boston Hotel, Boston, Massachusetts, 29 August–1 September 2002.

18. See David Hume, *An Enquiry concerning the Principles of Morals* III.ii, in Hume, *Enquiries concerning the Human Understanding and concerning the Principles of Morals,* 2nd ed., ed. L. A. Selby-Bigge (Oxford, UK: Clarendon Press, 1902), 197n. In this connection, see Patrick Riley, *The General Will before Rousseau: The Transforma-*

tion of the Divine into the Civic (Princeton, NJ: Princeton University Press, 1986), 3–180.

19. For a useful discussion, see David W. Carrithers, "Introduction," in Charles-Louis de Secondat, baron de la Brède et de Montesquieu, *The Spirit of Laws: A Compendium of the First English Edition*, ed. David W. Carrithers (Berkeley: University of California Press, 1977), 1–88 (at 26–30, 34–40, 44–51). Note the emphasis that Montesquieu placed on discovering *les causes physiques et morales* in his *Défense de L'Esprit des lois*, in Pléiade II 1137, and see Raymond Aron, *Main Currents of Sociological Thought*, tr. Richard Howard and Helen Weaver (New York: Basic Books, 1965–1967) I: *Montesquieu, Comte, Marx, Tocqueville, the Sociologists and the Revolution of 1848*, 11–56.

20. Cf. René Descartes, *Discours de la méthode pour bien conduire sa raison* V, in Descartes, *Œuvres et lettres*, ed. André Bridoux (Paris: Bibliothèque de la Pléiade, 1953), 153–67 (esp. 155–56).

21. See George Klosko, "Montesquieu's Science of Politics: Absolute Values and Ethical Relativism in *L'Esprit des lois*," *Studies on Voltaire and the Eighteenth Century* 189 (1980): 153–77 (esp. 153–67), and Michael Zuckert, "Natural Law, Natural Rights, and Classical Liberalism: On Montesquieu's Critique of Hobbes," *Social Philosophy & Policy* 18:1 (2001): 227–51 (esp. 231–39).

22. Stuart D. Warner, "Montesquieu's Prelude: An Interpretation of Book I of *The Spirit of Laws*," in *Enlightening Revolutions: Essays in Honor of Ralph Lerner*, ed. Svetozar Minkov, with Stéphane Douard (Lanham, MD: Lexington Books, 2006), 159–87, does a nice job of bringing this out. Note also Pierre Rétat, "Les Ambiguïtés de la notion de loi chez Montesquieu: Analyse du livre I de *L'Esprit des lois*," in *De la Tyrannie au totalitarisme: Recherche sur les ambiguïtés de la philosophie politique*, ed. Marie Cariou (Lyon: L'Hermès, 1986), 125–35.

23. See Catherine Volpilhac-Auger, "Une nouvelle 'Chaîne secrète' de *L'Esprit des lois*: L'Histoire de texte," in *Montesquieu en 2005*, ed. Catherine Volpilhac-Auger (Oxford, UK: Voltaire Foundation, 2005), 85–216 (at 185–94), and "Annexe A.2. Que faire des Muses?" in VF III cxlvi–clvi.

24. See Michel Jean Louis Saladin, *Mémoires historique sur la vie et les ouvrages de M. J. Vernet, ministre de l'Église de Genève, accompagné de 'l'Invocation aux Muses,' de Montesquieu, et de plusieurs lettres de J.-J. Rousseau et Voltaire, qui n'ont pas encore été publiées* (Paris: Bossange, 1790), 29–30, who reprints what purports to be the version excised by Vernet.

25. For a critical edition of the latter version, see Volpilhac-Auger, "Une nouvelle 'Chaîne secrète' de *L'Esprit des lois*," 193–94, and "Annexe A.2. Que faire des Muses?" in VF III clv–clvi.

26. Cf. David Hume, *A Treatise of Human Nature*, ed. L. A. Selby-Bigge (Oxford, UK: Clarendon Press, 1968) I.iv.6–7.

27. He did the latter by sending him a copy of *De l'Esprit des lois*: see Letter from David Hume to Montesquieu on 10 April 1749, in Nagel III 1217–22 (at 1222) and in *Letters of David Hume*, ed. J. Y. T. Greig (Oxford: Clarendon Press, 1932), I 133–38 (at 138).

28. Cf. Thomas Hobbes, *Leviathan*, ed. Edwin Curley (Indianapolis, IN: Hackett, 1994)

I.iii.3–5, viii.14–16, and Hume, *A Treatise of Human Nature* II.iii, with *LP* 31.22–34/33; note *CEC* 393–97, and see *EL* 3.19.27, p 577.

29. Consider the precise manner in which Montesquieu's brief account of the state of nature (*EL* 1.1.2), which he had first outlined for inclusion in his *Traité des devoirs* in the early 1720s (*MP* 1266, pp. 344–45), involves a correction of Hobbes's account (*Leviathan* I.xiii) and an anticipation of the evolutionary account sketched out at some length by Jean-Jacques Rousseau, *Discours sur l'origine et les fondemens de l'inégalité parmi les hommes* (1755), ed Jean Starobinski, in *Œuvres complètes de Jean-Jacques Rousseau*, ed. Bernard Gagnebin and Marcel Raymond (Paris: Bibliothèque de la Pléiade, 1959–95), III 109–223: see Zuckert, "Natural Law, Natural Rights, and Classical Liberalism," 239–51 (esp. 239, 240); Yoshie Kawade, "La Liberté civile contre la théorie réformiste de l'État souverain: Le Combat de Montesquieu," in *Le Travail des lumières: Pour Georges Benrekassa*, ed. Caroline Jacot Grapa, Nicole Jacques-Lefèvre, Yannick Séité, and Carine Trevisan (Paris: Honoré Champion, 2002), 203–23; and Paul A. Rahe, *Soft Despotism, Democracy's Drift: Montesquieu, Rousseau, Tocqueville, and the Modern Prospect* (New Haven, CT: Yale University Press, 2009) II.2. In this connection, note also Catherine Volpilhac-Auger, "Annexe B.1. L'*Antioccupatio* attribuée à Hobbes (*L'Esprit des lois*, I, 3)," in VF IV 897–98.

30. See Thomas L. Pangle, *Montesquieu's Philosophy of Liberalism: A Commentary on The Spirit of the Laws* (Chicago: University of Chicago Press, 1973), 161–99; Benrekassa, "D'une Naturalité du savoir politique: Montesquieu et le problème des déterminations géographiques," in Benrekassa, *La Politique et sa mémoire*, 205–26; Jean-Patrice Courtois, *Inflexions de la rationalité dans L'Esprit des lois* (Paris: Presses Universitaires de France, 1999), 70–103, and "Le Physique et le moral dans la théorie du climat chez Montesquieu," in *Le Travail des lumières*, 139–56, which is reprinted in *Lectures de L'Esprit des lois*, ed. Céline Spector and Thierry Hoquet (Bordeaux: Presses Universitaires de Bordeaux, 2004), 101–19; Carlo Borghero, "Libertà e necessità: Clima ed *esprit général* nell'Esprit des lois," in *Libertà, necessità e storia: Percorsi dell'Esprit des lois di Montesquieu*, ed. Domenico Felice (Naples: Bibliopolis, 2003), 137–201; and Ana Samuel, "The Design of Montesquieu's *The Spirit of the Laws*: The Triumph of Freedom over Determinism," forthcoming in *American Political Science Review*.

31. See David Hume, "Of National Characters" (1748), in Hume, *Essays Moral, Political, and Literary*, rev. ed., ed. Eugene F. Miller (Indianapolis, IN: Liberty Fund, 1985), 197–215, which was first published in the month immediately following that in which Montesquieu's *De l'Esprit des lois* appeared, and which has the appearance of being a pointed critical response to Montesquieu, *EL* 3.14–17. For elaborate detective work suggesting that, as much as a year before *De l'Esprit des lois* was actually published, Hume may have been more or less fully apprised of the thesis concerning climate advanced therein by Montesquieu, and for reasons for supposing that Montesquieu sent Hume a copy of his magnum opus after reading and puzzling over the latter's denial that climate shapes national character, see Paul E. Chamley, "The Conflict between Montesquieu and Hume: A Study of the Origins of Adam Smith's Universalism," in *Essays on Adam Smith*, ed. Andrew S. Skinner and Thomas Wilson (Oxford, UK: Clarendon Press, 1975), 274–305 (esp. 282–99).

32. Montesquieu was not, however, the first to deploy against slavery the natural rights theory of England's radical Whigs: note David Brion Davis, *The Problem of Slavery in Western Culture* (Ithaca, NY: Cornell University Press, 1966), 374–78, 402–9, and then see Rahe, *RAM* II.vii.8.

33. Montesquieu had long before read this work with care: cf. *LP* 101.4–16/104, which should be read in conjunction with *MP* 224 and 1252, with John Locke, *Two Treatises of Government: A Critical Edition with an Introduction and Apparatus Criticus*, 2nd ed., ed. Peter Laslett (Cambridge, UK: Cambridge University Press, 1970) II.xi.135, from which his own brief summary of English thinking is copied almost word for word.

34. Cf. John Locke, *Two Treatises of Government* I.i.1–II.ix.131, xvi.175–xix.243, with Montesquieu, *MP* 174 and *EL* 3.15.2.

35. This is drawn from *RMU* 8.8.109–12, 122–34.

36. In this connection, consider Albert O. Hirschman, *Exit, Voice, and Loyalty: Responses to Decline in Firms, Organizations, and States* (Cambridge, MA: Harvard University Press, 1970).

37. This is drawn from *RMU* 8.125–31.

38. See Shackleton, *Montesquieu*, 50–51.

39. In this connection, see *LP* 26.35–53/28, 75.46–49/78.

40. Note also Montesquieu, *MP* 1340.

41. Cf. Michael A. Mosher, "The Judgmental Gaze of European Women: Gender, Sexuality, and the Critique of Republican Rule," *Political Theory* 22:1 (February 1994): 25–44, and "What Montesquieu Taught—'Perfection Does Not Concern Men or Things Universally," in *Montesquieu and His Legacy*, ed. Rebecca E. Kingston (Albany: State University of New York Press, 2008), 7–28, with Montesquieu, *MP* 1062 and *EL* 4.23.21, p. 707; see Diana J. Schaub, "Montesquieu on 'The Woman Problem'," in *Finding a New Feminism: Rethinking the Woman Question for Liberal Democracy*, ed. Pamela Grande Jensen (Lanham, MD: Rowman & Littlefield, 1996), 39–66, and consider III.3, below.

42. [Jean Le Rond d'Alembert], "Éloge de M. le President de Montesquieu," in *Encyclopédie, ou Dictionnaire raisonné des sciences, des arts, et des métiers*, ed. Denis Diderot and Jean Le Rond d'Alembert (Paris: Briasson, 1751–1772; Neufchastel: S. Faulche & Compagnie, 1765; Amsterdam: M. M. Rey, 1776–1777; Paris: Panckoucke, 1777–1780), V iii–xviii (at vii).

43. In this connection, see Montesquieu, *LP* 125.53–70/131 and *CR* 6.211–34. Note also *MP* 699.

44. On this subject, see Carrithers, "Introduction," 23–30; Pangle, *Montesquieu's Philosophy of Liberalism*, 193–99; Francine Markovits, "Montesquieu: L'Esprit d'un peuple, une histoire experimentale," in *Former un nouveau peuple?: Pouvoir, éducation, révolution*, ed. Josiane Boulad-Ayoub (Quebec: Presses Universitaires de Laval; Paris: L'Harmattan, 1996), 207–36, which is reprinted in *Lectures de L'Esprit des lois*, 65–99; and Céline Spector, "Des *Lettres persanes* à *L'Esprit des lois*: Montesquieu, parcours d'une œuvre," in *1748: L'Année de L'Esprit des lois*, ed. Catherine Larrère and Catherine Volpilhac-Auger (Paris: Honoré Champion, 1999), 117–39. See also Émile Durkheim,

"Montesquieu's Contribution to the Rise of Social Science," *Montesquieu and Rousseau: Forerunners of Sociology*, tr. Ralph Manheim (Ann Arbor: University of Michigan Press, 1965), 1–64 (at 56–57).

45. Consider Montesquieu, *De la Politique* (1725), ed. Sheila Mason, in VF VIII 515, in light of Sheila Mason, "Introduction," in ibid., 505–10.

46. Cf. *EL* 1.2.4, 3.10, 5.24.2.

47. Cf. Pierre Manent, *The City of Man*, tr. Marc A. LePain (Princeton, NJ: Princeton University Press, 1998), 75–85 (esp. 79–85).

48. Note Arthur M. Wilson, "The Concept of *Mœurs* in Diderot's Social and Political Thought," in *The Age of the Enlightenment: Studies Presented to Theodore Besterman*, ed. W. H. Barber et al. (Edinburgh: Oliver & Boyd, 1967), 188–99, and see Catherine Larrère, "Droits et mœurs chez Montesquieu," *Droits* 19 (1994): 11–22, which is reprinted in *Lectures de L'Esprit des lois*, 233–46.

49. Consider *EL* 1.4.6–8 in light of 2.12.30, p. 458, n. a, 4.23.7, and see II.1, above.

50. With regard to the consequences, see Montesquieu, *CR* 4.60–64, which should be read in light of Montesquieu, *MP* 210.

51. On this point, see Michael A. Mosher, "The Particulars of a Universal Politics: Hegel's Adaptation of Montesquieu's Typology," *American Political Science Review* 78:1 (March 1984): 179–88.

52. See also *LP* 61/63, 96–97/99–100, along with *EL* 3.19.5–6, 8–9, 12, 14–15.

53. Cf. *LP* 49.43–56/51

54. In the original edition of the book, the second volume began with the twentieth book, and the epigraph headed the volume; in the last edition supervised by Montesquieu it was placed at the head of *EL* 4.20—where it has appeared ever since.

55. Cf. Xen. *An.* 4.7.21–27 (esp. 24). David Hume and many another reader, then and since, have found the allusion puzzling: see Letter from David Hume to Montesquieu on 10 April 1749, in Nagel III 1217–22 (at 1222) and in *Letters of David Hume*, I 133–38 (at 138).

BOOK THREE, CHAPTER TWO.
COMMERCIAL CIVILIZATION

1. For an extended meditation on Montesquieu's "design" and on the place reserved within it for the eighteenth book of his *Spirit of Laws*, see William B. Allen, "That All Tragedy Is Local: Book 18 of *The Spirit of the Laws*," *Interpretation: A Journal of Political Philosophy* 31:2 (Spring 2004): 193–216.

2. In this connection, see *MP* 38.

3. Cf. Raymond Aron, *Main Currents of Sociological Thought*, tr. Richard Howard and Helen Weaver (New York: Basic Books, 1965–1967) I: *Montesquieu, Comte, Marx, Tocqueville, the Sociologists and the Revolution of 1848*, 39–40.

4. For a thoughtful exploration of this theme, see Rolando Minuti, "Ambiente naturale e dinamica delle società politiche: Aspetti e tensioni di un tema di Montesquieu," in *Leggere l'Esprit des lois: Stato, società, e storia nel pensiero di Montesquieu*, ed. Domenico Felice (Naples: Liguori, 1998), 137–63, which is reprinted in French as "Milieu naturel et sociétés: Réflexions sur un thème de Montesquieu," in *Le Temps de Montesquieu:*

Actes du colloque international de Genève (28–31 octobre 1998), ed. Michel Porret and Catherine Volpilhac-Auger (Geneva: Droz, 2002), 223–44.

5. See Montesquieu, "Projet d'un histoire de la terre ancienne et moderne," 1 January 1719, ed. Lorenzo Bianchi, in VF VIII 183–84.

6. See Montesquieu, *Considérations sur les richesses de l'Espagne* (ca. 1727), ed. Pierre Rétat, in VF VIII 595–623.

7. Elsewhere, he described Spain and Portugal as being "in tutelage in Europe": *MP* 2220.

8. Cf. Montesquieu, *LP* 116/120 and *CR* 17, n. r, where some such scheme is already presupposed. Montesquieu's contention that there were four stages in the development of civilization had a considerable impact on subsequent thought: see Ronald L. Meek, *Social Science and the Ignoble Savage* (Cambridge, UK: Cambridge University Press, 1976), 5–176, who attributes to Anne-Robert-Jacques Turgot and to Adam Smith a theory of economic and political sociology that had already been more or less fully worked out in Montesquieu—as they recognized, and we shall soon see. All that Turgot added was an all-too-quick dismissal of Montesquieu's argument concerning the influence of climate and terrain and the arguably false presumption that progress from one stage to the next is not adventitious but inevitable. In this connection, see Istvan Hont, "The Language of Sociability and Commerce: Pufendorf and the Theoretical Foundations of the 'Four Stages' Theory," in *Wealth and Virtue: The Shaping of Political Economy in the Scottish Enlightenment*, ed. Istvan Hont and Michael Ignatieff (Cambridge, UK: Cambridge University Press, 1983), 253–76, which is reprinted in Hont, *Jealousy of Trade: International Competition and the Nation-State in Historical Perspective* (Cambridge, MA: Harvard University Press, 2005), 159–84. Cf. Arist. *Pol.* 1256a. Note also Montesquieu, *MP* 38.

9. Note Montesquieu, *LP* 125.53–70/131 and *CR* 6.211–34, and see Catherine Larrère, "Montesquieu et les sauvages," in *L'Ethnologie à Bordeaux: Hommage à Pierre Métais* (Bordeaux: Publications de l'Université de Bordeaux, 1995), I 59–68.

10. In this connection, see Paul A. Rahe, *Soft Despotism, Democracy's Drift: Montesquieu, Rousseau, Tocqueville, and the Modern Prospect* (New Haven, CT: Yale University Press, 2009) II.

11. Cf. Henry C. Clark, *Compass of Society: Commerce and Absolutism in Old Regime France* (Lanham, MD: Lexington Books, 2007), 114–21 (esp. 116), who fails to recognize the significance of the distinction that Montesquieu draws in *EL* 3.18.8 between a society that is merely agricultural, though it presupposes the existence of money and does involve commerce on a modest scale, and commercial society, which is itself built on exchange.

12. After reading Catherine Larrère, "Montesquieu on Economics and Commerce," in *Montesquieu's Science of Politics: Essays on the Spirit of Laws (1748)*, ed. David W. Carrithers, Michael A. Mosher, and Paul A. Rahe (Lanham, MD: Rowman & Littlefield, 2001), 335–73, see Thomas L. Pangle, *Montesquieu's Philosophy of Liberalism: A Commentary on The Spirit of the Laws* (Chicago: University of Chicago Press, 1973), 200–215, 240–43, who errs in supposing that Montesquieu intended to place the "Invocation to the Muses" at or near the beginning of *EL* 4: see Catherine Volpilhac-Auger, "Une nouvelle 'Chaîne secrète' de *L'Esprit des lois*: L'Histoire de texte," in *Montesquieu en*

2005, ed. Catherine Volpilhac-Auger (Oxford, UK: Voltaire Foundation, 2005), 85–216 (at 185–94), and "Annexe A.2. Que faire des Muses?" in VF III cxlvi–clvi. In this connection, see also Albert O. Hirschman, *The Passions and the Interests: Political Arguments for Capitalism before Its Triumph* (Princeton, NJ: Princeton University Press, 1977), Pierre Rosanvallon, *Le Libéralisme économique: Histoire de l'idée de marché* (Paris: Seuil, 1989); and Claude Morilhat, *Montesquieu, politique et richesses* (Paris: Presses Universitaires de France, 1996).

13. On the subject of *préjugés destructeurs*, see I.3, note 54, above.

14. When, on his travels in the late 1720s, Montesquieu visited the imperial cities of Germany, Genoa, Holland, and England, he was astonished and deeply offended by the manner in which commerce, all-pervasive, had transformed mores: see Montesquieu, *Voyage de Gratz à La Haye*, in Pléiade I 628–29; NA 863–64, 876–78, 880, 883; and MP 552, 592. Cf. Céline Spector, "Montesquieu et la question du 'doux commerce' dans *L'Esprit des lois*," in *Actes du colloque international, tenu à Bordeaux, du 3 au 6 décembre 1998*, ed. Louis Desgraves (Bordeaux: Académie de Bordeaux, 1999), 427–50, and *Montesquieu: Pouvoirs, richesses et sociétés* (Paris: Presses Universitaires de France, 2004), 232–48, who, in her eagerness to downplay the significance of Montesquieu's celebration of the *esprit de commerce*, tends to give to the initial, passing impressions that Montesquieu recorded in his notebooks upon arriving in these commercial societies priority over the more nuanced, complex, and thoughtful analysis he later provides in *The Spirit of Laws*.

15. Cf. Ferdinand Tönnies, *Community and Society* (London: Routledge & Kegan Paul, 1955).

16. Consider Bernard Mandeville, *The Fable of the Bees: or, Private Vices, Publick Benefits*, ed. F. B. Kaye (Oxford, UK: Clarendon Press, 1924), I 47, 51, 78–80, 342–44, 369, II 128–34, 147, 188–89, 268, in light of F. B. Kaye's introduction, in ibid., I xxxiii–cxlvi, and see Ronald Hamowy, *The Scottish Enlightenment and the Theory of Spontaneous Order* (Carbondale: Southern Illinois University Press, 1987). See also Mandeville, *The Fable of the Bees*, I 41–57, 323–69. Note, in this connection, Thomas A. Horne, *The Social Thought of Bernard Mandeville: Virtue and Commerce in Early Eighteenth-Century England* (New York: Columbia University Press, 1978); J. A. W. Gunn, "Mandeville: Poverty, Luxury, and the Whig Theory of Government," *Beyond Liberty and Property: The Process of Self-Recognition in Eighteenth-Century Political Thought* (Kingston, Ontario: McGill-Queens University Press, 1983), 96–119; M. M. Goldsmith, *Private Vices, Public Benefits: Bernard Mandeville's Social and Political Thought* (Cambridge, UK: Cambridge University Press, 1985), 47–77; E. J. Hundert, *The Enlightenment's Fable: Bernard Mandeville and the Discovery of Society* (Cambridge, UK: Cambridge University Press, 1994); Pierre Force, *Self-Interest before Adam Smith: A Genealogy of Economic Science* (Cambridge, UK: Cambridge University Press, 2003); and the discussion of Pierre Nicole in II.3, above.

17. Consider Montesquieu, LP 11–14, 85/87, MP 1266, and EL 1.1.2–3, in light of Diana J. Schaub, *Erotic Liberalism: Women and Revolution in Montesquieu's Persian Letters* (Lanham, MD: Rowman & Littlefield, 1995), 29–39, and see Michael Zuckert, "Natural Law, Natural Rights, and Classical Liberalism: On Montesquieu's Critique of

Hobbes," *Social Philosophy & Policy* 18:1 (2001): 227–51, and Yoshie Kawade, "La Liberté civile contre la théorie réformiste de l'État souverain: Le Combat de Montesquieu," in *Le Travail des lumières: Pour Georges Benrekassa*, ed. Caroline Jacot Grapa, Nicole Jacques-Lefèvre, Yannick Séité, and Carine Trevisan (Paris: Honoré Champion, 2002), 203–23.

18. See Pierre Rétat, "De Mandeville à Montesquieu: Honneur, luxe et dépense noble dans *L'Esprit des lois*," *Studi francesi* 50 (May–August 1973): 238–49, and Celine Spector, "Vices privés, vertus publiques: De la *Fable des abeilles* à *L'Esprit des lois*," in *Montesquieu and the Spirit of Modernity*, ed. David W. Carrithers and Patrick Coleman (Oxford, UK: Voltaire Foundation, 2002), 127–57.

19. See also Montesquieu, *LP* 61/63, 85/87, 96–97/99–100, and *MP* 1062, 1439, 1553. In this connection, note Michael Sonenscher, "Fashion's Empire: Trade and Power in Early Eighteenth-Century France," in *Luxury Trades and Consumerism in Ancien Régime Paris: Studies in the History of the Skilled Workforce*, ed. Robert Fox and Anthony Turner (Aldershot, UK: Ashgate, 1998), 231–54.

20. In this connection, see Stephen J. Rosow, "Commerce, Power, and Justice: Montesquieu on International Politics," *Review of Politics* 46:3 (July 1984): 346–66. In the note that he drew on when composing the pertinent paragraph of *EL* 4.20.23, Montesquieu expressly mentioned the English and the Dutch: see Montesquieu, *MP* 45, and note what is missing from *MS* 514–17 (esp. 515). As Clark, *Compass of Society*, 106 n. 69, points out, Montesquieu appears to have borrowed the phrase *esprit de commerce* and the notion that it is opposed to the *esprit de conquête* from Charles Rollins, *Histoire ancienne des Egyptiens, des Carthaginois, des Assyriens, des Babyloniens, des Medes et des Perses, des Macedoniens, des Grecs* (Paris: Estienne, 1740), V 557, which first appeared in French in 1730 and in English the following year.

21. See Pangle, *Montesquieu's Philosophy of Liberalism*, 240–43; Guillaume Barrera, "Montesquieu et la mer," *Revue Montesquieu* 2 (1998): 7–44; and Eluggero Pii, "Montesquieu e l'esprit de commerce," in *Leggere l'Esprit des lois*, 165–201, which should be read in light of Catherine Larrère, "Montesquieu et le commerce selon Eluggero Pii," *Il pensiero politico* 34:2 (May–August 2001): 190–99; and Larrère, "L'Histoire du commerce dans *L'Esprit des lois*," in *Le Temps de Montesquieu*, 319–36, whose analysis is penetrating, but who nonetheless misses the mark in the criticism (ibid., 323–26, 329–33) she directs at Pangle who never draws a metaphysical distinction between antiquity and modernity but who rightly insists on the profound significance of a fact that she acknowledges as well—that the *esprit de commerce*, which was marginal in antiquity, has become hegemonic in modern times. Cf. Spector, *Montesquieu: Pouvoirs, richesses et sociétés*, 97–100, 221–70, who follows Larrère closely and makes a similar mistake in attempting to drive too large a wedge between Montesquieu, on the one hand, and Adam Smith and Benjamin Constant, on the other. In assessing the reasons for the great transformation underway, Pangle, Pii, Larrère, and Spector rightly emphasize the transformation of rulers' calculations occasioned by the invention of the letter of exchange, but none of the four attends sufficiently to the consequences for the conduct of war in Europe deriving from the changes that took place in the *ius gentium* as a consequence of the achievement of hegemony in Europe by the Christian faith: see I.1, above. In their

eagerness to downplay the importance of the distinction that Montesquieu draws between antiquity and modernity, both Larrère and Spector misread his treatment of Athens: see below, III.4, note 39.

22. In this connection, see Muriel Dodds, *Les Récits de voyages, sources de L'Esprit des lois de Montesquieu* (Paris: Honoré Champion, 1929), and Bertrand Binoche, *Introduction à De l'Esprit des lois de Montesquieu* (Paris: Presses Universitaires de France, 1998), 199–242.

23. In this connection, see David W. Carrithers, "The Enlightenment Science of Society," in *Inventing Human Science: Eighteenth-Century Domains*, ed. Christopher Fox, Roy Porter, and Robert Wokler (Berkeley: University of California Press, 1995), 232–70; Sheila M. Mason, "Les Héritiers écossais de Montesquieu: Continuité d'inspiration et métamorophose de valeurs," in *La Fortune de Montesquieu: Montesquieu écrivain* (Bordeaux: Bibliothèque Municipale, 1995), 143–54; and James Moore, "Montesquieu and the Scottish Enlightenment," in *Montesquieu and His Legacy*, ed. Rebecca E. Kingston (Albany: State University of New York Press, 2008), 179–95. Note also Paul E. Chamley, "The Conflict between Montesquieu and Hume: A Study of the Origins of Adam Smith's Universalism," in *Essays on Adam Smith*, ed. Andrew S. Skinner and Thomas Wilson (Oxford, UK: Clarendon Press, 1975), 274–305, and see Pierre Manent, *The City of Man*, tr. Marc A. LePain (Princeton, NJ: Princeton University Press, 1998), 86–108. If one overlooks the manner in which Montesquieu's argument unfolds dialectically in stages requiring that one think over a question and then rethink again, one is likely to miss as well the fact that, in *EL* 3.18–4.21, he jettisons "static" analysis and the propensity for his account to seem "synchronical even when episodes of the past are illustrated" and anticipates what Roberto Romani calls "stadial theories of social development on the Scottish model": cf., for example, Romani, "All Montesquieu's Sons: The Place of *Esprit Général*, *Caractère National*, and *Mœurs* in French Political Philosophy, 1748–1789," *Studies on Voltaire and the Eighteenth Century* 362 (1998): 189–235 (esp. 192–202).

24. Cf. Spector, *Montesquieu: Pouvoirs, richesses et sociétés*, 249–67, who, in outlining what the Scots owed Montesquieu, wrongly denies that he was as much an enthusiast for commercial society as they were. If he failed to celebrate, as they did, the manner in which commerce sapped the foundations of the feudal order, it was because he had reasons for reticence that they did not share: see III.2–3, below.

25. In this regard, the printing press is crucial: see *MP* 1745.

26. In this connection, one should consider the epigraph to this chapter: Jean-Jacques Rousseau, *Émile, ou De l'Éducation* (1762) V, ed. Charles Wirz, in *Œuvres complètes de Jean-Jacques Rousseau*, ed. Bernard Gagnebin and Marcel Raymond (Paris: Bibliothèque de la Pléiade, 1959–95), IV 829–30.

27. In this connection, see Georges Benrekassa, "La Position de la Romanité dans *l'Esprit des lois*: L'État moderne et le poids de son histoire," in Benrekassa, *La Politique et sa mémoire: Le Politique et l'historique dans la pensée des lumières* (Paris: Payot, 1983), 257–358; Umberto Roberto, "Diritto e storia: Roma antica nell'*Esprit des lois*," in *Leggere l'Esprit des lois*, 229–80; Vickie B. Sullivan, "Against the Despotism of a Republic: Montesquieu's Correction of Machiavelli in the Name of the Security of the Individ-

ual," *History of Political Thought* 27:2 (Summer 2006): 263–88; and Céline Spector, "'Il faut éclairer l'histoire par les lois et les lois par l'histoire': Statut de la Romanité et rationalité des coutumes dans *L'Esprit des lois* de Montesquieu," in *Généalogie des savoirs juridiques contemporains: Le Carrefour des lumières,* ed. Mikhaïl Xifaras (Brussels: Bruylant, 2007), 15–41.

28. Elsewhere, Montesquieu implies the opposite: cf. *CR* 6.211–27.

29. On this theme, see Roberto, "Diritto e storia: Roma antica nell'*Esprit des lois*," 247–69.

30. On this question, Montesquieu was astonishingly acute: see Rahe, *RAM I.* Montesquieu's complex, nuanced treatment of Athens has confused a number of scholars: see III.4, note 39, below. In the working manuscript of *The Spirit of Laws,* he was even more emphatic in his depiction of Athens' martial character: *MS* 540–41.

31. Montesquieu is alluding to Pierre Daniel Huet, *Histoire du commerce et de la navigation des anciens,* 2nd ed. (Paris: Antoine-Urbain Coustelier, 1716), and he made this explicit in the working draft of his *Spirit of Laws:* see *MS* 531.

32. See Montesquieu, *MP* 77, 280.

33. Within *The Spirit of Laws,* Montesquieu's allusions to these events are infrequent but telling: see, for example, *EL* 2.9.7–9, 3.14.2.

34. For the details, see Pléiade II 1479–81.

35. In this connection, see Michel Rosier, "Les Marchandises et le signe: Turgot versus Montesquieu," and Maurice Lagueux, "À Propos de Montesquieu et de Turgot: Peut-on encore parler de la monnaie comme d'un 'signe'?" *Cahiers d'économie politique* 18 (1990): 81–96, 97–107. Montesquieu's remarks are, of course, doubly true where specie has been replaced by paper currency.

BOOK THREE, CHAPTER THREE. MONARCHY'S PLIGHT

1. See also *LP* 61/63, 85/87, 96–97/99–100 and *MP* 1439, 1553, and consider Michael Sonenscher, "Fashion's Empire: Trade and Power in Early Eighteenth-Century France," in *Luxury Trades and Consumerism in Ancien Régime Paris: Studies in the History of the Skilled Workforce,* ed. Robert Fox and Anthony Turner (Aldershot, UK: Ashgate, 1998), 231–54.

2. For an extended meditation on the logic underpinning this prohibition, see Catherine Larrère, "Montesquieu, noblesse et commerce. Ordre social et pensée économique," in *Il pensiero gerarchico in Europea, XVII–XIX secolo,* ed. Antonella Alimento and Cristina Cassina (Florence: Olschki, 2002), 31–48.

3. For an attempt to disprove the case, presented here, that monarchy was fast becoming an anachronism, cf. Céline Spector, *Montesquieu: Pouvoirs, richesses et sociétés* (Paris: Presses Universitaires de France, 2004), 145–287.

4. For the origins and significance of the distinction that Montesquieu draws between the two species of commerce and the debate that he is engaging, see Catherine Larrère, "Montesquieu: Commerce de luxe et commerce d'économie," in *Actes du colloque international, tenu à Bordeaux, du 3 au 6 décembre 1998,* ed. Louis Desgraves (Bordeaux: Académie de Bordeaux, 1999), 467–84, which is reprinted in *Lectures de L'Esprit des lois,* ed. Céline Spector and Thierry Hoquet (Bordeaux: Presses Universitaires de Bor-

deaux, 2004), 121–43, and Henry C. Clark, *Compass of Society: Commerce and Absolutism in Old Regime France* (Lanham, MD: Lexington Books, 2007), 1–72, 89–95, 117–29. For the revival of this distinction and its deployment against the Physiocrats by the abbé Galiani, see ibid., 153–91. See also ibid., 257–80.

5. In this connection, see Lionel Rothkrug, *Opposition to Louis XIV: The Political and Social Origins of the French Enlightenment* (Princeton, NJ: Princeton University Press, 1965), 193–211. Note also Montesquieu, *MP* 1690.

6. After reading John Brewer, *The Sinews of Power: War, Money, and the English State, 1688–1783* (Cambridge, MA: Harvard University Press, 1990), see Michael Sonenscher, "The Nation's Debt and the Birth of the Modern Republic: The French Fiscal Deficit and the Politics of the Revolution of 1789," *History of Political Thought* 18:1 (Spring 1997): 64–103 and 18:2 (Summer 1997): 267–325, and *Before the Deluge: Public Debt, Inequality, and the Intellectual Origins of the French Revolution* (Princeton, NJ: Princeton University Press, 2007), who documents this obsession on the part of the French and attempts to make sense of the various schemes devised for coming to grips with the problem. In this connection, see also Clark, *Compass of Society*, passim (esp. 164–66, 236).

7. Cf. Sonenscher, *Before the Deluge*, 95–172, who contends that Montesquieu thought the contrary, with Clark, *Compass of Society*, 111–14, 121–29, who demonstrates that Montesquieu was far less sanguine with regard to French than with regard to British commerce.

8. After digesting David Bien, "Offices, Corps, and a System of State Credit: The Uses of Privilege under the Ancien Régime," in *The Political Culture of the Old Regime*, ed. Keith M. Baker (Oxford, UK: Pergamon Press, 1987), 87–114; Michael Kwass, *Privilege and the Politics of Taxation in Eighteenth-Century France: Liberté, Egalité, Fiscalité* (Cambridge, UK: Cambridge University Press, 2000); and Gail Bossenga, "The Patrimonial State, Markets, and the Origins of the French Revolution," *1650–1850: Ideas, Aesthetics, and Inquiries in the Early Modern Era* 11 (2005): 443–509, see David Stasavage, *Public Debt and the Birth of the Democratic State: France and Great Britain, 1688–1789* (Cambridge, UK: Cambridge University Press, 2003).

9. See also *LP* 56/58.

10. In this connection, see Montesquieu, *LP* 125.53–70/131 and *CR* 6.211–34. Cf. Annelien de Dijn, *French Political Thought from Montesquieu to Tocqueville: Liberty in a Levelled Society?* (Cambridge, UK: Cambridge University Press, 2008), 24, who claims that, in "his discussion of feudalism," Montesquieu "never mentioned representative institutions or participatory rights," with Johnson Kent Wright, "A Rhetoric of Aristocratic Reaction? Nobility in *De l'Esprit des lois*," in *The French Nobility in the Eighteenth Century: Reassessments and New Approaches*, ed. Jay M. Smith (University Park: Pennsylvania State University Press, 2006), 227–51, who notes the allusion but fails to give it due weight.

11. In this connection, see Domenico Felice, "Francia, Spagna e Portogallo: Le monarchie Europee 'qui vont au despotisme' secondo Montesquieu," in *L'Europe de Montesquieu: Actes du colloque de Gênes (26–29 mai 1993)*, ed. Alberto Postigliola and Maria Grazia Bottaro Palumbo (Oxford, UK: Voltaire Foundation, 1995), 283–305, which appears in

revised form as "Le forme dell'assolutismo europeo," in Felice, *Oppressione e libertà: Filosofia e anatomia del dispotismo nel pensiero di Montesquieu* (Pisa: ETS, 2000), 119–47.

12. See Montesquieu, *Mémoire concernant les moyens d'acquirer les dettes de l'état* (1715), in VF VIII 55–64. Note his interest in the estates of Languedoc and Brittany: MP 859.

13. In this connection, note François Furet and Mona Ozouf, "Deux légitimations historiques de la société française au XVIIIe siècle: Mably et Boulainvilliers," *Annales ÉSC* 34 (1979): 438–50, and see Harold A. Ellis, *Boulainvilliers and the French Monarchy: Aristocratic Politics in Early Eighteenth-Century France* (Ithaca, NY: Cornell University Press, 1988), and Diego Venturino, *Le ragioni della tradizione, nobiltà e mondo moderno in Boulainvilliers (1685–1722)* (Turin: Casa editrice Le Lettere, 1993).

14. Note Montesquieu, MP 100, 927.

15. See Letter to l'abbé Ottaviano, comte di Guasco, on 19 October 1747, with the attendant note by Guasco, in Nagel III 1096–97 (with particular reference to n. a). I see no reason for discounting Guasco's testimony. Cf., however, Henri Augustesen, "L'Histoire de Louis XI," *Revue philomathique de Bordeaux et du Sud-Ouest* 1 (1897–98): 569–78, and Barckhausen, *Montesquieu: Ses Idées et ses œuvres d'après les papiers de La Brède* (Paris: Librairie Hachette, 1907), 339–42.

16. Consider the secondary literature cited in I.1, note 47, above, with an eye to the secondary literature cited in I.2, note 29, above, and see Montesquieu, MP 1525.

17. That, at least some of the time, Montesquieu thought it easy to answer these last two questions in the affirmative is clear: note MP 1273; see Denis Richet, "Autour des origines idéologiques lointaines de la Révolution française: Élites et despotisme," *Annales ÉSC* 24:1 (January–February 1969): 1–23, and Mark Hulliung, *Montesquieu and the Old Regime* (Berkeley: University of California Press, 1976), 15–107 (esp. 15–53), 173–230; and consider Ran Halévi, "The Illusion of 'Honor': Nobility and Monarchical Construction in the Eighteenth Century," tr. Mary Schwartz, in *Tocqueville and Beyond: Essays on the Old Regime in Honor of David D. Bien*, ed. Robert M. Schwartz and Robert A. Schneider (Newark: University of Delaware Press, 2003), 71–85, which should be read in conjunction with David D. Bien, "Manufacturing Nobles: The Chancellerie in France to 1789," *Journal of Modern History* 61:3 (September 1989): 639–52, and "Aristocracy," in *A Critical Dictionary of the French Revolution*, ed. François Furet and Mona Ozouf, tr. Arthur Goldhammer (Cambridge, MA: Belknap Press, 1989), 616–28.

18. See Thomas L. Pangle, *Montesquieu's Philosophy of Liberalism: A Commentary on The Spirit of the Laws* (Chicago: University of Chicago Press, 1973), 215–17. See also Pierre Manent, *The City of Man*, tr. Marc A. LePain (Princeton, NJ: Princeton University Press, 1994), 82–85.

19. Note also the letter on this subject added to the posthumous edition: *Lettres persanes* 124, in Pléiade I 315–16; and, in this context, consider LP 107/110 and MP 1254.

20. Note also Montesquieu, MP 1610.

21. For the context within which Montesquieu frames this charge, see Clark, *Compass of Society*, 75–89.

22. In this connection, see *LP* 126.1–32/132, 132/138.

23. Note also the observations attributed to an unnamed French visitor to Spain: *LP* 75/78.

24. In this connection, see Pangle, *Montesquieu's Philosophy of Liberalism*, 249–59, and Diana J. Schaub, "Of Believers and Barbarians: Montesquieu's Enlightened Toleration," in *Early Modern Skepticism and the Origins of Toleration*, ed. Alan Levine (Lanham, MD: Lexington Books, 1999), 225–47, especially the latter. Note also Robert C. Bartlett, *The Idea of Enlightenment: A Post-Mortem* (Toronto: University of Toronto Press, 2001), 13–43.

25. See Paul Kléber Monod, *The Power of Kings: Monarchy and Religion in Europe, 1589–1715* (New Haven, CT: Yale University Press, 1999).

26. After reading *LP* 22.24–42/24, see Montesquieu, "Discours sur les motifs qui doivent nous encourager au sciences," 15 November 1725, ed. Sheila Mason, esp. 1–52, in *VF* VIII 495–502 (esp. 495–98), and *MP* 1252, 1265, 1983.

27. See Peter Burke, *The Fabrication of Louis XIV* (New Haven, CT: Yale University Press, 1992), 1–133 (esp. 125–33); then consider Jeffrey W. Merrick, *The Desacralization of the French Monarchy in the Eighteenth Century* (Baton Rouge: Louisiana State University Press, 1990).

28. In this connection, see John Pappas, "La Campagne des philosophes contre l'honneur," *Studies on Voltaire and the Eighteenth Century* 205 (1982): 31–44, and Clark, *The Compass of Society*, 121–29 (esp. 123–25); then note Montesquieu, *MP* 1062, 1272, 1340, 1491.

29. Note also *EL* 1.5.19, p. 304.

30. Note also Montesquieu, *MP* 534. Cf. Michael A. Mosher, "What Montesquieu Taught—'Perfection Does Not Concern Men or Things Universally'," in *Montesquieu and His Legacy*, ed. Rebecca E. Kingston (Albany: State University of New York Press, 2008), 7–28 (esp. 16–20).

31. See David B. Young, "Libertarian Demography: Montesquieu's Essay on Depopulation in the *Lettres persanes*," *Journal of the History of Ideas* 36:4 (October 1975): 669–82.

32. See Merle L. Perkins, "Montesquieu on National Power and International Rivalry," *Studies on Voltaire and the Eighteenth Century* 238 (1985): 1–95 (esp. 72–82), and Marc Belissa, "Montesquieu, *L'Esprit des lois* et le droit des gens," in *Le Temps de Montesquieu: Actes du colloque international de Genève (28–31 octobre 1998)*, ed. Michel Porret and Catherine Volpilhac-Auger (Geneva: Droz, 2002), 171–85.

33. Cf. François de Salignac de La Mothe-Fénelon, *Supplément à l'Examen de conscience sur les devoirs de la royauté* (1734), in Fénelon, *Œuvres*, ed. Jacques Le Brun (Paris: Bibliothèque de la Pléiade, 1983–1997), II 1003–9, which was penned at some point prior to Fénelon's death in 1715, with Montesquieu, *EL* 2.10.1–2, and see 5.26.23 with *MP* 1900. Although Fénelon's *Examen de conscience sur les devoirs de la royauté* was not published until 1747, an abortive attempt at publication, stymied by Cardinal Fleury, was made by his great-nephew, the marquis de Fénelon, in 1734, and he it was who added to the *Examen de conscience* the *Supplément*: see the editorial comments of Jacques Le Brun, in Fénelon, *Œuvres*, II 1664–68. Subsequently, Montesquieu must have gained access to the manuscript of the *Supplément*, now lost, or to one of the hand-

ful of printed copies that escaped destruction in 1734, for his argument with regard to preventive war and universal monarchy is indistinguishable from that advanced by Fénelon.

34. Cf. Michael Walzer, *Just and Unjust Wars: A Moral Argument with Historical Illustrations* (New York: Basic Books, 1977), who makes a distinction between pre-emptive war, which he regards as just, and preventive war, which he condemns as unjust, that Montesquieu would have judged not only confused and unrealistic but highly irresponsible and likely to play into the hands of a would-be universal monarch such as Louis XIV. For a useful corrective, see Raymond Aron, *Paix et guerre entre les nations*, 8th ed. (Paris: Calmann-Lévy, 1984).

35. Cf. Michael A. Mosher, "Montesquieu on Conquest: Three Cartesian Heroes and Five Good Enough Empires," *Revue Montesquieu* 8 (2005–6): 81–110 (at 90–93), and "Montesquieu on Empire and Enlightenment," forthcoming in *Empire and Modern Political Thought*, ed. Sankar Muthu (Cambridge, UK: Cambridge University Press, 2010), whose defense of the moral significance of the distinction that Walzer draws between pre-emptive and preventive war rests on a failure to appreciate precisely what, in Montesquieu's opinion, it is that stands in the way of the establishment of universal monarchy in Europe.

36. See Letter to l'abbé Niccolini on 6 March 1740, in Nagel III 1000–1001, where Montesquieu reports that Paris has devoured the provinces in its vicinity.

37. See Catherine Betty Abigail Behrens, *The Ancien Régime* (New York: Harcourt, Brace, & World, 1967), 138–62, and Bailey Stone, *The Genesis of the French Revolution: A Global-Historical Interpretation* (Cambridge, UK: Cambridge University Press, 1994), 20–63.

38. Note *MP* 1452, 1466,1623; see Letters to Martin Ffolkes on 21 January 1743 and to François, comte de Bulkeley, on 20 October 1748, in Nagel III 1033–34, 1137–38; and consider Charles-Jacques Beyer, "Le Rôle de l'idée de postérité chez Montesquieu," in *La Fortune de Montesquieu: Montesquieu écrivain*, ed. Louis Desgraves (Bordeaux: Bibliothèque Municipale, 1995), 65–72.

39. Cf. Montesquieu, *MP* 1729, which was drafted for inclusion in *EL* 2.10. Note also *MP* 1518, 1899.

40. Note also Montesquieu, *MP* 1271.

41. Cf. Michael A. Mosher, "The Judgmental Gaze of European Women: Gender, Sexuality, and the Critique of Republican Rule," *Political Theory* 22:1 (February 1994): 25–44, and "What Montesquieu Taught—'Perfection Does Not Concern Men or Things Universally'," 7–28, whose account is, to say the least, one-sided.

42. For the details, see Andrew J. Lynch, "Montesquieu and the Ecclesiastical Critics of *L'Esprit des Lois*," *Journal of the History of Ideas* 38:3 (July–September 1977): 487–500. See also Charles-Jacques Beyer, "Montesquieu et la censure religieuse de *L'Esprit des lois*," *Revue des sciences humaines* 70 (1953): 105–31. For a list of the passages singled out for criticism, see David W. Carrithers, "Jansenist and Jesuit Censures of *The Spirit of Laws*," in Montesquieu, *The Spirit of Laws: A Compendium of the First English Edition*, ed. David W. Carrithers (Berkeley: University of California Press, 1977), 467–68. See also Claude Lauriol, "La Condamnation de *L'Esprit des lois* dans les archives de la

Congrégation de l'Index," in *Montesquieu, Œuvre ouverte?* *(1748–1755): Actes du Colloque de Bordeaux (6–8 décembre 2001, Bordeaux, bibliothèque municipale)*, ed. Catherine Larrère (Oxford, UK: Voltaire Foundation, 2005), 91–114.

43. In this connection, see Cecil Patrick Courtney, "Montesquieu and Revolution," in *Lectures de Montesquieu: Actes du Colloque de Wolfenbüttel (26–28 octobre 1989)*, ed. Edgar Mass and Alberto Postigliola (Oxford, UK: Voltaire Foundation, 1993), 41–61.

44. After contemplating the eulogy of Montesquieu in Edmund Burke, *An Essay towards an Abridgment of the English History* (1757), in *The Writings and Speeches of the Right Honourable Edmund Burke* (Boston: Little, Brown, 1901), VII 157–488 (at 315), and its fullsome restatement in *An Appeal from the New to the Old Whigs* (1791), in ibid., IV 211–12, consider Burke, *Reflections on the Revolution in France* (1790), in ibid., III 231–563. In this connection, see Cecil Patrick Courtney, *Montesquieu and Burke* (Oxford, UK: Blackwell, 1963).

45. This is a theme to which Montesquieu frequently returned: see *LP* 96–97/99–100, and *EL* 3.19.5–6, 8–9, 12, 14–15. Note also *LP* 61/63.

46. See Felice, "Francia, Spagna e Portogallo: Le monarchie Europee 'qui vont au despotisme' secondo Montesquieu," 283–305, and "Le forme dell'assolutismo europeo," 119–47.

47. See also *MP* 1746.

48. See the thoughtful essay by Guillaume Barrera, "La Figure de l'Espagne dans l'œuvre de Montesquieu: Élaboration conceptuelle d'un exemple: Stratégie d'écriture et mode d'avertissement," in *Actes du colloque international, tenu à Bordeaux*, 153–71.

49. It is with this in mind that one should read the epigraph to this chapter: Jean-Jacques Rousseau, *Émile, ou De l'Éducation* (1762) III, ed. Charles Wirz, in *Œuvres complètes de Jean-Jacques Rousseau*, ed. Bernard Gagnebin and Marcel Raymond (Paris: Bibliothèque de la Pléiade, 1959–95), IV 468.

50. Cf. Michael Oakeshott, *On Human Conduct* (Oxford, UK: Clarendon Press), 185–326 (esp. 246–51), and Michael A. Mosher, "Civic Identity in the Juridical Society," *Political Theory* 11:1 (February 1983): 117–32; "The Particulars of a Universal Politics: Hegel's Adaptation of Montesquieu's Typology," *American Political Science Review* 78:1 (March 1984): 179–88; "The Judgmental Gaze of European Women: Gender, Sexuality, and the Critique of Republican Rule," 25–44; "Monarchy's Paradox: Honor in the Face of Sovereign Power," in *Montesquieu's Science of Politics: Essays on the Spirit of Laws (1748)*, ed. David W. Carrithers, Michael A. Mosher, and Paul A. Rahe (Lanham, MD: Rowman & Littlefield, 2001), 159–229 (esp. 202–15); and "What Montesquieu Taught—'Perfection Does Not Concern Men or Things Universally'," 7–28, who argue for continuity between Montesquieu's monarchy and the liberal pluralism thought to be characteristic of civil association in modern Europe, with Celine Spector, *Cahier Montesquieu* 5 (2001): 199–200, 6 (2002): 264, who quite rightly finds the argument implausible, and see Sharon R. Krause, "The Politics of Distinction and Disobedience: Honor and the Defense of Liberty in Montesquieu," *Polity* 31:3 (Spring 1999): 469–99, and *Liberalism with Honor* (Cambridge, MA: Harvard University Press, 2002), 32–66, who emphasizes the manner in which human beings in Montesquieu's monarchy are, though self-assertive, nonetheless honor-bound—and emphatically not, in the sense

prized by Oakeshott, existentially free. Note also Alain Pons, "Amour des lois et amour de la liberté chez Montesquieu," in *L'Amour des lois: La Crise de la loi moderne dans les sociétés démocratiques* (Montreal: Les Presses de l'Université Laval, 1996), 187–95 (esp. 193–95).

51. Cf. David W. Carrithers, "Montesquieu et l'étude comparée des constitutions: Ses Analyses des régimes anglais et français," in *Actes du colloque international, tenu à Bordeaux*, 235–42, with Ran Halévi, "La Modération à l'épreuve de l'absolutisme: De l'Ancien Régime à la Révolution française," *Le Debat* 109 (March–April 2000): 73–98.

BOOK THREE, CHAPTER FOUR.
DEMOCRACIES BASED ON COMMERCE

1. Cf. Albert Mathiez, "La Place de Montesquieu dans l'histoire des doctrines politiques du XVIIIe siècle," *Annales historiques de la Révolution française* 7 (1930): 97–112; Franklin L. Ford, *Robe and Sword: The Regrouping of the French Aristocracy after Louis XIV* (Cambridge, MA: Harvard University Press, 1953), 222–45; Franz Leopold Neumann, "Montesquieu," in *The Democratic and the Authoritarian State*, ed. Herbert Marcuse (Glencoe, IL: Free Press, 1957), 96–148 (at 106–13); and Louis Althusser, *Politics and History: Montesquieu, Rousseau, Hegel and Marx*, tr. Ben Brewster (London: NLB, 1972), 26–29, 96–106, with Denis Richet, "Autour des origines idéologiques lointaines de la Révolution française: Élites et despotisme," *Annales ÉSC* 24:1 (January–February 1969): 1–23, and Jean Ehrard, "La Signification politique des *Lettres persanes*," *Archives des lettres modernes* 116 (1970): 33–50.

2. Cf. Élie Carcassonne, *Montesquieu et le problème de la constitution française au XVIIIe siècle* (Paris: Presses Universitaires de France, 1927); Gabriel Loirette, "Montesquieu et le problème de France: Du bon Gouvernement," in *Actes du Congrès Montesquieu réuni à Bordeaux du 23 au 26 mai 1955* (Bordeaux: Impriméries Delmas, 1956), 219–39; Jean-Jacques Chevallier, "Montesquieu, ou Le Libéralisme aristocratique," *Revue internationale de la philosophie* 9 (1955): 330–45; Harold A. Ellis, "Montesquieu's Modern Politics: *The Spirit of Laws* and the Problem of Modern Monarchy in Old Regime France," *History of Political Thought* 10:4 (Winter 1989): 665–700; Céline Spector, *Montesquieu, Les Lettres persanes: De l'Anthropologie à la politique* (Paris: Presses Universitaires de France, 1997), and *Montesquieu: Pouvoirs, richesses et sociétés* (Paris: Presses Universitaires de France, 2004); Michael A. Mosher, "Monarchy's Paradox: Honor in the Face of Sovereign Power," in *Montesquieu's Science of Politics: Essays on the Spirit of Laws (1748)*, ed. David W. Carrithers, Michael A. Mosher, and Paul A. Rahe (Lanham, MD: Rowman & Littlefield, 2001), 159–229; Johnson Kent Wright, "A Rhetoric of Aristocratic Reaction? Nobility in *De l'Esprit des lois*," in *The French Nobility in the Eighteenth Century: Reassessments and New Approaches*, ed. Jay M. Smith (University Park: Pennsylvania State University Press, 2006), 227–51; and Annelien de Dijn, *French Political Thought from Montesquieu to Tocqueville: Liberty in a Levelled Society?* (Cambridge, UK: Cambridge University Press, 2008), 11–39 (esp. 20–32), with Paul Alexandre R. Janet, *Histoire de la science politique dans ses rapports avec la morale*, 4th ed. rev. (Paris: Félix Alcan, 1913), 323–28, 361–65.

3. Consider Letter from Claude Adrien Helvétius in 1747, in Nagel III 1102–5 (esp. 1102–3).

4. For a fine piece of literary detective work, see Frances Acomb, *Anglophobia in France, 1763–1789: An Essay in the History of Constitutionalism and Nationalism* (Durham, NC: Duke University Press, 1950), 124–28, and Robert Koebner, "The Authenticity of the Letters on the *Esprit des lois* Attributed to Helvetius," *Bulletin of the Institute of Historical Research* 24:69 (May 1951): 19–43. There is reason to suspect that La Roche tampered as well with the works of Helvétius: see Marie-Thérèse Inguenaud and David Smith, "Un disciple d'Helvétius: Martin Lefebvre de La Roche (1738–1806)," *Studies on Voltaire and the Eighteenth Century* 374 (1999): 29–52.

5. Note Letter to Pierre Samuel du Pont de Nemours on 13 March 1771, in *Œuvres de Turgot et documents le concernant*, ed. Gustave Schelle (Paris: Librairie Felix Alcan, 1913–1923), III 476–78 (at 477), and see [Antoine Louis Claude Destutt, comte de Tracy], *A Commentary and Review of Montesquieu's Spirit of Laws*, [tr. Thomas Jefferson] (Philadelphia: William Duane, 1811), wherein one can also find a translation of Concorcet's critique of Montesquieu, *EL* 6.29 and of the two letters on Montesquieu's *De l'Esprit des lois* that La Roche fobbed off on Helvétius.

6. See Letter from Claude Adrien Helvétius in 1747, in Nagel III 1102–5 (at 1105), whose rejection of what Montesquieu called *modération* typified what subsequently presented itself as the dominant strain in the French Revolution. In this connection, see Bernard Manin, "Montesquieu," in *A Critical Dictionary of the French Revolution*, ed. François Furet and Mona Ozouf, tr. Arthur Goldhammer (Cambridge, MA: Belknap Press, 1989), 728–41.

7. See also *LP* 76.16–27/129.

8. In this connection, see Alberto Postigliola, "Forme di razionalità e livelli di legalità in Montesquieu," *Rivista di storia della filosofia* 49:1 (January 1994): 73–109.

9. In this connection, see Catherine Larrère, "Montesquieu and Liberalism: The Question of Pluralism," in *Montesquieu and His Legacy*, ed. Rebecca E. Kingston (Albany: State University of New York Press, 2008), 279–301, whose argument is defective in only one particular: see notes 36–39 in context, this chapter.

10. See Robert Shackleton, *Montesquieu: A Critical Biography* (Oxford, UK: Oxford University Press, 1961), 320; then cf. Letter to Pierre-Louis Moreau Maupertuis at the end of June 1747, Letter from Pierre Mussard on 8 July 1747, and Letter to Pierre Mussard on 24 August 1747, in Nagel III 1088–95 (esp. 1090–93), with Letter to Monsignor Gaspare Cerati on 28 March 1748, in Nagel III 1114–17 (at 1116–17), and see Letters from Jacob Vernet on 5, 24, and 29 June; July–August; 4, 11, and 20 September; and 4 November 1748, in Nagel III 1117–22, 1130–32, 1134–37, 1141–43.

11. Note François Furet and Mona Ozouf, "Deux légitimations historiques de la société française au XVIIIe siècle: Mably et Boulainvilliers," *Annales ÉSC* 34 (1979): 438–50, and see Harold A. Ellis, *Boulainvilliers and the French Monarchy: Aristocratic Politics in Early Eighteenth-Century France* (Ithaca, NY: Cornell University Press, 1988), and Diego Venturino, *Le ragioni della tradizione, nobiltà e mondo moderno in Boulainvilliers (1685–1722)* (Turin: Casa editrice Le Lettere, 1993). In this connection, note Montesquieu, *MP* 1184.

12. The swiftly changing ideological needs of the monarchy required on the part of Dubos considerable flexibility in argument: see Thomas E. Kaiser, "The Abbé Dubos and the Historical Defense of Monarchy in Early Eighteenth-Century France," *Studies on Voltaire and the Eighteenth Century* 267 (1989): 77–102, which should be read in conjunction with Kaiser, "Rhetoric in the Service of the King: The Abbé Dubos and the Concept of Public Judgment," *Eighteenth Century Studies* 23:2 (Winter 1989–1990): 182–99.

13. That Montesquieu wanted to do this is clear enough; that his main purpose in *The Spirit of Laws* was to shore up the existing order is not. Cf. Wright, "A Rhetoric of Aristocratic Reaction? Nobility in *De l'Esprit des lois*," 227–51, who, in taking a small part for the whole, fails to come to grips with the fact that the two books central to his thesis (*EL* 6.30–31) were not composed until the type for Montesquieu's magnum opus was already being set and that they were added to that work at the last possible moment as an appendix of sorts and clearly identified as such on the title page of the original edition.

14. See Jean Le Rond d'Alembert, "Analyse de *L'Esprit des loix*," in Nagel I xxxiv–lii (at li–lii).

15. See Jean Ehrard, "La 'Chaîne' de *L'Esprit des lois*," in Ehrard, *L'Esprit des mots: Montesquieu en lui-même et parmi les siens* (Geneva: Droz, 1998), 179–92 (at 189).

16. See Paul O. Carrese, *The Cloaking of Power: Montesquieu, Blackstone, and the Rise of Judicial Activism* (Chicago: University of Chicago Press, 2003), 11–104. In this connection, note also Diana J. Schaub, "The Regime and Montesquieu's Principles of Education," in *Montesquieu and the Spirit of Modernity*, ed. David W. Carrithers and Patrick Coleman (Oxford, UK: Voltaire Foundation, 2002), 77–100 (at 96–98), and Sharon R. Krause, "History and the Human Soul in Montesquieu," *History of Political Thought* 24:2 (Summer 2003): 235–61. When he added *EL* 6.28, 30–31 to his *Spirit of Laws*, Montesquieu also added 3.18.21–31: *MS* 435–54 (esp. 435–38). For an analysis of the logic underpinning these changes, see William B. Allen, "That All Tragedy Is Local: Book 18 of *The Spirit of the Laws*," *Interpretation: A Journal of Political Philosophy* 31:2 (Spring 2004): 193–216.

17. See Stephen A. Siegel, "The Aristotelian Basis of English Law, 1450–1800," *New York University Law Review* 56 (1981): 18–59, and James R. Stoner, "Common Law and Natural Law," *Benchmark* 5 (1993): 93–102.

18. First, cf. J. G. A. Pocock, *The Ancient Constitution and the Feudal Law: A Study of English Historical Thought in the Seventeenth Century: A Reissue with a Retrospect* (Cambridge, UK: Cambridge University Press, 1987), with Glenn Burgess, *The Politics of the Ancient Constitution: An Introduction to English Political Thought, 1603–1642* (University Park: Pennsylvania State University Press, 1993); note Alan D. T. Cromartie, "The Constitutionalist Revolution: The Transformation of Political Culture in Early Stuart England," *Past & Present* 163 (May 1999): 76–120, and consider with care James R. Stoner, *Common Law and Liberal Theory: Coke, Hobbes, and the Origins of American Constitutionalism* (Lawrence: University Press of Kansas, 1992), 11–175 (esp. 152–61); then, in this light, read Cecil Patrick Courtney, *Montesquieu and Burke* (Oxford, UK: Blackwell, 1963); Orest Ranum, "Personality and Politics in the *Persian Letters*," *Political Science Quarterly* 84:4 (December 1969): 606–27 (esp. 608–12); K. M. Schönfeld,

"Montesquieu et 'la bouche de la loi': Jacques 1er, Edward Coke et l'antithèse 'rex judex'," in *La Fortune de Montesquieu: Montesquieu écrivain*, ed. Louis Desgraves (Bordeaux: Bibliothèque Municipale, 1995), 207–23; and Jacob T. Levy, "Montesquieu's Constitutional Legacies," in *Montesquieu and His Legacy*, 115–37, and note the presence in Montesquieu's library of a work by John Selden: see *Catalogue de la bibliothèque de Montesquieu à La Brède*, ed. Louis Desgraves and Catherine Volpilhac-Auger (Oxford, UK: Voltaire Foundation, 1999) no. 3220. On the neo-Aristotelianism of the moderate Enlightenment, see Paul A. Rahe, "The Idea of the Public Intellectual in the Age of the Enlightenment," in *The Public Intellectual: Between Philosophy and Politics*, ed. Arthur Melzer, Jerry Weinberger, and M. Richard Zinman (Lanham, MD: Rowman & Littlefield, 2003), 27–52.

19. In this connection, after reading II.Pref., note 3, above, see Georges Benrekassa, "Philosophie du droit et histoire dans les livres XXVII et XXVIII de *L'Esprit des lois*," in Benrekassa, *Le Concentrique et l'excentrique: Marges des lumières* (Paris: Payot, 1980), 155–82, and Céline Spector, "Quelle justice? Quelle rationalité? La Mesure du droit dans *L'Esprit des lois*," in *Montesquieu en 2005*, ed. Catherine Volpilhac-Auger (Oxford, UK: Voltaire Foundation, 2005), 219–43.

20. Cf., however, Montesquieu, *CR* 6.211–27.

21. In this connection, see Montesquieu, *MP* 774, 1799 (especially, the latter), and note Guillaume Barrera, "Montesquieu et la mer," *Revue Montesquieu* 2 (1998): 7–44 (at 29, n. 51); Catherine Volpilhac-Auger, "Montesquieu et l'impérialisme grec: Alexandre, ou L'Art de la conquête," in *Montesquieu and the Spirit of Modernity*, 49–60; Catherine Larrère, "L'Histoire du commerce dans *L'Esprit des lois*," in *Le Temps de Montesquieu: Actes du colloque international de Genève (28–31 octobre 1998)*, ed. Michel Porret and Catherine Volpilhac-Auger (Geneva: Droz, 2002), 319–36 (esp. 324–25, 329–30); and Pierre Briant, "Montesquieu, Mably et Alexandre le Grand: Aux Sources de l'histoire hellénistique," *Revue Montesquieu* 8 (2005–6): 151–85. Where my friend and former colleague Michael A. Mosher, "Montesquieu on Conquest: Three Cartesian Heroes and Five Good Enough Empires," *Revue Montesquieu* 8 (2005–6): 81–110 (esp. 103–10), and "Montesquieu on Empire and Enlightenment," forthcoming in *Empire and Modern Political Thought*, ed. Sankar Muthu (Cambridge, UK: Cambridge University Press, 2010), is inclined to think that Montesquieu saw in Alexander a genuine willingness to acknowledge the subjectivity of the subjected, I am inclined to think that he had an appreciation for Alexander's canniness as a manipulator—eager to avoid provocation and rebellion and prepared to let commerce soften mores over time.

22. Cf. Stephen J. Rosow, "Commerce, Power, and Justice: Montesquieu on International Politics," *Review of Politics* 46:3 (July 1984): 346–66 (at 363–64), and Mosher, "Montesquieu on Conquest," 94–110, and "Montesquieu on Empire and Enlightenment," passim.

23. Cf. Montesquieu's use of the pertinent adjective in *EL* 1.6.13, p. 323, in a phrase added to the posthumous 1757 edition (*MP* 1897 with the attendant note in Montesquieu, *Pensées, Le Spicilège*, ed. Louis Desgraves [Paris: Laffont, 1991]), to describe the manner in which "a wise legislator" would act when confronting a people, such as the Japanese,

who are "opinionated, capricious, determined, whimsical [*bizarre*]," and accustomed to despotic rule.

24. See Mosher, "Montesquieu on Empire and Enlightenment," who suspects that the phrase *la tyrannie sourde* is an allusion to the dominion of the Roman Catholic Church. In this connection, consider Montesquieu, *LP* 113.55–63/117, and *MP* 1252, 1265, 1983.

25. Until quite recently, the seraglio narrative was neglected, if not treated as a defect, in the secondary literature on the work: see Philip Stewart and Catherine Volpilhac-Auger, "Introduction: Pour une 'Histoire véritable' des *Lettres persanes* II. Lectures," in VF I 44–71.

26. Note Montesquieu, *MP* 1252, and cf. John Locke, *Two Treatises of Government: A Critical Edition with an Introduction and Apparatus Criticus*, 2nd ed., ed. Peter Laslett (Cambridge, UK: Cambridge University Press, 1970) II.xi.135, and see Rahe, *RAM* II.vi.1–vii.10 (esp. II.vi.6–vii.9).

27. See *LP* 2–4, 6–7, 9, 19–20/20–21, 24–25/26–27, 39–41/41–43, 45/47, 51/53, 60/62, 62–63/64–65, 68–69/70–71, 77/79, 93/96, 139–48/147–56, 149/159, 150/161. The posthumous edition of 1758 includes a number of additional letters pertinent to the narrative of the harem: see Montesquieu, *Lettres persanes* 15, 22, 157–58, 160, in Pléiade I 154, 163, 369–70, 372.

28. See Jean Starobinski, "Exile, Satire, Tyranny: Montesquieu's *Persian Letters*," in Starobinski, *Blessings in Disguise; or, The Morality of Evil*, tr. Arthur Goldhammer (Cambridge, MA: Harvard University Press, 1993), 60–83 (esp. 73–83). See also Michael A. Mosher, "The Judgmental Gaze of European Women: Gender, Sexuality, and the Critique of Republican Rule," *Political Theory* 22:1 (February 1994): 25–44; Diana J. Schaub, *Erotic Liberalism: Women and Revolution in Montesquieu's Persian Letters* (Lanham, MD: Rowman & Littlefield, 1995); and Corey Robin, "Reflections on Fear: Montesquieu in Retrieval," *American Political Science Review* 94:2 (June 2000): 347–60, as well as Mosher, "Montesquieu on Conquest," 87–90, and "What Montesquieu Taught—'Perfection Does Not Concern Men or Things Universally'," in *Montesquieu and His Legacy*, 7–28 (esp. 23–27).

29. Cf. the morbid curiosity of Leontius: Pl. *Rep.* 4.439e2–440c5.

30. In his youth, when he attempted to compose his *Treatise on Duties*, before he came to recognize the *rapports* existing between laws, mores, and manners on the one hand and forms of government on the other, Montesquieu imagined an ideal *esprit de citoyen*, which would be common to public-spirited men in monarchies and republics alike, and which would be in no way oriented toward aggrandizement (*MP* 1269), but there is no reason to suppose that he ever thought that this *esprit* actually typified the attitudes of citizens in actual republics and monarchies.

31. See, however, Bernard Manin, "Montesquieu, la république et le commerce," *Archives Européennes de Sociologie* 42:3 (2001): 573–602 (esp. 582–94), and Catherine Larrère, "Montesquieu, noblesse et commerce. Ordre social et pensée économique," in *Il pensiero gerarchico in Europea, XVII–XIX secolo*, ed. Antonella Alimento and Cristina Cassina (Florence: Olschki, 2002), 31–48 (esp. 35–41), and "Montesquieu and Liberalism," 279–301 (esp. 281–83).

32. See Catherine Larrère, "Montesquieu: Commerce de luxe et commerce d'économie," in *Actes du colloque international, tenu à Bordeaux, du 3 au 6 décember 1998*, ed. Louis Desgraves (Bordeaux: Académie de Bordeaux, 1999), 467–84.

33. For a discussion of the origins and character of Machiavelli's conviction in this regard, see Rahe, *ATA* 56–100.

34. See Schaub, "The Regime and Montesquieu's Principles of Education," 82, n. 6.

35. As I have intimated in II.2, above, it is not fortuitous that *vertu* and its cognates loom large in Part One of *The Spirit of Laws* and pass almost unmentioned in Part Two, where Montesquieu's focus shifts to the political options available within Christendom in modern times: see Ehrard, "La 'Chaîne' de *L'Esprit des lois*," 189.

36. Athens might seem to be an exception to this rule (*EL* 1.3.3, 5.6, 4.20.4). But, as we have seen, Montesquieu makes it clear that Athens never achieved its potential as "a commercial republic"—presumably because, at Athens, "the spirit of commerce" was "crossed by another" spirit alien to it: consider 4.21.7 in light of 1.5.6.

37. If one neglects the significance of the distinction that Montesquieu draws between antiquity in Europe and modernity, one will also be confused concerning the distinction that he draws between democracies based on virtue and those based on commerce: cf. Manin, "La république et le commerce," 577–94, and Larrère, "Montesquieu and Liberalism," 281–83.

38. Cf. Manin, "Montesquieu, la république et le commerce," 582–94 (esp. 583); Larrère, "L'Histoire du commerce dans *L'Esprit des lois*," 319–36 (esp. 323–26, 329–33); and Spector, *Montesquieu: Pouvoirs, richesses et sociétés*, 97–100, 221–70 (esp. 237–42), who fail to recognize the degree to which in antiquity commercial republicanism was an abberation and who therefore interpret its survival into modern times as proof of a fundamental continuity between antiquity and modernity, with Giuseppe Cambiano, "Montesquieu e le republiche greche," *Rivista di filosofia* 45 (1974): 93–144, and see Cambiano, *Polis: Histoire d'un modèle politique*, tr. Sophie Fermigier (Paris: Aubier, 2003), 297–354. If this element of continuity were sufficient to justify dissolving the distinction, there is no reason why one should not take the survival of despotism to be sufficient as well.

39. Cf. Manin, "Montesquieu, la république et le commerce," 590–94; Catherine Larrère, "Montesquieu et le commerce selon Eluggero Pii," *Il pensiero politico* 34:2 (May–August 2001): 190–99 (at 197), "L'Histoire du commerce dans *L'Esprit des lois*," 324–26, 332–33, and "Montesquieu and Liberalism," 281–83; and Spector, *Montesquieu: Pouvoirs, richesses et sociétés*, 237–38, 241–42, who, in their eagerness to deny that Montesquieu is intent in *EL* 4.21 on contrasting antiquity with modernity, fail to see that the point of 4.21.7 is to underline the significance of this very distinction as it pertains to the spirit of commerce—by contrasting Athens in this fashion with England.

40. Consider *EL* 3.19.27, p. 580, in light of the characterization of Henry VIII's rule at 2.12.10, 22, 5.26.3. Note also S 450, 534, 670, and *MP* 187, 373, 583, 626, 651, 787.

41. He owned a copy of *Oceana* and the complete works of Bacon: see *Catalogue de la bibliothèque de Montesquieu à La Brède* nos. 1405, 2376.

42. Cf. Montesquieu, *De la politique* (1725), ed. Sheila Mason, in VF VIII 512, with Montesquieu, "Réflexions sur le caractère de quelques princes et sur quelques événements

de leur vie" (ca. 1731–33), ed. Sheila Mason, VI, in VF IX 51–65 (at 59–60), and see Montesquieu, *MP* 75, 373, 583, 626, 651, 787, 1302, p. 381.

43. See Montesquieu, "Réflexions sur le caractère de quelques princes et sur quelques événements de leur vie," VI, in VF IX 51–65 (at 59–60).

44. For the import of the Englishman's characteristic "independence," cf. *EL* 3.19.27, pp. 575, 583, with 1.5.12; note 1.1.2, 2.11.3, 5.26.15; and then see 5.24.2, 5.

45. Note Montesquieu, *MP* 814.

46. See NA 883–84.

47. The English, Montesquieu observes in his notebooks (*MP* 767, 1531), are distinguished by their preference "that men be men." In consequence, they are free from the "prejudice" in favor of "war, birth, dignities, men of good fortune," and "ministerial favor," and they reserve their esteem for "riches and personal merit." To "personal merit," they, in fact, give greater consideration "than any nation in the world." In contrast with a certain, unspecified but easily recognizable "nation nearby," they show that they have "more pride than vanity."

48. When he visited England, Montesquieu found that the English took little care to treat one with *politesses* and that they never descended to *impolitesses*: NA 883. Note also 876–77, and *MP* 780, 784, 1271.

49. See Larrère, "Montesquieu: Commerce de luxe et commerce d'économie," 467–84 (esp. 475–80).

50. See Shackleton, *Montesquieu*, 77–78.

51. Letter from Montesquieu to William Domville on 22 July 1749, in Nagel III 1244–45.

INDEX

Constitution of England, The (continued)
  liberty to be lost when legislative more
      corrupt than executive power, 118,
      136–43, 240
  longest and most famous chapter in *The
      Spirit of Laws*, 42
  Madison on, 41, 61
  on political liberty in relation with the
      citizen, 95
  particular attention paid to judicial
      power, 98
  political liberty established by laws but
      not enjoyed, 96–102, 113–19, 136–43
  polity's principles, 278
  presupposes second essay on foreign pol-
      icy, religion, mores, manners, and
      character produced by English insti-
      tutions, 52–54
  prudently dropped from triptych, 52
  separated powers rarely at rest, 100
  Spirit of Laws chapters on distribution of
      powers at Rome follow, 134
Corinth, 226
Corneille, Pierre, 10, 208
Coste, Pierre, 107, 294
Crete, 64, 72, 116
Crillon, Louis Balbis de Berton de, 81
Cromwell, Oliver, 9, 232
Cyrus, Achaemenid king of Persia, 254

d'Alembert, Jean Le Rond, 64, 86–88, 217
democracy based on commerce, 58, 224–
    38, 325
  aberration in antiquity arising from pe-
      culiar local conditions, 228
  Athens only seems to be, 180, 225–30,
      312–14, 325
  commercial, pacific, 92
  does not ordinarily exhibit political
      virtue as such, 227–28
  England is, Athens is not, 229–38, 325
  English polity best-constituted, 55, 59,
      229–38
  excessive wealth can destroy spirit of

commerce and inspire disorders of in-
    equality, 225
  exists in ancient and modern times, 226
  inclination to regulate and manage com-
      merce, 143
  only species of republic exhibiting spirit
      of peace and moderation, 92–94,
      224–30
  only species of republic to survive into
      modern times, 212, 228
  partitive inheritance preferable, 225
  patronage corrupts, 143
  practices commerce of economy, 226
  spirit of frugality, economy, moderation,
      industry, wisdom, tranquillity, orderli-
      ness, regularity, 225–28
  Tyre, Carthage, Corinth, Marseilles,
      Rhodes, Florence, Venice, Holland
      exemplify, 226
  works best where spirit of commerce
      crossed by nothing else, 225
democratic republic, the, 69–74, 119–23,
    134, 174, 226, 280–81, 325. *See also* de-
    mocracy based on commerce; Greece,
    classical, cities of; Roman republic;
    Rome, classical
  absent dread tends towards corruption,
      75, 124
  account presupposes reason never pro-
      duces any great effects on minds of
      men, 71
  agriculture Achilles heel, 173–74
  ancient understanding versus Mon-
      tesquieu's understanding, 70–71
  banishes luxury with corruption and
      vice, 122
  can join wisdom of good government
      with force of faction, 73
  can only within limits approach modera-
      tion, 75
  censorial supervision of women neces-
      sary, 121–22
  Christianity subverts, 86, 92–94, 176, 228
  commerce subverts, 175–76, 228

English form of government, the, 40–45,
 49–59, 84–85, 90–91, 96–117, 136–43,
 229–38, 292. *See also* democracy based
 on commerce
 abolition of powers intermediary opens
  way to state popular or despotic, 85,
  90, 142, 193, 240–41
 absence of courtiers, flatterers, pleasers,
  234
 account deliberately cryptic, 88
 all the passions left free, 101, 235
 best exploits religion, commerce, liberty,
  230
 best-constituted democracy based on
  commerce, 229–38
 capacity for self-correction, 44, 49, 52,
  90, 137
 changes in *ius gentium* effected by
  Christianity make world safe for, 92–
  94, 147
 citizens accept heavy taxes for sake of
  liberty, 55
 citizens given to *inquiétude*, 99–108,
  113–17, 136–43, 240
 citizens more public-spirited and vigilant than their representatives, 139,
  140–41
 citizens unhappy, unsociable, 101–2
 clergy exhibit moderation, 234
 commerce crucial for sustaining liberty
  therein, 139–41
 commercial, maritime orientation prepared by expulsion from French soil,
  53, 90
 commercial, pacific, moderate, 230,
  235–38
 compared with Rome, 43–45, 56, 58,
  132–37, 231
 conducive to multiplicity of sects, 234
 conducted by passions, not reason, 100
 conducts commerce as other nations do
  war, 56
 confidence renders fictive wealth real

 for power projection, 54–55, 115, 172,
  189, 269–70
 court procedures singled out as practices
  typical of republic, 90
 criminal law highly praised, 98
 deliberately not made thematic until
  Part Two of *The Spirit of Laws*, 90
 direct object political liberty, 68–69, 74,
  85, 94–99, 108, 113–17, 148, 185, 234
 distribution and separation of powers,
  44, 52, 95–100, 96–102, 113–19, 136–
  43, 236, 289, 302
 distribution of powers at Rome illumi-
  nates, 132–36
 does not fit political typology laid out in
  Part One of *The Spirit of Laws*, 85,
  147–48
 Domville's query, Montesquieu's response, 136–41, 238, 300–302
 early reader suggests terror the principle
  setting it in motion, 99
 economically and morally superior to
  monarchy, 239
 elections an antidote to corruption,
  301
 eliminates dangerous prejudice, men
  judged on merit, 234, 326
 ethos of solitude and independence, 101,
  114, 140, 143, 233–34, 236, 326
 executor of the laws above the laws, 71
 exemplifies moderation in government,
  84–85, 91, 210, 230, 235–38, 281
 exhibits peace and moderation, 94, 225
 exported to colonies, 57
 extreme liberty, 97
 fails to engender desire for conquest, 56
 far better suited than monarchy to enlightened, commercial world order,
  236–38
 favorable to liberty, 289
 favored by the passions and favors them
  in return, 99
 favors solid luxury, not frivolity, 235